THE
LITIGATORS

THE LITIGATORS

Inside the Powerful World
of America's High-Stakes
Trial Lawyers

JOHN A. JENKINS

Doubleday
New York   London   Toronto   Sydney   Auckland

To My Wife, Susan,

and My Daughters, Jenny and Christina.

Published by Doubleday, a division of Bantam Doubleday Dell Publishing Group, Inc., 666 Fifth Avenue, New York, New York 10103

Doubleday and the portrayal of an anchor with a dolphin are trademarks of Doubleday, a division of Bantam Doubleday Dell Publishing Group, Inc.

Portions of the fourth and sixth chapters previously appeared, in a different form, in the *New York Times Magazine*.

LIBRARY OF CONGRESS CATALOGING-IN-PUBLICATION DATA

Jenkins, John A.
  The litigators: inside the powerful world of America's high-stakes trial lawyers/by John A. Jenkins.—1st ed.
     p.   cm.
  Includes index.
  ISBN 0-385-24408-8
  1. Lawyers—United States—Biography.   2. Trials—United States.
I. Title.
KF372.J46 1989
349.73'092'2—dc19
[B]
[347.300922]
[B]   88-28236
                                           CIP

BOOK DESIGN BY KATHRYN PARISE

BG

Acknowledgments

I am indebted to my assistant, Allison Porter, a paralegal, and my wife, Susan Raleigh Jenkins, an attorney, for their research assistance on this book. Each spent many hours evaluating and summarizing some 200,000 pages of transcripts and trial materials from the various cases I have written about.

Legal assistants in the offices of the lawyers profiled here were essential intermediaries and valued providers of documents and transcripts. This is to express my gratitude to Paula Miller, Betty Davis, Kay Frapart, Bernadette Lyons, Toni Caldwell, Sue Stearns, Allison Randall and Mimi Eagleton, each of whom greased the wheels of this project in important ways. Luis Díaz, Ashok Mathur and Minu Mathur did translations for the Bhopal chapter. John Blue, David Gidmark, Catherine Upin and Rita Malley also went out of their way to provide trial materials unobtainable elsewhere, as did David Snively of Monsanto and Brian Owen of the *Chicago Daily Law Journal.* My editor at Doubleday, Paul Breswick, was tremendously supportive of this project and kept me pumped up when things looked overwhelming. Mark Garofalo and Lisa Wayer were also valued compatriots. My agent, Jane Dystel, was the best advocate any author could possibly ask for. Ron Plesser and Ralph Nader suggested lawyers to be profiled and offered useful guidance early on.

More than 250 interviews were conducted during the research for this book. Most interviews were on the record; some were not. For understandable reasons, some of those whose assistance was particularly invaluable asked not to be mentioned here. To everyone who helped, whether named here or not, I offer heartfelt thanks. This book couldn't have been written without you.

Contents

Introduction

Tort (from Lat. *torquere,* to twist; *tortus,* twisted, wrested aside). A private or civil wrong or injury, other than breach of contract, for which the court will provide a remedy in the form of an action for damages.

Philip Corboy earned more than $3 million a year as one of the country's greatest plaintiffs' lawyers representing the victims of accidents, injuries and catastrophes—the law of torts.

Even though he had been at it for more than a generation, a courtroom battle still held for Corboy the same childhood fascination as discovering a strange liquid metal that skittered every which way when he let it go. "Quicksilver. Every trial's like that." Its unpredictible course was the challenge of a trial, and trial law was the sport the greatest lawyers were bred for. A battle of equally matched foes was a test not just of the lawyer's will to win, but of his ability to come back—to recover the skittering quicksilver and forge it into pure gold.

Corboy, like every successful plaintiff's trial lawyer, had built his lucrative practice by betting his own money on his courtroom skills. Lawyers like Corboy didn't ask or expect their clients to pay for the spirited advocacy they provided. Instead of charging an hourly fee to handle a case, they took an ownership interest that gave them a clear financial incentive to push for the best judgment.

What the plaintiff's lawyer earned was called a *contingent* fee in legal parlance—contingent on *winning.* But what that really meant was that the trial lawyer was gambling on his own resourcefulness when he accepted some client's case. A plaintiff's lawyer paid all the expenses and sometimes even lent money to his client. If the lawyer lost, the client could just walk away. But if the lawyer were able to successfully market his client's misfortune to the jury, or to get a good settlement before the case went to trial, that trial lawyer would be rewarded handsomely. His share would be one third or more of whatever the client was awarded, plus expenses. Right off the top.

That was the beauty of the contingent fee, and that was what had transformed the law of torts from what it was in ancient times to what it is today: from the Judeo-Christian notion of individual moral responsibility, in which people were entitled to get compensation from anybody they could prove had harmed them, to an insurance-based system that sometimes paid tens of millions of dollars to victims who filed lawsuits to collect for lost wages, medical expenses, and even intangibles like pain and suffering.

Such was the incredibly lucrative world of the plaintiffs' trial lawyers. And, understandably, such was my interest in it. Trial lawyers —used here, the term refers to the advocates for victims of what the law calls torts—are a virtually unknown class of the bar, and they shy from the mantle of their own astounding success the way anybody who has a good thing going would. That was why I set out to reveal their small, powerful world, a world where trial lawyers became *entrepreneurs* of adversity, taking advantage of the business opportunities that the contingent fee provided.

This world of the plaintiff's lawyer is one where pain meets possibility: The worse the injury, the higher the contingent fee, because, after all, a third of a lot of money is a whole lot more than a third of a little. To the lawyer as entrepreneur, the financial incentive of the contingent fee is what moves the freight and keeps the market efficient. Marginal claims are discounted for quick settlement or written off altogether. Bad percentage shots simply aren't taken. Trial lawyers claim they need their whopping percentage to compensate them for the losers they take. But the fact is, they don't knowingly take losers. *Ceteris paribus*, the trial lawyer spends his time on the winners. And if a client has a promising case, the lawyer will stake him to it out of sheer self-interest. In the world of the trial lawyer, victim and advocate have a strange kind of economic symbiosis: Each needs the other to succeed.

The result has been the creation of a hidden legal industry in

America, one with its own culture, its own mores, and a rich tradition of keeping competitors and regulators out. Maintaining an oligopoly —which is the classic economic model for what the trial lawyers have, with their secret clubs and their well-entrenched ways of dividing business among themselves—requires discipline and money. The trial lawyers have enough of both to do whatever needs to be done to ensure their own self-interest, whether it's publishing a slick newsstand magazine about "everyday law" or lobbying the states and Congress to defeat those who would limit their fees.

The law is an industry that's rapidly headed for the $100 billion mark, in terms of the total amount spent in America on legal goods and services. And, just as in any other industry, things run best for the players who got there first. There's a good reason why the same core group of trial lawyers can move so adroitly from one mass disaster to another; and why the Inner Circle of Advocates, the secret society of million-dollar-verdict trial lawyers, is dedicated to keeping its number at exactly 100. The best lawyers like it that way, thank you very much, and can you blame them? People who call themselves trial lawyers comprise only a tenth of the nation's 700,000 lawyers, but they take home half of the estimated $18 billion earned by practicing lawyers in this country, which means the very best of the contingent-fee lot are outearning their hourly-wage brethren by a whole lot more than the nine-to-one ratio the numbers suggest.

This is a book about those world-class litigators, the plaintiffs' trial lawyers who are the swashbucklers of American jurisprudence. How they win. And how they lose.

It is a book that will take you right into the courtroom with the country's greatest lawyers as they pursue the biggest verdicts in history.

In the legal profession, as in every other, there is a well-ordered hierarchy of status. At the very top are the litigators, flamboyant risk capitalists in a profession that can often seem decidedly colorless. They're the judicial combatants who invest their egos and their personal wealth in the cases they bring into the courtroom.

Trying a case before a jury is the law's most demanding task, one that melds a lawyer's knowledge with an actor's panache and a bluffer's guile. Those few who truly master it can earn millions of dollars a year. These litigators, comprising no more than several hundred of the nation's lawyers, literally set the pace for the entire legal profession: Their advocacy in the relatively few cases that actually reach trial establishes a market rate for other, similar cases that will later be settled, and in that way their influence grossly exceeds their small number. On another level, the litigators are the embodiment of a legal system that the average American otherwise little understands and probably will never experience.

If Philip Corboy was one master of this unique craft, Rex Carr was another. The strutting, bantam of a lawyer from East St. Louis, Illinois, earned $1 million a year, but his most notorious distinction was as the instigator of the longest jury trial in history: a three-and-a-half-year trial against Monsanto for that company's alleged negligence when dioxin spilled from a tanker car during a Missouri train wreck. The trial became the private crucible of a feared litigator who boasted to me, in better times as the trial began, that "I frequently get more money in settlements than I believe I can get at trial. It's asinine, but some insurance companies, they hear my name and they say, 'Pay that sucker what he wants!' They're fools to do that! But they believe in my reputation, and they pay."

For the Hunt brothers—Nelson, Herbert, and Lamar—a fortune was at stake in the lawsuits being pursued by their lawyer, Steve Susman. Having failed a few years before to corner the world silver market, the brothers needed a way to stave off the twenty-two banks who collectively held the $1.5 billion debt the brothers ran up during the fiasco. The courts offered the only chance for the Hunts to beat the bill, and even that possibility seemed remote. It took a skilled trial lawyer like Susman to turn the legal system against itself so that it would start working for the Hunts.

For the lawyer representing Rose Cipollone, the debate came down to this: Who will pay for the deaths that cigarettes have caused? The fifty-eight-year-old New Jersey woman smoked for forty years, but before she died she filed a massive unsafe-products lawsuit against the tobacco companies whose products helped to kill her. No one had ever won such a case, but Cipollone's lawyer—a young, earnest man named Marc Edell—was going to give it his best shot. Problem was, so were the tobacco companies. For them, it was a bet-your-company case, a case so important they couldn't afford to lose it. Apart from that, the litigation offered a fascinating glimpse into a new kind of public interest law. The lawyers representing Cipollone's estate were being aided by the Tobacco Products Liability Project, a coordinating group that was generating hundreds of lawsuits against cigarette makers around the country.

In the case of Wayne Newton, the issue was one of reputation—for NBC, which linked him to the Mafia in a 1980 broadcast; for the network's noted libel lawyer, New York's Floyd Abrams; for the distinguished reporters who stood by their stories; and for Newton himself, who was represented by the most successful personal-injury lawyer in Las Vegas, Morton R. Galane. "This is a case," Galane told his jury, "about a man who had a good name." But could Galane really beat the system, even in Las Vegas? Could he win the largest libel verdict in history?

Forty percent of whatever he won would go to Galane, for he, too, was a legal entrepreneur who took an ownership interest in the cases he brought.

Advocates of this uniquely American system of compensating lawyer and victim saw the contingent fee as the average person's key to the courtroom, helping to maintain a measure of equality in our legal system. Detractors, on the other hand, called it a means of promoting more litigation.

Ask Washington's John P. Coale about the contingent fee, though, and you got a refreshingly different perspective. He likened the lawyers' share of damages to the million-dollar paydays on the professional tennis circuit. "They're [always] the same players," he said of the lawyers like him who literally moved across the globe from one calamity to another. When the Bhopal accident occurred, Coale was one of the first on the scene, and at one time he claimed to have 60,000 clients there. When San Juan's Dupont Plaza Hotel burned on New Year's Eve, it was Coale who filed the first lawsuit.

To combat the disaster lawyers, corporate defendants have begun using some sophisticated tactics of their own. A case in point is Delta Air Lines, whose lawyers swung into action immediately after one of the airline's planes crashed short of the runway in Dallas, killing 137 people. The lawyers quickly began settlement negotiations with the victim's families—and if a family didn't settle or sued instead, Delta hired private investigators to find out all they could about the victim and his lifestyle. The strength of a marriage, bonds to children, drinking, and even sexual conduct were among the factors included in the dispassionate equation of how much someone's life was worth.

During a year spent interviewing, analyzing and studying the world of the great trial lawyers, I developed respect for these lawyers and the legal system they embody. The contingent fee arrangement has its flaws, as anyone who reads on will see. But the system also works so well that the real shame is that it does not help more people. Six million lawsuits are filed each year in the United States, but that, alone, isn't a sign of crisis, and the sheer number of lawsuits we as a nation file isn't a reason to batter the trial lawyers. If anything, the "efficient market" engendered by the contingent fee has probably kept the number of lawsuits down, not up. The insurance industry has an $81 billion conflict of interest when it says otherwise, because that's what the General Accounting Office says the industry's profits were during the last ten years of this "crisis."

If I have a quarrel with the trial lawyers and their contingent fee system, it's that they've been able to make so much off so relatively few cases, while many victims get little or nothing. (According to the Rand Corporation, the average personal-injury plaintiff whose case ended in 1985 received $18,536; the plaintiff's and defense *lawyers* in that typical case together got $13,902.) The efficient market is brutally so. Without a serious injury and a deep pocket from which to seek recompense, a victim is out of luck. Instead of looking for ways to keep more people out of the courthouses, under the guise of a crisis that never existed, we ought to find ways to open the legal system to those who've been shut out. Until then, our unique litigation system will only continue to better serve the ambitions and financial imperatives of the trial bar than the ends of justice.

A few final comments about the lawyers I have selected are in order. There are many great trial lawyers who *aren't* profiled here. Exigencies of time and space being what they are, this book is about six lawyers in disparate specialities whose recent cases were in some way truly unique: biggest libel verdict against a news organization, longest jury trial in history, most important product-liability case, bankruptcy of some of the country's richest men, greatest mass disaster of all time. The most publicity-conscious lawyers often aren't the best ones; if the names of the protagonists here aren't instantly recognizable to you, read on and enjoy their stories anyway.

The world of the trial lawyer is still overwhelmingly white and overwhelmingly male, and these lawyers reflect that world. Like others, I look forward to the day when that isn't so.

All of the trial lawyers described in this book are skilled entrepreneurs taking advantage of the opportunity that the contingent fee provides. They like the money and the adulation, but they are motivated by more than just economic self-interest or egocentricity. These lawyers are mavericks, practicing solo or in very small firms, and they have an innate passion for combat, a pure zest for competitiveness, that sets them apart from the legion of lawyers who are merely foot soldiers in the courtroom. They have something to prove. To us. And to themselves. As Rex Carr would tell me at the start of his dioxin trial, "This is an arena; it's combat. Me against the other lawyers. And I want to win!"

The importance of examining the motivations and conduct of America's premier litigators lies in what can be revealed not only about them, but about our country's legal system as well.

Washington, D.C.
September 1988

Mr. Las Vegas:
Mort Galane and the
Case of *Wayne Newton*
v. NBC

In hard-fought litigation where the stakes are high, lawyers say and do a helluva lot of things in anger, and only
a psycho would view it as heinous! You're not injuring
anyone physically. You're not stealing their money.
What's the big problem?

MORTON GALANE

It was a Saturday night, October 4, 1980, and an
exultant Wayne Newton—the Las Vegas icon of the double-knit generation—had just sealed the biggest deal of his charmed life.

Little more than a week before, the Nevada Gaming Commission
had approved the singer's purchase, with a partner, of the Aladdin
Hotel & Casino on the Las Vegas Strip. Now, the entertainer sat down
and carefully penciled out his own lyrics to a song he would sing later
that night:

Long ago and far away, I dreamed a dream one day.
That dream was not denied me.
Chills run up and down my spine.
Aladdin's lamp is mine, and now you're here beside me.

The child soprano who'd been discovered by Bobby Darin and
become a star at sixteen with the schmaltzy hit called "Danke
Schoen" now was a beefy man of thirty-eight who dyed his thick hair

1

jet black and sported a pencil-thin, Cesar Romero-style moustache. The high voice had become raspy and deeper, and Newton had changed in other ways, too. He was a power on the Strip, a drawing card so big he could make $8 million a year just working the big rooms in the town that greed built.

Newton had so much going for him: wealth and fame, and all that they buy. Arabian horse ranches. A private jet and a helicopter he piloted himself. An exquisite collection of rare automobiles. The friendship and adulation of politicians, astronauts, his fellow entertainers—and at least one member of the mob.

If you were anybody special in Vegas it was hard *not* to at least cross paths with a few unsavory characters now and then. After all, the glitzy casinos were just about the only place on earth where it was *customary* to keep millions of dollars in cash, no questions asked— and that was what attracted organized crime. The town wasn't just for gamblers. It was a money launderer's delight, a skimmer's paradise. At the Stardust and the Tropicana alone, the mob families from Kansas City, Milwaukee, Chicago and Cleveland from 1976 to 1979 skimmed $2.3 million from the casino counting rooms before taxable revenues had been declared.

The city fathers did their best to keep things clean, to the point of requiring convicted felons to register with the sheriff upon arrival. The gaming board was tough on the undesirables, too. But as long as pliable front men could be found, the gangs had a way in.

Once inside, the mobsters ruled ruthlessly. Consider the case of Carl "Toughy" DeLuna, the underboss and comptroller of the Kansas City gang. When DeLuna and his compatriots thought they could get a bigger skim at the Stardust and the Fremont if they put in a new mob front man, DeLuna paid a visit to Allen R. Glick, the licensed owner of the two hotels, and made Glick an offer he couldn't refuse: Sell out or your two children will be murdered. Glick sold.

The mob had moved in on the Aladdin, too. In 1979, its owners were convicted in federal court in Detroit of fronting for the mob, and Nevada authorities moved swiftly to shut down the big Strip gambling palace.

But that had been good news for Newton, because Mr. Las Vegas wasn't content to be the highest-paid star on the Strip. He wanted to *own* a piece of it. He wanted to buy the Aladdin.

Newton wasn't the only one eying the Aladdin, though. Television personality Johnny Carson was in on the bidding, and so were two Las Vegas businessmen, Ed Torres and Delbert Coleman.

The issue of who would get the Aladdin hinged not so much on money as on who could get past the Nevada gaming authorities. They were the gambling industry's cops on the beat, and they'd already denied Torres and Coleman the Aladdin license because of their unsavory connections.

By May 1, 1980, Newton and his then-manager Jay Stream were the new darlings of the Aladdin's deposed owners. They had come to terms on a $105 million buy-out deal. But Newton didn't have that kind of money himself, and everyone he asked—from the owner of the Riviera Hotel on the Strip to the Pritzker family who had the Hyatt Hotel chain—turned him down when he asked for it.

Then, during that summer, two financial angels came forward, offering Newton some better deals.

Meyer Blinder ran a stock brokerage company that made its money the old-fashioned way, suckering clients into investing in overpriced, outrageously speculative penny stocks. It was a churn-'em-and-burn-'em business where the people who made the big money were Blinder's own thousands-strong force of salesmen. And, of course, Blinder himself. His Denver-based brokerage was named Blinder, Robinson & Co., but on Wall Street and inside the Securities and Exchange Commission (SEC) it had a different name: "Blind 'em and Rob 'em." The securities industry's watchdogs had been chasing after Blinder since at least 1971; by 1986, Blinder had been banned for life from the securities industry by the SEC, a punishment that he then began vigorously appealing up through the courts, staying in business all the while.

But here was a chance for Blinder to get into a new line of work, one that, although heavily regulated, offered the prospect of a handsome return on his or someone else's money. Newton was obviously willing to listen to a high-class con man if it would help him get his hotel. Blinder invited an eager Newton to New York for a meeting.

On the evening of August 5, Newton checked into the posh Pierre Hotel on Fifth Avenue across from Central Park. He was going to hear Blinder's business proposition the next morning. But that night

Newton got a call at the Pierre from the chairman of the Valley Bank of Nevada. The banker wanted to head off the Newton-Blinder deal.

"I have the ideal partner for you," the banker, E. Parry Thomas, told Newton.

Newton asked who.

"Ed Torres," Thomas replied.

Newton knew exactly who Torres was. Not only had Torres and the banker Thomas both been part owners of the Riviera, and not only had Torres already tried and failed to buy the very hotel that Newton was now going after, but Torres had years earlier been the entertainment director at the downtown Fremont when Newton got his first Vegas gig there as a lanky, high-voiced sixteen-year-old. This sure was a coincidence, Newton told Thomas. Yes, he would meet with Torres the next day, right after his meeting with Blinder.

Torres waited in the next room the following morning while Newton spoke to Blinder. Then Torres and his retinue spoke to Newton. Since the gaming authorities had already nixed Torres once, the key to any deal, they told him, would be Newton's solid reputation. Valley Bank was already on board as the source of Newton's $10 million down payment on what was now an $85 million deal. Wayne Newton was going to get his hotel after all.

Ira Silverman, a field producer for NBC News, was in Los Angeles a few months earlier when a source told him about a mobster named Guido Penosi, a member of the Lucchese crime family who also had connections to the Gambino organization. The Los Angeles police believed Penosi was a central figure in the West Coast drug trade, the most dangerous man in Los Angeles, and they had been watching him closely, staking out his Beverly Hills house and trailing him when he left it.

Penosi's mob nickname was "The Bull," and the police told Silverman they were finding out just how apt the appellation was as Penosi tried to beat up the undercover guys he caught following him.

In New Haven, Connecticut, FBI agents were hearing some interesting things. The agents, supervised by federal strike-force lawyers, had been investigating organized crime there since December 1979, and they had tapped the telephone of a mafioso named Frank Piccolo.

To the outside world, Piccolo appeared to be just another Bridgeport entrepreneur, the owner of a truck leasing company. But he was actually a *caporegime*—Sicilian for "boss"—of the Gambino family, the nation's largest and most powerful Mafia organization, and he was stationed in Bridgeport to oversee the Gambino rackets there—loan sharking, robbery, phonograph records, and trade-union activities. It was Piccolo who was responsible for delivering Connecticut's organized-crime proceeds to the family leadership in New York.

The federal agents had been listening in on Piccolo's phone calls since May 16, and they were hearing the voice of a man they couldn't identify. Someone named Guido was calling Piccolo at his hangout at the Backstage Delicatessen in Bridgeport. They were talking about Newton and the Aladdin. The two men were obviously plotting about how they would earn money from Newton once he bought the Aladdin.

"I'm waiting for it to be over," waiting for Newton to buy the hotel, the feds overheard Guido tell Piccolo.

"Whenever it's over, then you call me to go in there and we'll go," Piccolo replied.

Guido: "I'll call to make arrangements for both of us."

Piccolo: "Right. I want to talk to him."

Guido: "Yeah. I'll let you, too."

Piccolo: "Who knows? Even if he don't buy the hotel. So what?"

Silverman was one half of a news reporting team that had earned an extraordinary reputation by breaking sensational stories about sensational crimes. Covering organized crime was one of the specialties of Silverman and his on-camera partner, Brian Ross, but they'd also scooped the world just a few months earlier when they revealed the Abscam "sting" against members of Congress. Ross and Silverman had such excellent sources of information that they even knew when and where some of the arrests would be made, and NBC cameras were waiting to reveal those arrests to the rest of the country that night.

In the world of television, it took many people to put together a story and get it on the air, and, as a field producer, Silverman played a crucial role. Moon-faced, beefy and balding, Silverman was the legman, a digger-up of facts and an arranger of interviews. The producer worked much as a print reporter would, except that instead of typing up the finished product he had to have it recorded onto videotape and edited into a compelling minidrama that would take no more than several minutes of air time. Ross, as slim and handsome as Silverman was homely and rotund, was the journalistic television performer. He was the one on camera, doing the interviews that Silverman often arranged, speaking the words that he or Silverman wrote.

Ross and Silverman cultivated law-enforcement sources all over the country, and they also knew something about their care and feeding. The reporters sometimes swapped information with the cops and federal agents they knew.

And so it was that one of the New Haven agents revealed to Silverman the extraordinary things that were now being heard through the Piccolo wiretaps. There had been threats of some sort to Wayne Newton, made by a man called "Dapper." Piccolo and the guy named Guido had both been talking to Newton about his problem, and then to each other about how they would earn money from Newton.

But the agents were still puzzled about this Guido character. Did Silverman know who it might be?

Silverman played an instant hunch and replied that it might be Guido Penosi, the mafioso he'd heard about from the L.A. cops.

Unbeknown to Newton, the two investigative reporters started pursuing the story, checking with their sources and gathering whatever information they could get about the phone calls between Newton and the mobsters. They learned that Penosi had made eleven phone calls to Newton to talk with him about solving some kind of problem. And when Newton and Torres announced they had a deal to buy the Aladdin, the two reporters asked another source, an IRS agent, to act as a go-between in arranging a secret meeting with two agents of the Nevada gaming board who had been doing the background check on Newton.

Newton and Torres were moving fast to close the Aladdin deal, and the state gaming board was going to hold a special public hearing on the Aladdin license transfer on September 25.

The meeting between Ross and Silverman and the two Nevada gaming-board agents was set for Thursday, September 11, at a place called the Village Pub. In the meantime, Silverman telephoned Henry Bushkin, the lawyer for Johnny Carson, to see what the Carson camp might know about their rivals for the Aladdin license.

It would take a record-setting libel trial, years later, to reveal the truth about Newton's relationship with the mobster Guido Penosi.

Although it wasn't known then by either the NBC reporters or, for that matter, even the many law-enforcement authorities who were poking into the darker recesses of Newton's life, Penosi was one of Newton's oldest friends.

As a twenty-one-year-old working the lounge of the Copacabana in New York City, Newton was befriended by a fan he came to know as Guido. Penosi, already a killer, was a Lucchese soldier, living in New York in those days, and he visited the nightclub as often as several times a week to watch Newton perform. Guido became Newton's protector, keeping undesirables away from the young singer with the effeminate voice. "Hey, lay off that kid. He's mine," Guido told other hoodlums who showed up at the Copa. Guido boasted that he was "claiming" Newton, and he even gave Newton and the boys in his band gold wristwatches that were engraved "From Guido and Carmine." Carmine Trumanti, a boss of the Lucchese family, was one of Newton's fans, too.

Penosi later moved to Miami, and when Newton performed there Penosi visited the show and invited the entire Newton entourage— mother, father, fiancee, brother and band members—to the Penosi home for an Italian dinner on a Sunday.

If Penosi needed a favor, the man he'd once "claimed" tried to oblige. Penosi's son was trying to make a pilot for a television variety show. Could Newton help? Along with his manager and three people from his band, the entertainer flew out to California from Vegas and sang some songs on the show for free.

When Penosi's wife died, it was a bereaved Guido who called

Newton in 1979 and told him he wanted to travel to Vegas. Newton thought that was a fine idea, and he even invited Penosi to be a guest at his house.

There was just one hitch, Penosi replied. As an ex-felon, he would have to register with the Las Vegas Metropolitan Police Department. Could Newton arrange for him to do that?

Newton could, and did, vouch for his buddy Guido with the lawmen, although he also told his friend that given the criminal record it would be better if Guido stayed at the Desert Inn, where Newton was then performing. The Newtons had a three-year-old adopted daughter, Erin, and Newton felt funny about having a criminal around the house.

Even if Penosi understood what made Newton so skittish, he also wanted to make a good impression on the Newton family. And when Penosi arrived in Las Vegas, he made it a point to visit his friend's house with a gift for the little girl—a silver-trimmed saddle. Newton was quite a horse fancier, too. On his ranches in Las Vegas and Reno he kept 250 prized Arabians.

On September 25, prodded along by Ross and Silverman, who already had told the gaming board agents that they were going to broadcast information about Newton that would embarrass the whole state of Nevada, the gaming board was waiting with questions about Newton's ties to the mobster Guido Penosi.

What was the nature of Newton's relationship to Penosi?

"Just as a fan and a longtime family friend," Newton lied. "On the basis on which I've known him, I don't think there has been a relationship."

Newton told the board members questioning him that day that he'd only seen Penosi four times in his life, and that Penosi had never been to his home. More lies.

Newton also said he didn't know anything about Penosi's mob connections. But he also allowed that, if Penosi *did* have such connections, he wouldn't associate with him anymore.

As Newton left the hearing, Ross followed him, down the stairs, out the door and into the parking lot, a camera rolling the entire time. Ross was doing what NBC paid him so handsomely to do. He pushed himself into Newton's path, still asking questions about Penosi. "Look, do me a favor," Newton finally told him.

"I'm not doing you any favors," Ross snarled back.

That night, the NBC reporters called the agent in New Haven who had originally tipped them off to the Piccolo-Penosi-Newton telephone conversations.

Newton testified that Penosi was just a fan, they explained. Is that true?

Their source laughed. Newton's not telling the whole story, he said.

The next day was Friday, September 26, and Ross and Silverman were in California interviewing Johnny Carson to see whether he had any pieces to add to the puzzle. The two surmised that Carson, as a frustrated bidder for the Aladdin, might have some dirt on Newton. But Carson couldn't help.

Newton, meanwhile, filed an affidavit that day with the gaming authorities that, he said, told the whole story about his relationship with Penosi. It did say that they'd been together when Penosi visited Las Vegas the year before—"my first and only meeting with him in approximately thirteen years"—but it didn't mention the gifts Newton had received from Penosi, or all the telephone calls between them, or the free TV-pilot guest shot that Penosi had arranged and viewed during its taping.

Ross and Silverman started preparing their story the following Monday, September 29, at the NBC studios in Burbank, California.

What they had was an intriguing tale of a famous singer's ties to the Mafia. They felt certain about their information from the wiretaps. Newton really wasn't telling the whole story about Penosi.

They also were sure Newton had asked Penosi for help with a problem, and that Penosi and Piccolo had taken care of that problem and now were plotting to cash in on the help they'd given Newton. All that came from the wiretaps. But what was the problem Newton needed help with? That was a vital part of the story, because it would explain Penosi's motive, and his opportunity for sinking his hooks into Newton.

Ross had heard something from a source about Newton's needing protection for his family, but when he asked Newton about that during the ambush interview that followed the singer's gaming-board testimony, the singer's attorney had cut him off. "Don't be silly," lawyer Frank Fahrenkopf said.

Ross and Silverman suspected the problem must involve money, then. But Ross also knew that Newton's financing for the Aladdin hadn't come from the mob, because he'd already verified that Newton's share of the up-front money was from the Valley Bank of Nevada.

Since Ross and Silverman didn't have the complete picture of Newton's "problem," they'd have to skate carefully around it. Nonetheless, the two reporters wrote up a script that talked about Newton's having financial problems.

Paul Greenberg, the executive producer of the "NBC Nightly News," saw the script and worried about it. Was there enough support for a statement that attributed Newton's "problem" to money? If Newton was going to the mob for money, the inference was that he would be fronting for the mob at the Aladdin. That was serious stuff. Greenberg penned a correction to the script that said Newton "may have had" financial problems. But Ross and Silverman persisted, and Greenberg's changes were removed from the script.

On Monday, October 6, 10 million viewers in 213 cities around the country heard anchorman John Chancellor read his lead-in to the dramatic piece of journalism that Ross and Silverman had created in Burbank the week before.

"Wayne Newton is an idol of millions of music fans," Chancellor began, "and they have made Newton one of the highest-paid entertainers in the world. But all that money has brought him some difficulties, some of which are now the subject of a grand jury investigation. Our Special Segment by Brian Ross is about Wayne Newton's problem."

What followed was great theatre, three minutes and nine seconds of crisply edited sequences that NBC called "Wayne Newton and the Law," an evisceration of Newton in sixteen scenes.

Video	*Audio*
Medium shot, car parked at inter-section, camera moves in on rear window, two men are seen inside.	This is Palm Drive in Beverly Hills, California. There are two men in this car, detectives from the district attorney's office, on a stakeout in an organized-crime investigation.
Medium shot, two men emerging from house, camera moves in close on one who walks around car, gets in.	The man they are watching, Guido Penosi, who says he is a roofing salesman. State and federal authorities say Penosi is a New York hoodlum from the Gambino Mafia family, a man with a long criminal record, now believed to be the Gambino family's man on the West Coast, in the narcotics business and also in show business.
Medium shot, Brian Ross with Aladdin Hotel in background.	Penosi is now a key figure in a federal grand jury investigation of the activities of the Gambino Mafia family in Las Vegas. An investigation that involves one of the big casinos here, the Aladdin; and one of Las Vegas' top performers, singer Wayne Newton.
Front view, Wayne Newton on stage singing.	Newton is said to make a quarter of a million dollars a week for his nightclub act, and late last month Newton and a partner were given state approval to buy the Aladdin Hotel in Las Vegas for
Rear side shot, three women on stage, Newton crosses in front, camera moves in on him alone.	$85 million. A federal grand jury is now investigating the role of Guido Penosi and the mob in Newton's deal for the Aladdin. Despite his big income, authorities say Newton

Freeze frame of Newton, which then recedes to left of screen, is joined by freeze frame of Penosi.	has had financial problems. Investigators say that last year, just before Newton announced he would buy the Aladdin, Newton called Guido Penosi for help with a problem. Investigators say whatever the problem was, it was
Close-up, still photo of two men, camera moves in close on man on right, Piccolo.	important enough for Penosi to take it up with leaders of the Gambino family in New York. Police in New York say that this mob boss, Frank Piccolo, told associates he had taken care of Newton's problem, and had become a hidden partner in the Aladdin hotel deal.
Close-up, Newton taking oath at gaming board hearing.	At a hearing of the state gaming board, Wayne Newton said he had no hidden partners, and Newton said under oath that he knew Guido Penosi—

(sound up as Newton says)

I do.

(narration resumes) but that Penosi was just a fan and a longtime family friend.

Medium shot, board members seated.	*(board member asks)* Did you know that he is a purported member of the Gambino organized crime family?
Close-up, Newton testifying.	*(Newton answers)* No sir, I did not.

(board member asks) Are you planning to continue any relationship with Mr. Penosi?

(Newton answers) Well, on the basis of which I've known him, I don't think there has been a relationship.

Tracking shot, Newton and party go down stairway	*(narration resumes)* Federal authorities say Newton is not telling the whole story, and that Newton is expected

and into corridor.

Tracking shot, outside as Newton crosses parking area to car.

to be one of the first witnesses in the grand jury investigation.

Newton became angry when we tried to talk to him about his relationship with Guido Penosi.

(Newton) I really don't care what you want.

(Brian Ross, off camera) Pardon me?

(Newton) I said I really don't care what you want.

(Brian Ross, off camera) I'd like to talk to you about Guido Penosi—

(Newton) Go ahead and talk.

(Brian Ross, off camera) and your relationship with him.

Medium close tracking shot, man moves past camera from car, toward house.

(narration resumes)

Guido Penosi told us *(man camera is following gestures toward camera and says, "Get lost." This is background sound, low audio level)* he doesn't know anyone named Wayne Newton. Federal authorities say they know of at least eleven phone calls Penosi made to Newton's house in one two-month period, and authorities say those phone calls and Penosi's relationship with Newton and other entertainment figures are now part of a broad year-long FBI investigation of the investment of East Coast mob money from narcotics and racketeering into the entertainment business in Las Vegas and Hollywood. Brian Ross, NBC News, Los Angeles.

Medium shot as man, back to camera, enters house and closes door.

Newton watched the broadcast that night with his wife and daughter, as well as his parents, who lived in another house on his ranch in the horsey part of Vegas called Paradise Valley.

His mother walked out of the family room with tears running down her face. Newton was shaken, too. He was being accused of having a hidden mob partner in the Aladdin deal. On the news that night, he had looked like a greaseball who ran from the camera because he had something to hide.

The next morning, Newton called a press conference and said he was going to sue NBC for libel. I'm going to vindicate my good name, even if it takes everything I have and the rest of my life to do it, Newton vowed.

A few weeks later, a letter from Newton's lawyer, Fahrenkopf, was on the desk of J. Marshall Wellborn, the NBC lawyer who had signed off on the reporters' script before it was broadcast. Newton was demanding a total retraction. But Wellborn kissed off Fahrenkopf with a terse reply. NBC stood by its story.

But the network *should* have been concerned about the broadcast it had aired, because there were some gaping holes in the reporting done by Ross and Silverman.

The reporters' biggest mistake was their guess about the nature of Newton's "problem": It didn't have anything to do with money. Instead, as the reporters had once suspected before Fahrenkopf misled them, Newton had gone to the mob for personal protection. A smarmy move, perhaps, but one far different from buying a casino as a front for the mob. Besides, Newton later would steadfastly maintain that he didn't know Penosi was in the mob, and the denial was plausible even if it did strain credulity.

Newton had invested $122,000 in a show-business magazine, but when his partner needed more, Newton said no. Angered, the partner and a second man showed up one night outside the Frontier Hotel dressing room of their gold-plated investor. Things got ugly. The second man dropped references to "the godfather," and, when they wouldn't leave, Newton forcibly showed them the door. After that, an anonymous caller, a gravelly voiced enforcer who went by the name "Dapper," started making telephoned threats. Even though Newton had a bodyguard at the hotel and was protected at home as well, someone had obviously been following his daughter to and from school, because Dapper knew her routine. He told Newton that if he didn't pay the money, little Erin would be abducted, and her father would get her body back in pieces.

The sheriff told Newton there wasn't really anything that could be done. That was when Newton called his friend Penosi for help. And it was Penosi who told Newton to telephone Piccolo, a man Penosi knew very well because his sister, Jean Penosi, was married to another mobster who was Piccolo's cousin.

Penosi actually delivered the kind of protection the sheriff couldn't. Piccolo got word back to Dapper to keep hands off, and the threats stopped.

Whether he knew his cohorts were mobsters or not, Newton certainly had been having a great many more dealings with the Mafia than he had led anyone to believe. But financial problems? They weren't there, unless you stretched things beyond reason and counted as a financial "problem" his refusal to sink more money into a losing publishing venture.

There were some other elements of the broadcast that should have concerned NBC as well. Just because Guido and his pals were boasting about earning money off Wayne Newton didn't make it so, and there wasn't any evidence that Newton knew anything about their braggadocio. He certainly hadn't made them his hidden partners.

Worse, the reporters had cooked the broadcast so that it left out an integral part of Newton's testimony to the gaming authorities. The tape showed Newton telling a real whopper when he said he didn't think he had a relationship with Penosi. But they omitted the next part of his answer, in which Newton added that if Penosi *did* have mob connections, he wouldn't continue any relationship with him at all. The omission had saved a mere five seconds of broadcast time, but the real reason it wasn't there was that neither "Nightly News" Executive Producer Greenberg nor Ross thought the excised answer fit in with the theme of the story about Newton and his mob connections. The story would have been a different one had that exculpatory footage been included—which was precisely why it should have been.

They had also shown Newton fleeing the gaming-board hearing like some two-bit hoodlum on the lam. But, once again, the broadcast had omitted important scenes that would have shown a different story. Waiting in ambush with his camera, Ross had bulled his way into Newton's path and, with a few choice remarks of his own, provoked Newton's venom that showed up so well on television that night.

NBC's response to Newton's demand for a correction came exactly a month later, when it broadcast a second story by Ross and Silverman about the singer and his ties to the mob.

This time the piece showed Newton arriving in New Haven after flying all night in his private jet to answer questions from the federal grand jury that had intercepted the Penosi-Piccolo-Newton telephone calls.

But in his November 6 broadcast, Ross was still harping on the alleged financial ties between Newton and the mob—ties that by now he should have known didn't exist:

"Federal authorities want to know why Frank Piccolo became involved in solving problems Newton was having last year with a business deal"—wrong again—"and whether Piccolo had anything to do with the Aladdin Hotel deal."

If Morton Galane turned on the television at all, it was usually to watch the old movies he could beam in on the big satellite dish in the backyard of his Vegas home.

Galane didn't know much about the NBC broadcasts, but he knew the law of libel and he also knew and liked Newton. The craggy-faced lawyer had once represented the singer in a case involving Newton's former booking agent, the William Morris Agency, which claimed Newton owed it commissions on the money he'd made from a fat contract with Howard Hughes' Summa Corporation hotels. Galane saved Newton by claiming the Morris Agency used undue influence to get Newton to sign the deal.

Now, Newton was asking Galane to take his case against NBC.

But suing NBC would pose enormous problems because of the strong free-speech protections accorded newspapers and broadcasters under the law of libel.

"You're taking a crapshoot," Galane's young associate, twenty-nine-year-old James J. Jimmerson, counseled. "Where's the malice?"

Jimmerson was clearly right. Because Newton was a public figure, the law put him in a special category of people who got almost no libel protections at all. Even if a story about Newton were completely wrong, he couldn't collect any damages unless he proved that the news organization acted maliciously.

Legally speaking, *libel* is published slander (or defamation) of a person—essentially, journalistic malpractice. But even though other professionals, like lawyers and doctors, have long had to contend with the threat of costly malpractice lawsuits when they make a mistake, journalists have always enjoyed a privileged status in this country, protected by First Amendment guarantees and by court decisions, most notably the U.S. Supreme Court's 1964 landmark decision in *New York Times v. Sullivan.*

The New York *Times* precedent gave reporters great leeway to report on the foibles and malfeasances of public officials and others in the public eye—encouraged it, even. The Warren Court decision held that a public official couldn't recover damages for defamation relating to his official conduct unless he proved that the statement was made with "actual malice." Actual malice was present if a statement was made with knowledge of its falsity or with "reckless disregard" of whether it was false or not. Three years later, in *Curtis Publishing v. Butts* and *Associated Press v. Walker,* the High Court extended the "actual malice" libel test to "public figures" who had enough access to the media to expose any falsehoods published about them. Wayne Newton definitely fell into that category.

Even if the public figure could demonstrate malice, his case against a news organization still wasn't treated like any other. For ordinary citizens, the common-law tort of libel was a unique offense—"an oddity of tort law," to quote the Supreme Court—because damages for a libelous statement were *presumed* from the mere fact of publication. Juries could award substantial damages without any proof of harm to someone's reputation. The *only exception* was when a public figure like Newton claimed to have been libeled by a news organization. Then, even if malice had been shown, no damages were presumed; every penny's worth had to be proved. And the burden was always on the aggrieved party to prove the report false.

Pretty lousy odds for Newton. And for Galane.

But this was precisely the kind of case the fifty-four-year-old Galane seemed to thrive on: the unusual, seemingly unwinnable case.

Fueled by his own inadequacies and driven by a zealot's sense of right and wrong, Galane was a confounding mix of Perry Mason and *Revenge of the Nerds*. He had a wide-eyed, where-am-I? look about him, and he had long ago given up driving his old Dodge Dart with its rusted-shut driver door—had literally turned in his license at city hall and started walking the three miles from home to work—because he couldn't drive and try cases at the same time. Every trial seemed to produce a daydream-induced fender bender. Or, remembered Don Tingey, one of his former law partners, "he'd be driving in the left lane on the freeway and be talking so intently about a case that he'd forget to keep his foot on the gas pedal, and the next thing you know he'd be almost stopped cold, with traffic whizzing by all around him!" Galane's seventy-one-year-old bookkeeper, a grandmotherly type named Edith, doubled as his chauffeur. Because of his single-mindedness, something broken would invariably stay that way: Galane's telephone, with its cord so tightly twisted that he couldn't lift the receiver to his ear, was a classic example. Galane made do by putting his ear almost to desk level, a distance the cord could still momentarily be stretched. And yet the absentminded Galane also was gifted with a photographic mind that enabled him to commit entire documents and court opinions to memory, there to be summoned up years later in the heat of a courtroom battle.

Courtly and charming in private, he was inflammable as a truckload of dynamite in the courtroom, and Mort Galane stories were the stuff of legend in the Vegas courts. He had sobbed in front of juries and he had had at least one fistfight with an opposing lawyer. Other lawyers who'd worked for him said he was a great teacher but an intolerable colleague, a screamer and a perfectionist and, maybe worst of all by the lights of his brethren, an abysmal businessman.

In fact, Galane was the antithesis of the plaintiff's-trial-lawyer-as-entrepreneur: Although he took $500,000 a year out of the firm in salary and deferred compensation, he hadn't given himself a pay raise in a decade, and at least once he'd spent so much of his own money on a case that he ran completely out of funds midway through the trial. He took too many longshot cases, and when he got one, the last thing he thought of was settling.

Tingey finally quit Galane's firm in frustration over his mentor's steadfast refusal to take the steady, well-paying personal-injury (PI) cases that would have amply subsidized Galane's other legal work.

"He never cultivated the PI work," Tingey remembered, "and instead he'd be taking in all these dogs. He'd be representing some poor widow whose husband had been burned to death, spending years trying to prove who was at fault. Or a stuntman named Harry Wham who got hurt by diving between the wings of an airplane! Mort *made* that case; it was a nothin' case. He got seventy-five thousand dollars for it, but he could have been making ten times that amount on other things."

Only Galane would have sued the Riviera in the 1960s for the unique tort of dance-band piracy. His client was a local bandleader, Benny Short, and twenty years later Galane was still talking about how he got the courts to uphold his allegation that the Riviera, the musicians' union, and another bandleader had all conspired to steal Short's relief band.

Then there was the time Galane sued Union Oil for putting a car wash out of business. Jimmerson lost the case the first time, but then Galane got the verdict reversed and tried it again to win a $1.5 million verdict—which Galane split fifty-fifty with his grateful client. And it was vintage Galane when he sued Dun & Bradstreet, the big credit reporting company, in the tiny borough of Doylestown, Pennsylvania, over a bad report it had given his client. He won the case— Galane almost always won—but he didn't get even one dollar in damages for his client. They're still laughing about that one in Galane's office, too, because that was the case in which Galane, who'd stayed out too late dancing one night, dropped dead asleep at the counsel table the next morning and the judge thought he'd had a heart attack and died.

Around the courthouse, the worst case for a defense lawyer to have was the kind generically known as "a Mort Galane case."

"Nobody wanted to be on the other side from Mort Galane,"

Tingey recalled. "You knew you were going to have to double your defense budget."

Mort Galane did one thing better than any lawyer in Vegas. He beat you to death. And by beating you he beat the demons of self-doubt that tortured him.

"You have to have two things to really succeed. One, you've gotta have some self-doubt, and I have all kinds of self-doubt, all the time. That's why you work so hard. And second is, you have to have felt the pain of losing."

With his rapid-fire speech and the occasional hint of an instantly recognizable Bronx accent in a voice that, in excitement, spanned three octaves, Galane was still the native New Yorker, the only child of an uneducated plumber.

It was 1954 when Galane first arrived in Las Vegas. With an engineering degree from the City College of New York and a night-school law degree from George Washington University in Washington, D.C., Galane became a patent attorney for a small Washington firm. He had a client in Vegas, and when he went out to the desert for the first time he immediately fell in love with it, not just because of the climate, but because Galane smelled an opportunity.

"This was a place where they needed good professionals and they didn't have many," Galane recalled. "It was the chance to be a big fish in a little pond. To excel at something. To have power." Galane wasn't happy with the kind of practice a lawyer had to have in Washington or any of the other legal centers. There, an attorney specialized in one area—antitrust, patents, litigation, securities—"and you told people how exciting and important it was, but basically it was pretty dreary." By contrast, Vegas was a beckoning boomtown.

And yet the Vegas culture also bred a defensiveness into Galane, a feeling that lawyers from outside Las Vegas would never accept him as one of the best. Galane's reaction was to vindicate himself, to refute what he *thought* those other lawyers thought of him by mercilessly beating them in the courtroom. Nothing stood in his way. He walked to the office and often was at his desk before sunrise. His workaholic's idea of a vacation was to visit the law library in another city.

Galane's was a paranoiac's reaction to a threat perceived. He became even more of a loner—made few friends, did his own legal research, took in no law partners. "The reason Mort wouldn't ever go to a football game," teased Paula Miller, his secretary of eighteen years, "is because he'd think those eleven men in a huddle were talking about *him.*" Galane always denied that, of course, but hearing him say, "I'm not paranoid" was like hearing Nixon say, "I am not a crook." Galane was a lawyer built for survival. Always tightfisted, he now got free of every debt, even his home mortgage, so he could survive any financial calamity.

There was a paradox to Galane. He worried about what people thought of him and puzzled over the hatred he engendered, but he also reveled in his reputation as a take-no-prisoners lawyer. Paranoia about the opposition kept him on constant alert. In the obloquy of others he found an order of battle, and he used it to impell him to victory. "I'm a very hard-hitting lawyer—*very* hard," Galane said proudly. "And I *win.*"

When Galane learned once that lawyers he'd beaten in a jury trial ten years earlier were still spreading rumors about his alleged misconduct in the case, he roiled with the kind of anger that won cases. "I know exactly who they were, and which cases, and they're LOSERS!" he shouted, the last word so tinged with his suddenly returned Bronx accent that it came out *"LOOS*-ahs," a big punch on the first syllable.

"Big shots with credentials of law review editors, and LOSERS! What the hell can I say? If a guy's a loser, and he goes that far, he's SICK! What can I say? So, obviously I know what I'm talking about. I can tell you this: I'd never do it. You can quote me on that one. I'm more of a man than they could ever be! Not in a million years! I think you gotta be SICK to harbor a grudge for a decade! A mental case! To harbor a grudge, for a DECADE! I can't believe that any professional man would do that! I must have been a helluva man to do that to someone! What the hell could I have done that was that good that people can wait ten years to get their satisfaction?"

The lawyers who didn't like him had "sour grapes" because Galane had beaten them, he told himself. "Some of them might be extraordinarily vain, and have had their bubbles burst." As Galane saw it, vanity bred overconfidence—and that was every opponent's window of vulnerability. Yet he also didn't mind having his ability underestimated by the other side. That just made it easier for him to win.

"In the vast majority of my cases," Galane claimed, voice suddenly rising above a shout once more, "opposing lead counsel have given their clients opinions, which I learned about, that there'd be no damages, no liability, and no recovery. I know it as a fact! In case after case! In some instances, the lawyers have gone on record that I'm to get nothing, because there's no merit to my case!

"And let's say I became aware of it. And let's assume that case goes to trial. And let's assume the verdict comes in that's unique in history. How do you think the lawyer feels who may have signed the letter that said 'No liability and no damages'! Case after case after case!

"And that led to situations where either nobody would even talk to me, or, if the time came as trial approached and they did talk to me, it was in a very condescending manner, as if this were a nuisance suit where they had to give some money in order to show their clients that they don't want to appear intransigent. And then there's a verdict with a historically high award! How does the lawyer explain that to his client?"

Galane softened his voice now. "That does not breed fondness."

Certainly, Galane knew that. "I'll give you a list of enemies the likes of which you've never seen!" he boasted when I first asked him for the names of people who could tell me something about him. Then he cackled. "I wouldn't run for public office! Even my wife wouldn't vote for me! She's too perceptive!"

Galane saw himself as a reflection of his father. "You talk about a workaholic! This guy was a real breadwinner. Worked until he was seventy-eight years old and then he died. I begged him: Why don't you retire? Move out West. He would've *died* if he'd retired." Galane said the same thing about himself. "So, I figure it's in the genes."

In the genes. Everything predetermined.

Nobody liked his father, either, and whatever provoked that animus must, Mort reckoned, be in his genes, too. "It's *all* in the genes! What the hell!"

"What's meant to be is meant to be," Galane always said. He didn't think anyone's scope of free will was very great. "We're boxed in. We need a couple of breaks."

And yet, despite his fatalism, despite his avowed acceptance of the hands life dealt him, Galane was also an extraordinarily superstitious man. He was Sin City's version of a latter-day Calvinist who believed everything was preordained—but he sure wanted to see some good omens now and then. Galane reconciled fatalism and superstition by saying he didn't want to "dare" the bad cards to come his way. Once, when they were returning to their office from the courthouse at dusk, a black cat crossed the path of Galane and Tingey and ran up the alley behind the Four Queens casino next door. Galane threw down his papers and bolted into the alley, hot on the trail of the cat and hell-bent on finding it so he could walk around it. Galane spent half an hour hunting for the cat, but it was just too dark and he returned to the office disheveled and glum.

Galane: "You saw some white on that cat, didn't you?"

Tingey smiled inwardly, but he knew his boss needed assuaging. "Yeah," he replied impishly. "I think I saw some white around the neck."

People hired Mort Galane not because he was suave or dignified or any of the other things that lawyers can be, but because once he took their case he would stop at nothing to win. Well-publicized victories produced clients who wanted more of the same. That, in fact, was what persuaded Newton to hire him: Galane had just won a $675,000 libel verdict against one of the local television stations on behalf of a mobile-home dealer who'd run unsuccessfully for governor. It was an impressive judgment, considering that the owner of the station had merely accused the candidate, falsely, as it turned out, of paying for his TV advertising with a check that bounced, a foolish accusation, maybe, but one that Galane was able to make into a huge verdict. Trouble was, every judge always had the last word on Galane's success, and in this case the judge later reduced the judgment to a paltry $50,000. That was the flip side of Galane's talent: He was so effective that judges frequently felt compelled to overrule his juries.

Sometimes, the loser in a case against Galane decided to switch sides and hire Galane himself the next time he had a problem. That was exactly what Robert Maheu had done.

Maheu was Howard Hughes' chief of operations in Las Vegas during the billionaire's heyday there. Even though Maheu and Hughes both lived at the Desert Inn, the two had never even met—Maheu had only glimpsed his boss twice from a distance, and Hughes communicated with him through telephone calls and hundreds of notes scribbled on sheets of yellow paper and passed along to Maheu via Hughes' Mormon aides. But Maheu had been Hughes' aide-de-camp and general factotum since 1959, the doer of whatever needed to be done. Maheu oversaw Hughes' vast and expanding gambling empire, and when Hughes wanted to make a political contribution or send a message to some politician, Maheu was the bagman. He was also Hughes' alter ego, representing his boss before government agencies and maintaining contacts with the outside world from which Hughes had withdrawn.

At first blush, it was hard to conceive of someone less suited to the task than Maheu, a portly, balding character and a great spinner of yarns who cast himself as a master of stealth but who, ever since his FBI days, had seemed to botch and bumble his way through one cloak-and-dagger episode after another. On his very first FBI assignment, conducting a background investigation of a federal clerical worker, the new G-man accidentally locked the keys in his government car and had to break the driver-side window with the butt of his gun. Maheu actually enjoyed telling such stories on himself, and one of his favorites was about the time, in 1944, that the government sent him to Washington to convince two German agents that the D-Day invasion would be in Southern France, rather than Normandy. He had lived under the assumed name of Robert A. Marchand "for about forty-five minutes when I bumped into one of my best friends from Holy Cross College." So much for that assignment. He hadn't done very well, either, in arranging the exploding-cigar assassination of Cuba's Fidel Castro. But Maheu was Hughes' man and there were those who so marveled at the organization's pathological secrecy that they believed Maheu possessed a cunning that simply wasn't apparent.

While the Hughes organization was still furtively assembling its gambling properties in Vegas in the late 1960s, Maheu tried to buy one of the last big, undeveloped parcels on the strip and promptly ran head-on into Galane.

Maheu was trying to get the piece of land cheaply by buying it through a ringer. Galane's client, the parcel's owner, also happened to be the man Galane had earlier beaten in the Benny Short band-pirating case—the loser had switched sides after Galane trounced him. As Galane did some digging through the Las Vegas land records, he sniffed out Maheu's scam and slapped the Hughes organization with an antitrust suit for monopolizing the Vegas casino business!

"We'd set out to buy every piece of raw land on the Strip, and I didn't think anybody but Hughes knew this!" Maheu marveled later. He telephoned Hughes and told the billionaire that Galane had found them out. "I can't believe it," Maheu told Hughes. "He knows every piece of property we've bought—even the ones where we used shills" to disguise the real purchaser.

"Settle the goddamn thing, quick!" Maheu recalled Hughes' replying. And settle it Maheu did, making a fast friend in the process. Not long after that, Galane and Maheu and their wives vacationed together in Mexico.

The Hughes people paid Maheu handsomely in those freewheeling days—$520,000 a year during the late 1960s (a sum worth many times that today), plus perks like cars and jets and a yacht and housing. But if Maheu deserved that much as a vaunted Vegas straw boss for Hughes, Maheu told the tax man a decidedly different story when it came to his personal finances. From 1961 to 1971, he reported the comparatively paltry sum of $40,368 as his average annual after-tax earnings. During the five years from 1967 to 1971, the average was an astoundingly miniscule $2,661—1/250 of what he was being paid by Hughes!

The IRS suspected something fishy. But, then again, perhaps so did some of the other key people in the Hughes organization, because on the night of Friday, December 4, 1970, they threw Maheu out in a palace coup. Hastily, Maheu directed one of his subordinates to enter the casino cage at the Frontier Hotel and bring him $10,000 that he could use to file a lawsuit to prevent his firing. And then he called Mort Galane.

The fifty-three-year-old Maheu told anyone who would listen that Hughes couldn't possibly have ordered his dismissal; that, far from being dissatisfied with Maheu, Hughes had once begged him not to quit and had tearfully offered him a job for life. As far as Galane was concerned, his friend had a breach-of-contract lawsuit, and that was what Galane filed in state court the next morning.

Maheu, insolvent and despondent, couldn't find a job during all of 1971, and Galane's breach-of-contract lawsuit for him wasn't going anywhere, either. But right after the new year, Hughes surfaced, bringing with him the makings of a new lawsuit.

McGraw-Hill had just announced plans for an autobiography of Hughes, based on interviews the hermit had supposedly given to a writer named Clifford Irving. It was all a hoax, but Irving was counting on Hughes to continue his hermitic ways and thus not to spoil Irving's crime. Instead, Hughes' aides called a news conference, and on January 7, 1972, Hughes spoke for hours by telephone from his hotel room on Paradise Island in the Bahamas to seven newsmen assembled at the Sheraton Universal Hotel in Los Angeles.

"Was Maheu fired on your orders?" NBC's Roy Neal asked. Hughes had already been talking to the reporters for two hours, and he was getting testy.

"Specifically," Hughes replied, probably ending whatever hopes Maheu had of getting his old job back by order of the Nevada courts.

"Why?" Neal asked.

"Because he's a no-good, dishonest son of a bitch, and he stole me blind," Hughes blurted out. "I don't suppose I ought to be saying that at a news conference, but I just don't know any other way to answer it. If you, if you would even—you wouldn't think it could be possible with modern methods of bookkeeping and accounting and so forth for a thing like the Maheu theft to have occurred, but believe me it did, because the money's gone and he's got it."

Galane told Maheu he had a new cause of action against Hughes: slander. And Galane's modus operandi in prosecuting that lawsuit against one of the world's richest men presaged the kind of battle Galane would wage more than a decade later against NBC.

Galane filed his case against the Hughes Tool Company (later known as Summa Corporation) in Los Angeles the following month. Since Maheu was a citizen of Nevada and Hughes had once lived there, the choice of venue and defendant was calculated to make sure Galane got the case out of the inhospitable Nevada state court and into federal court. Under the doctrine known as *diversity*, a federal court could have jurisdiction as long as the plaintiff and the defendant were from different states. Had Galane sued Hughes personally instead of going after only Summa, he risked keeping the case in Nevada by Hughes' lawyers claiming he was still a Nevada citizen who was just visiting the Bahamas.

The Hughes case was going to be a pitched battle from Day One. There was no possibility of a settlement because the Hughes people, sitting atop their boss' millions, couldn't afford to encourage lawsuits by making themselves easy targets. And yet, with Maheu already broke, the litigation against Hughes & Co. threatened to bring down Galane because he would have to put his own money up front.

Galane had the case on a contingency, which meant he'd ultimately collect a third of whatever Maheu was awarded. In the meantime, Maheu was supposed to be paying Galane's out-of-pocket expenses— expenses which ultimately came to $300,000—but the management-consulting job that the sad-sack Maheu had finally gotten with Checker Cab hardly provided enough to pay Maheu's rent, let alone Galane's expense bills. So Galane had no choice but to start plowing his own savings into the case.

Worse, since the case was going to go to trial in Los Angeles, Galane would literally have to move his three-lawyer firm to that city for the duration of the proceedings.

Everything was done on a shoestring. Galane's young associate, Tingey, a Mormon who by then already had ten children, and who now has twelve, was making a mere $28,000 a year. He and his young colleague took rooms in a cheap downtown motel, while Galane rented an apartment four blocks from the courthouse for $300 a month, plus another $100 a month for the furniture. Maheu took a room in a men's club downtown. When it came time to ship to Los Angeles the documents Galane was going to need for the trial, it was Tingey who loaded the filing cabinets into a U-Haul truck and drove them there himself.

Despite Hughes' comments at the telephone news conference, it was Galane's theory that others in the Hughes organization had conspired to kick Maheu out. To prove his point, and, thus, to prove the falsity of what Hughes had said, Galane served notice that he was going to take the depositions of all of the key Summa officials. He was going for punitive damages, and his intent was to gather evidence of "ill will" against Maheu to support his claim.

But the Hughes people, almost as maniacally secretive as their boss, seemingly wanted to avoid having their depositions taken at almost any cost, knowing, as they must have, that Galane would take full advantage of his opportunity to undertake a microscopic examination of the mysterious world of Hughes.

Even the trial judge, Harry Pregerson, fifty-one years old, a crusty, battle-scarred ex-Marine who'd been a judge in the Central District of California since Lyndon Johnson appointed him seven years earlier, didn't seem to think much of Galane's chances of winning, so he suggested a compromise: There could be two stages to the trial, a liability phase and a damages phase. If Maheu lost on liability, there obviously wouldn't be any need to establish punitive damages, and thus no need for the exhaustive depositions Galane was contemplating.

Summa's chief trial lawyer was Norbert Schlei, a trim, silver-haired forty-five-year-old partner in the Los Angeles office of Hughes Hubbard & Reed. Schlei was heavy-duty: Yale Law, Supreme Court clerk, assistant attorney general of the United States under Kennedy and Johnson. He was assisted by Howard Jaffe, a New York lawyer whose firm, Davis & Cox, had close ties to Summa, and whose partner, Chester Davis, was one of Summa's corporate officers.

Ordinarily, the burden would be on Maheu, as the plaintiff, to prove that Hughes had lied. But Pregerson obviously thought so little of Maheu's prospects for doing that that he suggested something to simplify the case even further: Pregerson asked Schlei whether Summa would be willing to switch places with the plaintiff and assume the burden of proof instead. Yes, Schlei replied, he would be glad to prove that what Hughes said about Maheu being a crook was entirely true.

"That's not good enough," Galane countered. "What about the malice issue?" Proving malice was the key to winning punitive damages.

Pregerson asked Schlei, If you don't discharge your burden of proving truth, would you then admit that there was malice in what Mr. Hughes said? Yes, a confident Schlei replied again.

"That's still not good enough, Your honor," Galane shot back. "What about the *degree* of malice, because that also affects punitive damages?"

This time, Pregerson asked Schlei whether he would be willing to admit that, if Summa lost on the truth issue, the greatest degree of malice would be presumed. Yes again.

"I protest!" Galane shouted. "That doesn't mean that the whole Summa board of directors admits it, and under the complicity rule of California law we have to have an admission on this."

Yes, yes, yes, Schlei replied, the whole board of directors will admit the greatest degree of malice if we don't prove truth.

Summa was going to almost any length to avoid intensive depositions of its officers—to the point where even Schlei's fellow lawyers were puzzled at the handicap he was letting Summa assume.

John Blue, a thirty-year-old second-year associate at Schlei's firm, couldn't figure out what his senior partner was doing, but there were some things a young associate didn't say to a presumably wisened partner. Blue and another Hughes Hubbard second-year man, twenty-seven-year-old Bill Bisset, were Schlei's grunts and gofers. They both wondered whether Schlei had made some kind of deal with the other side, and they speculated—wrongly, Galane later maintained—that Summa had assumed the burden of proof in exchange for Galane's agreement not to name Hughes personally as a defendant, an action which, had Galane taken it, would almost surely have produced a no-show defendant and a default judgment for Maheu.

"If there was no deal," Blue told me during my research for this book, "then Davis & Cox and Hughes Hubbard & Reed committed egregious malpractice by not moving to dismiss Summa as a defendant." (Bisset disagreed, telling me it was obvious that Summa wanted to protect Hughes and had ordered its lawyers to keep him out of the litigation.) Hughes, both young lawyers theorized at the time, though, had been speaking as a private citizen: Maheu stole *him* blind. Hughes had no role in the management of Summa, and there was no reason for Summa to take responsibility for what Hughes said. But Blue and Bisset kept these thoughts to themselves then rather than antagonize Schlei. That was the way the big law firms worked.

Galane had already formed his own opinions about Schlei and Jaffe. He loathed them. To some extent, working up a good hatred for the lawyers on the other side was just Galane's way of limbering up for the main event. He was a method actor in front of a jury, a lawyer whose preparation always included self-induced animosity for the other side.

But Galane's feelings about the Summa lawyers far transcended that. Galane even blamed Jaffe for the heart attack that he had suffered as he rushed from his Beverly Hills hotel to a pretrial hearing in Pregerson's court in September 1972. The defense lawyers had been waiting in the courtroom for Galane, but it was Pregerson who found out the reason for the delay in a phone call from Galane. "I can't come to court, Judge," Galane told the stunned Pregerson from his doctor's office. "I'm having a coronary."

Jaffe rushed to the hospital, beating Galane's ambulance, so that he was waiting at the emergency room door when his foe was wheeled in. Galane took one look at Jaffe and grasped the hand of his doctor: "Don't worry, Doctor," he said. "I'll be the best patient you've ever had, because my competition will never get the edge on me over this!" The next morning, Galane woke up to find his first visitor: Jaffe. All this was just too much for such a superstitious man. Galane started telling people he thought Summa had put out a contract on his life.

"Jaffe could really push Mort's hot button and he did it again that day," Blue recalled. "I still remember Mort backing down the hall at the Davis & Cox offices some time later, absolutely enraged, shaking a finger at Jaffe and saying: 'Don't come any nearer to me! You were the first person I saw after my heart attack, and you wished me DEAD!' "

There was no love lost between Galane and Schlei, either. Galane, always sensitive about what the big-city lawyers thought, felt Schlei had demeaned him after they appeared in court together for the first time on a pretrial motion.

The truth was, Schlei was the best orator Galane, three years Schlei's senior, had ever been up against. Galane silently acknowledged that to himself as soon as Pregerson ruled in Schlei's favor on the routine motion.

But when Schlei invited Galane to a downtown sushi restaurant afterward, what had been an innocuous conversation became more interesting to Galane as the two walked back to Schlei's office. "You know," Schlei boasted to Galane when they arrived there, "I have a golden tongue."

Galane still recalled the incident vividly. "He was telling me what a great lawyer he is. The man was *very* vain. I have a favorite expression when someone talks like that. And it comes because when I was a youngster I was raised in a family that earned its livelihood in the building trades. In the trades, a man was supposed to be paid union scale. But to hold a job, at the height of the Depression, workmen always worked below scale. They were never given union scale.

"So, in the building trades, when you had a top man, he'd always talk about getting scale. Nobody got it, but that's how they talked. So, when this man said to me, he has a golden tongue, I quietly said, 'For what it's worth, I don't work below scale.' In other words, I'm no slouch, either.

"I remembered it afterward, because you size up a lawyer, and if you've got a vain lawyer, you can beat him. Vanity is a sign of someone who's so wrapped up in himself that he can't have any feeling for jurors. A vain person is a person who, when he looks in a mirror, all he can see is how beautiful he is. He doesn't know anyone else is alive! Such people cannot try jury cases. They're no good because they can't relate to the jury."

Galane returned to Vegas and told Tingey and Shearing, "We have found a vulnerable opponent, and we're going to beat him!"

Galane was seeking $17 million in damages from Summa. As previously agreed, Schlei was going to defend the case on the ground that the statement was true—that Maheu was, indeed, a thief—and he was going to present more than a dozen specific examples of Maheu's alleged dishonesty. To find for Summa, the jury had to believe the truth of only one of those examples.

Since Schlei had assumed the burden of proof, he would be the first to deliver his opening statement on Thursday, February 28, 1974, in Pregerson's Los Angeles courtroom, sketching the outline of the case that would gradually be filled in over the next four months of trial.

In one scam alone, Schlei told the jury, Maheu had stolen more than $750,000 from Hughes by overbilling him for guard services at an airport Maheu leased for Hughes in Tucson. But there were other sizable swindles as well: Maheu had also been pocketing some of the money that was supposed to be used for the Tucson airport lease payments, and Summa was more than $70,000 in arrears when the lease finally ended.

There was also the matter of the $50,000 cash political contribution that Maheu was supposed to have given Vice President Hubert Humphrey on Hughes' behalf. Hughes wanted Maheu to use the money as an inducement for Humphrey to stop the Nevada atomic-bomb tests if he became president, because Hughes thought the bomb tests hurt his gambling business and kept people away from Las Vegas. Maheu claimed he'd left the cash in a briefcase in Humphrey's limousine, but Humphrey swore Maheu hadn't, and Schlei said Maheu had pocketed it himself. Maheu, Schlei went on, blended into the Vegas mixture of ready cash and no-questions-asked very well: He had withdrawn another $209,000 in cash from various casino cages and from Hughes' personal bank account, virtually all of it to take care of whatever cash-flow squeeze he was experiencing at the moment.

The third major area of misconduct asserted by Schlei was Maheu's alleged acceptance of hundreds of thousands of dollars in kickbacks from persons with whom he dealt on behalf of Summa and Hughes. Maheu, Schlei claimed, had received a $150,000 kickback from Las Vegas newspaper publisher Hank Greenspun and another $150,000 under the table during negotiations for Hughes' purchase of the Desert Inn and the Sands. There was a pattern, Schlei asserted, that whenever someone got money from Hughes, part of it wound up in Maheu's pocket, at least a million dollars in all, maybe as much as $2.5 million.

"Now, again, ladies and gentlemen, your purpose here is not to determine whether Mr. Maheu should be punished or whether he should pay any money back to the company," Schlei said, all politesse and self-confidence, as he finished his opening statement that day. "In this proceeding that is now before you, we cannot win anything from Mr. Maheu. All that we can do is *not lose,* so the question is whether we have made out a defense to the claim that Mr. Maheu has made, and whether he is entitled to more dollars to go with those he has already received. Thank you."

Even before the end of Schlei's opening statement, though, Galane was doing what he was best known for in court, going into his usual start-of-trial tirade, this time shouting at Schlei because "he concealed, and intentionally lied to the jury" about the damages Maheu and Summa were seeking from each other.

Pregerson reacted with equanimity. "You had better keep your voice down, Mr. Galane. I am only about two feet from you."

Galane's defense of Maheu was straightforward enough: Hughes knew everything that Maheu was doing—knew about all the money that was being raked off—and in every single case either explicitly or implicitly approved of it. Galane ticked off each deal that Schlei had mentioned the day before and furnished his client's innocuous, if implausible, explanation for each. After all, Galane seemed to say, Howard Hughes' world was a crazy one, and what his people did didn't have to make sense to the average man. As far as Hughes was concerned, things the rest of us might consider suspicious were all in a day's work for Maheu.

As Galane neared the end of his opening statement and spoke of how Maheu was forced out of the Hughes organization, he was beginning to sound more and more like the keynoter at an Elks Club testimonial for Hughes' most loyal retainer.

"The evidence will show you that Robert Maheu could *not* resign," Galane veritably shouted, "because the Nevada Gaming Commission and the governor of Nevada had years before made an arrangement that they would not require Howard Hughes to appear before them, and in fact not even require fingerprints for a gambling license, provided one man, *and one man alone,* took the responsibility to be the spokesman for Howard Hughes before the entire officialdom of the State of Nevada, and that one man was Robert A. Maheu! And if he had resigned without adequate proof in documentary form of what Howard Hughes indeed wanted, Robert Maheu would have forfeited whatever position of trust would have been lodged in him by the government of the state of Nevada. That's what the evidence will show!"

There were two people who knew the truth or falsity of that defense, but only one of them was going to testify. And if the jury believed Robert Maheu, Summa was going to lose.

"It became their 'Prince of a Man' theory versus our 'He's a Thief' theory," Blue recalled.

"My case was a credibility case," Galane explained. "You either liked and believed Robert Maheu, or you didn't. A guy says, 'I had these conversations with Hughes.' There was nobody to contradict!

"I told Maheu, 'The best thing you can do is get on that witness stand and tell your story.'"

And that was precisely what Maheu did, spending day after day on the witness stand regaling the court with incredible tales of the mysterious world of Howard Hughes, tales Maheu earnestly claimed he fully expected his old boss to come walking right into the courtroom to corroborate. It was quite a performance.

Schlei's lengthy questioning of Maheu gave Maheu the chance to be an Ollie North-style witness. Even the judge began to see Maheu in a sympathetic light—a bungler and a bumbler, maybe, but also a guy who was trying to do right by his eccentric boss.

Schlei either didn't see what was happening or didn't worry about it, so certain was the defense team that it had the goods on Maheu. Secure in his oratorical gifts, Schlei was winging the trial, showing up each morning a few minutes before the eight o'clock start. But Blue and Bisset, the two young associates assigned to help him, feared the lack of preparation would some day catch up with the defense, so they started preparing a color-coded "script"—that's what they called it—that Schlei would use each day. Blue was responsible for outlining the deposition testimony that would be read into the record, while Bisset took charge of scripting out what Schlei should ask the live witnesses.

On the night before a defense witness' testimony, the entire defense team—Schlei, Jaffe, Bisset and Blue—would take the witness to dinner, with Schlei's asking the witness questions while the two young men furiously scribbled notes so they could re-create the scenario back at their Century City offices later that night for use in the next morning's script. Pregerson fancied himself a scholar of the law and would frequently ask both sides to prepare briefs on some esoteric legal point that had come up that day, and it also fell to the young $25,000-a-year associates, who hadn't yet even taken the California bar exam, to stay up all night writing the defense responses.

The judge had also introduced a novel device to help the jury keep track of all the evidence that was flying past it: Pregerson periodically stopped the trial and let Schlei and Galane spend a little time summarizing the evidence they'd just presented. It was a welcome tool for the jury, and one that would also be used in the Newton libel trial twelve years later. But for Blue and Bisset, it only meant more work, because they scripted out every word of each minisummation for Schlei, an amazing feat considering that Blue, at least, didn't even understand what Schlei was trying to prove until well into the trial.

"We had a bunker mentality," Blue recollected. "So much work to do. So little time. I was married and working my ass off, billing over 300 hours a month. I didn't have time to see the forest; we were always confronting the trees. It was like being in the middle of a pack during a marathon. Not in front, not behind, just exhausted and waiting for the finish line."

As the four-month liability phase of the trial drew to a close, it was finally becoming clear to the defense team that the absence of their best witness, Hughes, was going to hurt them greatly. So was their strategy, once deemed so expedient, of keeping the other Summa executives out of trouble by assuming the burden of proof and defending the slander case purely on the basis of truth.

Schlei saved his best rhetorical flourishes for what he saw as the strongest part of his case: Maheu's overbilling for the Tucson airport guards. Maheu, Schlei pointed out, had claimed that Hughes asked him to falsify the bills—"the damnedest lie that was ever told in an American courtroom. That is the biggest whopper you will ever hear if you stay in courtrooms for the rest of your life. . . . This Tucson thing must have been like Banquo in *Macbeth*. I mean, it was something that Mr. Maheu kept thinking was behind him, and the ghost would keep rising!" But all that Schlei could offer in response were the defense *theories* about Hughes' dissatisfaction with Maheu. Hughes wasn't there to contradict anything Maheu said.

"This lawsuit is the capstone of Mr. Maheu's career," Schlei proclaimed. "It is, in itself, an instrument of a kind of extortion, of blackmail. It is Maheu's way of getting one last chunk of that Hughes money. . . . He is seeking to use you, ladies and gentlemen, as the very instrument of this last effort to get money wrongfully from his employer."

Galane's closing argument went on for four days. He saw closings as the time to etch in every tiny detail that came out during the trial, and if the judge didn't stop him Galane always filibustered. Painstakingly, he took the jurors through Maheu's version of each disputed transaction. And he pounded away relentlessly at the absence of Hughes and the Summa executives: in essence, putting everyone *except Maheu* on trial.

"Only two men, only two men are involved in the determination of the justice of this cause," Galane began. "Robert Maheu. Howard Hughes."

Galane said Hughes couldn't avoid responsibility for his actions simply by not showing up. Nor, he said, could the other Summa executives: "The failure of a party to obtain the testimony of a person peculiarly available to that party allows you in your discretion to draw an inference that that party was afraid to face cross examination, and therefore it is Mr. Maheu who told the truth!"

It was a pitch for the stars by a desperate lawyer—a lawyer out of money and out of luck if he lost. Galane was living the ignominy, too, right along with his client, and you could hear that in his voice.

"If Howard Hughes had had the human decency to place a telephone call to a man with whom he had had a business relationship for as many years as Robert Maheu and Howard Hughes had had such a relationship, *that* would have been an effective termination. However, Mr. Hughes saw fit to disappear!" Hughes, Galane thundered, wasn't a man; he was just "a disembodied voice who did not see fit to show his face to the world as he destroyed another human being, but hid behind an electronic box." Hughes was a coward who had "the moral obligation of one who destroys the character of another to come forth and justify the weapon of destruction that he utilized."

It was up to Pregerson to instruct the jury on the applicable law, and then to send them out to begin their deliberations. But no one was ready for the two-cents-worth that Pregerson decided to add to the debate over Maheu's credibility.

Pregerson, who had been droning on with his jury instructions, suddenly announced that he intended to comment on the evidence, and thereupon he launched into what he undoubtedly thought would be a helpful summation of his own.

"To me," Pregerson began, "Robert A. Maheu is an enigma, a puzzlement. On one hand he can be described as affable, intelligent, imaginative, articulate. He is a friendly man with important friends in high places." Maybe Maheu was an overly trusting man whose personal affairs were in a state of disarray, Pregerson speculated. He was "possessed of some unusual talents, but like all men he has his share of foibles."

That was it—a personal character reference for Maheu! No mention whatsoever of any of the defense evidence of Maheu's fraud.

The trial was over. Pregerson asked the lawyers for both sides whether they had any objections, and both Schlei and Galane said they didn't.

But Schlei and his defense team had made a terrible error in not immediately objecting to Pregerson's blatantly one-sided judicial summation, and within minutes they learned just how badly they'd blundered when Schlei's wife, Barbara, walked to the front and, in effect, told her husband that Pregerson had just destroyed his case.

Quickly, Blue looked into the jury room and verified that deliberations hadn't yet begun. The jurors were off to lunch. There was still time to raise an objection, and the defense lawyers sent a note to Pregerson asking that he summon the jury and take back what he'd just said. But Pregerson wouldn't do that, and on Tuesday, July 1, a week and a day after their deliberations began, the jury found for Maheu. Tingey packed up another U-Haul truck that afternoon and transported all the trial records back to Vegas.

Winning that first trial was just a prelude to the payoff, though. It meant Galane would next have to establish the extent of his client's damages—in other words, if Maheu couldn't get a job because of what Hughes said about him, how much was he really losing? Galane's case for big damages still seemed weak, because after a long stretch of unemployment Maheu had finally gotten a $40,000-a-year job. The after-tax income Maheu declared in his years with Hughes had been even lower. If that were what Maheu was really worth, and assuming he had perhaps ten more years of gainful work ahead of him, the damages were going to be quite small. But what the defense lawyers hadn't anticipated was the fanciful theory Galane and Maheu concocted to vastly inflate Maheu's real worth on the job market.

The theory was this: What Maheu picked up from his day job was nothing compared to what he could do during evenings and on weekends! Maheu divided his spare time into six equal parts and said he had been planning, before the Hughes news conference, to sell each for $100,000, for a potential annual income of somewhere around $600,000. Galane could only afford one expert witness, a business economist who calculated that Maheu's lost earnings were thus somewhere around $8,633,850. After four weeks of desultory testimony during the summer of 1974, the same jury that had found in Maheu's favor awarded him roughly a third of what Maheu said his "spare time" was worth: $2,823,333.30.

As weak as Maheu's case seemed, and as laughable as his damage theory was, Summa would probably have ended up paying that judgment had Pregerson not made his last-minute Maheu's-not-such-a-bad-guy-after-all speech to the jurors. Almost as an afterthought, the defense lawyers threw their quarrel with Pregerson's little speech into their appeal brief, and that turned out to be the one thing that the U.S. Court of Appeals for the Ninth Circuit thought warranted a new trial for Summa. The ruling finally came on January 12, 1978.

"A lying, prevaricating, equivocating, mendacious, dishonest, deceitful, untruthful, tergiversating witness," the three appellate judges said of Maheu. The judges couldn't understand what Pregerson saw in him. If there were any other synonyms for describing Hughes' former factotum, they obviously weren't in Roget's.

Now it was Galane who faced a crucible. After six months devoted to one case in Los Angeles, his Las Vegas law practice had been in shambles and it was only now financially healthy again. Maheu couldn't pay him a cent, and Galane was deeply in hock from the first case. He couldn't possibly afford to retry the case, but he bluffed and told Summa he intended to—unless they settled with him.

Summa's insurance carrier, which had the burden of paying all the legal costs if a second trial took place, offered a settlement that benefited everybody but Maheu. The insurance company would pay $1.5 million into a settlement pool that would be divided into thirds: Galane would get $500,000 as his fee; Summa would get another $500,000 in satisfaction of a counterclaim it had against Maheu; and the final $500,000, Maheu's share, would be turned over to the IRS, which was trying to collect $3 million in back taxes it claimed Maheu owed from the Hughes days. The IRS had a lien on anything and everything that Maheu owned.

"I ended up with zilch," Maheu grumbled. "I never saw any of it. They think I'm filthy rich. I didn't even get my travel expenses paid for."

The Maheu victory heralded heady times for Galane. Defeating the entire Hughes organization was a showstopper, and Galane returned to Vegas with a mythic reputation as the city's lawyer of choice. Hotel owners steered lucrative legal business his way, and soon Galane was paying himself a $250,000-a-year salary and sinking another $250,000 annually into a deferred-compensation plan. The good times had finally arrived for Mort Galane.

"I had a couple of years, after the Maheu case, where I cleaned up representing hotels here," he said later. "And we've got lawyers here who'd give their right arm to represent big hotels, as if it's a big deal. And I was cleaning up! And the work was duck soup! My wife and I would be invited to the biggest dinners. We'd get a call, 'Come to the Century Plaza.' I'd come in a tuxedo and be an honored guest at $1,500 a plate. And we had nothing but money coming out of our ears—and I was goddamned bored to death!

"Contracts. Civil cases. I could go into court and try those cases blindfolded. Quite candidly, I was bored to death. I knew what it was that I really wanted to do."

Galane wanted the challenge of the tough cases, the ones that were seemingly impossible to win. And he saw the libel case he took several years later, on behalf of the Nevada gubernatorial candidate who'd been accused on television of passing a bad check, as the start of his road back. His victory in the candidate's case then brought him Newton, and "I could feel the intense excitement all over again." Galane was back doing what he wanted to do.

The irony of Galane's success was that everybody acknowledged his legal prowess except Galane himself. Insecure as ever, Galane continually tried to find a new peak to climb. It was a catch-22: He wanted the respect of his colleagues but he thought so little of them that he didn't have confidence that they'd ever recognize his outsized achievements.

And it was this hubris that kept pushing Galane onto paths he should not have taken.

Already at work on the Newton case, Galane now decided he wanted to be a federal judge, and he passed the word to his friend, then-senator Paul Laxalt, who arranged to have him nominated in 1983.

But it was hard to conceive of a lawyer more poorly suited to the role of being an arbiter. Galane's hot temper and thunderous demeanor—the qualities that sometimes made him so effective as an advocate—had no place on the bench. Everybody saw that but Galane. "I wanted to be a judge. It was an honor. I thought it was a nice thing," he would later recall. A joke went around the courthouse that Galane was precisely the kind of judge *nobody* wanted—he worked fifteen hours a day, seven days a week, and no lawyer wanted to have to match that!

The judicial nomination proved to be yet another crucible for Galane. He arranged to sell his practice to young Jimmerson, but as the FBI's background investigation proceeded, Galane began to fret over a malpractice case that had been pending against him for nearly five years, and that was about to come to trial. It was a minor case, really: Galane had let the statute of limitations run out on a debt-collection case, and so now the client was coming after him to make good on the $77,253 bad debt.

Part of Galane's hubris was that he apparently didn't think the local press possessed his own high standards of fairness and accuracy, because as the malpractice case neared its trial date, Galane became so worried about how the local reporters would cover it that he offered a $200 cash "early-Christmas gift" to journalists from the two Vegas dailies. A horrible mistake. "I was very sensitive. I wanted the truth reported. I didn't want to have the situation distorted in any way, and I felt I'd be building goodwill with them if I gave them the gift."

Even Galane's devoted secretary, Paula Miller, saw it for what it was. "He bribed a reporter. He called the $200 an early Christmas present, but it was really just a bribe." The reporter from the Las Vegas *Review-Journal* took the money shortly before Galane's malpractice trial began in April 1983; the reporter from the Las Vegas *Sun* refused the envelope with the money in it and reported the whole incident to the FBI. (The malpractice case against Galane was settled during the trial for $90,000.)

Galane's judicial nomination was thus imperiled more quickly than anyone could say "res ipsa loquitur." The American Bar Association judicial evaluation panel, which had first given him an excellent recommendation, reconvened and called him unqualified. Facing certain defeat for what even Galane readily confessed was an error in judgment, he sent the president a letter withdrawing his name and delivered copies to the local newspapers. As if he could somehow avoid personal responsibility for the whole sordid mess, Galane found solace in his own superstitions. "If it was meant to be, for me to be a judge, it wouldn't have come out that way. And if it wasn't meant to be, it saved my life. Maybe what occurred revealed some innermost subconscious drive that being a judge wasn't what I really wanted. Possible."

But the miniscandal tore apart his law firm. Angered that Galane wasn't going to turn over the reins after all, Jimmerson left the firm, taking another lawyer with him, and opened up a competitive office across town. Galane gave big raises to all the remaining staff in hopes of keeping them.

The only person who appeared thrilled by the turn of events was Newton. Anticipating Galane's departure for the bench, the singer had hired a Washington law firm to continue his libel case against NBC. The morning after Galane withdrew his name, Newton sent a beautiful crystal vase to Galane's house, with a handwritten note: "The gods have smiled upon me today. Wayne." Galane knew he was back in the case to stay.

Floyd Abrams was, like Galane, a native New Yorker, but he was also everything that Galane was not—a patrician from a silk-stocking law firm; a respected, oft-quoted member of the bar; the embodiment of the lawyer's lawyer.

Short, soft-spoken and elegant, and ten years younger than Galane, Abrams had already gained the respect that still eluded the Las Vegas lawyer. Abrams was the nation's preeminent First Amendment attorney, and he was one of the senior partners at the respected Wall Street firm of Cahill Gordon & Reindel. Through his representation of the New York *Times,* Abrams had argued the Pentagon Papers case before the Supreme Court as a thirty-five-year-old in 1971, and he had gone to the mat for his newspaper client on other cases of great notoriety, including the 1978 "Dr. X" case in which Timesman Myron A. Farber was jailed for not turning over his notes to a New Jersey court in the Mario Jascalevich murder trial. Abrams had argued a host of other First Amendment cases before the Supreme Court, representing, in addition to his main clients NBC and the *Times,* such others as Metromedia Broadcasting Corporation, *The Nation,* and the Columbia Broadcasting System (CBS). He represented all three networks in their 1981 efforts to secure the Abscam videotapes and their 1978 attempts to get the Nixon White House tapes.

In their litigating styles, though, Galane was fire to Abram's ice. The latter was mainly an appellate lawyer: despite his impressive credentials, Abrams had tried a mere ten cases, only six of those before a jury, by the time *Newton v. NBC* came to trial in 1986. Just a single one of those ten trials had been in a libel case, back in 1978, and he'd lost it. One-on-one, Abrams was witty and persuasive, but he was inexperienced before a jury and he was coming into a city where he readily acknowledged he was going to "start out behind the eight-ball."

Even under the best circumstances the courtroom is unfriendly turf for a libel defendant. Few libel cases ever go to trial; the strong media protections that began with *New York Times v. Sullivan* see to that. But when libel cases do go to trial, juries vote for the plaintiff 70 percent of the time.

The bias against the media defendants may be understandable. Juries see an individual against a faceless corporation, an injured person seeking recompense. There is also a counterintuitive nature to libel cases that makes them difficult for the layman to apprehend. Common sense tells the juror that the person suing shouldn't have to prove that what's been said is false, regardless of what the law requires. Nor does it make sense to the average man that, even if the plaintiff *does* meet his burden of proof, the public-figure plaintiff isn't entitled to collect unless he can prove *malice.* And so what happens is that libel-case jurors frequently do what they consider to be "the right thing," regardless of what the law requires. They award big money, and then the media defendants appeal the case and get the judgment reversed somewhere down the line.

But Abrams knew that this courtroom would be unfriendlier than most. "The trial was going to be in Las Vegas, and it was about a broadcast that attacked Las Vegas itself!" At least that's how Abrams thought the locals were going to perceive it—not as Newton against NBC, but as Glitter Gulch versus the heartland.

"It really *did* matter that the case was in Las Vegas and that the person we were up against was Wayne Newton," Abrams said. "It became Wayne Newton and Las Vegas against NBC and all the people who don't understand Nevada." It got even tougher, Abrams believed, when a sitting Las Vegas federal judge was impeached shortly before the Newton trial was to begin. The nightly news programs had carried the sorry sight of one of Las Vegas' most esteemed citizens in the dock, being ridiculed by members of Congress. "The Las Vegas people were intense in their feelings, and there was a degree of estrangement. They felt people didn't understand Las Vegas."

Abrams sought to have the trial transferred to another venue, and when that gambit didn't work, he asked the judge to prohibit any mention of the fact that NBC's lawyers were New Yorkers, an extreme, almost comical request, but one Abrams felt Galane's own conduct warranted.

Galane had, in fact, been playing to the hometown crowd a few months before the start of the trial, when he said in a May 30, 1986, pretrial hearing that Abrams and NBC "don't even understand our people and why we live here and what we're made of. And we're very proud to be Nevadans." Abrams thought a repetition of that kind of thing during the trial would be disastrous for his client, but Judge Myron D. Crocker, the seventy-one-year-old jurist from Fresno, California, who'd been brought in to preside over the lengthy trial, was amused by the irony of Abrams' argument.

"Your honor," Galane later recalled saying, "the juries in Nevada comprise people who've come from all over the country, and they're relatively sophisticated. And this jury is going to know in thirty seconds flat that *both* lead counsel originate from the City of New York! And the judge interrupted me, in his own inimitable style, and said, 'Yes, Mr. Galane, but Mr. Abrams' accent isn't as bad as yours!' Everybody laughed. The judge denied their motion. And that was the end of that nonsense!"

But the animosity between Abrams and Galane ran deep, and once again it was fueled by Galane's perception that his foe didn't respect him, an impression that Galane had formed early on, when he surmised that Abrams had told NBC's libel insurance carrier, the Fireman's Fund Insurance Companies, that NBC shouldn't settle Newton's case because it was meritless. Whether Abrams had done that or not, Galane had convinced himself that it was so, and in doing that Galane had psyched himself up for the battle that lay ahead.

"No damages, no liability, and no recovery!" Galane shouted. "I know it as a fact! And that led to situations where either nobody would even talk to me, or, if the time came as trial approached and they did talk to me, it was in a very condescending manner, as if this was a nuisance suit where they had to give some money in order to show their clients that they don't want to appear intransigent."

It put his beef with NBC on a personal level, one from which Galane could be driven by his own instincts. That was part of Galane's method. And when Abrams argued that NBC couldn't get a fair trial in Las Vegas, that played right into Galane's style, too. As Galane saw it, Abrams thought he was coming into some legal backwater, the last bastion of frontier justice. If now his Yale Law–educated nemesis didn't respect a night-school lawyer whose office was around the corner from the Tunnel of Love Wedding Chapel, he surely would later on. Galane would see to that.

All those demons in Galane's mind simply reinforced the arrogance and elitism Galane already ascribed to Abrams, and they made Galane want to work that much harder to show Abrams and NBC what happened when big-city lawyers didn't take him seriously.

Even Newton was amazed at how personally Galane seemed to take every little incident. "The difference between Mort and every other attorney," Newton observed after the trial, "is his personal input. He *lived* this case. When he stepped out of it when he was going to become a judge, we brought in numerous different legal brains"— Newton sneered when he said the words, and he sliced the air with his fingers to put quotation marks around the phrase—"but there wasn't one who could even begin to comprehend where Mort was leading off, to say nothing of where he was going from that point.

"To them, it was a legal issue. But Mort *lived* this thing with me. *It happened to him.*"

Galane, as usual, became so wrapped up in the case that his own conduct became an issue. At one time or another, Galane accused every member of Cahill Gordon and the two law firms assisting it of being "liars." The entire Cahill Gordon firm, Galane contended, bore him malice. He called one young lawyer a "baby" and a "boob" and told him to "grow up." One of Abrams' partners, Tom Kavaler, was, Galane told him on the record, "an asshole. . . . I have analyzed you, sir, Mr. Kavaler. . . . The record should indicate from my sincere viewpoint that [Kavaler] has a problem with envy, self-hatred" and "should have his head examined."

If Galane disagreed with a point being made by one of his foes, he sometimes uttered the obscene noise commonly called a Bronx cheer or defiantly raised his middle finger—a nasty jab he insisted was in emulation of his hero, Nelson Rockefeller, who once did the same thing to some college students who were heckling him. (Galane had been Rockefeller's southern Nevada chairman in his 1964 bid for the Republican presidential nomination, and had served as Rockefeller's statewide chairman in 1968.) When the NBC lawyers objected to one of his deposition questions, Galane would reply with one of many possible characterizations. The objections were either "smart-ass remarks," "verbal diarrhea," "out of line," "jealousy," "whining," "lawyers' chatter," "kindergarten," or some derivative thereof. You get the idea. And when one of the depositions was running late one afternoon, Galane replied with an ethnic slur on the religious background of Abrams and his fellow lawyers: "Can you finish this objection . . . before Friday, sundown?"

Sometimes his opponents replied in kind, as when, during Galane's 1981 deposition of producer Ira Silverman, Kavaler told Galane: "Your arms are spread apart. I wish that I had a nail."

"It was," Abrams said in characteristic understatement, "never a good relationship." What Abrams failed to understand was how effectively Galane was using the self-induced friction to ignite himself and his case.

Newton and Galane had made a settlement demand of $7 million early in the case, and as trial neared they tried again, naming a slightly lower figure and giving NBC forty-eight hours to respond. The network let the deadline pass without comment; no libel judgment against a news organization had ever been upheld for even $1 million, let alone what Newton was asking. Besides, NBC had, after all, put its own "healthy six-figure" settlement offer on the table, a tacit acknowledgment of the level of the network's concern. To deter lawsuits, news organizations rarely even offer to settle libel suits for anything other than a correction.

Despite Galane's theatrics and whatever animus the locals might be harboring against NBC, though, Abrams still had a very strong case.

The NBC broadcast—the first one, the one that generated all the ruckus—was, after all, substantially true. Newton *had* gone to the mob for help with a problem, and he really *hadn't* told the whole story to the Gaming Commission. He *did* have ties to the mob, and both Piccolo and Penosi *had* been indicted for trying to extort money from Newton and his business manager, Mark Moreno. (Piccolo was gunned down, gangland-style, three months later at a phone booth in the North End of Bridgeport; Penosi's first trial ended in a hung jury, and he was acquitted at a second trial in 1982. An ex-convict was arrested for Piccolo's murder, but two successive grand juries refused to indict him.)

Abrams' strategy would be to admit that the script written by Ross and Silverman was suceptible to more than one interpretation, including the interpretation that Newton had ties to the mob and therefore was himself an unsavory character. But Abrams was also going to stress that the statements in the script had been chosen carefully, and that each one, taken alone, was literally true no matter what the "sting" of the broadcast might seem to be.

That was important to his second line of defense. Galane was arguing that the literal meaning of the words in the script wasn't as important as the inference a viewer drew from the broadcast, with its slick graphics and film of mobsters juxtaposed with an evasive Newton. Abrams' response was, So what? Newton still hasn't proved his case because he can't show that NBC acted with malice. *New York Times v. Sullivan* protected even the shoddiest journalism as long as the falsehoods weren't intentional.

Abrams, still concerned about the home field advantage he thought Galane had, wanted jurors who'd lived the shortest possible time in Las Vegas, and who'd attended college. They would have, he theorized, the "vision" to see Newton's case for what it was. Each side had three peremptory challenges, and Abrams used them all, "even the last one, which is always tough, because you don't know who you're going to get after that." The jury of six regulars and four alternates he ended up with had four women on it. The average juror was a forty-four-year-old blue-collar worker with a high school diploma but no college education at all.

"You ought to see the ones who *didn't* get on," Abrams said. "The last guy we threw off looked like he came right out of a Ku Klux Klan meeting."

A trial lawyer's opening statement is a set piece, a carefully drawn blueprint of how the lawyer is going to build his case. The statement itself isn't evidence, but its importance can transcend the days or even months of testimony that will follow. During the opening statement, the lawyer gets his first feel for how the jury will react to him. Each side takes the other's measure.

The players—judge, jury, lawyers, spectators—were all assembled on Wednesday, October 15, 1986, in a makeshift courtroom at the Cashman Field convention complex beyond the Strip, a venue chosen of necessity since the downtown courthouse didn't have the extra space for a trial that was expected to last at least four months. As he would throughout the trial, each lawyer had his clients at his counsel table, Newton with Galane, Ross and Silverman with Abrams. If sitting there hour after hour took a toll on Newton, who was also performing two shows a night at the Bally Grand Hotel and didn't finish until 3 A.M., it didn't show.

Galane's counsel table was nearest the jury, and he used that to advantage as he stood alongside it, facing the jurors but also resting his notes on the table so that he could read from them with glances that were almost imperceptible. The effect was one of a lawyer who was looking each juror in the eyes from just a few feet away, and it was an effect that Galane had perfected over his thirty-year legal career. He believed in eye contact. Galane had watched politicians work the crowd in a room and gotten some insight into the way the eyes convey sincerity: "Watch their eyes. They shift! You know that you're not the person they're really talking to. They're scanning the room to see who else they can talk to.

"I've learned from that. If I'm sensitive to that trait in a politician, then a juror will be sensitive to that trait in a lawyer. And if the lawyer gives the slightest indication that his words are for the media, or his words are for the audience, or even for the judge, that juror, whether conscious of it or not, will become sensitive to it and may resent it. Because the juror wants you to talk to him.

"I watch that like a hawk. And when I talk to the jury, my words are only for them. Absolute, total concentration. Remember, you're being evaluated by people with common sense. And they're sitting there with nothing to do but watch you. And it's going through their mind: Is this guy a phony?"

"May it please the Court, ladies and gentlemen of the jury, this case is about a man who at one time had a good name."

Galane, standing almost directly in front of the jury box, began his opening statement. "This case is also about a television news broadcast to a nationwide audience on October 6, 1980, and what this broadcast did to the good name of that man."

Like some tour guide piloting a visitor around Newton's den, Galane described the mileposts and mementos of the singer's career: Learned to play the guitar at the age of four. Performed on radio as a six-year-old. Had his own Phoenix television show at age ten. Starred in the Fremont lounge at sixteen. Befriended by Bobby Darin, who propelled him into a recording contract and the big showrooms of Miami, Tahoe and Vegas.

Galane had a strategy: Straight off, he was going to tell the whole story of Newton's mob connections. That would demystify it for the jurors—Galane wouldn't be talking so much about all that mob stuff if Newton had done something wrong, would he?—and it would also leave nothing for Abrams to surprise the jury with later on. Abrams was pleased as he heard Galane go into painstaking detail about how the singer first met Penosi, how Newton was protected as a youth by the mobster, how he received gifts from him and, finally, how Newton went to Penosi for help. Galane talked about the wiretaps and what they showed. "Piccolo was scheming," Galane intoned, "to sink his claws into Wayne Newton." Abrams, who didn't realize how effective Galane's strategy would be, thought Galane was making NBC's case for him.

Next, Galane described the NBC reporters and their "extraordinary sources of information within law enforcement authorities." He let the tension build as he explained, without yet naming them, how the reporters painstakingly put their stories together, and how the two were so good at what they did that they'd been sought by the two competing networks when their contracts expired. Ross and Silverman were among the best in their business, and Galane didn't deny that. If anything, what Galane wanted to do was to build them up even more, because that would show that the errors and selective editing in their broadcast couldn't possibly have been mistakes. He was laying the groundwork for proving malice, and later on in his opening statement he would buttress it by asserting that even after NBC management knew there were problems with the broadcast they did nothing except "to screen and shelter and protect Brian Ross and Ira Silverman."

Galane's legal theory on NBC's culpability was a novel one. He told the jurors that the overall *impression* conveyed by the broadcast was what was at issue in the trial. Abrams could argue the literal truth of the script if he wanted to, but Galane was telling the jurors to judge NBC by a different set of rules:

"You will see that broadcast in this courtroom, and I ask you, ladies and gentlemen, to view it as the average viewer who watched it and listened to it in his or her living room understood the broadcast. And please remember that the average American viewer does not have a script in front of him or her to read, cannot ask the narrator to repeat the words, and cannot study after the conclusion of the broadcast the visual representations and the words uttered."

"I want to start my opening today by telling you a little bit about the evidence of some other people's reputations, because I represent clients, too, and they are real live people, too, and they have real live reputations, too."

Abrams addressed the jury like the consummate appellate lawyer he was, professorially standing behind a lectern about eight feet away from the jurors, far enough back so that he could look directly at all of them without moving his head from side to side.

He at once fell into the trap Galane had set for him. Abrams began by building up the reputations of his clients, Ross and Silverman— exactly what the jurors *shouldn't* have been hearing if NBC wanted to preserve the plausibility that two reporters could have made some innocent mistakes in the hot pursuit of a story.

Abrams felt he had to walk a fine line in telling the jury about Newton. Since he was defending the broadcast on the grounds of truth, he had to persuade the jurors that Newton really did lie to the gaming authorities about his ties to the mobsters. A strategy that had Abrams arguing truth and totally standing by his reporters required Abrams to be *at least* as tough on Newton as his own reporters had been. He should have relentlessly hammered away at Newton's credibility. But, fearing a hometown backlash from too fierce an attack on the city's number-one entertainer, Abrams also thought he had to be careful not to hit Newton *too* hard. Thus, all through the lengthy trial, when Abrams talked about the lies Newton told, he often called them "untruths" or said, as the broadcast earlier had, that Newton "hadn't told the whole story." Explained Abrams: "That was an easy way to understate it. There was no advantage to being stronger. Newton was distraught [about the threats to his little daughter]. Most people would understand you'd do strange things to save a member of your family." But by lionizing Ross and Silverman while frequently being too easy on Newton, Abrams was inadvertently affirming the plaintiff's case: that two reporters who knew exactly what they were doing took advantage of a pretty nice guy, and that once they did that, their vaunted reputations precluded admitting an error.

Abrams continued his opening: "The testimony will show that Brian Ross and Ira Silverman do a rather specialized form of reporting. They're not just award-winning journalists. They do a certain sort of journalism. It is not," Abrams stumbled, "not entertainment reporting. There's nothing wrong with that. It just happens not to be what you will hear that they do. It's not reporting about stars. It's not a sort of 'Lifestyles of the Rich and Famous,' one of the many programs Mr. Newton has been on long after he claims he was destroyed. Their specialty, the evidence will reveal, is not reporting about stars, but reporting about crime, organized crime, and otherwise, crime directed by mob figures, crimes of unions, crimes of businesses, crimes which threaten us all.

"And you'll hear, the evidence will show, the honors they have received, these two deliberate liars, the honors they have received in the course of their work as journalists. You'll hear about the Emmy awards they have received, the TV equivalent of the Oscar, the duPont award of Columbia University. You'll hear, the evidence will show, that they've been chosen by their colleagues as the best investigative reporters on television, these deliberate liars. You have a lot of reputations at stake here."

Abrams' opening was also a spellbinding recitation of an incredible story of two mobsters plotting to make money off a famous singer. Abrams called it a "chilling tale," and it certainly was that. It also, Abrams said, was a tale that had nothing to do with NBC.

"It is a portrayal of high-ranking mob figures at work, plotting and planning to earn off Wayne Newton, who had come to them for resolution of a problem. And it was before anyone from NBC had anything to do with anything! That is not NBC's fault! If there is any fault in that, and I'm not even saying there is, if there is any fault, we will argue to you, it's not NBC's. . . .

"And so I start my opening with two facts that we believe the evidence will show: One, Wayne Newton went to the mob, whatever he did, he went to the mob for help with a problem. . . . NBC had nothing to do with that. And Guido Penosi was not, not, contrary to what Mr. Newton said in public and implied in private to the Nevada gaming authorities, not just a fan, but a lot, a whole lot more than that."

Although Galane was putting the *inference* of the broadcast at issue, Abrams' strategy was to argue the *literal truth* of each sentence in the total of four broadcasts that NBC had run about Wayne Newton and the mob. (Each broadcast after the first had been successively more cautious, and the fourth, in May 1982, was done by a different NBC reporter and was a virtual on-air exoneration of Newton.) Abrams painstakingly took the jurors through the scripts of each broadcast and explained why every word was true. But Abrams didn't deal with the inference issue at all, and he skated around the most vulnerable part of his case: that, despite their reference to Newton's "financial problems" and the inference that mob money was being used for the Aladdin deal, the two NBC reporters had known *before the broadcast* that money for Newton's share of the Aladdin purchase had come from a $10 million loan from the Valley Bank of Nevada. Abrams had to hope that the reporters' error wouldn't be enough to hang his two clients.

Abrams ended his opening with a statement he would use frequently during the trial: "Wayne Newton should look in the mirror for the cause of his problems, not at his television set."

The problem for Abrams, though, was that the NBC broadcast had mistakenly cast Newton's "problem" as a financial one, rather than one of parental fright that someone might harm his little girl. Newton had panicked and called Penosi; even Abrams didn't want to hit him too hard for that. And Galane was able to make NBC's mistake seem to be a callous error.

"Did you have information at this time that Guido Penosi was associated with the Mafia?" Galane asked his first witness, an emotional, choked-up Newton.

"No, sir."

Galane: "If you had such information, Mr. Newton, would you still have called him?"

Newton: "Absolutely."

Galane: "Tell this jury and his honor exactly why."

Newton: "To save my daughter's life."

Galane's questioning and Newton's tearful performance had turned Newton's admission, clearly a potential low point, into high drama instead.

On the stand for days at the beginning of the trial, Newton mirrored Galane's act, turning hostile, even arrogant, when Abrams cross-examined him. Abrams stayed with it because he thought the jury could see the bitterness that, as Abrams put it, was stuck all over Newton. Abrams reasoned, incorrectly, as it turned out, that such obvious rancor wouldn't play well with the jurors.

But what Newton was able to do was to turn Abrams' questions around and put NBC on trial instead. When, for instance, Abrams asked Newton whether he would ever do anything to hurt Penosi, Newton replied: "I have no reason to hurt Guido. What he is in his life is his business, and until your boys over there decided to include me I wasn't included and I'm not included." Later, when Abrams tried to establish that Newton had lied to Ross when Ross asked Newton how recently he'd spoken to Penosi, Newton acknowledged the lie but tartly added: "I didn't realize that I was under oath to Mr. Wimp over there," gesturing toward the slightly built Ross.

Abrams spent hour after hour, day after day, trying to break Newton down, but, just as in Schlei's cross-examination of Maheu, Abrams' rambling questioning of a witness as glib as Newton merely reinforced Newton's story in the jury's mind. Example:

Abrams: "Do you remember when I questioned you and I asked you, You have some doubts about whether Mr. Penosi is a member of organized crime? And you said, I really don't spend a lot of time thinking about it, Mr. Abrams.

"And I said, Do you believe as you sit here today that Mr. Piccolo was a serious and active member in organized crime? And you said, I have no opinion on the matter. And I asked you the next day, Did you believe Mr. Balmer [a gaming agent] that Mr. Penosi was involved in organized crime?

"You said, I have no reason to consider it either way, Mr. Abrams.

"I said, Is it a matter of indifference to you? And you said, Relatively so, yes.

"Does that refresh your recollection that at some point after that you came to your current view that Mr. Penosi is involved in organized crime?"

Newton: "It just simply reminds me of how eloquent you can be in putting words in people's mouths, Mr. Abrams."

"Did Abrams have a goal?" Galane later asked as he puzzled over Abrams' cross-examination. "Cross-examination has to be short, to the point—to the jugular. You have to have depositions with a few key points of impeachment. Five minutes of a good cross-examination, with two or three items of contradiction, are worth more than all the days he spent!

"Cross-examination must be short: Did you, on direct examination, tell this jury as follows? I show you your deposition, sworn to five years ago. Read page so-and-so, line so-and-so. Was that your testimony? Yes or no! *That's* a cross-examination!"

Unlike in the Maheu libel trial, this time Galane had an ample budget to pay for the kind of expert assistance he would need.

And, unlike in the Maheu case, this time Galane was getting paid up front, with his $350-an-hour bills offset against a 40 percent contingency "kicker" if he won the case. In other words, Galane was earning handsomely—already as much as $1 million overall—at an hourly rate, and if the long shot paid off, he stood to win, potentially, millions of dollars more. All told, each side had spent well in excess of $2 million getting the case to trial.

Galane had used his expense money wisely. One of the country's leading experts on the Mafia, Notre Dame Law School Professor G. Robert Blakey, was brought in at a cost of $50,000 to interpret the mob lingo for Galane and, later, to serve as an expert witness at the trial. Galane also found a former TV journalist to testify that Newton's exculpatory answer to the Gaming Commission—when Newton said he wouldn't see Penosi any more if he had mob ties—was left out by the reporters even though it would have taken up only five more seconds of air time. Galane had a full-time technician on duty in the courtroom so that videotapes and wiretaps could be cued up and played whenever necessary.

Judge Crocker had also adopted another suggestion by Abrams, which, whether Abrams and Crocker knew it or not, had been employed years earlier in the Maheu case. Abrams' suggestion was that the lawyers be allowed to make interim summations, just as they had in another recent and celebrated libel case, *Westmoreland v. CBS.* Every Monday morning, for the full two months of the trial, the jury watched a one-on-one verbal duel between Galane and Abrams.

The summations themselves were revealing, not just about the evidence but also about the two men's contrasting styles. In the early going, while Galane was putting on his case, Abrams often played the aggressor, telling the jury, for example, at the start of the third week of trial that Newton had made "a string of false statements" (never lies, of course), "some little ones . . . and some whoppers!" But as the trial progressed, Abrams seemed to grow more conservative as Galane became bolder. By the start of the sixth week of trial, Galane was crashing through Abrams' case like a bowling ball with a wicked hook spin, immediately opening his minisummation with a savage attack on the credibility of a government lawyer named Richard Gregorie who had tipped off Silverman to the grand jury investigation of Piccolo and, thus, put the NBC reporters on Newton's trail.

"May it please the Court, ladies and gentlemen of the jury, how should we evaluate the credibility of the leaker Gregorie . . . ? He denies under oath that he ever made a declaratory statement leaking investigative information. It is a cock-and-bull story, insults the intelligence of the jury, and is a lie under oath . . . ! Once Gregorie made up the story concerning the leak, NBC had him in its hip pocket. They own him lock, stock and barrel! His career, his livelihood is at stake! And everything he said thereafter was to serve their interests against Wayne Newton, ladies and gentlemen."

It was in that same minisummation that Galane began driving home to the jury a key point in his case: that, with their negative broadcast about Newton, Ross and Silverman were "talent stroking" Johnny Carson, the NBC star who was Newton's rival in the Aladdin bidding.

During a deposition of Silverman, Galane had discovered what he considered the "smoking gun" of his case. Ross and Silverman had visited Carson at his home less than two weeks before the first Newton broadcast, ostensibly, they maintained, in a fruitless attempt to see whether Carson knew anything about Newton's mob connections.

Around Galane's office, they called it the "Holy Shit" deposition. Newton had become obsessed with the Carson angle, to the point of being suckered into buying, for $2,500, two forged memoranda, allegedly written by the then-president of NBC, showing that "Mr. C." had initiated the NBC news story and was to be kept informed of its progress.

Even if it was just, as Galane put it, "talent stroking," Ross' visit to Carson was enough to provide a plausible motive for a journalistic vendetta, enough of a wedge to let Galane drive home to the jurors his case for malice.

"You must use inference and circumstantial evidence to look into the minds of Ross and Silverman," he thundered. "Their direct testimony will be meaningless. Any man can deny what's in his state of mind, because you can't put a microscope into it. But circumstances can speak louder of what they intended to achieve by going to the meeting with Mr. Carson, and how they felt when the board voted to recommend approval, and how they felt when, the next day, they had to face this majestic figure in national television, Johnny Carson, to show what they had accomplished. A total failure they were!

"And from that moment on, the next ten consecutive days were nothing more than distortion of information, evidence, videotaped, reconstruction of phraseology, all for the purpose of making it appear to the American people on television that Wayne Newton acquired his 50 percent interest in the Aladdin as a front for mob money! Let's never get away from that meaning of the broadcast . . . ! The ultimate goal was to curry favor at the highest levels of corporate management. And the plan went awry."

Abrams' retort to the jury that morning was that Galane's lambasting of Gregorie was a diversionary tactic to hide the fact that Galane's case was crumbling, and that whatever involvement the reporters had with Johnny Carson was beside the point because the broadcast was the truth, period. Even if everything Abrams said was true, it was hardly sufficient to smother Galane's fire.

Later that week, Abrams asked Silverman on the witness stand how he felt about Galane's imputation of talent stroking to the two award-winning reporters. Silverman replied that he felt "sick" about it. But all that did was give the fired-up Galane a chance to take still more hits at NBC the following Monday morning:

"[Silverman] said, 'I was sick.' At least Wayne Newton is giving him a federal judge, a federal jury, due process of law and evidence! I point out that it was Ross and Silverman who arrogated to themselves, ladies and gentlemen, the triple role of judge, prosecutor and jury without ever giving Wayne Newton a day in court—without ever giving him a hearing destroyed his character before the entire American people! It's amazing what sensitivity Ira Silverman showed on the witness stand. He looked like a seething volcano about to explode twice when I committed the cardinal sin on cross-examination and suggested words that interrupted him. Did you see his face?

"Ladies and gentlemen, do you remember four weeks ago I said to you there is the wordless language that should be looked at, when I discussed the credibility of Wayne Newton? Did this jury examine the demeanor of *this* witness? Did you see [Silverman's] traits? Unnaturalness, uneasiness, nervousness, hesitation, affectation, concealment, deceit, all of the elements of insincerity?"

Galane wasn't holding anything back. He wanted the jury to believe his version of what they had seen. And after Ross, appearing much more composed than Silverman had, testified later that week, Galane was roaring back the following Monday with more wisdom for the jury: "He is a very photogenic, presentable witness. Believe me, he is a sharp contrast to Ira Silverman. But the testimony is pretense, I suggest to you! Indifference to oath belies a pretense of humility, and that pretense is designed to cause the emotion of sympathy toward him as a witness."

Abrams had his moments, too. After Galane had produced a pollster, Richard Wirthlin, who said many Americans didn't like Newton because they thought he had mob connections, Abrams gleefully pointed out that more than twice as many people said it was Newton's *moustache* and his *hair* that they didn't like. And in his final minisummation, Abrams did some slashing of his own, revealing that Newton's mob friend Penosi had been arrested at age sixteen for homicide and deingrating Newton for being "indifferent" to organized crime while Ross and Silverman "believe that Guido Penosi is a murderer, scum, a killer, a person who fills our children with drugs. . . . It's all true, a murderer, a convicted heroin dealer, cocaine dealer, the largest drug dealer on the West Coast."

But, by now, Abrams was also backpedaling from his earlier, unquestioned defense of the broadcast—a smart move, albeit one that was coming too late to do him much good. "The key question before you, if there's anything false in the broadcast, is whether Mr. Ross and Mr. Silverman are deliberate, willful, purposeful liars. . . . Anyone can make mistakes," he now said. "These people can make mistakes. But lies—that's something else."

When Crocker, the energetic seventy-one-year-old senior judge who'd traveled from Fresno to hear the Newton case, asked Abrams and Galane how much time they wanted for their closing arguments, the two lawyers were, as usual, at polar extremes. Abrams, well aware of Galane's penchant for the long stem-winder of a closing statement, wanted a one-and-a-half-hour limit. Galane wanted his usual four days.

Galane was at his best when he moved in close and worked the jury for days on end, recounting every piece of testimony and repainting the jury's entire image of the case. The high-strung lawyer had railed at the Maheu jury for four days straight, and in the trial that Galane had finished right before *Newton v. NBC* began, he'd also spent four days delivering his closing argument and snared a $24.6 million verdict on behalf of the builders of a nearby waste-water treatment plant who claimed they were underpaid by the county.

Crocker laughed when he heard Galane's request, telling the Vegas lawyer that the federal judge in the wastewater case had confided that giving Galane four days to close his case was the biggest mistake he'd ever made. You can have six hours, Crocker told both sides. No more. Since the burden of proof was on Galane, he would speak first, for two and a half hours, and he would also address the jury again in a rebuttal after Abrams had spoken. Galane would use the majority of his time for that final jeremiad.

Galane's closing argument began at nine o'clock on the morning of Monday, December 8, 1986.

"Let me illustrate by a simple homespun analogy the weight and value of circumstantial evidence," Galane patiently, carefully started off. He had a case, after all, that was built largely on circumstantial evidence, particularly as to the crucial, malice-proving talent stroking of Carson by Ross and Silverman. He was going to give the jury an everyday example by which to judge the two reporters.

"You walk into your kitchen, and on the table is a jar of jam. The cover is off, the jar is open, the knife is lying by the jar of jam, with jam upon the knife. And little Johnny stands there and around his mouth is the jam. The inference that little Johnny opened the jar, took out the jam, and ate it is overwhelming, yet that is what we call circumstantial evidence. And even if little Johnny denies that he did so, which would be direct evidence, the circumstantial evidence is so powerful as to clearly and convincingly prove the proposition! That is what we are going to talk about this morning."

Galane was asking the jury to disregard everything that the NBC witnesses had said, and instead to view the circumstantial evidence— the editing decisions that were made, the calls and the visit to Carson —in the worst light. Once again, he used Abrams' praise of the two reporters to make a telling point against NBC, telling the jury repeatedly that "they knew exactly what they were doing. . . . I repeat, thirty years of [cumulative] experience in electronic journalism strips from Ross and Silverman any effort to try to hint to this jury that this was some kind of mistake."

"Mr. Newton," Galane told the jurors, "is going to win this case."

Witness by witness, Galane took the jury back over the testimony they had heard during the nearly two-month-long trial. He was warming up now, gathering speed, voice rising, his anger barely bridled and his hands shaking like bundles of rapid-firing neurons.

He reminded the jurors that NBC put the first Ross and Silverman "Special Segment" on its schedule a month before it actually aired, long before the reporters could possibly have gathered all the facts they knew they were going to need. That proved the two had "a mindset" against Newton. He reminded the jury of the outtakes—videotape shot but never used in the broadcast—that they had been shown during the trial.

"Just think of the videotape! Did you see anger in the eyes and expressions of Brian Ross? Did you see the pursuit down the corridor after Wayne Newton had very clearly and rather courteously said that from his perspective this was not the time for an interview? Did you see the finger pointing at Wayne Newton with the repeated motion saying, 'I'm not doing you any favors!'? Why? What had Wayne Newton done to them in his whole life? What has he done to *anybody,* except good?

"The only explanation for it, ladies and gentlemen, is such an extreme frustration on the part of Ross and Silverman that they did not get their way in the effort to intercede in the licensure proceedings that they reacted to what they must have deemed some type of real or fancied insult on the part of the Nevada gaming authorities as to simply direct their hostility to Wayne Newton.

"Now, that's on videotape for the jury to see."

Galane was painting the picture all over again, telling the jury exactly what he wanted them to remember about his case, shading elements to put the most favorable light on his best subject. Galane's trick in a closing argument was to tell the jurors exactly what they thought and felt, *to make his partisan advocacy their reality.* It didn't matter whether Galane's description of Ross was real or fancied, so long as he made it so vivid that the ten men and women in the box remembered Galane's description when they walked into that jury room.

He burned home the fact that the reporters knew Newton didn't have money problems but put it into the script anyhow. Then he rammed ahead to the Carson connection, for he needed to tie that down in the jurors' collective mind in order to get even one cent in damages.

"I don't understand the attempt to *deceive* the jury with the statement that the motive for going originally to Mr. Carson was to get his input concerning his dealings with the sellers of the Aladdin. Look how the trust and confidence in NBC is *forfeited* as far as this jury is concerned! . . . How do they explain Ira Silverman's telephone call of Tuesday, October 7, 1980, the day *after* the broadcast, to [Carson lawyer Henry] Bushkin's office? Ira Silverman never addressed it. You didn't hear one word out of his mouth to try to explain the call because he knows and the lawyers for NBC know they cannot reconcile that call with this *fairy tale* that the only reason for contacting Johnny Carson was to ascertain from him what his dealings were with the sellers of the hotel!"

Galane was on the rampage, demanding that the jurors ask themselves why the reporters would call a source after a broadcast, unless "here was an opportunity to bring ourselves to the attention of Mr. Carson. . . . I'm not faulting ambition; I'm faulting *blind* ambition."

Despite Galane's screaming and everything that he'd said, Abrams began his closing argument confident that he had proved his case, and so angry at Galane that the two had stopped even acknowledging each other's presence some three weeks before. Quietly, carefully, in crisp sentences that parsed much better than Galane's, he began by asking the jurors a question: Why did Newton "want so much to believe that NBC did this? . . .

"The Johnny Carson theory makes sense." Abrams was taking a real gamble with that statement. "It's a lie, of course, it's an absolute lie, but it makes sense. It makes sense in that if that's what they were doing, if they were doing it to curry favor with Johnny Carson and Johnny Carson and Wayne Newton didn't get along and Johnny Carson had wanted the Aladdin, well, at least there is some relationship there.

"The problem with that, though, is it's not true. It's nonsense. It's madness to suggest to you that these two journalists who had built a lifetime, a career of trying to tell the truth, who won their awards reporting about the mob, would suddenly get it into their heads to curry favor with Johnny Carson, and to come and prepare what is in essence a lie on television. . . .

"One of the reasons that I believe, and I would urge upon you, that Wayne Newton has appeared so angry in this courtroom—and he is angry, I don't deny that for a moment—is that he very well knows that everybody now knows something that he didn't want anybody to know. He went to the mob."

Abrams continued for almost another hour, tediously dissecting the federal investigation into the relationship between Piccolo and Penosi and Newton, but neglecting to tell the jury *why* he was doing that. Returning to court after the afternoon recess, it was as if Abrams had suddenly realized that he might have lost the jury among his own musings, so he explained: "It goes to the truth of the broadcast. . . . NBC had nothing to do with that investigation. All NBC did was to find out about it." Abrams then settled back into his notes and spent the rest of the afternoon playing tapes of the FBI wiretaps and continuing to lay out what the tapes and testimony had shown about the mob conspiracy to hoodwink Newton. "The point of it is this: Are these [mob] people interested in Wayne Newton getting the hotel? Of course they are! Did NBC make that up? I mean, is this some creation of NBC? Are these people interested in Wayne Newton? Are they planning to try to earn from Wayne Newton in some way? Of course they are!" Abrams would continue in the morning with a painstaking, sentence-by-sentence defense of the broadcast. He went back to his suite at the Alexis Park Hotel, a place near the airport where, since it didn't have gambling, Abrams could get away from "that oppressive, clockless, Las Vegas bright-lights aura" he abhorred.

Finally, by midmorning on the following day, Abrams had completed his top-to-bottom run-through of the relationship between Newton and the two mobsters. The evidence, Abrams insisted, proved beyond a doubt that Newton hadn't told the whole story to the Nevada gaming authorities—"a central statement in the broadcast."

Next, Abrams took the jury on the same kind of exhaustively detailed description of how Ross and Silverman had put their broadcast together. He was still trumpeting their credentials, still arguing that two men as revered in their profession as Ross and Silverman wouldn't possibly be out to "get" Wayne Newton. Abrams had thirty-six separate story boards, and now he went through each one to show the support the reporters had for their statements.

"Financial problems I want to pause for a moment on," Abrams said. If there were an Achilles heel to the broadcast, this was it, and Abrams carefully skated around it. "I think there may be some dispute as to [Newton's financial problems]," Abrams continued, "although I don't think there should be." He matter-of-factly named the banker who was concerned about Newton overextending himself, and the gaming board accountant who figured Newton was already $75,000 a month short in meeting his current obligations.

But Abrams was still ignoring a key facet of Galane's case: that the juxtaposition of the statement about Newton's money problems with the revelation that Newton had asked Penosi for "help with a problem" made it seem that Newton had given the mob a secret interest in the Aladdin. Ross' erroneous report—the only one Abrams acknowledged—that Newton's call to Penosi occurred at the same time Newton announced he would purchase the Aladdin (in fact, the two events were many months apart) further entrenched the false impression that Newton was fronting for the mob. There was just no getting around that, and Abrams didn't even try. He tried to breeze right past it.

"They had to *mean* it," Abrams finally told the jury. Ross and Silverman had to have fully intended to hurt Newton; otherwise, they were guilty of nothing. Even if Galane was absolutely right when he said viewers got the wrong impression from the juxtaposition of so much television razzle-dazzle with Ross' somber narration and a few shots of Newton ducking the cameras, Ross and Silverman still couldn't be guilty unless they acted maliciously. "Even though you think there is an impression, they had to *mean* it." Abrams had to hope the jury would pick up this lawyerly nuance that he was trying to slip in without breaking faith with the two reporters whose reputations were on the line: Abrams was arguing that the broadcast was true, and that even if it wasn't, so what? There was no malice.

Then there was the ambush interview of Newton in the parking lot after the gaming hearing. Abrams dismissed it as "an attempted interview in a situation of stress." Ross and Newton, Abrams said matter-of-factly, simply "weren't getting on."

Nearing the end of his closing argument, Abrams now returned to the Johnny Carson connection. It was outlandish, maybe, but way out in the realm where absurdity met reality, Galane's theory could be made to seem plausible. Abrams had conceded that already. Worse, though, there was no way for Abrams to shake Galane's theory conclusively. How could Abrams prove the negative? How, other than by scoffing at a theory that Abrams himself had already admitted was plausible, could Abrams show that these two boys with jam all over their mouths really hadn't done anything wrong? Abrams did what he could. "So ridiculous, so absurd, so totally off the wall that it is fair to say it's nonsense," Abrams said of Galane's argument.

It appeared from the way Abrams talked to the jurors that he saw his low-key defense as an asset. "I haven't yelled at you; I haven't cried at you," he said. "I haven't done other things that other lawyers do. I have tried to talk sense as a lawyer to you, tried to persuade you." The contrast with Galane was obvious, and Abrams told them Galane's bombast was just a clever way of covering up for a weak case. But at least one of the jurors thought Abrams' placidity was an indication that he didn't really believe in his clients. "My fault," Abrams said when he heard that. "I never had clients I believed in more."

Galane pointed out the discrepancy in their styles, too. Abrams had spoken with "a very winning, quiet voice of reason," Galane said when he addressed the jury again later that afternoon to give his rebuttal. But Abrams hadn't made his case.

The next morning, Wednesday, December 10, Galane was back again to finish his rebuttal. He wanted to drive home once and for all the theory that words can have a meaning beyond their literal truth, and he carried with him a children's storybook to help him make his point.

Galane started reading to the jury from Lewis Carroll's classic *Through the Looking Glass:* " 'When I use a word,' Humpty Dumpty said, in a rather scornful tone, *'it means just what I choose it to mean.* Neither more nor less.' " It was an effective way for Galane to make his key point, using an analogy that the jurors would certainly remember when they began their deliberations. Before he was through on this day, Galane would quote from Shakespeare and the Bible, too. Unlike Abrams, who had facetiously suggested one dollar as the proper recompense for Newton, Galane wasn't going to ask the jury for a specific amount in damages. But he reminded them of a poll taken by Wirthlin nine months after the broadcast, a poll showing that 11.6 million Americans thought Newton had connections to the mob. "How much per American?" Galane demanded. You didn't have to reach far to grasp Galane's unstated premise.

Wayne Newton had been sitting at the counsel table, beside Galane, throughout every day of the trial. If there's any justice at all in this world, he said to himself now, we have to win this case.

Instead of releasing the jury's four alternates, Crocker gained both lawyers' permission to let all ten jurors deliberate—seemingly a plus for Abrams, since the likelihood of a holdout might be greater among ten people than six. The verdict would still have to be unanimous. But Abrams had given Galane so much room to maneuver that all ten jurors never seriously considered *not* finding for Newton. Taking Galane's advice and watching the broadcast from the standpoint of an ordinary viewer, they had seen NBC's report just as Newton had. And, for all Galane's bombast and showmanship, he was still the picture of a lawyer who believed in his client. Abrams lacked fire. His nitpicking, truth-of-the-matter defense might have played well in a lecture hall, but in the heat of battle his earnest, low-key approach just withered away. The proof of that was in the astounding damages the jurors awarded: $7.9 million for lost income, $5 million for reputational damage, $5 million in punitive damages, $1.1 million for loss of future income, and $225,000 for pain and suffering.

The $19.2 million libel verdict was the largest ever rendered against a news organization! If it held up on appeal, the verdict would also mean a potential $7.7 million payday for Galane. Abrams was stunned. Right up to the end, he thought his case had been going better than he could have possibly imagined, a feeling generally shared by the newspaper reporters who covered the trial daily, but evidence of just how out of touch with the jury they all were.

Abrams blamed the defeat on the hometown jury. He wanted a new trial in a different city, and he wouldn't mind a different lawyer at the other table the next time around, either. Stories that alleged rampant misconduct by Galane through his six years of litigation against NBC —rumors that certainly detracted from his big win—were all over the legal grapevine. In his office late one afternoon, Galane fidgeted and fretted about who was spreading them, spinning fanciful theories about the "conduit" through which one or another of the stories about him had passed. He pleaded for some confirmation of his suspicions. "Am I right? Am I right?"

Then Mort Galane stopped himself. "Who cares!" he bellowed, as if the real importance of his win had only now been revealed to him. "I just want to get the judgment affirmed and bank the money! What the hell are they boasting about? They LOST!"

Bhopal and Beyond:
John Coale and the
Disaster Hustle

When there's a mass disaster, I want to know: Why did it
happen, what can I do to prevent it from happening
again, and, in the meantime, make some money, get excitement, be in a big game, and have everything that goes
along with that.

JOHN P. COALE

We're just humanitarians, capitalist style.

TED DICKINSON, COALE'S ASSISTANT

Lawyer John Coale, a courthouse hustler who represented drunk drivers, was in the backseat of a taxicab near his
Washington, D.C., home when he heard the first radio reports of the
worst disaster the world had ever known. A Union Carbide India Ltd.
chemical plant in Bhopal, India, had spewed forth toxic gases that
killed 1,861 people and gravely injured at least another 26,874. It
was December 3, 1984.

"This is going to be the biggest case in a long, long time," Coale
thought to himself as his cab headed down Massachusetts Avenue
near the Capitol Hill section of Washington. That was Coale, always
playing the angle. He brought in plenty of business with his cornball
television ads, but he aspired to something more than defending
drunk-driving cases. Matter of fact, he'd already begun to gin up
publicity with a few high-profile cases: representing some of the Iran

hostages in a suit against the U.S. Government, suing Blue Cross and Blue Shield after they refused to pay for a heart transplant operation, and going after his own city government to strike down a new no-fault auto insurance law. And Coale, who was nothing if not an opportunist, immediately saw in this awful disaster a chance to change his luck —a chance to attain the fame and wealth that surely would be his if he could break into the supercharged ranks of the nation's greatest mass-disaster lawyers.

The thing about being a disaster lawyer, Coale knew, was that the game was always over before most people knew it had begun. The key to success was in getting clients, and in controlling the committee of lawyers that the courts invariably appointed to oversee the litigation when there were many lawsuits and a common disaster.

Whereas other plaintiffs' lawyers would prepare a case knowing that it might yield an uncertain result at trial, the disaster lawyers *knew* their cases would settle: The airlines and multinational companies whose negligence killed someone couldn't very well deny culpability, and their corporate wealth invariably guaranteed a sweet payday for any lawyer fortunate enough to land a contingent-fee client. The arena of combat wasn't the courtroom, but, rather, the *back* room, and the clash of lawyer against lawyer wasn't between plaintiff and defendant, but between the plaintiffs' lawyers themselves. The simple fact was that these cases were so lucrative—such *sure winners* —that the tight fraternity of mass-disaster plaintiffs' lawyers made sure they controlled the cases, and their fees, by swapping favors among themselves and keeping newcomers like Coale on the outside.

But Coale, a cherubic, curly-haired five foot nine lawyer with a chipmunklike giggle and an extra fifty pounds around his midsection, had an iconoclast's knack for bashing the establishment. He'd never played in the big leagues of mass-disaster law, but he had a resourcefulness borne of hustling those drunk-driving cases at the local courthouse.

A few years earlier, Coale and another lawyer, a roly-poly, Danny DeVito-type character named Arthur Lowy, had developed an assembly-line approach to soliciting driving while intoxicated (DWI) clients and copping pleas for them. It was "a great deal for the consumer," Coale said, even if it did rile every other lawyer who had a good thing going at the courthouse. Coale and Lowy, eighteen years Coale's senior and a Harvard Law School graduate, generated such volume that they slashed the customary $1,500 DWI legal fee by two thirds. The duo sublet space from an orthodontist whose office was atop a Capitol Hill restaurant, and they had so much business that the overflow of drunk-driving clients had no choice but to cool their heels in the adjoining orthodontist's waiting room, fidgeting there along with all the kids in braces, as they awaited their interview with the two characters that the rest of the courthouse regulars called "Fat and Rat."

Coale had his own raps to beat. There has to be an easier way to earn a buck, the lawyer thought whenever he pulled an all-nighter, cutting and pasting and retyping some motion he would file the next morning in a drunk-driving case. "I was going toe-to-toe with excellent lawyers every day in the courtroom. What I was doing in Superior Court was *more* complex than the disaster stuff."

Coale's gift even then was in snaring the clients, hundreds of them, all with the same problem. And that's what the Bhopal case would be like, too, Coale reasoned. He'd be happy if he could hustle twenty death cases and one hundred injury cases. Coale went upstairs to his office and called his live-in girl friend, Greta Van Susteren, an aggressive young criminal defense attorney who had once been his legal assistant but now had her own practice near the courthouse. I know this sounds crazy, Coale began, but there's this poison-gas leak in India and I'm thinking about going there to sign up clients. Ah, well. Coale was irrepressibly adventuresome. Go if you want to, she said.

To the outside world, Ted Dickinson and Tyrone Roberts were known as Coale's "investigators," but, in fact, they played much more important roles as Coale's "runners," nonlawyers who lined up clients for Coale. Roberts was a suave black man whose wardrobe put Coale's and Lowy's to shame. It was Roberts who made the rounds of the local police precincts every morning to copy down the names and addresses of those who'd been arrested for drunk driving the previous night, so that they could be lined up as new clients.

The smooth-voiced Dickinson, a friend of Coale's since high school, was best at working the phones. He could talk the saddle right off a horse, and the telephone-solicitation scams Coale and Dickinson had run were legendary among other lawyers—and, by the rules of the D.C. Bar, perfectly legal, too, because the District of Columbia had the nation's most permissive regulations on a lawyer's soliciting clients. (A bar member could hustle clients all he wanted, as long as he didn't lie or try to sign up cases in front of the local courthouse.) Dickinson's father was a prominent Washington lawyer, and his ex-stepmother, Tandy, was a socialite well known for her romance with a corrupt South Korean influence peddler in Washington named Tong-sun Park.

Coale talked to Lowy, Dickinson and Roberts right after he got off the phone with Van Susteren. The chase to Bhopal was on, Coale told them, and what he promised was the kind of adventure they'd never have in an orthodontist's waiting room.

But a few problems remained. Coale needed more expense money than he alone could provide. Where would that come from? Roberts always seemed to be the one in the office who had the most cash. Could he lend Coale $10,000? Roberts said he'd have the money the next day. Meanwhile, Roberts would also start working on getting visas for Coale, Lowy, and Dickinson.

They would also need a translator, a combination guide and scout who could be trusted to help them when they got to Bhopal. "Who do we know who's an Indian?" Coale asked Lowy. "We can't go to India alone because we don't know anything."

A tailor named C. S. Sastry had made Coale some custom suits at his shop in nearby Virginia, and it was Sastry, who was from the southern Indian city of Bangalore and who'd worked for the Singer Company as a marketing manager in South Asia, to whom Coale turned the next day. First, Roberts softened the beach with a phone call to Sastry, then Coale followed up with a call of his own. Their proposition was attractive to Sastry. He'd get an all-expenses-paid trip back to his homeland, and Coale would repay Sastry for the $3,000 in business his tailor shop would lose while he was away. Yes, Sastry told them on December 5, he would join in their adventure, too. They would all depart at week's end, provided the Indian Embassy came through with the necessary visas.

But the embassy processed visa applications with the same indifference and capriciousness that marked the rest of India's hopeless bureaucracy, and a functionary soon informed Coale and his group that their application for a business visa had been denied. The four of them—Coale, Lowy, Dickinson and Sastry—had tickets for Pan American flight 66, which was bound for Bombay from Kennedy

Airport in New York City on the night of Friday, December 7. But, short of a miracle, they wouldn't be on it, unless Sastry could somehow wheedle the necessary visas out of the embassy.

Coale thought they might be able to get tourist visas more quickly. "We're not tourists, but we're gonna lie," he said in an impish deadpan. "So we lie. Shoot me."

Sastry telephoned the Indian Embassy that Friday morning and informed the man in charge of the Consular Division that there had been a terrible mistake. Coale and Company weren't going to India on business at all! They were simply tourists who wanted to see the erotic temple carvings at Khajaraho, and Bhopal happened to be the closest airport! The consular official was suspicious. He asked Sastry, an Indian citizen, to visit the embassy in person and make his explanation, and Sastry did that, with Dickinson tagging along. Whatever Sastry said, it sure enough did the trick, because right at the close of business, the passports of all three of the Americans were handed over to a grateful Dickinson. They would all meet a few hours later for the 7:30 Pan Am flight from Washington National Airport to Kennedy.

What was so amazing about all of this was the unprecedented brazenness of Coale's first foray into mass-disaster law. Here was a lawyer with absolutely no experience in mass torts, who'd never even hustled—to use the street lawyer's lingo—a single disaster victim, and he was about to journey halfway around the world to a country he'd never visited so that he could offer aid and representation to the victims of the worst disaster in history! His itinerary consisted of nothing more than his plane ticket. He was going to that strange country without even a hotel reservation. Despite seeming to do everything wrong, Coale was becoming a key player in the global disaster business.

From Coale's diary:

You start to smell Bombay as the airline comes down to the 10,000-foot level. And then the beggars—as we were going to the American Express place—the beggars at each stop light surround the car and I usually try to take about 100 or so rupees in 5-rupee notes, and I give the women and children money, but not the men. Incredible place. India is where man is going if we don't get our act together. There is almost total corruption, total misery, which somehow breeds this incredible arrogance where they will not ask for help, and they won't recognize that we in the West may have some answers to their problems. It is just incredible.

The flight from New York to Bombay takes a day and a half, so it wasn't until the morning of Sunday, December 9, that Coale and his retinue finally arrived in Bhopal.

Coale expected the competition for clients to be fierce. After all, the King of Torts himself, San Francisco's Melvin Belli, had filed a $15 billion class action the previous Friday, December 7, on behalf of two Bhopal survivors, clients whom other lawyers accused the publicity-hungry Belli of pulling out of thin air, just so he could have the distinction of filing the first lawsuit. It was well known that Belli was on his way to Bhopal, too. But Coale had been cooped up for so long in the cocoon of his Pan Am 747 jet that he hadn't heard any news for almost two days and didn't have any idea how many other American lawyers he might encounter when he reached the site of the tragedy.

"We expected there'd be twenty to thirty American attorneys already there," Coale recalled later. "We had no idea. But, when we walked off the plane and across the tarmac, we saw probably a hundred reporters and TV cameras waiting there, and it suddenly became quite clear that there weren't any American lawyers there yet! We get up to the terminal and some reporter says, 'Where's Melvin Belli?' And I said, 'Who? You mean that asshole who filed a suit when he didn't even have a client?'

"Belli's going across the world, stopping every place for one night to hold press conferences," Coale giggled. "So this whole town is just waiting for this saviour, this American lawyer, to come. But *it's me! I* show up! *I'm* the first saviour that comes down the pike."

Coale was amazed. He was a rookie, and yet by some incredible fluke he'd become the designated hitter for every disaster lawyer in the world. The media touted him as the First American Lawyer on the Scene. Reports of his arrival ran in the New York *Times* and the Washington *Post* (which quoted him—incorrectly, Coale maintains— as boasting that he was on "the greatest ambulance chase in history"), and on all the American network television news shows. He'd been instantly legitimized, a nationally known figure. "Now, they've got a story!" Coale said of the waiting reporters who suddenly began chronicling his every move.

As Coale viewed it, Bhopal was a place right out of the thirteenth century, an ancient civilization whose people nonetheless had autos and radios. "Like a Mexican town with 800,000 people. Wall-to-wall people. Very hot. Dusty. Polluted." Sastry tried to get some rooms for his group at the Imperial Sabre Hotel, where he'd stayed when he worked for Singer, but it was booked solid. Finally, Sastry found four rooms at the Ramson Hotel. He left Coale there in the lobby with a bunch of reporters and rushed to a meeting with the Bhopal mayor.

The mayor, R. I. Bisarya, was a practicing surgeon who also ran a private clinic in Bhopal, and it was at the clinic that Sastry found him on that Sunday morning.

Sastry wanted to arrange a meeting between Coale and Bisarya. Fine, the mayor replied, tell Mr. Coale to come around at eleven o'clock tomorrow morning. Sastry casually asked the mayor whether he had been contacted by any other American lawyer. When the mayor replied no, Sastry offered to have Coale and Lowy come right over. An Indian lawyer was brought in, too, and when the group got together Coale was quickly hired as the city's lawyer. He told them that he would file a lawsuit in the United States on the city's behalf and that he would charge as his fee the usual American cut of 33 1/3 percent of any recovery. The Indians said that wasn't a good idea, because contingent fees were illegal in India. No problem, Coale replied. He'd write the retainer agreement so as to assure he'd simply be paid the "customary" American fee. Nothing more.

That was fine with the mayor. Bisarya seemed to like Coale, so much so that the he suggested Coale and the Indian lawyers who were present join forces so they could immediately start signing up clients in the squatter villages whose residents had been ravaged by the deadly gray cloud of methyl isocyanate gas. Lowy drew up a retainer agreement, it was translated into Hindi, and the mayor told his nephew, who ran a print shop, to have 3,000 copies of the retainer ready for distribution the next morning.

What happened next is itself the subject of a lawsuit. According to Sastry, "the mayor hinted as to how the system works" and Lowy immediately "offered $250,000 to the mayor for his trouble and efforts, plus a few trips to the U.S.A., all expenses paid," and then everybody shook hands on the deal. Coale denies there was such a bribe offered, and Lowy won't talk about it. But it is clear that the mayor did get some trips to the States and some money—about $20,000, according to Coale and to documents that surfaced in a lawsuit between Coale and Sastry—out of his association with Coale. The trips and at least some of the money were ostensibly given to Bisarya for being a consultant on a since-aborted movie deal about the Bhopal tragedy.

"We got a helluva deal," Coale said later in defending the payments to the mayor. "He put us in touch with *everybody.*"

In any event, after their first meeting with the mayor on that Sunday morning of Coale's arrival in Bhopal, Coale & Company were flying high. They returned to the Ramson Hotel for their first shower in nearly two days, and at lunch there were repeated toasts to their having accomplished so much in those first few hours in the strange land. The mayor invited everybody back to his house that night for dinner.

On Monday, December 10, the Bhopal gold rush began in earnest.

With his blank retainer agreements in hand, Coale, still marveling that he was the only show in town and determined to make the most of it, set out that morning for the vast hut village just south of the Union Carbide India Ltd. plant.

In a country like India, wealth is relative, and a man who can put his family into one of these illegal hut settlements is far better off than the squatter who has only a tent, or, worse, the open air, to live in. For the squatters, vacant land becomes a crossroads where a permanent community forms. In a perfect completion of the food chain, the one-room huts are built with bricks made of hardened cow dung, with a cast-off piece of burlap, wood, or corrugated metal for a roof. If somebody in the squatter community dares to risk his life to attempt it—and, invariably, someone does—there will even be a bootleg hookup to an electrical pole so that residents can siphon off power for the one amenity that many huts don't do without: television. Thousands of people can be crammed into each of these small, permanent settlements, and the government looks the other way because it has to. There is nowhere else for the squatters to live.

This is what Coale's freshly printed blank retainer agreement said:

I hereby retain ARTHUR LOWY & JOHN P. COALE & Associates ATTORNEYS AT LAW 1019 19th STREET N.W. WASHINGTON D.C. U.S.A. to represent me in connection with injuries resulting from UNION CARBIDE Plant leak on night of December 2nd & 3rd on the following conditions:

ARTHUR LOWY & JOHN P. COALE & Associates are to receive compensation in accordance with the United States customs in personal injury cases.

Within minutes, a throng of people assembled around Coale. As Coale walked through the hut village, everybody was clamoring for a retainer to sign. People who couldn't write their name placed a thumbprint on the document. Walking among the teeming dark-skinned masses, trailing reporters and cameramen behind him, Coale saw himself in messianic terms: "I'm there. I'm concerned. It's covered by the media. It's like Palm Sunday and Christ for me."

By 11:30 Monday morning, Coale already had 1,500 retainers signed. He turned the task over to students hired by S. C. Godha, the Indian cocounsel whom the Bhopal mayor had set Coale up with the day before, and to whom Coale had already paid a retainer of $4,000 in traveler's checks. Three days later, the Coale contingent had signed more than 30,000 people to retainer agreements, a tribute not so much to Godha, who in the few days that followed his first meeting with Coale had begun demanding more money and more control over the cases, but rather to the Bhopal mayor. Bisarya, bribed or not, turned out to be Bhopal's answer to Boss Daley. The mayor had his own version of the City That Works. He commanded a formidable political machine, and with it the workers who went from hut to hut gathering in two days a total of 10,000 signatures for Coale.

On Tuesday, December 11, a second contingent of lawyers arrived in Bhopal on the same flight with Mother Teresa. Jay Gould and

Frederico Sayre, the latter a former partner of Belli, had a Los Angeles firm that was involved in the mass-tort Dalkon Shield litigation. On the day they reached Bhopal, their office filed in New York the second class action against Union Carbide, this one for $20 billion.

Belli, whose class action was for a mere $15 billion, finally arrived on Wednesday, December 12. "I am here," he declared upon his arrival, "to bring justice and money to these poor little people who have suffered at the hands of those rich sons of bitches." A typical Belli-ism.

All the lawyers had the same objective: to sign up as many clients as they could, and to file suit on their behalf against Union Carbide in the United States. Filing in the United States was crucial, because the Indian courts were slow and corrupt, and they charged outrageous filing fees. Moreover, only in American courts could the lawyers receive their contingent fees, and only there would the doctrine of strict liability apply. As Belli rather inelegantly explained the doctrine, "It doesn't matter that you didn't intend to bring harm. What matters is that it happened. In this Bhopal case we can damn well prove that it happened. We'll have videotape of all those poor bastards who are sick and dying. We will have a brochure on every single person who was killed."

Now the various groups of lawyers were competing for clients, and for media attention. Coale derided Gould for filing his case so quickly, without a more thorough investigation. "I don't believe in just pulling a figure out of the air," Coale said.

And Gould, who claimed he was on a long-planned trip to China and had intended all along to stop in India, called a news conference and mocked Coale for what Gould characterized as ambulance chasing: "We have not come here to run out and indiscriminately sign victims to documents."

An angry Coale walked up to Gould. "Jay," he said, "the only thing you're pissed off about is, you have a shitty travel agent."

The allegation of ambulance chasing hit Coale where it hurt the most, though, because outright solicitation of clients was certainly illegal in India, just as it was virtually everywhere else except in Coale's hometown. The rule against solicitation made sense; after all, it protected victims of misfortune from being besieged by hordes of hungry lawyers, and it prevented unseemly bidding wars among competing lawyers.

But the clever Coale answered his critics by saying that he wasn't soliciting at all—that the clients came to *him* as he and his people walked from hut to hut, and what was wrong with answering the plaintive cries of those who undoubtedly needed him? Besides, Coale told his media interviewers and the authorities who questioned him, he'd been *summoned* to India by none other than Godha, the hotshot Bhopal lawyer who'd joined with him in signing up clients.

Coale's story was that Godha had contacted an "intermediary," who, in turn, called Sastry and asked Sastry to send over the best lawyer for the job—namely, Coale. That's what Coale told everybody from the *American Lawyer* newspaper to Ted Koppel on "Nightline."

It was a lie.

Sastry had a slightly different story. He said his cousin, a Bhopal engineer, hired Godha, and that the cousin then called Sastry, who called Coale. But that was a lie, too.

The resourceful Coale, having traveled to Bhopal entirely on his own, now needed a way to cover his tracks. He needed to be able to prove that he really *had* been invited over on legitimate business. So, on December 14, not long before Coale was due to *leave* Bhopal, Godha typed up an invitation for Coale & Co. to *come* to Bhopal "because of our business relationships and common problems," and then he back-dated it to December 4, so that it appeared to have been sent to Coale just one day after the tragedy.

At the same time, Coale, Lowy and Godha executed another agreement with Godha, calling themselves "partners" with him and promising to divide equally among themselves any fees they received. It was a great deal for Godha: Coale and Lowy were going to advance all the expenses.

But things were beginning to get too intense for Coale. Waves of lawyers were beginning to arrive, and the allegations of ambulance chasing by American lawyers were heightening. Godha still wasn't in line, and he had threatened to have Coale arrested for signing up clients to illegal contingent-fee agreements. The police were, in fact, already harassing Coale, following him everywhere he went.

Get out of town right now, Sastry advised Coale. That night, Coale and Dickinson left for Delhi by train without informing anyone, taking all 30,000 of their retainers with them. They didn't take the plane, for fear of having the signed retainers confiscated by the government during the rigorous antiterrorist searches that every airline passenger must undergo.

The next morning, December 15, Sastry and Lowy met the mayor and explained that Coale had to leave suddenly to make an important call from Delhi to the States. Reassured, the mayor summoned his official car to take his two remaining guests to the airport for their flight to Delhi.

Coale *was* making an important call: to his brother, Howard, a $150,000-a-year stockbroker for Prudential-Bache Securities Inc. who lived in Greenwich, Connecticut. Coale wanted to let his family know he'd be returning home the next day. Then Howard told his brother the bad news: "They're really killing you," Howard said of the American news media's coverage of Coale's adventure. "In the United States and in the whole world you're being trashed as a vulture."

Coale was stunned. He hadn't seen a newspaper or heard a television or radio broadcast, aside from the local Indian media, since his arrival. He really thought he was doing the Bhopal people a favor. Sure, Coale might make some money, but so what? The Bhopal victims would make money, too.

Coale was still jet-lagged when, having just returned to Washington, he attended a bar group luncheon the following Tuesday. The Association of Plaintiffs' Trial Lawyers was celebrating the successful lawsuit striking down the D.C. no-fault auto insurance law, a lawsuit that Coale had filed and worked hard on. Coale was proud of what he'd done.

But, instead of praising Coale, the speaker dubbed him "the star of that new movie, *A Passage to India.*" Some savage Coale jokes were in reserve, but when the lawyer-comedian asked whether Coale were in the audience, and Coale's hand went up, he toned them down. Coale was humiliated. Here he was, trying to break into the big time, and all he got was condemnation. He went back to his office and wrote out a letter resigning from the bar group.

"I am used to getting criticism," Coale wrote. "It doesn't really hurt me. I don't care. But today was too much for me. . . . I get absolutely nothing but humiliation from your organization."

The Bhopal winter promised to be an interesting one.

Coale didn't like some of the things being said about him, but he sure didn't mind the publicity that was coming his way in such abundant quantities.

"I go with Huey Long," he said. "If they spell your name right, that's all that counts."

And Coale knew that all this publicity was going to be his ticket to soar away from the bill-by-the-hour anonymity that was no doubt fated for the rest of his classmates from the University of Baltimore Law School, class of 1972.

Coale grew up in Baltimore, a rich kid who came from a nice neighborhood and went to a pretty good private school until he got kicked out in the 11th grade for misbehaving. His family owned an envelope-manufacturing company in the city, and he was a good Catholic boy, one of seven children. His grandfather was one of the founders of the Baltimore Orioles baseball club.

But young John just couldn't seem to find his niche. He was married at nineteen, fathered a child, then was divorced at twenty-four while he was still in law school. A few years later, he remarried and had another child, but that match ended in divorce, too.

Maybe it was Coale's childhood wealth that gave him an identity crisis about the law and a blasé attitude about money. He kept dropping in and out of his law practice, picking up a fat fee and then splitting for the Colorado Rockies or Los Angeles. Along the way, he collected an array of angry creditors.

"I grew up around money and it was never a thing. Even when I've been down to nothing, I've always figured I can get money." The Superior Court docket room in Washington, D.C., still contains a record of some of the money problems that have plagued Coale even in recent years: his unsuccessful attempts to get back the deposit he placed on the yacht *Honest Pleasure* after he changed his mind about buying it; his failure to pay a $1,106.84 credit-card bill, a $3,027.65 license fee for his television advertisements and a $900 newsletter subscription, the latter resulting in attachment of his bank account;

his brother's Greenwich, Connecticut, rental house that Coale cosigned for, only to find himself on the business end of a $65,000 lawsuit for theft, fraud and nonpayment of rent; and, of course, the Sastry lawsuit claiming $300,000 in damages.

Then there were the problems with drugs and alcohol. No sooner had Coale passed the Maryland bar and gotten a job with the Baltimore prosecutor's office than he was arrested for drunk driving—and promptly fired. He moved out to California and became, by his own description, "a hippie," living on the salad and Coke he could get for a quarter a day at a Denny's.

Back in Washington four months later, he promptly racked up so many traffic tickets that he was summoned to the D.C. traffic court to explain.

"And I went to traffic court, and I looked around and just felt somebody's making a lot of money down here! So I started snooping around. These guys [lawyers] were making a fortune!

"The small group in traffic court was hanging out there and getting drunk-driving cases, or No Left Turns, and making a fortune! They're pulling in maybe two grand a week, in cash!

"So I started hanging out there. And I got real good at soliciting drunk-driving cases. I would have it where I wouldn't really solicit, because you couldn't solicit then. I'd just kind of make myself there, and look like a lawyer. Kind of beam in on a guy you knew was a drunk driver. And you'd just kind of beam in, smile at him, and he'd invariably come up.

"You'd say, 'How're you doing?' Just steer the conversation around. Most of 'em would be thrilled to find somebody to help 'em." There wasn't much that needed to be done. Maybe Coale could plead them to reduced charges or get them into a first-offender program. "You only worked from eight to twelve, and you'd make a thousand, fifteen hundred a week." Coale had a big grin on his face, just thinking about it. He giggled his chipmunk giggle. "That was in 1976, 1977. Makin' money in traffic court. Playin' the rest of the time."

Coale practiced drug law, too, defending "your clean-cut college guys making a lot of money." The dope dealers sometimes let him take his fee in trade, and Coale used acid, pot, and cocaine, until 1979, when his own fear about his "degraded" lifestyle caused him to flee to England, where he bought an old thirteen-meter steel-hulled yacht called the *Wuffenwood* and started sailing it from country to country.

Coale's boat had masts made of wood, rotten wood, as it turned out. And in a gale ten miles off the coast of Spain, both masts snapped off, entangling the sails in the boat's engine. The craft was swamped, and Coale, his seventeen-year-old brother, Richard, and another young teenage friend were saved when a fishing boat saw their emergency flares.

"That was the real stuff," Coale said. "That boat was going down, and we didn't know what we were going to do."

What Coale did was return to England and wait six weeks for his insurance money to come through. He lived off the $100 a day he made counting cards, a few hands at a time so as not to arouse suspicion, at the blackjack table in a Portsmouth casino.

Back in Washington, Coale's second marriage was breaking up. He moved in with his sister, who lived in a Maryland suburb, and got a ride back downtown.

"I walked into the courthouse. Spotted a guy. He comes up to me and says, 'Are you a lawyer?' I say, 'Yes.' He says, 'I got a DWI,' gives me $350, and I'm back in business!

"So I'm down. I have some money but it still hasn't come from England. So I started hustling cases. But the great thing was, I found out, since I'd gone, that the D.C. Bar had legalized solicitation!

"So I put together this scam, which turned out to be a riot. I met this guy, Tyrone Roberts, a black guy out of Philadelphia. We met at the courthouse. He was down and out, too. He was an investigator.

"So we planned and planned and I finally came up with the great scam: It was so simple! Tyrone went around to all the precincts. Opened up the arrest book, every morning. Copied down the names and addresses; everybody who'd been caught for DWI, we sent 'em a letter. I had Arthur Lowy working with me. Within a matter of weeks, we cornered the market in DWI cases."

Coale, Lowy and Roberts would meet their new clients—about seven a day—each morning at Jaybirds, a little cafe and beer joint across the street from the courthouse.

"We'd send 'em a letter, interview 'em over the phone, and then tell 'em to meet us down there at Jaybirds. Every morning we'd meet 'em down there and then we'd march 'em in to the courthouse to be arraigned—Lowy in the front, me in the back, and Tyrone working the flanks, because all the lawyers got so crazy they were actually grabbing the people, and they're trying to rough up Lowy. The other lawyers are going crazy! Because we've cornered the market and this is their livelihood!"

Afternoons, the trio would return to the dinky, one-desk office atop the American Cafe on Capitol Hill to interview new clients. "So you gotta see this office in the afternoon! Me and Lowy are fightin' over who gets to sit at the desk! Real wild stuff. But the funny thing is, the guy who rented us the office had an orthodontic practice. He said we could use his waiting room for the overflow. You gotta get this picture of these little kids and these drunks in the same waiting room!"

That was what Coale referred to as "seriously practicing law." He made some thirty-second television spots featuring football announcer John Madden: "If you've been in an accident, you have rights. . . . Call John P. Coale." And the ads started producing some interesting clients.

It was Coale's first real exposure to personal injury work, and there was no question that his paydays were going to get bigger. The family of three-year-old Melissa Gilbert hired him after their daughter was strangled when the strings of her parka caught in a Washington subway escalator. That case settled for $500,000, and Coale pocketed the standard one-third cut.

He had another client who was struck broadside by a Washington Redskins van driven by the son of team owner and big-time lawyer Edward Bennett Williams. Talk about deep pockets! Coale got another half-million-dollar settlement from that case, and he took a one-fourth contingency for himself.

It was an eclectic practice, but even the most quixotic cases taught the up-and-coming Coale some valuable lessons about how to win his points *outside* the courtroom. That was where he was at his best, after all. The last place Coale wanted to be was in a courtroom. No action for *him* there.

So even the pro bono cases helped Coale become more media-wise. There was the time Blue Cross/Blue Shield refused to fund a liver transplant operation for a three-month-old child in Washington state. Coale got on the phone to lawyers for K-mart, the employer of the child's parents, and was still getting nowhere two days later. So he called the company's public relations department. "I saw thirty or forty K-mart ads on the Olympics," he said. "I'm sure you must have spent millions of dollars on those ads. Well, if you don't pay up, I'll file a $10 million lawsuit. I'll call a press conference, and you'll have to spend millions explaining why you wouldn't pay for this little girl's transplant. Whether you win or lose the suit, you'll still lose." Coale was learning. Three hours later, K-mart agreed to pay for the transplant operation.

Four years before he went to Bhopal, Coale took the cases of twelve American Embassy workers who had been held hostage in Iran. First, he sued the Iranian Government for $400 million. But then the U.S. Government established an exclusive Iran claims tribunal at The Hague to consider all the lawsuits against Iran, and his cases were dismissed from the U.S. courts. Still, Coale persisted, next filing suit against *his own* country, on the grounds that *somebody* ought to pay his clients—if not the people who injured them, then their own government, by God! "I would expect the United States to step in and compensate my clients," he said indignantly.

He carried the hostages' case all the way to the Supreme Court, and the justices finally threw it out for good in 1984, the very week he left for Bhopal. But by then Coale had perfected his stratagem of calling a government's bluff. And the ploy was going to come in handy if the Bhopal case didn't go his way.

By January 1985, just a month after the disaster, there was a stampede among lawyers for control of the world's biggest mass-tort case.

Coale now had 60,000 retainer agreements, and that made him a player. But, amazingly, there were some other lawyers with even more clients. Mahendra Mehta, a Chicago immigration attorney who'd once been suspended from practice after being convicted of making false statements to U.S. immigration officials, claimed 100,000 clients. All told, the people of Bhopal had signed an estimated 498,000 retainers—and many residents, it was said, had gladly signed up again and again and again with every lawyer who came through, hoping to increase their chances of recovery.

Over 100 lawsuits had already been filed in more than a dozen federal courts from Maine to California. But soon those suits would all be consolidated into one gigantic case. That was what the federal rules dictated whenever a multitude of individual cases was filed because of a common disaster.

This was called *multidistrict litigation*, MDL for short. A special judicial panel on multidistrict litigation was going to decide where to send the Bhopal cases. Once that issue was settled, the judge assigned those cases would be appointing a few lawyers to coordinate everything. If the lawyers agreed among themselves as to who should be on that steering committee, the judge usually ratified their choices. If they didn't, the judge made his own selections.

The members of the steering committee controlled everything that happened: subpoenas, depositions, motions, the works. They divided up the work and held the purse strings. More importantly, the lawyers on the steering committee got what amounted to an ownership interest in every single case, and thus a much higher fee than everyone else. It wasn't unusual for a court, at the conclusion of a big multidistrict case, to deduct 6 percent or more from each lawyer's total fee and put that same amount into a big pot to be split among the steering committee members. In the $180 million Agent Orange toxic-tort case, the eight lawyers on the steering committee had such an entrepreneurial spirit that they guaranteed themselves a three-to-one return on their contribution to the common expense fund of nearly $2 million. Only after the elite had taken their share could the other lawyers who had worked on the case split what was left over. Such was the "new math" of disaster law.

And that was where the strategizing came in.

The disaster law business ran by the Rules of Three. The name of the game was seizing control of the litigation by being one of the few lawyers named to the steering committee, and there were three factors that judges usually considered: the lawyer's résumé, his firm's financial strength, and whether he had filed cases soon after the disaster occurred.

Because judges gave the positions of power to those who were most experienced in disaster litigation, and who could advance the hundreds of thousands of dollars that sometimes had to be expended on travel and experts, every lawyer pumped up his résumé to make it look good to the judge. And, since the number of claimants a lawyer represented and whether the lawyer had been one of the first to file also were taken into account, Belli and Gould had been quick to file suit. It was part of the overall strategy, a way of staking their claim.

But getting onto the steering committee was only the first of three ways that a disaster lawyer could get big money from other lawyers' cases.

The second was to be called in as a cocounsel by a lawyer who already had a case but who either couldn't or wouldn't work on it himself. Publicity in the legal newspapers, such as the *National Law Journal* and the *American Lawyer,* gave a lawyer a national reputation as an expert in a particular field, and that brought in the cocounsel referrals. The lawyer who originally signed up the client commonly kept 60 percent of his contingent fee and gave the rest to his cocounsel if there were a settlement, or split the recovery fifty-fifty if the case went to trial—a tacit acknowledgment that, short of a trial, the hardest part of a disaster lawyer's job was hustling the clients!

The third way lawyers gained a financial advantage was to trade legal-fee kickbacks for other favors. Let's say a lawyer wanted to guarantee himself a spot on the plaintiffs' steering committee. Since the judge allows the lawyers to select the committee members, the best way to guarantee yourself a spot was by good old-fashioned vote-swapping. A lawyer who knew he didn't have a shot at the steering committee might agree to vote for a colleague in exchange for a 10 percent kickback on whatever steering-committee fees that colleague got. Or, two lawyers might pool their cases and agree to split their fee awards fifty-fifty, so that if one lawyer got on the committee and the other didn't, the lawyer who was left out would still be protected.

"Stamina and cleverness," Coale said with bravado. "That's what makes you a mass disaster lawyer." But could Coale outswim all these sharks?

Coale hadn't filed any lawsuits yet, and that was going to be a big strike against him when the nut-cutting finally began. With a newcomer's naivete, he wanted to be the one to broker an agreement among the U.S. Government, the Indian Government and Union Carbide, and he thought his experience in suing the United States and

Iran during the hostage crisis would convince the other lawyers to cede that role to him. Coale thought that if he could develop some contacts at the State Department, he could see whether the striped-pants boys were going to help the plaintiffs' lawyers, or whether they were going to grease the skids for Union Carbide to somehow slide out from under its liability. "I know how State works," he told any-one who'd listen. "We have to deal with these people [at State], or else they're going to take the case away"—send it back to India, where the American lawyers couldn't get any contingent fees. "It's just a matter of time before the Indian Government steals the case, or the U.S. Government comes in and throws us out." There was merit to Coale's argument, but his fellow lawyers were too busy jostling each other to see it.

Amid those jockeying for position, a few key players were already emerging. Coale was a factor because of the sheer number of cases he controlled, but he was also an unknown, with no trial-lawyer allies from previous disasters. He had no favors to trade, nothing to bargain with except his own cases. Meanwhile, a second group of lawyers had entered the litigation. They had instant credibility because of their work in earlier disasters.

Stanley Chesley, white-haired and beefy at age forty-eight, had a seven-lawyer Cincinnati firm that specialized in mass torts and class actions, and he was Belli's cocounsel in the $15 billion Bhopal law-suit. Chesley had also played a key role in the big cases that followed the 1980 fire at the MGM Grand Hotel in Las Vegas and the 1977 Beverly Hills Supper Club fire in Covington, Kentucky. In the Agent Orange case, he had been awarded $525,000 in fees and expenses for less than a year's worth of settlement negotiations, but that was noth-ing compared to the upward of $3 million he had received out of the $49 million Beverly Hills Supper Club settlement, or the several million dollars he'd made from the MGM Grand case. Rumors circu-lated about how Chesley swapped favors and kicked back fees so that he could put himself in control of a case, but the cagey lawyer was careful to stay high enough above the fray to keep his reputation unsullied. Chesley's firm had a long, important-sounding name, but he had no partners. The firm's profit was all his, and a conservative estimate of his annual take was $1 million. The rest of the young lawyers in his firm were there for the experience of working alongside an acknowledged master of disaster.

Wendell Gauthier of Metairie, Louisiana, headed his own firm, too, and, at forty-one, he was the oldest lawyer in it. A pudgy man with thick brown hair, he had already served on the plaintiffs' steering committees resulting from the MGM Grand fire, the explosion at a Continental Grain Company elevator, and the crash of Pan Am Flight 759.

Michael V. Ciresi, thirty-eight, was an intense, cigarette-smoking lawyer from the big Minneapolis law factory of Robins, Zelle, Larson & Kaplan, and even though he wasn't cast in the lone-wolf mold of the typical plaintiff's lawyer, he was a Bhopal player here nonetheless. Robins, Zelle, with 125 lawyers, represented plaintiffs as well as defendants. To the latter, it sold itself as a frugal, aggressive alternative to the big, stuffy Washington and New York firms. To plaintiffs, it touted an impressive record of huge awards in disaster cases, including the MGM Grand fire and the Dalkon Shield litigation against A. H. Robins, in which Ciresi just the previous year had helped to mastermind a record $38 million settlement.

Chesley made the first move. In early January, he summoned sixty of the lawyers who had Bhopal clients to a meeting at the O'Hare Airport Hilton outside Chicago. Coale had been getting more Bhopal publicity than anybody else there, "so I go there figuring I'm in a power position," he later explained.

"Chesley comes up and introduces himself and says, 'Look, we want to work together.' He figures I'll give him all my cases. I play along. 'Fine. Sure. I'm sure we'll all work together.'

"Nothing comes of that Chicago meeting, except I realize that there's a tremendous amount of bullshit that's being slung here. Everybody's trying to throw their résumé on the table. They're standing up, touting what they've done. I just sat back, knowing I had 60,000 cases. I didn't say anything."

Chesley wanted to form an interim steering committee quickly, and another meeting was scheduled for January 23, this time in Gauthier's territory, at the downtown Hyatt Hotel in New Orleans. With the MDL panel scheduled to hear arguments in New Orleans the next day on where the Bhopal cases would be consolidated, all the lawyers would be flying in anyway. But Gauthier asked Coale and a few others to show up early and have lunch with him in advance of a bigger gathering of Bhopal-disaster lawyers scheduled for that evening. Coale took his sidekick Dickinson along.

There was quite a welcome for Coale and Dickinson at the airport. They were met there by an attractive female legal assistant who took them into town in Gauthier's Rolls Royce. "Didn't impress me," Coale harumphed. "I knew you could get an old Rolls for almost nothing out in L.A." Chesley owned a Rolls, too. Coale preferred his own sleek black Jaguar.

Over lunch, the various lawyers started pumping up their qualifications again. Coale stressed his experience "with sovereigns" in the Iran hostage case, and in another case in which he'd sued the nation of Brazil for $10 million after its ambassador's son shot and wounded the bouncer at a sleazy Washington bar. Coale was once again arguing for bringing the United States and Indian governments into the settlement negotiations at the outset, so that they wouldn't upset whatever accommodation the lawyers finally arrived at with Union Carbide.

"Look," Coale began, "I want to settle this case. But if we get it into the courts, it's going to go on for years and they're going to steal the case from us! Get it into the legal system too far and it'll never be heard from again. India or the U.S. is going to steal the case. If we get together and try to settle it, fine."

But Coale thought he wasn't getting any takers because an early settlement would prevent people like Chesley and Gauthier from claim-jumping all the cases that enterprising attorneys like Coale had staked out.

Rival factions had already begun to form. Belli, Chesley and Gauthier were working together, as were a group of New York lawyers that included celebrity lawyer F. Lee Bailey and his partner, Aaron Broder. At fifty-one, the enterprising Bailey was the best known of the bunch, having represented people like Patricia Hearst and the Boston Strangler, hosted two network game shows and published a skin magazine called *Gallery*. Broder and Bailey wanted the cases sent to New York City because Union Carbide was headquartered in nearby Connecticut.

Chesley and Gauthier beckoned Coale to join their alliance, but he held out. "My power is because I have a lot of cases," he reasoned.

"But, more importantly, I'm in the media more than *anybody*. Belli's in there a lot, but I'm in there whenever there's a comment about Bhopal. I give nice comments. I have a lot of media access.

"They also are finding out that I'm not a small-timer who's impressed by all the bullshit. A lot of small-timers were giving up cases, thinking these guys [Chesley and Gauthier] know how to work the litigation, not knowing they're getting pushed aside. They think they're going to split the contingency with Wendell [Gauthier] and Stanley [Chesley]. But Gauthier and Chesley will get on the committee, *and the judge awards the fee for what you did on the committee!* The guy who got the cases to begin with won't get much! These other guys don't know that. I know this! And I also know bullshit when I see it!"

"Number 626," the court clerk announced the next morning, January 24. "In re Union Carbide." Whereupon three dozen lawyers swarmed to the front of the courtroom.

Union Carbide's lawyers wanted the case sent to New York since that city was "a transportation hub" and nearly half of the thirty-seven cases already pending had been filed there. Belli argued for West Virginia, where he and Chesley had filed their class action, because Union Carbide had another plant there that also produced methyl isocyanate. Stanley Rosenblatt of Miami argued for Miami, because "the weather is good, which is as good a reason as some of the others I've heard."

Chesley had called another meeting for February 9, in Coale's hometown at the Washington Hilton. Meanwhile, the New York lawyers met at the Tandoor, one of New York's best Indian restaurants, and resolved to put up a united front to prevent Chesley and his cronies from taking over the case.

Coale was doing some lobbying of his own in advance of that next meeting. "I started to put it together. I see where the *power* is. The power's in the *death* cases. There's so much incredible stuff going on with the injuries. The only *real* cases are the death cases, 'cause you can prove them with death certificates.

"So I start to get a group together. I get together about ten guys and we agree to centralize our death cases. Now, I got like 600 or 700 death cases! We figured if we could start settling death cases, we could start the whole thing settling.

"I'm learning fast! I've seen how the game's played. So, now *I'm* calling meetings!"

The twenty or so lawyers who were invited to Coale's National Lawyers Club meeting the night of February 8 came from outside the inner circle of big-time disaster lawyers. They were under great pressure to close ranks, because the MDL panel had ruled only two days before that all the Bhopal cases would, indeed, be consolidated in New York City. Up to this point, the lower-caste lawyers like Coale had successfully prevented the Brahmins like Chesley and Belli from putting a steering committee in place by arguing that it was premature to elect anybody before the MDL panel ruled. Now, that condition had been satisfied, and Coale was sure the February 9 meeting would be the last battle for a committee. Belli was already predicting that all the cases would be settled by Christmas!

But Coale had seriously misjudged how much power he really had. The other lawyers weren't buying his act, media star or not, death cases or not.

They were voting for experience over everything else. And, at Chesley's five-hour meeting the following day, Coale was not only kept off the steering committee, but totally, unequivocally cut out of the picture altogether. "John Coale is a runner," Ciresi said. "He can't point to a thing he did in Bhopal. John Coale in Bhopal was a nonentity, except as a media figure." After much wrangling, what the lawyers finally approved that day was a committee that included one representative from each of the twenty-eight law firms that had filed federal cases. Chesley and Jerry Cohen, the latter a respected class-action lawyer from Washington, were elected cochairmen, with Chesley designated as the press spokesman. Since Coale hadn't yet filed a case, he was out in the cold, exactly where the other lawyers wanted him.

Coale was stunned. "Here I am with 60,000 cases and I'm not on the committee," he thought. "They got me. I'm out. I'm dead." Since the steering committee would control who worked on the case and, consequently, who got most of the fee award when the time came to split it up, "If I want any money at all, I've gotta give 'em my cases. We gotta do a deal." As Coale saw it, what was happening was pretty clear. He was being blackmailed.

Gauthier walked over, as if to offer his condolences. The two men had hit it off when they'd first met in New Orleans a few weeks before. Coale trusted Gauthier, though he certainly didn't trust Chesley.

"Whaddaya think?" Gauthier asked, a weak grin on his face.

"You guys really hit us with the old freight train," Coale answered, still feeling the shock of what had just happened.

"What are you gonna do now?"

"Wendell," Coale replied, reaching back for whatever was left of his old swagger, "I've had a lot of fun in this case. It's been exciting, a lot of action. You guys just took all my fun away. There's only one thing left to do where I can possibly have as much fun, because you guys know that's all I'm interested in. It's to fuck you guys, and really fuck you good! I'm gonna go out there and start talking. There's a guy out there from *Playboy* who wants to do an interview with me on all the shenanigans that have been going on. Now that you guys have beaten me out of the case, the only thing left to do is to take you guys with me!"

Gauthier wasn't amused. But with his bluster—there was no interviewer waiting outside—Coale had managed to gain a little bit of leverage on the powers that be. Better to have Coale inside their tent pissing out, Chesley and Gauthier decided, than outside their tent pissing in! Two days later, someone from Chesley's office called Coale and told him a ticket to Cincinnati was waiting for him at the airport. Once in Cincinnati, Coale turned his cases over to Chesley and Gauthier as part of a deal in which he and Lowy would divide 45 percent of whatever fee award his 60,000 cases ultimately produced. His new partners Chesley and Gauthier would get the rest. Plus, Chesley and Gauthier agreed to repay Coale the $80,000 in expenses he had already shelled out chasing the Bhopal cases, and to pay any other expenses he might have in the future as their chief "client contact person" in Bhopal.

"So I got in at the top on a free ride, is the way I looked at it."

John F. Keenan, a hard-nosed former criminal justice coordinator for New York's Mayor Edward Koch, was the federal judge to whom the Bhopal litigation was assigned. "Looks like a *Republican* judge," Coale sneered when he first saw Keenan.

In April, Keenan selected three top guns—Chesley, Bailey and Ciresi—as the executive committee for the plaintiffs.

The selection seemed to make intuitive sense. Chesley, after all, had taken the initiative from the start, and his election as their first cochairman and press spokesman showed his popular support. Bailey had an office in New York and had been a leader of that city's contingent. And Ciresi had confounded everybody by landing possibly the biggest account of all: He had just been hired the previous month to represent the government of India in its own suit against Union Carbide. Besides, Keenan said proudly if naively, none of the three, "nor anyone in their law firms," had gone ambulance chasing in India. If he wasn't aware of Chesley's fee-splitting arrangement with Coale, apparently no one was going to enlighten him.

But Keenan's seemingly sensible choice of the three-man executive committee was actually horribly flawed, because Ciresi had an irreconcilable conflict with the other two men. The conflict involved the Indian Government's passage, on March 29, 1985, of a law that gave the government of India the exclusive right to represent Indian plaintiffs in connection with the Bhopal disaster. Ciresi and his law firm, Minneapolis' Robins, Zelle, now carried the Indian Government's proxy in the litigation. As far as Ciresi was concerned, every one of the Bhopal clients belonged to him—*all 487,000 of them!*

But the Indian law wasn't enforceable unless the MDL litigation against Union Carbide were thrown out of the American courts and sent back to India. That meant Chesley, Bailey and all the rest of the American lawyers still had a shot at the action, but only as long as Keenan didn't send the cases back to India or declare Ciresi the only lawyer with a valid lawsuit. Chesley and Bailey obviously wanted to keep themselves and their lawsuits in Keenan's court; Ciresi understandably wanted them out of the action. The three lawyers had an alliance that was doomed from the start.

Union Carbide made no secret of its desire to have the litigation dismissed from the U.S. courts, for all the same reasons that the plaintiffs wanted to keep the cases there. Even the Indian Government didn't trust its own legal system to hand out the kind of money that the American courts would.

Keenan was willing to try to push for a settlement, but that was looking more and more doubtful as the lawyers piled into Keenan's courtroom in mid-April for a hearing. Even Belli and Broder, who were, after all, supposed to be *cooperating* since their counterparts Chesley and Bailey were overseeing the litigation, couldn't refrain from sniping at each other, even when they really should have been aiming at Union Carbide. Belli accused Broder of "chasing" his clients. Broder, who had been criticized in the past for running client-solicitation ads in the New York *Times* after airplane crashes, struck back by criticizing the Belli faction's "despicable" interest in its own contingent fees. Belli and his allies, said Broder, "aren't in the same league" as he was when it came to winning big jury verdicts.

As the Bhopal spring stretched into summer, there was another Union Carbide toxic chemical leak, this one at the company's Institute, West Virginia, plant. Coale & Co. lost no time in filing their suits. But the big payday still eluded them.

Keenan had secretly been trying to broker a settlement between Union Carbide and the plaintiffs' lawyers, and he was pleased by the progress that had been made. Starting with a dismally low initial offer of $78 million from Union Carbide, the judge had jawboned the giant company all the way up to $350 million. That was less than the $630 million that the Indian Government had been demanding, but a quick settlement for that sum now sure beat making the Bhopal victims wait while the lawyers slugged it out for years to come.

To keep the pressure on all the American lawyers to accept its secret settlement offer, Union Carbide was still publicly pushing to have the case transferred back to India. Keenan thought the case was only worth keeping in the States if there were a chance to get it settled quickly. He wasn't going to use the power of his robe unless all the parties cooperated, and he certainly didn't want to make the

Bhopal case his life's work. If there weren't going to be a quick settlement, Keenan reasoned, then he might as well grant Union Carbide's pending motion to send the litigation back to India, where he thought it really belonged. After all, that was where the accident happened, and that's where the victims were.

On the evening of February 10, 1986, Ciresi, Chesley and Bailey met for dinner at Sparks, the posh midtown steakhouse in front of which Mafia boss Paul Castellano had been gunned down the previous year. Castellano's last meal had set off a vicious gang war that still continued. So would this one.

Union Carbide's $350 million offer was final, and, with millions of dollars in fees hanging in the balance, Chesley and Bailey wanted to accept it. Chesley and Gauthier alone had already advanced $800,000 of their own money on the case; they wouldn't get a nickel of that back if the case went to India.

But Ciresi was adamantly opposed to the settlement. "It's ludicrously low," he told the two men. As far as Ciresi was concerned, the settlement talks were off.

But that surely meant Keenan would wash his hands of the whole thing and send the case back to India. Ciresi didn't mind that. The Indian Government was paying him by the hour, so he'd make his money either way.

When the three lawyers reported to Keenan that they couldn't agree on whether to accept the settlement, the judge reacted as the lawyers had expected, telling them he intended to begin writing his opinion on Union Carbide's transfer-to-India motion on March 17. There was little doubt about Keenan's intention to send the case back to India if there were no compromise before then.

It was time for Bailey and Chesley to make a desperation move. They secretly contacted their opposite numbers at New York's Kelley Drye & Warren, Union Carbide's outside counsel, and together the lawyers started making plans to settle the case and cut Ciresi out of the picture altogether.

The plan that emerged was for Bailey and Chesley to sweep the claims of all Bhopal victims into a huge class action that would be immediately settled for $350 million, thereby short-circuiting the Indian Government's claim that it represented all the victims. Union

Carbide wanted an end to all state and federal litigation over the Bhopal disaster, and this all-encompassing class action would produce it.

On the afternoon of Wednesday, March 19, during a conference in Keenan's chambers, Ciresi learned for the first time that Chesley and Bailey had that very morning reached a definitive agreement with Union Carbide on the sellout settlement.

Chesley telephoned Coale. "Get over there," he instructed. "You've gotta get over there" to sell the settlement to the Indian people. It was going to be Coale's fifth trip to Bhopal.

"Whenever there's heat," Coale said, "they call me to go 'cause I *like* the heat."

Ciresi had been expecting the end run all along. "We assumed," he told me later, "that the other lawyers would try to accept the offer. If they didn't at least make a stab at it, they were out of the litigation altogether, because the judge was going to send it back to India."

Ciresi couldn't have set a better trap for the others if he'd tried. As word spread about the Chesley-Bailey gambit—Ciresi wasn't exactly being tight-lipped about what had gone on—the settlement that so recently had been all but signed, sealed and delivered started to fall apart, its demise hastened by a series of fiascos that made Chesley, Gauthier and some of the other lawyers look like money-grubbing fools.

An angry Keenan called all the attorneys back to his chambers at 4:20 P.M. the following Monday, March 24. There was a gag order covering the settlement talks, but, over the weekend, the news of the Chesley–Bailey–Union Carbide deal had leaked on to the front pages of the New York *Times* and the Washington *Post,* and it had been reported by all the network newscasts. Articles about the settlement were *everywhere.* Union Carbide's public relations people had even put out a press release describing the whole thing, and Chesley, in trying to clarify *that* statement, had inadvertently given away even more information to *The Wall Street Journal*, which had carried his comments that day.

Keenan told the nine lawyers clustered in his office that he must be "operating under some kind of delusion." The judge thought everything was going to be kept secret. "If I am operating under a delusion, I would like to be advised of it right away," he fumed. "Now, can anybody tell me why yesterday's front page of the New York *Times* has as one of the lead stories, "Tentative Accord Reached to Settle Bhopal Lawsuits"; why the lead stories on the three national television networks last evening were the Union Carbide settlements; why today's New York *Times* on the first page of the Financial Section has an extensive story about the case and the settlement discussions; why today's New York *Post* has a story; why today's *Daily News* has a story; and, more interestingly than anything, why Mr. Chesley is quoted in today's *Wall Street Journal?*"

Chesley had foolishly given an on-the-record confirmation of the deal by cautioning reporters "there's no ink on it." He fell all over himself apologizing to the judge for what he said was a "mistake of judgment" in talking to the reporters, "because when you try and respond, they take it out of context." Some of the lawyers even wanted to put everybody under oath and find out who started the leaks.

"It has hurt us considerably," Chesley said in the one statement with which everyone who was there agreed. Whatever reasons Ciresi's client might have had for being conciliatory went down the drain when the articles quoted unnamed sources as saying that Chesley and Bailey wanted their own settlement because they thought the Indian Government was too corrupt and inefficient to administer the settlement itself.

"Whoever said that blew it insofar as the Indian Government is concerned," the chagrined Keenan commented. "It's the old story. You don't seek to obtain agreement from somebody after you kick them as hard as you can in the shins—or another part of their anatomy."

It was 4:50 P.M. the following afternoon when Keenan called the lawyers back for another conference. He was furious at the behind-the-scenes leaking that was still going on. It was clear from that morning's *Wall Street Journal* that someone had immediately run to the phone and given a blow-by-blow account of Monday's conference to the newspaper.

"I came down here in the morning," Keenan complained to the lawyers. "I get *The Wall Street Journal* here, and it's the same thing all over again. I eliminate myself unless I talk in my sleep and my wife called *The Wall Street Journal!* . . . Am I going to put everybody on the stand and cross-examine them?"

Keenan wheeled and fired at Ciresi's partner and corner-man, thirty-eight-year-old Bruce A. Finzen: "And where did *you* go when you left the courtroom yesterday, Mr. Finzen? Who did you have dinner with? Who did you speak to on the telephone?

"How about *you*, Mr. Allen?

"What did *you* do, Mr. Chesley?

"What did *you* do, Mr. Krohley?

"It's childish!" Keenan thundered. He'd never been more outraged in all his years on the bench.

"Somebody in the group who was here last Wednesday enjoys talking to the press, and, in my judgment, undermines whatever likelihood there was of a resolution to this."

Keenan told the lawyers he might as well lift the gag order since no one was following it anyway. "There are not going to be any more settlement discussions with me, anyhow," he added ominously. "I'll see you in the future."

Coale had just arrived in Bhopal. Lowy, who had already been there for a few days, gave him a big hug. Things were turning nasty, Lowy said. He was being followed around by the police, and the government was waging its own campaign against the $350 million offer that was now being widely reported.

As Coale saw it, his job was to counter the negative publicity by calling news conferences and distributing leaflets. He didn't think there were five people in the whole country who had any idea how much money Union Carbide was really offering. "If they're told it's small, they'll think it's small," he sputtered. "I'm over here trying to make it real to these people—what $350 million is. That's my job.

"There's a lot of racist crap going on. All the middle-class people can't stand the thought of the untouchables getting all this money. It's like, if you go to the South Bronx and make everybody there a millionaire, what do you think they're gonna think in Queens? They're gonna go crazy! They couldn't stand the thought!"

Bisarya, though still working for Coale, was no longer mayor of Bhopal, and the new administration wrote Coale a letter on March 31 firing him as the city's attorney.

From Coale's diary:

> *I have come back to Delhi to get Wendell [Gauthier] to wire me money and I am going back to virtually run a political campaign to change the opinion of the people. When you get the people on a one-on-one basis and it is explained how much money would be coming to them, they are very much in favor of the settlement. I think that it is getting across. I have Dr. Bisarya to start taking me to local leaders to explain our position. I will keep talking to the media and keep sending the boys out to see what they can do with the people.*
>
> *—March 31, 1986*

Coale returned to Bhopal from Delhi on April 2 and had thousands of handbills printed up and distributed.

"Compensation Settlement for Gas Victims: Truth and Reality," the eight-point Hindi-language handbill was titled.

Coale's version of the "truth" was that families of every person killed by the Bhopal gas leak would get anywhere from 300,000 to 800,000 rupees, or about $25,000 to $67,000 apiece. There were at least 2,000 people in this category. People with catastrophic illness— there were perhaps 25,000—would receive anywhere from $8,000 to $33,000, Coale assured everyone.

"This settlement is the largest ever given in a personal injury case," the handbill concluded. "This settlement includes penalties. If you accept this settlement, payment can begin in a few months instead of years."

Never mind that no such payments had been negotiated or agreed upon. Never mind that, aside from all the other payments for lesser injuries that Coale also promised, it would take well over $500 million just to compensate the families of those who were dead or seriously ill.

The Indian Government replied with front-page advertisements in all the local newspapers warning Bhopal residents about the evildoers in their midst. The government also printed up a Hindi-language handbill of its own:

GAS VICTIMS—BEWARE OF THE TEMPTATIONS
OFFERED BY SUSPECT MIDDLEMEN

The state government's attention has been drawn towards the activities in Bhopal of suspect middlemen who are conniving to get a meager compensation for gas victims—instead of getting them a suitable legal settlement. The government has also learned that the gas victims are being misinformed by these middlemen that if they do not accept their propositions, the cases of the victims will be dismissed from American courts. This misleading statement is being made to maximize the share that middlemen receive from any settlement.

The government of India has already filed suit against Union Carbide in an American district court and full attention is being paid toward it. Parliament has also passed a law which gives the right to represent gas victims exclusively to the government of India. These selfish self-appointed middlemen who are talking about a settlement have not been endorsed by the government of India. Neither will they ever be endorsed—because this would be completely inappropriate. The government will only accept a settlement by which all gas victims will be fully and appropriately compensated. The welfare of the gas victims is safe in the hands of the government. Gas victims should not be misled by temptations and assurances of middlemen. For obvious reasons, Union Carbide will make every effort to reach the smallest possible settlement. For this reason all people associated with this should watch out for middlemen who are tempting them to reach settlements by which they may lose their just and appropriate compensation.

The welfare of the gas victims is secure in the hands of the government.

From Coale's diary:

In this environment, it is interesting, one tends to start to become grubby. You start wearing the same clothes, kind of like the locals. As the British always do, I have instituted a policy with me and Lowy, that we have to wear well-pressed clothes every day and look spit and polished to keep discipline up. As strange as that may seem, it works well.
—April 2, 1986

Our plan is to try and call the Indian government's bluff. What we propose to do is to put out a press release and an ad in the paper stating that if the Indian government doesn't like the settlement, and they are so sure they can do better, why don't they guarantee to the victims $350 million. Then we will be happy.

I am in Bombay this morning. I flew out this morning. I just talked to Wendell. Apparently we are making some headway and the Indian government may want to start coming around a bit. I am going to American Express to get more funds for this campaign. . . . It was very encouraging, when I talked to Wendell, that Stan and Wendell and the boys understand what we are doing here and understand the danger and also what it can contribute to the settlement of this case, and, quite frankly, to the people of Bhopal, to get them some money.
—April 3, 1986

I don't know if there is any response to the press release. I haven't seen the morning papers. It is getting politically hot. Our inclination is to go back to the United States and tell the judge that it should be sent back to India, and let these bastards stew in their own juices. They are absolutely insane from A to Z. . . .

What has happened is that yesterday we gave the government 48 hours to agree to guarantee $350 million into the hands of the victims. Of course, we all feel that they have absolutely no intention of ever giving the victims anything, but this is at least a guarantee. I think this is going to *get some good press. [A] reporter said that he had talked with people in the government and they are very upset that this is happening. So, we will see what goes from here.*

—April 5, 1986

At 5:30 on the afternoon of Friday, April 4, Keenan's law clerk, Robin Roger, put through a conference call to Chesley, Bailey's partner Michael Zwal, Ciresi and the Union Carbide lawyers.

"Where in the world do the two American lawyers get off writing to what is essentially the governor of an Indian state and saying that there is a $350 million settlement?" Keenan screamed into the phone.

"Mr. Chesley, I want you—did anyone authorize this letter?"

Chesley: "Of course not, your honor—this is Stan Chesley talking. Your honor, I am outraged, and if I could speak in Yiddish, the word would be *chutzpah.*" Chesley said he wanted to get off the phone that instant so that he could have Gauthier contact Coale and tell him to come home.

"I am outraged," said Chesley, who, Coale said, had told him to go to Bhopal in the first place. "And I guess, you know, I am not my brother's keeper, but I urge—"

Keenan: "So you are saying you knew nothing about this?"

Chesley: "Of course not, your honor. I knew that—"

Keenan kept pressing Chesley. "You knew nothing about the letter?" He was skeptical.

Chesley wisely dodged the question this time. "I will get hold of Wendell Gauthier now."

Keenan thanked Ciresi's law firm for telling him about Coale's letter and then wished everybody a good weekend.

Gauthier telephoned Coale with the news that Keenan was ordering him back to the States.

"No way!" Coale replied. "This is WAR!"

From Coale's diary:

Col. Travis of the Alamo, sitting across from me, has just thanked me, David Crockett of the Kentucky Brigade, for coming to the Alamo. Santa Anna is outside the gates with 5,000 Mexicans.

—April 4, 1986

Our gun bearers have run off into the woods. We are looking for fresh gun bearers. We figure we have a couple more days of sanity before, either we go nuts, or they kill us.

—April 5, 1986

We are changing the tide.

—April 6, 1986

It was hard to conceive of a situation more farcical than that in which Coale & Co. already found themselves. Everything they tried seemed to backfire. Ciresi and his law firm, on the other hand, performed like masters of some arcane martial art. Whenever they saw Coale & Co. charging at them, the Minneapolis lawyers made a few deft moves and sent their foes crashing to the ground.

Coale hadn't been back in the United States even a week when he got still more bad news: His sidekick, Sastry the tailor, was suing him for $300,000! Although he'd promised to make Sastry a rich man once the cases settled, Coale had fired him a few months earlier because, Coale said, his Indian friend had double-crossed him by "selling" Bhopal cases to another lawyer. Sastry considered himself to be Coale's loyal retainer—the tailor had, after all, even signed over his house in India to the Bhopal mayor as collateral on a note from Coale. Sastry claimed *he* was the one who'd been cheated out of his money.

Sastry's April 16 lawsuit also contained the allegation that the mayor of Bhopal had been offered a $250,000 bribe—and somebody made sure that the Washington *Post* and *The Wall Street Journal* were notified of it right after it was filed. Both featured prominent stories about the alleged bribe, stories that further tainted the efforts of

"Stan and Wendell and the boys," as Coale called them, to drum up popular support for the $350 million settlement.

Coale thought he detected the fine hand of Michael Ciresi in this, too.

Coale had an informant who had done some odd jobs for Sastry's lawyer, and the informant remembered that he once had gone to the airport to pick up an important visitor: Ciresi.

The informant called Coale a few times, then agreed to meet Coale and Lowy on July 23 at the Waldorf-Astoria Hotel in New York.

The man told an incredible tale of how Sastry's lawyer met that April with Ciresi and another official of the Indian Embassy whose name he couldn't remember, a tall, thin man with a heavy British accent. "They would like to pressure you," the informant told Coale in rough English. They wanted to embarrass Coale, to drive him out of the case.

"Why?" Lowy blurted out.

"To do what?" Coale asked.

"To do what?" Lowy asked again.

"Because he was favoring the settlement," their source replied. The informant claimed he'd overheard that the Indian Government had offered to help the rest of Sastry's family settle in the United States and to arrange scholarships for Sastry's children.

Ciresi professed not to know very much at all about the Sastry lawsuit. Still, Ciresi made no secret of his animus for Coale, and he said the feeling was mutual. "There's no love lost," Ciresi explained drily. "They're out of the litigation. We're not."

But even if everything Coale's source told him in that July meeting was true, it still wasn't going to save the $350 million settlement. Coale's hopes for a high contingent fee were long dead by then.

Keenan sent the case back to India, just as he had threatened, on May 12. It was time, the judge said, for India to "stand tall before the world and to pass judgment on behalf of its own people."

Bhopal had, indeed, been a disaster—for John Coale. He'd been vilified by the lawyers whose favor he sought, and he hadn't made a cent from his year-and-a-half foray into big-time disaster law.

But Coale *had* accomplished one thing: He had become a genuine media personality, an acknowledged player among the masters of disaster. From the first days of Bhopal, Coale knew that the kind of media attention he was getting was something he could take to the bank.

And yet even though Coale knew it was time to start cashing in on all the free publicity he'd had, doing so wasn't *just* a matter of money to him.

"I'm not gonna bullshit you," he said. "I want the money. I want the excitement, and everything else. But to me, the real icing on the cake, after all is said and done, is that we can have a major impact on society." Coale truly believed this. Anybody who really knew Coale could understand how the twin motivations of earning big money and doing good could coalesce within him. Coale was bent on teaching the world that it had better show him some respect, even though he hadn't gone to the right schools or joined a white-shoe firm. He had the irreverent, antiestablishment streak that was found in many plaintiffs' lawyers.

"I'm the bad boy," Coale would cackle. "I'm a known *sleazebag!*"

He was the kind of guy who might have joined Nader's Raiders—if the pay had been better. And, of course, if they'd ever have let him in.

Coale's constant lament was that what he saw as his good work on the victims' behalf didn't earn him any credibility. "Ralph Nader has to run around in an old suit and dumpy shoes," Coale complained. "But if Ralph Nader were running around in a Jaguar and custom-made suits, like I am, he wouldn't have any credibility. To me, that's a bit bizarre. It just blows my fucking mind! If you want to help somebody, you're not allowed to make money! On the other side, you've got the industry spending billions of dollars to make money, and it's *industry*—not the lawyers—who's hurting these people! But society will come down on you if you try to make money off of helping the people that these guys are hurting! So you have a tremendously unequal balance here!"

Coale actually thought lawyers like him were much more potent weapons against corporate wrongdoing than the Nader's Raiders types. "Nader didn't do that much," he said. "Hitting GM and Ford in the *pocketbook*"—with big damage suits and class actions—"that's what hit 'em hard."

And that's what Coale wanted to do. He saw himself as a kind of global policeman of the multinationals.

The irony was that Coale was a trial lawyer who didn't believe in trying cases! He was "sue-and-settle John," a guy who relished the thrill of the chase but who couldn't get excited about the kill. Coale couldn't even remember the last time he'd ever actually tried a case!

"The cases that go to trial are usually lousy cases," he rationalized. "Because if you do a good job in preparing for trial, they'll give you a settlement you can't refuse. Your big mass disaster cases don't go to trial."

Coale didn't try cases; he *chased* them. "He's a runner," said Atlanta plaintiff's lawyer Guerry Thornton disdainfully. "A hound-dog agent for other lawyers. His first tactic is to stir up enough publicity so that he starts getting calls from other clients. Any time a disaster strikes, he counts the bodies and decides whether to hit the road."

Coale saw it differently. His job, he said, was to "create" money-making opportunities. After Bhopal, he merged his own one-man firm into a small Los Angeles outfit, forming the new eight-lawyer firm Coale, Kananack & Murgatroyd. He was on the payroll at $120,000 a year, he had free use of a brand-new Jaguar, and, best of all, he didn't have anything to do with management of the firm, so he could stay on the road as much as he needed to. "I got a great thing!"

Disaster law was like the world-class tennis circuit, Coale was fond of saying: the same pros going from city to city, all over the globe.

December 31, 1986. At the Dupont Plaza Hotel in San Juan, Puerto Rico, a fire set by a disgruntled Teamsters Union worker swept through the twenty-two-story resort, leaving 96 people dead and 140 others burned and maimed.

The most deadly fire on American soil in more than forty years was a spectator event, as people from adjoining hotels stood on the beach or in the pool area and watched in horror as desperate guests hurled themselves from windows and balconies while helicopters rescued others who'd climbed atop the roof.

Wendell Gauthier heard about the fire on television. For Gauthier, the year just passed had been an extraordinarily good one; despite losing out on the Bhopal largesse, he'd earned $485,000. Now, he wanted to get in on this latest disaster.

So did some of the local lawyers. One of those San Juan lawyers, Luis Davila Colon, had a physician brother who had been an expert witness for Gauthier. Luis Colon didn't have any clients yet, either, but, at his brother's suggestion, he called Gauthier anyway and asked him to come immediately to Puerto Rico. Any lawyer going to San Juan without a client was ambulance chasing, pure and simple. But Gauthier could have sworn he'd heard Colon say that he *did* have a client.

Gauthier was right in the middle of a trial, though, and there was no way he could just hop on a plane and start hustling cases. Besides, that wasn't his style. He liked to stay a little bit above the fray. Practicing disaster law, after all, also meant practicing the art of plausible denial.

Gauthier started checking around to see whom else he could send down to meet with Colon. He tried to call two other local attorneys he'd worked with before, but both of them were gone for the holiday. Desperate to move in quickly on the Dupont Plaza disaster, he next called one of the lawyers in his own firm, forty-year-old Pat McCabe.

McCabe, Gauthier knew, was a bright enough fellow, but he was too much of a gentleman. McCabe just didn't have what it took to be really aggressive when there was a son of a bitch on the other side. Gauthier would send McCabe, all right, but he was also going to make sure that John Coale went down with him. Gauthier liked Coale's mad-dog approach to getting things done. "He is by nature abrasive and aggressive and knows how to deal with obstinate people." The rumor was that this was a case of Teamsters arson, and if there were any trouble Gauthier wanted a hard-ass guy like Coale to be there.

Gauthier tracked down John Coale in New York, where Coale and his girlfriend had been ringing in the New Year with friends. Late the following day, on Friday, January 2, Coale and McCabe were on the scene in San Juan. In his briefcase, McCabe carried copies of the complaints that had been filed in the MGM Grand litigation. Those old complaints were going to be real time savers. The two planned to change the name of the defendants and use, word for word, as much of the rest of the old complaints as they could.

Coale assumed he was there to protect the interests of Gauthier's client, the client who, it turns out, didn't exist. "But we don't just want one client, we want a bunch of 'em," Coale later explained. "So, I have a lot of contacts in the media that were there, or they knew me from Bhopal. It was the same guys.

"Cable News Network and *USA Today* have been looking for me since the fire, figuring I was going to go down there. So when I got there, I was interviewed by CNN right away, right in front of the hotel."

But a lot of reporters were "hanging out," to use Coale's words, in front of the smoldering Dupont Plaza, and when the CNN interview began, the other reporters started crowding around to hear what was being said.

"They clustered me. You know that phrase? That's what these reporters call it. Somebody gives an interview and all of a sudden there's a cluster there. And, in a matter of minutes, you have more notepads and cameras in front of you.

"So this CNN interview turns into an international interview—it was on NBC and ABC that night. And the New York *Times.*

"Course, I'm telling them who I am and where they can contact me. There are a lot of local papers and television stations, so now I'm all over Puerto Rican television. And from then on I'm doing three, four, five interviews a day, on camera! The same thing that happened in Bhopal!

"Here, it's being written that John Coale, mass disaster attorney, is in Puerto Rico and is about to file suit. So I set up a network. First, I get the office set up in Puerto Rico. Wendell sends down some people. I bring in some more people. We get a big suite at the Condado Plaza Hotel. Within a few days we have secretaries, lawyers, then we start bringing in fire investigators.

"My talent is, I can get the ball rolling. Almost as if I'm the producer and this is a movie or a television show. I get all the players together; get things rolling."

In the weeks that followed, the plaintiffs' lawyers on the scene did, in fact, do a remarkable job of getting organized and making sure that evidence was gathered and preserved. Without waiting for the federal court to sanction an executive committee, the lawyers appointed their own, and it included Coale, Gauthier and Chesley, who had agreed to split the cases Coale hustled. The committee hired experts who analyzed the cause of the fire, scrutinizing burnt materials the way a detective would examine a fingerprint. As expenses ran to $20,000 a day, the lawyers accumulated over 5,000 photographs and over 900 exhibits that were later turned over in a report to the court. All the evidence that was gathered was made available to any lawyer who wanted it—a real public service.

But the order of battle in those first few days after the fire was to get as many clients as possible, and the key, as Coale already knew, was to control the media. He didn't have to solicit clients if he could get enough publicity, but he had to "handle it right. There are a lot of other guys down there trying to do the same thing."

By now, Coale had forgotten about the putative client of Luis Colon, because other victims were already starting to seek him out. Two women who had lost husbands in the blaze went up to his room at the Quality Royale Hotel and waited there for him. So did Jose Aponte, a San Juan supermarket butcher who was the last man to get out of the casino alive. Coale signed them all to agreements that gave him one-third of whatever award they got.

"Within ten days, we have probably twenty or twenty-five cases. No solicitation! You don't have to! Because they put in the stuff [in the news reports] about the hostages and Bhopal. *USA Today* had a small profile. And the 'Today' show was great! Bryant Gumbel introduces me as being in every major disaster there is! On every major network, I'm interviewed!"

But in the scramble for cases among the disaster lawyers, the same old story was unfolding: Victims became commodities to be traded and fought over. Instead of directing their fire at the hotel and the Teamsters, the plaintiffs' lawyers were squabbling with each other.

"It's a given that I'm going to be a hated figure," Coale said, seeming to relish his bad-boy image. "For the local lawyers, that's their retirement case. All of a sudden, right there on the street, they've got this giant personal injury case. And then Coale comes in and starts taking away the media and the case. The local bar says I'm a vulture and they're going to investigate me! They hate me!"

Guerry Thornton was an Atlanta plaintiffs' lawyer who had an office in San Juan and who had gone there on January 2 for a hearing on some Dalkon Shield cases he'd filed in Puerto Rico. His local cocounsel, Antonio Moreda, lived a mere one and a half blocks from the Dupont Plaza. Thornton and Moreda thought they, too, might pick up some cases from the disaster.

Thornton saw a throng of reporters interviewing someone outside the Dupont Plaza on Sunday afternoon, January 4. Thornton thought he might be a hotel spokesman, so he ambled over to listen.

It turned out to be Coale who was holding forth. The two had never met, but Thornton had heard of Coale's antics in Bhopal and had no use for him. When Thornton heard Coale boast to the reporters that he'd gotten a $350 million settlement in the Bhopal litigation, he became enraged and started asking his own embarrassing questions.

"Isn't it true that you are accused of bribing the mayor of Bhopal?" Thornton kept asking, much to the amazement of the other reporters, and much to the chagrin of Coale, who thought a lunatic reporter had arrived on the scene.

"Who *are* you?" Coale finally asked the guy wearing the rumpled suit and the scuffed wing tips without socks.

"Guerry Thornton." Coale had heard of him. A New York lawyer Coale occasionally worked with, Jan Levien, had told him Thornton had a crush on her.

Coale just wanted Thornton to shut up until he finished this interview. Thornton was interrupting everything. "We'll talk," Coale promised.

The two went back to Coale's hotel room and talked about the fire. Thornton thought there had been a videotape camera scanning the casino, and he wondered aloud what it might show if somebody found it.

Coale told Thornton about the Bhopal case and mentioned that he was friendly with Chesley. Thornton, Coale would later recall, started "foaming at the mouth." Thornton wanted to know how he could hook up with Chesley. So Coale called Levien, who acted as the coordinator of what Coale called the Chesley-Gauthier-Coale "strike force" in the Bhopal and Dupont Plaza cases, and put Thornton on the line so she could tell him how to reach Chesley.

What happened next became the subject of a heated debate. Levien, Thornton said, urged him to "call a news conference and announce you're bringing Chesley in." Thornton's side of the story is that he then called Chesley, who offered him the same deal Coale had had in Bhopal: all his expenses paid, in exchange for supporting Chesley as head of the plaintiffs' steering committee that would later be formed to guide the Dupont Plaza litigation.

"Chesley said, 'If I come in, you seal your lips and I speak for all of us, worldwide,' " Thornton related. "If I'd transfer my cases, he'd get worldwide publicity. Public relations people were already standing by!"

But Thornton balked because that would just get Chesley more clients without helping him. "If he alone gets the publicity, then he gets all the future cases and referrals. It isn't a true partnership. Moreda and I told him that and he was offended. He didn't understand that."

Thornton also said that he objected to any arrangements that would involve his working with Coale, and that Chesley thereupon denied he had any involvement with Coale. "Chesley said he didn't approve of Coale's methods, but it was obvious to me that he wanted any cases Coale could generate," Thornton said ruefully.

The next day, Monday, January 5, there was going to be a race to the courthouse. Every disaster lawyer worth his salt wanted to be the first to file. Coale thought the strongest case would be a death case, and that's what he wanted to file. But his death-case clients were shaky. They hadn't signed their retainers yet; some still had funerals to attend. He would have to go with Aponte, the butcher, who had nothing more than a dislocated right foot and a cut on his arm. It was the best Coale could do on such short notice.

Chesley called Thornton. Chesley wanted his name on the first lawsuit, he told Thornton, and Coale was on the verge of filing. Where did Thornton stand? Chesley asked. He was willing to wait for Thornton if they could work out a deal. Thornton said he'd think about it, and Coale filed his first lawsuit without putting Chesley's name on it.

Thornton considered Chesley's call to be evidence that Chesley was, indeed, working with Coale, and he said he decided not to join their group. Whereupon, Thornton claimed, Coale threatened to ruin him. "We were told by Coale that if we didn't cooperate, he would challenge our participation on the steering committee. Coale said:

'Does Antonio [Moreda] realize that if you don't come with us now, you'll get your nuts cut out later?' ''

"If major corporations did this—muscled in, cut deals, divided territories—these same lawyers would be suing them!" Thornton cried.

Coale denied everything. He claimed, quite literally, that Thornton had made it all up. "He has got deep-seated problems," Coale said. "It is fantasy."

Thornton took his allegations to the Association of Trial Lawyers of America (ATLA), the national trade group representing the plaintiffs' bar. Coale's membership had lapsed years before, but ATLA reinstated it without Coale's knowledge. Coale thought that was done just so he could be kicked back out. The group conducted its own investigation, but never took any action.

With good reason. Since the association had never adopted any rules of conduct for disaster lawyers, what could it accuse Coale of doing wrong?

But Coale, once again, had managed to get himself into so much hot water that there was no way the other lawyers would put him on the Dupont Plaza litigation steering committee. Chesley and Gauthier *were* on it, though—they'd stayed above the battle while Coale did the dirty work—and Gauthier had been elected chairman of the group. The only thing he could do was to rely on them to protect his interests.

May 19, 1987. A groggy Coale had just flown into Washington on the red-eye from Los Angeles. Now, he and another lawyer from his firm had to drive up to Baltimore for an early-morning strategy session with some other lawyers who represented clients in still another mass-disaster case.

Coale's latest big ticket was the crash of an Amtrak–National Railroad Passenger Corporation train and three blue Conrail locomotives. Amtrak's Colonial had been speeding to New York on the first Sunday of 1987, January 4, at 120 miles an hour when it rounded a curve and smashed into the freight locomotives that had blundered onto the tracks. Sixteen people had been killed, another 175 injured.

The Dupont Plaza and the Conrail-Amtrak crash were back-to-back disasters. Coale was still in Puerto Rico when the second tragedy struck, but this crash was in his own backyard, a few miles from Baltimore, and right after the accident someone who'd seen a big *People* magazine write-up about Coale's exploits in Puerto Rico sent the husband of one of the victims to Coale. It turned out to be a great case.

Jose Jesse Corti was an actor in the cast of the Broadway-bound *Les Misérables.* The show was at the Kennedy Center, and Corti's young wife, Laura, had spent the holidays with her husband in Washington. She was returning home on the Colonial. Now, she was dead.

Coale had a slam-dunk case. The Conrail engineers had been smoking marijuana, and there was no question that the Conrail locomotives shouldn't have been on the track in front of the fast-moving Amtrak train. Equipment that might have warned the Conrail engineers of the looming disaster apparently wasn't working either. It was a clear case of negligence—maybe even a case for punitive damages. And talk about deep pockets! "The doctrine of *res ipsa loquitur* applies," Coale said in his complaint. The thing speaks for itself: no way the two companies could dodge liability for this one.

Besides, said Coale, Jesse Corti was going to be "the greatest witness I've ever seen in my life. He's an actor and he can express himself."

Jesse and Laura were newlyweds, and Coale had a videotape of the wedding, the wake, and the funeral. Their wedding pictures had come back a few weeks *after* the accident, and Coale was going to get them, too. "We'll let the other side know about it, maybe show them the tapes."

Coale signed Corti to a one-third contingency fee and filed his case in the Baltimore federal court for $30 million: $10 million for Laura's pain and suffering, $10 million for Jesse's grief, and $10 million in punitives.

Someone else who was attending the meeting represented the family of Ceres Horn, a sixteen-year-old girl who had been smart enough to get into Princeton two years early. She'd had a vibrant future ahead of her.

Baltimore lawyer Read McCaffrey had already demanded an $8.7 million settlement from Amtrak, "and they didn't throw up," Coale explained to Dominique Hawker, the other lawyer from his firm, as they sped up to Baltimore that dreary, rainy morning. Coale thought that was a good sign.

But there were going to be the usual hassles along the way to the eventual settlement. For one thing, there were already three rival factions vying for control of the case. This was going to be an MDL case, and coalitions of lawyers had already formed in New York, Philadelphia, and Baltimore, all of them pressing to have the case sent to their home city.

"The guys in Philadelphia have minor cases," Coale groused. "What they want to do is get the case into Philadelphia, get on the committee, and take a piece of everybody's case."

But David Berger and Harold Kohn, the Philadelphia lawyers leading the charge, were acknowledged class-action heavyweights. They had already filed their own class action on behalf of all the Amtrak passengers, a suit which, if allowed to go forward, would nullify all the contingent-fee agreements that every other lawyer had. Even worse, from the other lawyers' standpoint, was the fact that the Philadelphia judge who had the class action had approved a notice that Berger and Kohn were sending to all the Amtrak passengers. The notice made it sound as if Berger and Kohn already represented everybody on the train! They were stealing the case! One of the other lawyers called the judge to complain. The judge hung up on him.

Coale was pushing for sending the litigation to Baltimore, and he thought this plan had the edge because firms from Washington and Baltimore had most of the death cases. The power's in the death cases, Coale thought, harkening back to his Bhopal days. The Baltimore coalition also had Williams & Connolly, the blue-chip trial-law firm from Washington, in their corner, and that would surely impress the MDL panel when it met in Washington in a few days to decide where to send the case.

Williams & Connolly, with its ninety-six lawyers, was best known as a defense firm. It was Williams & Connolly who'd gotten the insanity rap for John Hinckley. But the lawyers there had smelled the money in this case just as quickly as Coale had, and they had a contingency arrangement on three death cases. Plaintiffs' contingent-fee work was a little-known, but very lucrative, part of the Williams & Connolly business mix. Coale savored the irony. A few years before, as a semismarmy personal-injury lawyer who got his two-bit cases from television advertisements, Coale had sued Edward Bennett Williams and his Redskins in an auto-accident case. Now, he was working on the same litigation team with Williams' law firm, the best trial firm in the city. Early on, Coale, as usual, had brought in Gauthier as his cocounsel on the Corti case. But Williams & Connolly was in a different league altogether.

So, for that matter, was Whiteford, Taylor & Preston, a big Baltimore law firm that represented the family of two young girls, Corrine and Kirsten Luce, who had been killed in the crash. Read McCaffrey, the forty-four-year-old Whiteford, Taylor partner Coale had told Hawker about on the way up, was hosting the nine o'clock meeting that morning in the firm's plush conference room on the fourteenth floor of the Signet Bank tower in downtown Baltimore. McCaffrey was unctuous, white-haired and distinguished-looking, just like somebody who'd been sent down from Central Casting to play the role of the dignified barrister.

McCaffrey said he had already visited an Amtrak claims adjustor, Susan Hassinger. "We chatted about the applicable law and the value of our cases," he told the thirteen lawyers present.

"How much did you ask for from Amtrak?" someone wanted to know.

McCaffrey was more vague with this bigger group than he had been in his private conversation with Coale the week before. "Less than $10 million," McCaffrey replied. "We felt $10 million was a number that we did not want to exceed."

McCaffrey had put together a notebook that described the girls, the first step toward putting a dollar value on the two lost lives. The notebook contained a report from a Johns Hopkins physician estimating how much conscious pain and suffering the girls went through before their death, and an economist's report on their future earnings potential. "I also put into that notebook an essay that one of the children wrote at age eleven," McCaffrey went on. "She was making believe she was eighty and was looking back on her life. It was incredible, I'll tell you, as the father myself of two girls age eleven and thirteen. I saw Hassinger reading it, and she'll never survive as a poker player!" McCaffrey continued with a smile. "Her eyes watered. I want her on my jury!"

The MDL hearing would be held in Washington in a few days, and the Baltimore group needed to put up a solid front. Without that, the experienced Philadelphia crew—which *did* agree on where to send the case (Philadelphia, of course!) and was already out soliciting clients with the judge's blessing—would take over the game.

The Baltimore group saw two options: oppose consolidation altogether, an alternative Amtrak also supported; or fight for consolidation in Baltimore. Stuart Gasner, a thirty-two-year-old associate from Williams & Connolly, favored the first approach. He opposed consolidation anywhere. MDL cases, he said, were "a Roach Motel. They go in but they don't come out," meaning that once all the cases were consolidated in one place, individual lawyers who wanted their damage claims heard by sympathetic local juries were out of luck. No one thought Amtrak and Conrail would deny liability, but some of the lawyers thought they might have to put the issue of damages to a jury, and they wanted the home-field advantage. "Our clients are black," one lawyer worried, "and we want a black jury. Our clients lived for ten hours and when the jury hears that, some *big* number is going to come into their heads! I think I can get just as much in compensatory damages as I can in punitives."

The obvious advantage to Amtrak of *not* having an MDL consolidation was that individual cases could be picked off and maybe settled more cheaply than if all the lawyers made settlement decisions together and presented a united front. For the plaintiffs' lawyers, not having an MDL meant there would be no steering committee and, thus, no possibility of a court-ordered sharing of fees in what would obviously be a huge payday for each contingent-fee lawyer.

But Coale had thought of another angle, one that would preserve each lawyer's booty while allowing for consolidation.

Coale suggested that the Baltimore lawyers go for an MDL consolidation, but one in which work on the steering committee would be entirely pro bono, with the lawyers volunteering their time and paying their own expenses. If nobody were going to receive fees, there would be nothing for the Philadelphia interlopers to steal!

"Here, in this meeting, there are twelve death cases," Coale exhorted his colleagues. "Up against us is a lot of experience—Berger and Kohn. We have to emphasize that we're together, and that we are working together well."

As far as McCaffrey was concerned, the Baltimore contingent had a consensus. They would tell the MDL panel the following week that the Baltimore lawyers opposed consolidation, but that if consolidation were ordered, it should be in Baltimore.

At 10:15, a free-lance Baltimore photographer was ushered into the conference room. Marty Katz had donned a red hard hat, a red vest and a blue fireman's jacket when he heard about the crash, and he had sneaked onto the crash site. Now, he was selling hundreds of photographs and slides of the crumpled rail cars. Katz wanted $7,000 for the works. Marc Rosen, a smug, bearded, thirty-two-year-old lawyer and one of McCaffrey's associates at Whiteford, Taylor, told the group that Amtrak also wanted to buy the photographs, so it could destroy them.

The lawyers agreed to pitch in $550 each to buy them. They passed the contact sheets around the table and peered at tiny images through a magnifying glass. It was hard to see any dead bodies. Katz pointed out one such picture. The lawyers studied it intently: someone's client, perhaps.

Katz showed the group a slide of the Conrail engineer whose mistake had caused the tragedy. He was in the back of a police car, in handcuffs. "Get an autographed copy for everybody," McCaffrey called out to Katz before he was ushered out a back door. McCaffrey didn't want the two lawyers for Amtrak, who were waiting their turn to speak to the Baltimore lawyers, to see the photographer.

The Amtrak lawyers were ushered in at 11:13. "What you have, gentlemen, in this room are twelve of the death cases," McCaffrey boomed melodramatically.

The two lawyers for Amtrak wanted to discuss the coming MDL hearing. "The discovery [evidence gathering] is going to be on damages, not on liability," Mark S. Landman, a dark, dapper man who was Amtrak's lead counsel, told the group. He said it made more sense to have the cases filed where the victims lived, because in the local venues it would be easiest to assess the economic losses that families had suffered. Lawyers for both sides would be interviewing and maybe even calling as witnesses the victims' friends, family and coworkers, and the lawyers would be examining the victims' employment and financial records. All that argued against MDL consolidation. But Landman, almost as an afterthought, also mentioned that he thought there were plausible reasons for the MDL panel's choosing Philadelphia as the place to send all the cases. Conrail was headquartered there.

McCaffrey: "But if we advance no alternatives and the court decides on consolidation, they're left with no choice but Philadelphia."

Landman: "Okay. Right. We are opposed to consolidation. But we will tell the court that if they consolidate, it should be Baltimore," because of its proximity to Amtrak's corporate headquarters.

The plaintiffs' lawyers could hardly believe their good fortune. It was hard to tell just whose side Amtrak was on! Instead of coming in as their foe, Amtrak was actually *cooperating* with the Baltimore lawyers!

That was because the passenger railroad was, in fact, itself in litigation with Conrail over who was going to be responsible for paying the damages from the crash. The Amtrak-Conrail lawsuit involved a contract that Amtrak had foolishly signed with Conrail, allowing Conrail to use its tracks and excusing Conrail from liability for any accidents that occurred there. Amtrak maintained that the contract didn't cover Conrail's flagrant misconduct, but Conrail wasn't buying that argument.

Yet something told the lawyers that Amtrak was being *too* accommodating. The group that at first was so pleased by its seeming détente with Amtrak started growing suspicious after the Amtrak lawyers left the room.

"Here's a devious thought," McCaffrey told the others. "Are we being set up? Are we opposing any consolidation so that the court turns to Philadelphia, which is the briar patch that Brer Rabbit wants to be thrown into anyway?" McCaffrey thought maybe Amtrak was trying to trick them. "I'm very suspicious, for reasons that all of a sudden I cannot verbalize."

"We're in deep shit if it goes to Philadelphia," Coale whispered to Dominique Hawker.

"It's outrageous," another lawyer blurted out indignantly, "if the cases go to Philadelphia, a place where three plaintiffs who weren't even injured filed two days after the accident and where the judge chose lead counsel before he even saw the other cases!'"

"It's outrageous," Stuart Gasner, the young Williams & Connolly associate, chimed in. "Three crummy cases that are outrageously flawed."

McCaffrey cautioned them against such overt criticism of the Philadelphia lawyers during the MDL hearing. "Then you just get the sharks-circling-the-boat syndrome—a bunch of hungry plaintiffs' lawyers fighting with each other." But the surprising cooperation of Amtrak had made them nervous. McCaffrey and the others now changed their collective mind. Someone from Williams & Connolly, the most eminent of the firms represented around the table, would speak up during the hearing in favor of Baltimore. Everyone nodded approval.

As Coale got up to leave, he pointed out a lawyer who'd arrived late. "He's got a good case," Coale said. "He's got the Princeton girl."

Thursday, May 21, 1987, 10:20 A.M. "Docket 728," intoned the clerk at the U.S. District Courthouse for the Federal Circuit, just across Lafayette Park from the White House. "In re January 4, 1987, Rail Collision near Chase, Maryland."

The Conrail lawyer spoke first. Conrail, he said, wanted all the cases consolidated, and "if the panel thinks Baltimore is the right forum, we have no problem."

Another big break. To a man, the Baltimore lawyers broke out in broad grins. Even though the Philadelphia and New York contingents were going to plead for sending the cases farther north, the Baltimore lawyers now knew they had it locked up.

A few weeks later, the MDL panel did, indeed, send the litigation to the Baltimore federal court. McCaffrey and Coale both won spots on the steering committee, and the lawyers from Williams & Connolly were put in charge. Coale had finally won his first steering-committee assignment in a major disaster case, a breakthrough that surely would translate into more such assignments in the future.

"He's happy to sit back and let us make tons of money for him," one of Coale's colleagues on the steering committee said of him.

Besides, Coale was already on the trail of his next cases.

Coale had been using Ted Dickinson to call up families of GIs—"just Army kids"—who'd been killed in the Gander, Newfoundland, crash of a charter airliner taking them back home. It was Dickinson's job "to talk to people and see if they want to have an appointment; that sort of thing."

It was also Dickinson who had done a lot of Coale's legwork in Bhopal.

"When something exciting happens, I'll call him up," Coale explained.

To go angling for clients, all Coale had to do was to "get the list out of the newspaper. Same way a reporter would go about it. Just get the list and call Information. One way or another, you find out their number. And you call 'em, start up a conversation.

"He'd say, 'I'm Ted Dickinson. I'm from a law office. Tell me what happened.' They'll start talking. He's a very likeable guy. He's very good. And he'll start talking to 'em. And they may talk for months. And I might talk to 'em for months or weeks after that.

"He knows what to do. It's a matter of timing. You don't want to call them until after the funeral. They go through grief before the funeral. Then, after the funeral, they get pissed off.

"We'll ask them, 'Can we send you some literature on us?' And you might send them something like the *People* magazine piece, something like that.

"And they'll say, finally, 'I think you're the one I want.' Or not. 'Cause there are other lawyers they're also talking to. Everybody I talked to on the Gander case had been approached by at least a hundred lawyers."

Coale got three clients from the Gander crash.

On August 16, 1987, Northwest Airlines Flight 255 crashed on takeoff at the Detroit airport, killing 153 persons.

The next day, Coale flew to Detroit and checked into the Marriott Airport Hotel. He was there to "hang around," he said, so that he could be available for the inevitable media interviews that occurred when reporters had time and space to fill and couldn't get answers from anybody else.

Coale was interviewed on "Good Morning America." He was featured on the "ABC World News Roundup." The Baltimore *Sun* called him the "Master of Misfortune." In Phoenix, where the plane had been headed, the newspapers and television stations loved him.

"We'll probably get a couple of cases out of it. One is already biting hard."

A few weeks later, Coale went back to Michigan to visit the dairy-farmer father of a young man who was killed in the crash. The two talked awhile.

"I hate attorneys whose names are in the newspapers," said the father, who reckoned he had been contacted by just about every lawyer in the country.

"I hate 'em, too," replied the lawyer who once said his life story would be called "Disasters I Have Known and Loved."

Coale was wearing a navy blue flannel blazer and dark gray slacks with red suspenders that shone brightly against a starched white shirt, but when milking time came there was no doubting what Coale would do when the farmer asked him whether he wanted to help push the cows into the milking stalls. Coale hunkered down and did what needed to be done. "The farmer loved it!" Coale exulted afterward.

He soon got that case, as well as five others and an appointment to the interim steering committee.

Coale was on a roll. And when a Continental Airlines jet flipped over and killed twenty-eight people during a snowy takeoff attempt in Denver, the disaster hustle began anew.

"It's the John Coale show!" he giggled.

The Cigarette Wars: Marc Edell and the Litigators Against an Industry

I want to catch the sons of bitches. I'd like to get a good case and go after them.

MELVIN BELLI

Their strategy is, Money is no object. One of the tobacco lawyers said to one of the plaintiffs' lawyers once, "We only have two instructions: Don't settle and don't lose."

RICHARD DAYNARD, TOBACCO PRODUCTS LIABILITY PROJECT

In legal parlance, a "bet-your-company" case is one in which everything's riding on a single toss of the dice before a jury. The Hunt brothers versus their bankers, Texaco versus Pennzoil. Cases that carry the scent of catastrophe for the loser.

As the trial began in *Cipollone v. Liggett Group, Philip Morris, and Loews Theatres* (the parent of the Lorillard, Inc., tobacco company), those involved knew that this was even more than a bet-your-company case. Every cigarette products-liability trial was a bet-your-*industry* trial. The cigarette makers had to win every one. Even a single loss would push the litigation floodgates wide open, beckoning every plaintiff's lawyer in the country to make the cigarette companies a target.

The allegations in *Cipollone* were straightforward: Rose Cipollone smoked cigarettes for nearly forty years. Cigarettes caused her lung cancer because they were unsafe. The cigarette manufacturers knew how risky their product was, and yet they didn't warn her and conspired to hide the risks.

But behind those allegations lay troubling questions, not just for the tobacco companies, but for the entire legal system. Because if cigarettes could be held to a strict liability standard, what about other products that also aren't good for you even when they're used as intended: butter and sugar, wine and booze, handguns? If the cigarette plaintiffs made out, would the courts be inundated with lawsuits against the multitude of other products with known, inherent dangers?

Anybody who smoked a cigarette since 1966, when federally mandated health warnings first appeared, couldn't say he hadn't been warned of the dangers. To collect on their cases, the plaintiffs' lawyers would have to use some clever arguments to persuade jurors that the warnings did no good. They might try to prove, for instance, that advertisements showing youthful, vibrant smokers undermined the warnings. Or they might argue that nicotine was even more addictive than heroin, so that after a smoker got hooked the warnings were futile. The plaintiffs weren't entirely without options.

For their part, the tobacco companies were solidly entrenched in an economic system that forced them not only to deny the obvious danger of their product, but also to wage a pitched battle against anyone who claimed otherwise. The gods of this battle, after all, were the tobacco companies' shareholders, and their Holy Grail was price per share. Every lawsuit and every unfavorable *Wall Street Journal* article caused tobacco stocks to drop. RJR Nabisco, the parent of the R. J. Reynolds Tobacco Company, even considered allaying investor fears by spinning its cigarette business off as a limited partnership, thereby insulating the rest of its assets from hungry tobacco plaintiffs.

Investors needed to have confidence that the cigarette makers wouldn't lose, that their investment was protected. And the scorched-earth defense the cigarette companies mounted was calculated to provide that.

It was also calculated to dissuade all but the most determined plaintiffs and their contingent-fee attorneys—who, after all, were advancing all the expenses and wouldn't get paid unless they won—from ever bringing suit.

Tobacco companies, surmising that even one defeat in the 120 cases then pending would quickly produce more lawsuits, conferred and agreed on every move in every case, regardless of which of them were defendants. They published their own private newsletter on the litigation. They spent millions of dollars defending even the most trivial cases—at least $100 million a year overall, $15 million alone on one 1986 trial in which the plaintiff's budget was a comparatively tiny $100,000.

And when their delaying tactics couldn't keep them out of the courtroom any longer, the companies simply stonewalled, their chief executives and scientists alike feigning ignorance of the toxic effects of cigarette smoking.

But the tobacco companies used more than big money and delaying tactics to fight their cases. They pursued a strategy of intimidation. They stonewalled on depositions, denying any knowledge of the thousands of studies that proved a link between smoking and cancer. And they conducted such intimately thorough investigations and depositions of those who sued them that some plaintiffs simply gave up rather than subject themselves to it—doing, of course, exactly what the companies wanted. The tobacco lawyers called the exhaustive questioning to which they subjected a plaintiff "the lifestyle deposition," and by the time they finished, days or weeks later, there wasn't much they didn't know about a plaintiff.

"When did you become aware of the fact that you were unable to conceive children?" a lawyer asked seventy-three-year-old Dollie Root, a California widow who sued the General Cigar & Tobacco Co., whose pipe tobacco her husband had smoked.

A. "I knew before I was married I could not have children."

Q. "And I assume you discussed this with your husband?"

A. "Yes."

Q. "Did you make a decision prior to your marriage, just prior to your marriage, that you would adopt children?"

A. "No."

Q. "Was it your desire to have children or his desire to have children which caused you to decide to adopt children?"

The defense lawyers claimed they needed to ask these questions because the stresses and strains of life can cause or aggravate the heart disease and cancer that others claim has been brought on by cigarettes. Using that rationale, the tobacco lawyers also grilled Dollie Root about her adopted son's recent suicide, and they asked her how she felt after she found out that her daughter-in-law was a month pregnant when she and the adopted son were married. "I didn't know what to say," she recalled. "I didn't know she was. Besides, they were married twenty-five years ago. What does any of this have to do with my husband's death?"

When it came to Big Tobacco's bet-your-industry defense, there was no such thing as an unfair tactic. The amounts at issue were too great for compromise. The industry spent $2.7 billion a year on advertising. Every other billboard in America advertised cigarettes. Twenty-seven percent of all the adults in America smoked cigarettes. The industry sold 30 billion packages of cigarettes a year to 54 million Americans and produced $10 billion in excise taxes alone. Juxtapose that against the 315,120 premature deaths the Centers for Disease Control attributed to smoking in 1984 (the year chosen for an exhaustive study and the most recent government estimate available) and you got an idea of just how highly leveraged the risk-reward equation was for the cigarette companies.

Richard Daynard, who ran the Tobacco Products Liability Project, a Rockefeller Fund–supported clearinghouse for plaintiffs' lawyers at Northeastern University Law School in Boston, understood the tobacco companies' lethal economic incentives. "Once they get to the position where they have to settle, where they are handling them as any other case—you're talking about 350,000 deaths a year, to say nothing about injuries—at that point, the easier they make it to settle, the more people who are going to do it. If they settle 100,000 cases at $100,000 each, that's $10 billion. And that's real money, even for the tobacco industry. They want to keep it away from that. So they will spend, literally, billions of dollars in defense. They will do anything they can to discourage plaintiffs' attorneys."

In the end, after all, it came down to simple economics. Calvert Crary, a savvy Wall Street litigation analyst with the investment banking firm of Bear, Stearns & Co. Inc. crunched the numbers and decided this: The cigarette companies still had a hot-selling product, even though the proportion of American adult smokers had been steadily dropping from the 40 percent share attained in 1964, the year the Surgeon General first reported on the connection between smoking and disease. The companies, he calculated, could pay all the claims that might ever be filed against them simply by raising the price of each cigarette pack by a few pennies.

That "would generate billions of dollars of incremental revenues with which to pay claims," he reasoned. "The industry can pay claims without any meaningful financial impact much faster than the legal system can create and dispose of them." But, he finally concluded, the industry couldn't afford to do that for another reason: to admit liability would be to take from smokers their last plausible denial of just how unsafe their habit was.

In other words, too many people would quit smoking if the companies conceded fault. The cigarette barons couldn't let that happen. Their success depended on keeping people hooked.

Marc Z. Edell, a thirty-seven-year-old partner in the Short Hills, New Jersey, law firm of Budd Larner Gross Picillo Rosenbaum Greenberg & Sade, had been waiting more than four years for his trial against the tobacco companies to begin. Rose Cipollone went to him in the summer of 1983, referred to the young lawyer by the Fifth Avenue specialist who diagnosed her lung cancer.

"You're gonna be dissected. Chopped apart," Edell told her when they first met. "Nothing is going to be sacred." It took Rose a month to make her decision. But once she said yes, she made her husband promise to see the case through, no matter what happened to her.

There was a stark contrast between them: Cipollone, the dowdy, overstuffed wife of a cable splicer who'd been raised in a cold-water flat near Harlem by Italian immigrant parents, and who in her later years finally found a comfortable life for herself and her husband, Antonio, in Little Ferry, New Jersey; and Edell, the brash, moustachioed young lawyer with his fifty-dollar haircut, a small man with a physique built up by the judo lessons he took three times a week. Edell smoked Marlboros as a youth. "I was the Marlboro man. I wasn't macho enough to smoke Camels. But Marlboros were cool enough." As a teenager growing up in the exurbs of New Jersey, Edell had been packed off to military school—"Can't you tell by my military bearing?" he asked cockily. If nothing else, the experience seemed to have left him with a lingering need to challenge authority, and it was in the courtroom that he worked it off. Edell was irreverent and untamed, a master of jibes and quick retorts that were a constant irritant to his elders on the other side.

He wore the confidence of a lawyer who rarely lost: Of twenty-five jury trials, Edell had won twenty-three. He was also a man in a hurry. He drove his black Porsche hard and fast, and he kept its dash-borne fuzzbuster on constant alert.

And so it was that when the lucrative product-liability cases he was defending on behalf of some major asbestos companies ended up in bankruptcy court, Edell, barely thirty-two years old at the time, was impatient to find a new challenge.

He had, after all, spent the prior seven years, his entire professional career, coordinating the defense of those asbestos product-liability cases. He'd seen hundreds of cases of workers injured or killed by inhaling the tiny asbestos particles, "and it dawned on me that the tobacco companies were getting away with murder. Because what we saw in the asbestos litigation was, in almost every instance where somebody was injured, there was a smoking history! And in a substantial number, we saw *obstructive* lung disease," caused by tumors. "The long and the short of it is, asbestos diseases are usually *restrictive*"—that is, they attack the lung and immobilize it, causing slow suffocation. "But *cigarette* diseases are *obstructive*".

Edell wanted to build a new litigation industry around claims against the tobacco companies, just as lawyers had against the asbestos makers. If he succeeded, the resulting lawsuits against such a pervasive product might dwarf the asbestos litigation boom. And Edell, of course, might just get rich, just as other lawyers had until the Johns-Manville Corporation used the bankruptcy laws to wriggle out of the lawsuits it faced.

By the time Johns-Manville filed for bankruptcy-law protection in August 1982, there were 16,500 asbestos lawsuits pending against it, with an estimated 130,000 more claims yet to be filed. "But," Edell continued, "the cigarette companies were almost never joined as defendants, despite the fact that their product was contributing significantly to the development of the diseases, including lung cancers. And it had been my impression from a variety of discussions in that litigation that no one wanted to join the tobacco companies for fear of what the tobacco companies would do. Every asbestos company thought that if they tried to join the cigarette companies as defendants, the cigarette companies would gang up with the plaintiffs to prove the case *against* asbestos!"

What the asbestos companies came up with, instead, became known as the "empty chair" defense. They told the jurors the truth: that cigarettes acted in a synergistic way with asbestos to create deadly diseases. They said that the real culprits hadn't been brought before them. But, except in a few isolated test cases, the asbestos companies dared not bring them in. Better to put the empty chair on trial than to risk bringing into the courtroom a cigarette company which possessed unlimited resources, an iron will against settling, and every economic incentive to prove that liability lay with asbestos. The plaintiffs' lawyers didn't mind the empty chair, either, because after their breakthrough trial victory in 1971, they started winning or settling virtually every asbestos case they filed.

Winning or settling, that is, until the wave of asbestos-company bankruptcies. Overnight, the plaintiffs' lawyers saw their business dry up. So, too, did Edell and his fellow asbestos-industry defense lawyers.

But since Edell had spent so many years learning about lung pathology and the diseases caused by cigarettes and asbestos, he wanted to find another way to make money from his knowledge. He began toying with the notion of switching sides, of crossing over to the plaintiff's bar and suing the deepest pocket of them all: the cigarette companies that were making the most profitable product ever sold.

The asbestos cases were his exemplar. To defend the asbestos companies early in his career, Edell had prowled through the files of his foes, gathering up documents that proved his case. Edell knew what to look for: research materials and reports about marketing, public relations and trade association activities. That insider's knowledge turned out to be invaluable when Edell started serving subpoenas on the cigarette manufacturers. His demands for incriminating documents went right to the heart of their business.

Although he didn't realize it then, Edell's opportunistic decision to go after the cigarette makers marked the creation of a whole new kind of toxic-tort case. Motivated by the incentive the contingent fee gave him, Edell and a handful of other risk-taking lawyer-entrepreneurs were focusing resources where they were badly needed. If the lawyers induced the courts to adopt their new legal theory on cigarette-maker liability, millions of people would potentially benefit. There was nothing new about contingent-fee lawyers' moving in when they smelled the kill, but here was an instance when the public at large might benefit from the economic self-aggrandizement of the trial lawyers.

Edell discussed the idea of suing the cigarette companies with fellow lawyer David J. Novack, who was then also thirty-two years old and who, years later, still had the office next to Edell's. Novack had a friend who'd been on the plaintiffs' side in the asbestos litigation, Alan Darnell, thirty-six years old then, a beefy lawyer with droopy eyes, thick coal-black hair and a walrus moustache. His brand-new BMW sported an ALAN D license plate. Darnell was looking for a new game, too. The three of them pooled their resources and decided to take a run at the cigarette companies. So paranoid were the cigarette-industry lawyers that they incorrectly believed the trio was being bankrolled by asbestos companies who wanted revenge. It was a wrong guess, but who knew about the future? Documents discovered during the litigation would invariably reveal some dirty laundry. If Edell acquired documents showing, for instance, that the cigarette companies really did know that smoking exacerbated asbestos-related diseases, Edell's work might someday make it possible for the asbestos companies to put another culprit in the empty chair.

There is a saying among trial lawyers: You take your plaintiffs as you find them. It means that trial lawyers can't go out and drum up the perfect case. The canons of ethics don't permit it, and there's probably no such thing anyway. Each case has flaws; the lawyer's job is to minimize their effect.

With the cigarette cases, though, the flaws were magnified even though the link between smoking and cancer—documented by 45,000 scientific studies—appeared unquestioned. The reason was that nobody ever has a clean medical history. We've all had our share of illnesses, taken over-the-counter and prescription drugs, eaten fried or barbecued foods, drunk alcohol or coffee and been exposed to pesticides or maybe even workplace chemicals. And the strategy of the cigarette companies was to ascribe a smoker's cancer to each and every one of those factors—almost anything *except* cigarettes. There would come a time when hundreds of cigarette cases would be pending. But, in each, the causation issue would be a persistent worry for the plaintiffs.

That had been apparent in Edell's very first cigarette case, in which he represented a friend's father who was dying of lung cancer. Edell started talking to the man's doctor, gathering other medical information, drafting his complaint and figuring out theories of liability. As he dug deeper into the case, though, he realized that exposure to toxic substances at the man's workplace might have contributed to the cancer. It wouldn't be a winner, Edell thought. He dropped it.

But physicians to whom Edell and his confederates had touted this new enterprise were talking to their patients, "and that produced some interest," Edell recalled. "And once we started getting some publicity on the litigation, other people called us up. And that's how the litigation came in."

Edell and his partners were staking their own money on the seven cigarette cases they'd brought in. On the Cipollone case alone, they'd spent upward of $1 million out of pocket, for depositions, travel, medical experts and so on. The lawyers took nothing, betting their uncompensated time against the prospect of taking as much as one-third of the potentially huge damage award that hung in the balance. But if they'd been billing at their customary rates of between $100 and $200 per hour, they would have rung up another $2 million in fees.

In July 1981, Rose and Antonio Cipollone both visited their family doctor for their annual checkups. Unlike in past visits, though, this time the doctor saw a large, dark spot on the X-ray of Rose's chest.

"Rose," he told her over the telephone the day after her exam, "there's something wrong."

The doctor arranged for Rose to see a lung specialist in Manhattan that very day. The specialist told her the spot might be tuberculosis or a fungus infection. Or it might be lung cancer. Rose was scared. A few weeks later, when antibiotics hadn't cleared up the spot, she was admitted to the Lenox Hill Hospital in New York. There, during exploratory surgery, a portion of her lung was removed, and with it the tumor that the doctors had discovered. Right up to the time of the operation, Rose was smoking, bumming cigarettes off another patient's daughter. A few weeks after that surgery, she furtively started smoking again, but whenever the doctors asked her, she told them she'd quit.

In May 1982, Rose developed a cough that wouldn't go away. Her doctors checked her into the Lenox Hill Hospital again, and this time they discovered an even larger tumor. When she awakened from surgery, the doctors told her they had removed her entire lung. They also said her chances of recovery were good.

But in the summer of 1983, Rose developed a chronic pain in her right side, and she was admitted to the hospital again, this time for the removal of a cancerous tumor in her adrenal gland. The doctors started her on chemotherapy. They also told her to contact Marc Edell.

Q. "Has there been any recurrence of the cancer since your operation in 1983?"
A. "I hope not."
Q. "As far as you know, there has not been?"
A. "I hope not. I got my fingers crossed. Please."

Rose Defrancesco's parents were born in Montalbano, Sicily. Her father was a barber who raised his family in a ten-family building on 115th Street in one of the poorest parts of upper Manhattan. After her father died, Rose's mother took a job in the garment district, sewing straps onto slips. Rose was a simple child who learned early to accept life as she found it, or, perhaps more aptly, as it found her—

the poverty, the religion that dictated a year of black-clothed mourning after her father's death, all the other old-fashioned ways.

For a poor girl from New York, the movies were a vicarious ticket out. "We used to like a lot of movie stars," Rose recalled many years later, when she was dying from the cancer that ravaged her lungs, her glands, and, finally, her brain. As she sat in a lawyer's office, answering the harsh deposition questions of cigarette-company lawyers, it was almost as if she'd returned to the carefree days of her youth.

The purpose of a deposition is to give the other side a chance to explore, in virtually unrestricted questioning, every possible piece of evidence or testimony that might be used against them later at trial. A person's deposition answers become a baseline against which his later courtroom testimony can be compared. In Rose's case, though, the deposition took on much more importance. If she died before the trial, she would still speak to the jury through her deposition answers.

"You want to know something?" she asked the lawyers. It wasn't really a question, but, rather, a segue into her memories. "Most of [the movie stars] smoked. I remember they used to be so glamorous; they always used to wear evening gowns and we couldn't understand why they wore evening gowns and not regular dresses like we did, short. And they always used to have the cigarette. Bette Davis was always smoking. I remember a lot of that in the movies."

Rose and her brother and sisters were devoted to the movie magazines. "There was a junk man around the corner from us. His name was Herman. He used to collect—this is true! Don't laugh! He used to collect old newspapers, magazines, rags, bottles, and we couldn't afford to buy magazines, so we used to go around the corner and we used to ask Herman could we have this magazine, could we have that, and he was a very nice gentleman, he was a friend of my father's and he used to say, Take! So, instead of taking one, we used to take five and we used to run home and we had all the magazines.

"We used to play that we were the movie stars. The woman downstairs from us had daughters that were a lot older than us, and she used to give us all their long dresses and old shoes, high heels, and we used to put them on in the back yard and we used to roll up little pieces of paper and we used to walk around with these high heels and these old-fashioned long dresses and with the cigarettes and we were playing movies stars, or grown-up. That's how we played."

Not too long after that, Rose moved up to the real thing, buying unfiltered Chesterfields, one or two at a time, at the corner candy store on her way to school. "I thought that it was cool, as you would call it today, to smoke. And grown-up. And I was going to be glamorous or beautiful. I really thought it was really fantastic to smoke."

Q. "Can you tell me, as best you can, what ads that you saw that led you to start smoking?"

A. "I remember there was a pretty girl with a beautiful big hat, and she had a belt. That one I will never forget, because it was in the candy store where we used to go on the corner. More or less, that was the type of ads that we saw in those days."

Q. "Do you recall anything that the ads said?"

A. "They were mild."

Q. "Anything else?"

A. "Not really. I don't recall."

Q. "So, really, you saw attractive people in the ads?"

A. "Yes."

Q. "And you wanted to be like them?"

A. "I wanted to imitate. I definitely did. . . . I thought I would be Joan Crawford or Bette Davis."

It was 1942. Rose Defrancesco was sixteen years old. A year later, she would "graduate," as she put it, to a pack a day and the start of a forty-year habit she simply could not break.

Not that she hadn't tried. She switched to cigarettes she thought were safer, from L&M to Virginia Slims to True. Antonio pestered her to quit smoking altogether, and she even did so for a while when she was pregnant, at age twenty-one, with their first child. But when she went into labor, a male nurse "asked if I wanted anything and I said, 'Yes, please let me have a cigarette and a glass of orange juice.' And they brought me a pitcher of orange juice and put it on the little table by my bed, and he gave me a pack of cigarettes and I smoked them all before I had the baby."

The cigarette lawyers wanted to know about her television-watching habits, because the airwaves were rife with cigarette ads during much of the time Rose Cipollone smoked.

"I never watched the soaps. I never watched the soaps on TV. I would watch a movie on television, but my TV was mostly in the evening, after dinner, when we would clean up the dishes and we would put the TV on, and the children would watch their programs, and when they went to bed and my husband went to bed, then I could sit there with all my cigarettes and nobody would tell me to stop. And I could sit there and watch TV until I went to bed. . . .

"Tony was always after me to stop smoking," she said of her husband. "He really was. Then, there were articles about tests that they were doing with monkeys and that smoking was no good for the lungs and it caused diseases, heart disease, cancer, emphysema. . . . Of course, I didn't want to believe that, because it was very hard to quit and I figured, How true can it be if they strapped a monkey twenty-four hours to a machine? Of course he was going to get something, and, I figured, I'm not strapped to a machine and the government was there and there was no real proof. Tobacco companies wouldn't do anything that was going to kill you."

Even when Rose got a scratchy throat and a cough that wouldn't go away in 1965, she couldn't level with her doctor about the one and a half to two packs a day that she was smoking.

Q. "One of the reasons that you didn't want the doctor to hassle you is because you got a lot of pleasure—you just told us—in many situations out of smoking. Isn't that [so]?"

A. "True. I was a smoker."

Q. "And you didn't want the doctor to hassle you because you didn't want him to interfere with that pleasure. Isn't that true?"

A. "Yes."

But Rose was so terrified of getting cancer that she went to church and said a novena to St. Jude. "I prayed that I wouldn't have cancer."

Q. "You said that you were scared and you had the coughing and the pain in your throat?"

A. "Right."

Q. "And when you were talking to St. Jude, it was a serious matter for you then, wasn't it?"

"Well," Rose began sternly, "I don't know if you know anything about my religion. Maybe I'll clarify a point or two. A saint can only intercede in your behalf. He can't do anything. He can intercede for you so you ask him to intercede in your behalf."

Q. "What was it that you wanted him to intercede for you about?"

A. "That I wouldn't be sick."

Q. "You wouldn't be sick with lung cancer. Isn't that true?"

A. "That I wouldn't be sick, yes."

"You thought you could die from lung cancer, didn't you?" the lawyer shouted as he stung her with question after question. Opposing lawyers have great latitude in the questions they may ask during depositions, and the cigarette-company lawyer was taking full advantage of this as he bored in on Rose. She bristled. "You wanted St. Jude to intercede for you because you were afraid of getting lung cancer! True?"

A. "Yes, I was."

Q. "And you knew you could die from lung cancer! True?"

A. "Oh, yes."

Q. "And you knew at that time that it was the cigarette smoking that you were afraid of causing your lung cancer! Isn't that true?"

A. "Yes."

Q. "You weren't telling God, or this saint, anything that was false, were you?"

A. "No, I don't think so."

Q. "You really believed at that time that you could get sick from cigarette smoking, didn't you?"

A. "Let's say I was afraid of getting sick."

Q. "You were afraid of getting sick to the point where you went to a saint to intercede for you on your behalf!"

A. "Right."

Q. "Isn't that true?"

A. "Yes."

Q. "You were serious about the fact that you thought you could get sick from smoking?" Now Rose bristled with anger again. Clearly, the questions were calculated to prove that she knew all along the dangers cigarette smoking posed; that she willingly assumed the risks. Debilitated by chemotherapy, she found all this questioning about her talk with the saint too much to endure.

"You are going to fool around with a saint?" she barked back. "*Of course* you are serious!"

Q. "At that time you didn't tell the saint that you thought cigarettes were safe, did you?"

A. "Did I tell the saint cigarettes were safe? Come on, now. Give me a break, too. I was going to say to the saint that cigarettes are safe? St. Jude? Why would I go, then? Phrase the question in another way."

Q. " 'Why would I go then if I thought cigarettes were safe.' Say it! This is what you were going to say!"

A. "That is *not* what I was going to say. How can you know what I'm going to say? Don't put words in my mouth."

Q. "You were afraid because you thought cigarettes were unsafe! Isn't it a fact?"

A. "I was afraid because I had a pain in my throat and I didn't want to get sick."

Q. "From cigarettes?"

A. "From cigarettes."

Q. "You had read about the Surgeon General's Report as it appeared in the newspaper. Isn't that true?"

A. "Right."

Q. "You had been talked to by your husband for years. Isn't that true?"

A. "Correct."

Q. "You had avoided talking to doctors about cigarettes. Isn't that true?"

A. "Correct."

Q. "Because you didn't want them to tell you not to smoke. Isn't that true?"

A. "Correct."

Q. "You knew very well that you were going to continue to smoke but the thing that you didn't want to do was get the cancer you thought it could cause. Isn't that true?"

"Correct," Rose Cipollone replied cooly. Then she added, from behind icy eyes: "I did get the cancer, didn't I?"

Nine months before the *Cipollone* trial began, Edell and Darnell sat in Edell's stark, modernistic office and talked about this case that had outlived the victim it was supposed to help. Darnell, an intense man with huge gold wedding band and a nervous tic in his right eye, had spent so much time on the case that he saw some of the little things of everyday life through a haze of metaphorical smoke. Example:

Darnell thought he weighed too much, but he cheerfully said that "if I smoked I'd be thinner: 'Reach for a Lucky instead of a sweet!' "

Edell had been telling people he wanted "to win this case for Rose Cipollone." But by now she had ceased being anything other than a vehicle for the ultimate vindication of his lawyerly prowess.

"Some people think we're crazy," Edell said. A million dollars was, after all, a lot of money to be advancing on the kind of case that nobody'd ever won. "That's only a fraction of what it's cost us. We've spent, in legal fees, two million dollars more. I could have been billing that to something else. So, it's a big ticket.

"Why? Because, in the long run, if the cases are successful, it will be money well invested."

First and foremost, this litigation was a business proposition. An investment. Edell had pushed the numbers and decided that if one case could win, others could, too, and the millions of dollars that had been spent on gathering evidence and questioning experts could be written off against many cases instead of one.

Edell also considered this case "one of those rare instances where a lawyer can accomplish something for a client and also, at the same time, have a substantial positive impact on our society. Those chances come around once in a lifetime."

Finally, there was, he said, "the litigator's natural attraction to a challenge. And where the challenge is great, the attraction is greater. For me, that's important in any litigation I get involved in. That's my nature. The harder the litigation, the better I like it. The more pressure, the better I like it.

"I'm a competitive person. I do everything competitively. I like it. I thrive on it. When things are not hopping, I'm bored and I don't like it. In this litigation, you have that competition. You have clients who you develop relationships with. And you have the broader cigarette-smoking-and-health issue. It's got tremendous appeal! Financially, in the short run, it obviously does not. But we feel that there's a substantial likelihood that we'll win."

Darnell, the "self-righteous" one, as Edell teasingly called him, saw the litigation as a litmus test for the free enterprise system. "I believe in corporate responsibility," he said. "That's the essence of capitalism: Companies are responsible to the people they sell to. And we don't believe that the tobacco companies have been responsible about the product they sell. And they should pay the consequences.

"All we're saying in these lawsuits is, If you want to sell your product, fine. But if people get sick from them, you've gotta pay for what your product has done to them.

"The only reason people say the tobacco companies shouldn't have to pay is because so many people have died from smoking that they'd have to pay billions of dollars in damages. There's something wrong with that logic! They're saying, If you kill a lot of people, you're immune. If you kill only a few, then you should pay."

Edell flashed a satisfied grin. "I gotta remember that, Alan. Nice line."

In May 1981, the staff of the Federal Trade Commission (FTC) prepared a confidential report that raised troubling questions about the advertising practices of the cigarette industry.

The marketing plans for the various cigarette brands showed that they all were aimed at persuading young people to start smoking. Salem, an R. J. Reynolds cigarette, was to be associated

> with emulatable personalities and situational elements that are compatible with the aspirations and lifestyles of contemporary young adults, [so that] this important target segment will be attracted to the brand.

The same 1977 marketing plan said that a primary theme for Salem advertising would be to associate the cigarette with the lifestyle of "young adult males" who are "masculine, contemporary, confident, self-assured, daring/adventurous, mature." A Winston man was projected as "a man's man who is strong, vigorous, confident, experienced, mature."

Liggett & Myers' marketing plan for Larks said that by showing a balloon high above land, the Lark ads would give smoking an aura of "lightness and exhilaration." Lark would be positioned as a "youthful, contemporary brand that satisfies the lifestyles of the modern smoking public," in ads that emphasized "moments of post tension and relaxation." Every Liggett & Myers' Eve smoker would be portrayed as a "sophisticated, up-to-date, youthful and active woman who seems to have distinct ideas about what she wants."

What all the ads and marketing plans boiled down to, the staff said in its secret report, was a simple, psychological ploy to make people forget about the dangers of smoking. The ad themes, the FTC staff said, were designed to undercut the warnings that appeared on every cigarette package and in every cigarette advertisement.

As Brown & Williamson Tobacco Corporation's advertising agency, Ted Bates & Company, put it after conducting a number of focus-group interviews to help develop a new image for the Viceroy brand, even many smokers perceive their habit as a "dirty" and dangerous one engaged in only by "very stupid people." "Thus," Bates wrote,

> the smokers have to face the fact that they are illogical, irrational and stupid. People find it hard to go throughout life with such negative presentation and evaluation of self. The saviours are the *rationalization* and the *repression* that end up and result in a defense mechanism that, as [with] many of the defense mechanisms we use, has its own "logic," its own rationale. . . . Thus, smokers don't like to be reminded of the fact that they are illogical and irrational. They don't want to be reminded by either *direct* or *indirect* manner.

Another chapter of the report described how the company could introduce "starters" to the Viceroy brand:

> For the young smoker, the cigarette is not yet an integral part of life, of day-to-day life, in spite of the fact that they try to project the image of a regular, run-of-the-mill smoker. For them, a cigarette, and the whole smoking process, is part of the illicit pleasure category. . . . In the young smoker's mind a cigarette falls into the same category with wine, beer, shaving, wearing a bra (or *purposely* not wearing one), declaration of independence and striving for self-identity. For the young starter, a cigarette is associated with introduction to sex life, with courtship, with smoking "pot" and keeping late studying hours.

The Bates report had a final chapter entitled "How to Reduce Objections to a Cigarette." The answer: Since there "are not any real, absolute, positive qualities and attributes in a cigarette," the most effective advertising is that which presents a situation ambiguous enough to provide a smoker with an excuse for smoking.

The scene in the San Francisco law offices of Melvin Belli was a caricature of the man himself. On every wall were journalistic paeans to the King of Torts, because the country's best-known trial lawyer long ago learned that printer's ink brought in the clients. Never mind that Belli was nearly eighty years old before he won his first million-dollar damage verdict, and that there other were lawyers half his age who'd reached the million-dollar milestone years before. Melvin Belli, an outrageously profane, hugely obese man who stood barely five-foot-eight in his high-heeled cowboy boots, got the publicity—and the clients—because there was simply no one else like him.

A generation earlier, Belli had revolutionized personal-injury litigation by being the first to use "demonstrative evidence" in the courtroom. If a client wore an artificial limb as a result of an accident, Belli wouldn't just tell the jury that—he'd wrap the limb in butcher paper and drop it onto the counsel table, to be melodramatically unwrapped and passed around the jury box during the closing argument. That was how Belli showed the jury that leather and steel couldn't substitute for flesh and bone, and almost every plaintiff's lawyer worth a damn acknowledged, grudgingly or not, the insufferable Belli's contribution to the craft.

The sign hanging outside 122 Montgomery Street said BELLI, BELLI & BELLI, lest there be any doubt about the identity, or the ego, of the proprietor. A plaque commemorating Belli's first term as president of the Association of Trial Lawyers of America, in 1950 and 1951, hung in the waiting-room toilet. A big black bank vault sat in one corner of the brick-walled waiting room, a totem for the deep pockets Belli liked to reach into. THE HOLY GRAIL INSURANCE COMPANY it said on the safe's side. ASSETS: THE ADEQUATE AWARD. There were enough pseudo-old-time signs to wear thin: COUNTY JAIL #1—VISITING HOURS 1:30–3:30 P.M., one said. Another warned that PERSONS OTHER THAN WARDERS ARE FORBIDDEN TO PASS TO THE CONDEMNED CELLS WITHOUT BODILY INSPECTION.

Belli's shop was a clearinghouse: fifty cases a day came in unsolicited, and one lawyer spent all his time just culling through them for the three or four of those the firm would eventually accept. In such cases a well-heeled defendant, usually an insurance company or a big corporate defendant, was assured, and liability seemed clear. Of the cases taken, many would be referred to other lawyers, all of them happy for the business and only too glad to give Belli a perfectly legal kickback of a fourth or a third of whatever contingent fee the case ultimately paid. This way, Belli and the lawyers he employed—no partners for Belli; he owned his firm all by himself—could keep their own caseload lean and concentrate on getting the media attention that burnished Belli's reputation as a celebrity lawyer and brought in still more cases. Though few realized it, the lawyer who'd represented the likes of Jack Ruby and Jim and Tammy Bakker was running what amounted to a gigantic public-relations pyramid scheme. He wasn't so much a trial lawyer as an enterprise unto himself.

While Edell and Darnell were plotting their next moves in the carefully choreographed minuet of evidence gathering in their cigarette cases, Belli was preparing an assault of his own on the cigarette companies. Unlike his East Coast counterparts, who were pursuing a slow, deliberate path and laying careful groundwork for months of trial and years of appeals, Belli wanted to get his case to trial *quickly*. He wanted to be the first lawyer in a generation to haul a cigarette company into court. Win or lose, he would get the publicity.

Adding to the media appeal was the fact that Belli was a genuine pioneer. He had been one of the prime movers in an earlier wave of litigation against the tobacco companies. Starting in 1954 and stretching midway into the next decade, scores of lawsuits, Belli's among them, had been filed against the tobacco companies. Even the widow of singer Nat King Cole, who died of lung cancer in 1965 at the age of forty-five, filed such a suit.

When Belli brought his first cigarette case before a Louisiana jury on a muggy March day in 1958, he was already at his bad-boy best. Belli's client was Victoria Lartigue, whose husband, Frank, smoked Camels and died of lung cancer. She wanted $779,500 in damages. Belli's cocounsel, former state senator H. Alva Brumfield, was a rumpled character Belli called "The Kingfish." When the judge discovered that Brumfield had hired a private detective to spy on the jurors and find out their opinions on smoking, he declared a mistrial and shoved Belli's case all the way to the bottom of his docket. It took two years for the case to work its way back up, but only an hour and forty minutes for the jury to find in favor of R. J. Reynolds and Liggett & Myers.

Liability theories weren't so well developed then, so Belli and the other plaintiffs' lawyers had to fashion legal theories that didn't quite fit the special circumstances presented by a product with such well-known risks as cigarettes. The doctrine of *strict liability*, under which a product can be held unsafe even if it works exactly as it's intended to, didn't even exist. Most of those early cases claimed the tobacco companies sold an unsafe product despite their "implied warranty" that cigarettes were fit for human consumption. The evidence on that was considered weak, and it was the rare case that even got to a jury. In the few that did, the tobacco adversaries proved just as formidable then as they are now. Nobody got a penny from the cigarette makers.

But Belli thought that the climate had changed. The causal link between smoking and cancer was clearly established now, and the "nonsmokers' rights" movement was well entrenched, particularly in California, where strong no-smoking laws had even been enacted. He started looking around for the right case.

In California, it's generally illegal for a lawyer to drum up business by directly contacting prospective clients. That's called *solicitation*, otherwise known as ambulance chasing. But there's an important loophole in the California solicitation rule: A lawyer *can* contact clients if he takes the case for the good of the public, and without profit. And that is what Belli decided to do. If he got the right case, he would take it for free, because a good result in that first case would be a public-relations goldmine.

Belli, an ex-smoker since 1963, visited hospices and contacted doctors at major research hospitals throughout the United States, each time carrying the same message: "I'm looking for a cancer cigarette case. I want a squamous cell, bronchogenic carcinoma, located at the juncture of the bronchi." He was quite specific because he believed the medical evidence was strongest on the connection between smoking and that particular type of cancer. "I want to prove that cigarettes cause cancer," Belli told them, "and I want the tobacco companies held responsible for it!"

In 1982, a nurse attending a meeting of hospice professionals in

San Francisco heard Belli's request and contacted him. She had such a patient.

John Galbraith was a Goleta, California, man who'd been a three-pack-a-day smoker since he was fifteen years old. Now, at age sixty-nine, he was near death from the small-cell carcinoma that was eating away at his lungs, spinal column, eyes and brain.

Belli took the case to Paul Monzione, a young lawyer who'd joined his office the year before. Blond-haired and blue-eyed, Monzione was a Boston native who'd stayed in the West after attending law school at Southwestern University in Los Angeles. His clean-cut good looks and his obvious enthusiasm for his cases made him one of Belli's greatest assets.

Monzione saw some problems with the case. Galbraith did have cancer, and it appeared to be smoking-related. But he also had other lung and heart diseases that weren't connected to smoking. He'd actually outlived his parents and siblings—all of whom had died of the same hereditary heart and lung diseases that Galbraith had—by a considerable number of years. Clearly, the cigarette companies could be expected to claim the lung cancer was irrelevant to his death.

"The evidence was weak for us," Monzione admitted. "He was very sick. He wasn't a clean plaintiff, in terms of medical proof. But what he did have, which we felt was very strong, was a squamous-cell-type carcinoma, located at the juncture of the bronchi. That's an area where tobacco deposits—condensate from the smoke—generally is found.

"We had good evidence of the causation of his lung cancer being smoking. But where we didn't have good evidence, scientifically, was whether that lung cancer was a significant or substantial factor in bringing about his death."

Unlike lawyers who are paid by the hour and who thus may not care what their ultimate chances of success are so long as the client keeps paying his bills, the contingent-fee trial lawyers must analyze every case as a business proposition: Can they afford to risk their money against the prospect of a great reward later on? In the absence of special factors like a case's publicity value, a contingent-fee trial lawyer can't take a case that even remotely looks like a loser. The cash flow simply won't allow it.

Legal-ethics rules required the contingent fee agreement to be a written contract between the lawyer and his client. The Association of Trial Lawyers of America, which was composed of contingent-fee lawyers, went further, saying the percentage fee should be the subject of arms-length bargaining between the two parties. But even the association conceded that was seldom the case. Usually, the client simply accepted the lawyer's proposal, and the lawyers rationalized away any resultant problems by saying, in the words of ATLA's former president, Philadelphia's David Shrager, that "the client understands what one-third means. There are no extra charges. There is no easier-to-understand agreement between two adults."

Charles H. Baron, a Boston College Law School professor and an expert in legal ethics, said the trial lawyers were ignoring an inherent conflict of interest with their clients: "The client can't shop around, and he doesn't have the power to negotiate. He doesn't know any better. Trial lawyers claim their whopping percentage compensates them for the losers they take. But the fact is, they don't take losers. They're pretty good at smelling them out. They're mostly taking winners and charging people as if they're also getting some losers, when in fact they're not. And I really think that's disturbing."

In looking at the Galbraith case, Belli and Monzione made the kind of cold, hard calculations referred to by Baron. Galbraith, Monzione pointed out, had "a perfect smoking history. He was a person who was addicted before warning labels were put on cigarette packs. A person who took up the habit as a teenager living in Nebraska, thinking it was the macho thing to do. He was a smoker who was heavily influenced by the advertisements and by the tobacco industry's position on smoking." Galbraith was so hopelessly addicted to cigarettes that, even when he was close to death, he would pull out his oxygen tubes just for the satisfaction of a deep drag. His lawyers saw that as a plus for their case, because they intended to show that cigarette advertising had lured him into that addiction without warning him of its awful consequences.

"We also had a good lung cancer," Monzione explained, "which sounds horrible to say. But we did have a squamous cell tumor, located where we wanted one to be located in terms of proving the causal connection. And for those reasons we felt we had a good case."

Belli and Monzione decided not only to take the case, but to push it to trial as quickly as possible. Because of the California rule against solicitation, Belli would be spending his own money on the case and wouldn't get a fee even if he won, so time was money and the sooner this case went to trial, the less it would cost him. "Save your money and try your lawsuit," Belli said.

There was also obvious publicity value in being the first to get a case to trial. Monzione reasoned that the spectacle of a cigarette trial would be important, regardless of its outcome. "We felt that if we could go in there and have a jury say to the American public, and really to the world—because this is a case that received international attention—not only that cigarettes cause cancer, but that in the case of John Galbraith, they caused him to just whittle away in front of his family and killed him, horribly, that we'd have an impact on a lot of people who are either smoking now or will take up the habit. So, we pushed it. The scientific evidence was strong that he'd gotten cancer from cigarette smoking. Very strong."

But the lawyers also took a calculated risk. Instead of ordering an autopsy that would have pinned down the cause of Galbraith's death, they counseled against it. The reason given at the time was that Galbraith himself had told his wife, "They've poked enough needles into me; when I die, I just want to rest. I want to be comfortable." But there were so many other things wrong with Galbraith that everybody except the cigarette companies was afraid of what might be found.

Indeed, the death certificate signed by Dr. George Fisher, Galbraith's lung specialist, listed Galbraith's two non-smoking-related hereditary diseases, "arteriosclerotic heart disease and pulmonary fibrosis," as the two principal causes of his death. Cigarette-related maladies were listed in a part of the form entitled "Other conditions contributing but not related to the immediate cause of death," where Fisher wrote, "lung cancer and emphysema."

"I'm not so sure an autopsy would have helped us. It probably would have helped the defense. We took our chance," Monzione said.

Belli's lawsuit was not against just R. J. Reynolds, but also two local markets where Galbraith bought his cigarettes. That was another strategic ploy by Belli, because without the local defendants he would have to try his case in federal court as specified by the doctrine of diversity. The legal presumption is that cases like this belong in a state court as long as at least one plaintiff and one defendant are from the same state. But the federal courts may take over when there's no such common bond.

By deciding either to add or to keep off a local defendant, Belli could, in essence, choose his court. There were benefits to being in federal court: To win in this civil case, he'd need just the unanimous vote of a six-person jury, instead of a nine-to-three vote mandated for the state's twelve-person juries. Furthermore, the federal courts would probably allow him greater latitude, under the federal "hearsay rule," in presenting the Surgeon General's reports on smoking. And his case would probably get to trial faster, because the federal courts are less clogged.

But Belli finally decided he didn't want to be in federal court because of another legal doctrine: *preemption.* According to that doctrine plaintiffs couldn't file an unsafe-product lawsuit if they'd already been adequately warned about its dangers. A federal judge might say that the federal cigarette labeling law provided such a preemptive warning, although a state judge might not feel as tightly bound by the federal law. So, to defeat diversity and guarantee a state court trial, Belli added the markets. Then, right as the trial was beginning, he just as strategically dropped them from his lawsuit, betting—correctly, it turned out—that the cigarette companies would go ahead with the state-court trial anyway, instead of placing it at the bottom of the federal court docket.

Belli wanted $100 million in punitive damages and another $1 million in compensatory damages for Galbraith's widow and children. The lawyers for R. J. Reynolds, leaving nothing to chance in the litigation, began their usual thorough investigation. They interviewed all of Galbraith's coworkers at the Occidental Life Insurance Company, where he'd been an office manager; talked to neighbors and friends; even tracked down the ex-wife of one of Galbraith's sons, to see what she could tell them.

Her story proved to be so useful that the tobacco-company lawyers subpoenaed her for a formal deposition. Did she ever see John Galbraith smoke? Yes, of course. Did he ever tell her anything about smoking? Back in 1978, she said, Galbraith had told her that she shouldn't smoke, because it would kill her just as it was killing him.

Under California law, a plaintiff seeking punitive damages has to bring a lawsuit within a year after he becomes aware of the injury he has suffered. So the tobacco lawyers went into court and said Galbraith hadn't brought his lawsuit soon enough. The judge agreed and threw out the $100 million claim. That left Belli's $1 million wrongful death action.

As the case edged toward trial in 1985, the lawyers for R. J. Reynolds scheduled a September 11 deposition of Dr. George Fisher, the Santa Barbara lung specialist who treated John Galbraith.

Monzione had already spoken with Fisher. Right after Galbraith's death, when he saw the death certificate, Monzione had called and asked whether, in Fisher's opinion, cancer was also a cause of Galbraith's death.

"Absolutely, Paul," Fisher replied. "No doubt in my mind."

F. John Nyhan, one of the Los Angeles lawyers Reynolds had hired to handle its courtroom defense, was a forty-one-year-old partner in the firm of Lawler, Felix & Hall. He was also a formidable opponent, made all the more so by the millions of dollars Reynolds was spending to investigate every aspect of the case.

"You were not able to confirm the presence of the metastasis [cancer] in John Galbraith at the time of his death, were you, Doctor?" Nyhan asked Fisher near the end of his deposition.

A. "No, because he didn't have an autopsy."

Q. "And you don't have any opinion as to whether he had cancer at the time of his death, do you?"

Monzione held his breath. This would be a crucial answer. Nyhan wanted Fisher to say that the cancer was gone by then; that Galbraith couldn't have been killed by it because it didn't even exist at the time of his death.

A. "Yes, I think my opinion is that an autopsy would have shown that he had residual cancer."

Monzione smiled inside. The doctor, an advocate for neither side, had given an answer favorable to the Galbraith side. Then, unaccountably, Fisher blundered on:

"But I think it would have to be shown it had nothing to do with his death." In other words, Galbraith had cancer, but cancer *wasn't* what killed him. "I think his death was caused by his heart disease and his pulmonary fibrosis."

Monzione was stunned. He tried not to react outwardly. "Maybe

Nyhan doesn't know what he's got," he thought to himself. But Nyhan had brightened. Nyhan knew.

"No further questions."

Monzione would have to rehabilitate this witness as best he could. He grabbed the death certificate and cross-examined Fisher: "Did Mr. Galbraith's lung cancer play any role at all in causing his death, in your opinion?"

A. "I think that the radiation therapy that he received for his lung cancer caused further damage to his lungs, and aggravated the fibrosis and obstructive disease he had, and contributed to his hypoxemia. But I would place it below his heart disease and his pulmonary fibrosis as the cause of his death. So, I would consider it a contributing cause."

Fisher was changing his testimony *again*.

Q. "So, you would consider his lung cancer a contributing cause of his death, and you so noted that on his death certificate; isn't that correct?"

A. "I did."

Monzione had received the answer he wanted, but he also knew his case was in trouble. "What we've got," he thought, "is, at best, inconsistent testimony from the same witness. No way I can get that earlier statement out of there."

The case would soon be coming to trial, and, compared to R. J. Reynolds, Belli and Monzione had done precious little to prepare. The plaintiffs intended to present a strict-liability case showing that cigarettes caused the cancer that killed John Galbraith, but, as Fisher's deposition testimony had already shown, that link was tenuous at best. Monzione and Belli also anticipated that R. J. Reynolds and its expert witnesses would adamantly deny the dangers of smoking, and, incredible as those denials were, the two lawyers didn't have any smoking-gun proof that the cigarette company was stonewalling.

But Belli also knew that Edell, sitting atop a vast discovery machine back in his New Jersey office, had been subpoenaing hundreds of thousands of documents from the cigarette companies' private files. Less than a week before Belli's trial was scheduled to begin, Edell told me a desperate Belli telephoned him.

The two lawyers had never met, so Belli introduced himself over the phone and Edell, pleased at this recognition of his ascending importance in the plaintiffs' bar, did the same.

Belli stammered around uncomfortably for a few moments before coming to the point: "Um, ya got some discovery I can use in my trial?"

Edell had no idea what Belli wanted. Moreover, all the documents he'd subpoenaed were covered by a protective order, which meant they couldn't be made public or turned over to another lawyer without the court's permission. The young lawyer explained that. "Unless you can give me some indication of what you're looking for," he replied, "it's going to be very difficult."

"You gotta give me something to cross-examine these bastards on!"

"Mr. Belli," Edell replied, "I really can't give you this stuff I've subpoenaed. But we've gotten a lot of information from other sources. If you'll tell me what issues you're concerned with, I'll be happy to send you some stuff."

But Belli didn't know what to ask for. "God damn it," Belli replied in a huff, "after fifty years at the bar as a plaintiffs' lawyer, this is how I'm treated!" Belli slammed the phone down.

Edell and Darnell, meanwhile, were mired in problems of their own.

The coordinated strategy of the cigarette defendants had three prongs: attacking the lawyers, wearing down the plaintiffs and challenging the validity of the lawsuits that had been filed. The tobacco-company strategy was to tie cases in knots, delaying them for years through blizzards of pretrial motions.

Edell and Darnell were vulnerable to attack because another lawyer from a New Jersey firm representing the Brown & Williamson Tobacco Corporation switched to Darnell's firm in 1986. Under ethical rules covering lawyer conflict-of-interest and attorney-client privilege, a lawyer can't switch sides in a case without the permission of his former client, and, foolishly, nobody asked Brown & Williamson. Thus, as soon as Darnell's new partner came aboard, the tobacco companies filed motions alleging that Darnell's entire firm was tainted by conflict of interest. Moreover, the companies claimed the taint extended beyond Brown & Williamson, to cases involving every other cigarette company as well, because the tobacco companies were closely coordinating their defense. If the tobacco companies prevailed, Darnell would be out of business as far as these cases were concerned. He fought back, claiming that he'd already spent thousands of hours on the litigation and that no other lawyer could possibly take over for him. But the defense tactic took its toll. As the procedural wrangle dragged on, cases that Darnell had the principal responsibility for preparing for trial had to be put on hold, and the lawyers spent countless hours fighting a diversionary battle.

"If they lose, and I'm still in this case, God help 'em," Darnell intoned. "Because they knew that they were raising the ante when they started this." But the cigarette companies didn't lose. They beat Darnell on the disqualification motion, eliminating one of their major threats. Darnell was allowed to help Edell in the Cipollone case, but he was precluded from being paid for his work from that point forward and he wasn't allowed to take any more cigarette-liability cases.

The defense attorneys also kept Edell off balance by accusing him of reneging on a promise not to use in litigation other than *Cipollone* the corporate documents Edell had subpoenaed. That was a serious allegation, too, but Edell claimed he'd never made the promise to protect each and every document, no matter how innocuous, that he'd ever been given. Quite to the contrary, Edell's avowed intention was to eventually use in his own other cases and also turn over to friendly reporters and other plaintiffs' lawyers the cigarette companies' internal documents, documents which might show how the companies ignored the scientific evidence about smoking and undermined the health warnings in their own advertisements.

Edell hoped to find a smoking gun among the hundreds of thousands of documents he'd subpoenaed. "What we're looking for," he explained, "is some type of concrete evidence that supports what a large number of people believe has occurred over the years: that they were conducting research which resulted in a finding that cigarette smoking causes disease in human beings, and that they either suppressed or ignored it, didn't make it available to the general public, and never warned about it on their products."

"We also want concrete evidence that the cigarette companies intentionally tried to mislead smokers about the health hazards. And that they, in their advertising and promotional activities, directed an effort to the smoker to neutralize the effects of their health warnings.

I think that's very powerful. If you can show to the jury that there is a document or testimony that supports these propositions, that would be very compelling.

"One of the things we've seen the tobacco companies play up in the litigation is the idea that it's American to be able to choose what you want to do and what you don't want to do. 'Freedom to Choose. The American Way. We're just all-American, just like everybody else. The people who smoke enjoy their smoking and they know what's going on. We're just giving them a product, we're not forcing them to smoke it.'

"That's what the cigarette companies claim. And it's a very compelling argument. The problem with it is that they knew people became physically and psychologically dependent on their product. And they knew what they were doing, with their advertising efforts and their trade association efforts to fund research which led nowhere, but which they could use in press releases that said, 'We're spending $10 million to see whether smoking is hazardous.' A smoker reads that and says, 'They wouldn't spend $10 million if it was really proven already.' "

Cigarette-company lawyers dragged Edell into court on September 25, 1986. There had been a front-page article on the cigarette litigation in the New York *Times* ten days earlier, which quoted Edell at length. Murray Bring, a fifty-one-year-old senior partner in the Washington law firm of Arnold & Porter (and the lawyer who, one year later, would become the general counsel of Philip Morris), took his complaints about Edell to H. Lee Sarokin, the liberal federal judge from Newark who was going to preside over the Cipollone trial.

"He characterized the documents," Bring, Arnold & Porter's top cigarette-litigation lawyer, said of Edell's New York *Times* quotations, "and what he thought the documents meant to him, and you can imagine it was not very flattering to the interest of the defendants in the cases, and it was exactly this kind of characterization, and in my judgment, inaccurate characterization, which concerned us very much, because it was—it would have appeared to be the first shot in a public relations media campaign to discredit these parties before any issue came to trial, and it was the first shot in a media campaign to try to persuade the press and public [that] if Mr. Edell could only release the documents, everyone would see how nefarious the companies were." Bring claimed Edell was welching on a promise not to seek to use the documents in any case other than *Cipollone.*

Edell was furious. He told Sarokin that being able to share the documents and use them in other litigation was imperative. "I'm not sitting here with thirty lawyers. I'm not being paid on an hourly basis. I can't afford to go and fight each case like I'm fighting *Cipollone.* Doesn't make sense. There's no reason to do it."

After the hearing, Edell called Bring a liar and vowed to stop acknowledging his existence. "I will not correspond with him, I will not talk with him on the phone, and I will not shake his hand or talk to him when we're face to face. That particular lawyer, in order to try to get [something for] his client, lied. And every other lawyer who was involved in those negotiations knew damn well that he was totally misrepresenting what occurred. I will not stand for that."

Bring, a balding Arnold & Porter elder with a paunchy build and a rough complexion, was not particularly enamored of Edell, either. He scoffed at the image he thought Edell and the rest of the plaintiffs' lawyers tried to project as poor, impoverished lawyers up against a corporate monolith.

Rigorous investigations of the plaintiffs proved to be just as irksome as the attacks against the lawyers. As R. J. Reynolds had already shown when its lawyers tracked down the ex-wife of Galbraith's son and extracted from her an admission that demolished Belli's punitive-damage case, the cigarette companies were resourceful at using depositions to ferret out the information that could win their case. As with Rose Cipollone, they also left nothing to chance in their depositions, spending day upon day asking lifestyle-related questions from the two-inch-thick standardized deposition notebook that was the defense-lawyer's bible in these cases.

"The tobacco companies have an interesting outlook on what causes cancer," Darnell explained. "Their standards of cancer causation are rather loose, *for everything but tobacco!* So, they will go into questions about the exposures of your client to anything other than tobacco: Did the decedent ever eat brussels sprouts? Did he ever eat charcoaled meats? But when it comes to tobacco, they say nothing's been proven!"

That was certainly the case with Susan Haines, a young Philadelphia paralegal who retained Edell and Darnell to sue Liggett, Philip

Morris, R. J. Reynolds and Lorillard over her father's lung-cancer death. Twelve lawyers from five different law firms attended the three-day-long 1984 deposition during which Haines was asked about such topics as her two marriages, including the names of all the guests at both weddings; her mother's health (even though it was her late *father* whose health was in issue); all her stepbrothers and step-sisters; the churches her family attended; the names of guests she saw at some yacht club dances in the 1960s; the names of people who attended the funeral of her paternal grandfather; whether her grand-mother ever told her father not to smoke (She did, and he had re-plied, "Mom, it's not that easy"); how and when Susan Haines started smoking, and what brands she smoked; how and when her various brothers and sisters started smoking; how deeply her father inhaled and whether there was air pollution in the area of her father's New Jersey home.

Q. "What kinds of food did your father like to eat?"

A. "He liked all kinds of food."

Q. "Did he like spicy or highly seasoned food?"

A. "Not to my knowledge."

Q. "Did he like Mexican food?"

A. "I don't know. . . ."

Q. "Did he like smoked or charcoal-broiled foods?"

A. "I don't know. . . ."

Q. "Did he use mustard on his food?"

A. "Yes."

Q. "What food?"

A. "Sandwiches."

Q. "Horseradish?"

A. "No."

Q. "Did he eat beef?"

A. "He ate beef. . . ."

Q. "Well done, rare, or to what extent was it cooked?"

A. "Rare to medium."

"Did he eat liver?" the lawyer asked. Freshly caught fish? Smoked fish? "Three specific types of fish that I'm interested in," he went on, "trout, crab and eels. Do you remember whether he ate any or all of those three?" What about mushrooms? Celery? Parsnips? Parsley?

Sweet potatoes? Baked potatoes? Fava beans? Lima beans? Okra? Alfalfa sprouts? Radishes? Carrots? Brussels sprouts?

The lawyer asking the questions was David Hardy, who was then the lead counsel for Philip Morris and a senior partner in the respected Kansas City law firm of Shook, Hardy & Bacon. Incredibly, Philip Morris was paying top dollar for an eminent defense lawyer to do little more than read down a grocery list! As Hardy recited his produce-counter litany during the third full day of Haines' deposition, Edell would periodically interrupt him:

"All these things are relevant, right? That's why you are asking them? You are nodding your head affirmatively."

Hardy: "As far as I'm concerned, I haven't asked any irrelevant questions in this deposition. Every question I've asked has been relevant."

Hardy also wanted to know whether Haines had seen the autopsy report about her father, whose name was Peter Rossi. Specifically, Hardy was interested in something called an anthracotic scar that the pathologist had found on Rossi's lung. Hardy seemed to think that the scar might be evidence that some other kind of lung disease had caused Rossi's death. But when he started bearing down on Haines, her answer surprised him.

"I spoke to my mother about any prior lung problems that my father may have had and she told me that he had psittacosis at one point in the 1950s."

"How do you spell psittacosis?" a puzzled Hardy inquired.

Haines spelled it.

"What do you understand psittacosis to be?"

"It's a virus similar to pneumonia which is contracted from exposure to bird droppings."

By now, Darnell and Edell were stifling laughter. Hardy, meanwhile, was solemnly pressing on, attempting to get the complete story of this odd medical history. "Do you remember anything else from that conversation with your mother?"

A. "We discussed the fact that my grandfather's hobby was parakeets."

Q. "Which grandfather?"

A. "My paternal grandfather, my father's father."

Q. "What did your mother say about that in this conversation?"

A. "We simply said it must have been from the parakeets."

Hardy followed up with question after question about the parakeets: How many were there? Ten. Where were they kept? In the basement.

Darnell had been doodling on a piece of scrap paper. After all, he said, "when you've heard the fourteenth question about brussels sprouts, you start to get punchy." Now, an amused Darnell started a new doodle, drawing a cartoon of an eagle heeding nature's call. Darnell passed it to the smiling Edell. On the basis of Hardy's questions, Darnell was anticipating the tobacco companies' next line of defense, and so the caption on his cartoon read:

"The bird-shit defense. Will it fly?"

In product liability law, there are two basic types of cases:

- strict liability, which applies when a product has inherent flaws that make it unavoidably unsafe

- negligence, a much more common type of action, in which the manufacturer has failed to adequately warn people of a product's danger

When someone uses the strict-liability theory to sue a manufacturer over a product that's unavoidably unsafe, the lawsuit boils down to whether the benefits of the product exceed the risks it poses. If the product causes distinctly more harm than good, it can be held defective. In legal jargon, this is called the *risk-utility theory,* and it was a crucial one in the *Cipollone* case. If Edell could convince a jury that the risks of cigarettes exceeded their benefits, he might be able to win.

Proving cigarettes to be *inherently* dangerous under the risk-utility doctrine was clearly Edell's best shot at victory because it didn't require him to prove a company's bad motives, or its failure to warn smokers about known dangers, or anything else. All strict liability required was proof that, despite all efforts, cigarettes couldn't possibly be made safe—that they hurt people even when they were used exactly as intended.

Even if Edell couldn't persuade anyone that cigarettes were inherently dangerous, he might be able to show that they were risky under certain circumstances, and that the cigarette companies failed to warn people about those dangers. Those were the negligence and related counts.

But the cigarette companies had a seemingly credible defense against any failure-to-warn allegation.

Cigarette packages had, after all, carried congressionally mandated warnings since 1966. The first warnings had simply read: CAUTION: CIGARETTE SMOKING MAY BE HAZARDOUS TO YOUR HEALTH. In 1970, the warning was changed to read: WARNING: THE SURGEON GENERAL HAS DETERMINED THAT CIGARETTE SMOKING IS DANGEROUS TO YOUR HEALTH. And then, in 1985, new labels that listed specific maladies caused by smoking—cancer, emphysema, fetal injury among them—had begun appearing on cigarettes on a rotating basis.

The cigarette companies claimed that these federally mandated warnings insulated them from failure-to-warn lawsuits based on state laws. The point was arguable, for the federal labeling law did provide that "no statement relating to smoking and health [other than the federally specified warning] shall be required" on cigarette packages, and that "no requirement or prohibition based on smoking and health shall be imposed under state law with respect to the advertising or promotion" of cigarettes.

Clearly, the federal law prohibited states from requiring any warnings other than those imposed by federal law. But did the federal law also apply to lawsuits involving the *adequacy* of those warnings or involving cigarette-industry efforts to wage advertising and public relations campaigns to *undercut* the required warnings?

Edell and Darnell thought not. They argued that they were entitled to their day in court to prove that the warnings were inadequate. And in a crucial 1984 decision, Sarokin, the Newark federal judge, agreed.

Sarokin found that the tobacco industry had been undercutting its own health warnings with massive advertising that showed healthy people smoking, and with repeated statements that the scientific case against cigarettes was unproved—statements that contradicted the very health warnings the industry now was trying to hide behind.

"Efforts to convince the public that risks do not exist or that they are minimal or unsupported by medical and scientific data may, in and of themselves, give rise to a cause of action," Sarokin wrote.

It looked as if Edell and Darnell might yet be able to introduce some of the cigarette-industry documents they'd subpoenaed, which, they hinted, showed what the companies really knew about the safety of cigarettes, as well as when they knew it. Moreover, Sarokin's opinion seemed solid, since it closely followed two Supreme Court opinions and another court of appeals opinion on the issue. Just the previous year, the High Court had held that federal laws establishing safety regulations for nuclear power plants didn't preempt a California law that restricted plant construction. In another case, the Supreme Court had permitted the estate of Karen Silkwood to sue Kerr-McGee for her radiation-related injuries, even though a federal law limited a nuclear plant's civil liability. And the U.S. Court of Appeals for the District of Columbia Circuit had ruled that Chevron could be sued for failing to adequately warn about the dangers of the insecticide paraquat, even though it *had* fully complied with the federal labeling laws.

But when the cigarette companies took their appeal of Sarokin's ruling to the U.S. Court of Appeals for the Third Circuit, in Philadelphia, the result was a complete reversal of Sarokin's lower-court ruling, and a major setback for Edell and Darnell. The three-judge appeals-court panel held in April 1986 that there was *implied* preemption of any failure-to-warn claims. As if that weren't bad enough, the Third Circuit's opinion was written by a judge who, twenty years earlier, had defended American Tobacco in a cigarette-liability trial. The plaintiffs' lawyers cried foul when they learned about Judge James Hunter III's earlier incarnation as a cigarette-industry defense lawyer, but three of Hunter's judicial colleagues affirmed his impartiality and let the decision stand.

Other trial-court judges had followed Sarokin's landmark ruling allowing the failure-to-warn claim, but now, taking their cue from the only appeals court to rule on the matter, federal appeals courts elsewhere started following the Third Circuit. The Eleventh Circuit, in Atlanta, and the First Circuit, in Boston, issued implied-preemption rulings that tracked the Third Circuit's and threw out failure-to-warn claims. Edell's only hope was for a Supreme Court review of one of the cases, but, in the absence of any conflict among the circuits, that was unlikely. His own last-ditch appeal on the preemption issue was turned down by the Court in December 1987.

Yet the risk-utility part of the *Cipollone* case was still standing. Even as the Third Circuit was demolishing his 1984 ruling on preemption, Sarokin had helped the plaintiffs with another key ruling in favor of the risk-utility theory. The judge held not only that the theory could be applied at trial, but also that the cigarette makers couldn't include benefits to the general economy in the risk-utility equation. This meant that the cigarette companies wouldn't be allowed to show that they helped society by generating profits, hiring workers or paying taxes. "Strict liability law is intended to *temper* the profit motive," the judge groused.

But not all the players agreed with Sarokin on the salutary effects of New Jersey's concept of strict liability for the makers of unsafe products, particularly not the cigarette companies, who used one of their lawyer-lobbyists to make an end run around an unsuspecting Edell.

A new product-liability law was being written by the New Jersey state legislature, and it would severely limit the risk-utility doctrine's future applicability to defect-free products. The examples of products that would be affected by the new law were innocuous enough, but the cigarette companies saw an opportunity to undo Sarokin's earlier ruling on risk utility. Apparently unbeknown to the legislators voting the bill into law, someone inserted into the legislative history of the bill language that made the risk-utility ban *retroactive*. Edell's foes promptly filed a motion asking Sarokin to strike the risk-utility part of his case.

Edell, already overwhelmed by the paper flying back and forth between the parties so close to the trial date, thought it was just one more diversion, and he didn't even bother to answer the defense motion. But Sarokin, immediately apprehending the importance of the retroactive language in the legislative history, said he had no choice but to grant the defense motion.

Now Edell and his thirty-eight-year-old associate on the case, Cynthia Walters, had to try to dig up some dirt on how the retroactive language had been slipped in. Walters suspected it had been inserted by John P. Sheridan, a lobbyist for five tobacco companies that had spent nearly $1 million on lobbying and campaign contributions in

New Jersey. Sheridan's Morristown law firm represented R. J. Reynolds, and Sheridan himself had been hired by Covington & Burling, the big Washington law firm that represented the Tobacco Institute, to do the cigarette industry's lobbying work on the New Jersey product-liability law. Walters subpoenaed Sheridan for a deposition so that he could be questioned about his role in getting the anti-*Cipollone* bill passed.

But Sheridan and all the tobacco companies said they wouldn't answer questions about their lobbying, because it was covered by the First Amendment. "It goes without saying," Sheridan's law firm complained in a letter to Sarokin, "that all persons, including manufacturers of tobacco products, have an indisputable right to advance their position in the legislative process."

Sarokin, who seemed almost as angry as Walters and Edell about the turn of events, nonetheless agreed with the defendants. It wasn't a judge's job to revise the legislative process.

Sarokin didn't permit Walters to take Sheridan's deposition, and he grudgingly let stand his elimination of Edell's risk-utility claim, even though he said it was "offensive . . . that a litigant in the midst of ongoing litigation can prevail upon the legislature to eliminate a cause of action pending against it, particularly if that legislation is procured through the submission of intentionally misleading facts."

"So there's no risk-utility, and we'll never know who did what to whom," said an obviously disappointed Cindy Walters. "This is the kind of game they play." Motion by motion, the cigarette companies were winning the case even before it got to trial. Now, Darnell was disqualified, and their two best shots at recovery—risk-utility and post-1966 failure to warn—had been shot down by the other side.

Antonio Cipollone was holding his wife in his arms when she died on October 21, 1984, at age fifty-eight. "Tony, I love you," she told him.

"I love you, too."

"I know. I know."

Edell and Darnell still saw Antonio Cipollone and their other clients from time to time, but the legal battle had become so complex, and the stakes so great, that it was hard to remember who the beneficiaries of these cases really were. Platoons of lawyers sat around the conference table at Edell's firm, planning their next moves like the zealous corporate strategists they might have been. Rose Cipollone's misfortune, after all, was a commodity to be marketed. The jury would determine its fair market value.

In his office, Edell reflected on the long battle being waged. Before he filed his first case, he got the docket sheets from every case that had been brought during the first wave of cigarette litigation in the 1950s and 1960s. He wanted to see how the cigarette companies had defended those cases.

"The main defense strategy was a war of attrition," Edell remarked. "They did the same thing then as they do today. They make the litigation as financially and economically burdensome as possible, to dissuade plaintiffs' lawyers from getting involved in it. They use whatever procedural tactics they can employ. And they do a lot of clever lawyering. They hire very, very good lawyers and they divert your attention from the main issues. You end up in the Third Circuit on writs of mandamus and disqualification motions.

"None of us anticipated the kind of money that would be thrown at this litigation. In the beginning, I thought we could win the war of attrition. But we can't win it. It's impossible. We can only survive."

If everything else about Melvin Belli was outsized—from his ample girth to his own reputation—so, too, was his mode of travel to the venue where the Galbraith case was to be tried. Belli didn't fly or drive to picturesque Santa Barbara. He *sailed,* aboard his 105-foot yacht *Fifer* that was appropriately nicknamed the *Adequate Award.* Loaded up with the finest steaks and lobster, the festive boat became Belli's floating office and hotel, and it was one more tool for getting the publicity that set Belli apart from other trial lawyers.

Though they arrived in November 1985 with a flourish of media attention over the possibility of an anticigarette verdict, Belli and Monzione knew they had a weak case. They had already signaled that by their failure to get an autopsy, and they'd had it driven home to them when Galbraith's own doctor had expressed doubts about whether his patient even had cancer when he died.

The Santa Barbara Courthouse is a beautiful old Spanish period structure, perfectly matched to the rest of the wealthy seaside community. Bruce Dodds, forty-seven, a UCLA Law School graduate who'd previously worked as the Santa Barbara deputy county counsel and in the California Attorney General's Office, had been a judge there since he was first elected to the bench in 1977.

Dodds knew Belli's reputation for courtroom theatrics, and the judge was determined not to let the King of Torts ride roughshod over him, even if it meant holding Belli in contempt.

Belli had his own views about Dodds: "An utter, complete idiot," Belli called him. "A miserable, stupid son of a bitch! You can forgive a lot of things, but not stupidity. He ought to recognize his stupidity and not go on the bench. And that's what everybody thought about him down there, but they were afraid to say anything. Jesus, I wasn't! I just didn't like him from the time I first saw him."

Even in the courtroom, Belli made no secret of his scorn, and it did not work in his favor. The real irony was that, despite their mutual animus, Dodds was a believer in the kind of case Belli had brought him. The judge thought that the cigarette companies had, indeed, used their advertisements to negate the health warnings, and he was convinced that sooner or later a plaintiff would beat the industry. As Dodds saw it, though, Belli was so ill-prepared that he had no choice but to rule against him on key evidentiary points. In one crucial setback for the plaintiffs, Dodds refused let Belli introduce any of the reports of the Surgeon General describing the link between smoking and cancer, a devastating ruling but one Dodds felt compelled to make because Belli didn't have any expert witnesses to interpret the reports' findings for the jury.

"He wanted to read it in," Dodds explained later. "That's not the law in California. He had to have somebody there to present it."

Each side had lined up its experts. Monzione had persuaded Dr. Michael Shimkin of the University of California and Dr. Raymond Yesner of Yale University to donate their time to the case. Both were eminent cancer specialists, and each would play a specific role in this case. Shimkin would be one of the opening witnesses, testifying as to the link between smoking and cancer. Yesner, going last for the plaintiffs, would testify that cancer was what killed John Galbraith.

The participation of Yesner and Shimkin gave some lustre to Belli's case, yet his lack of preparation was also quite evident. Even the judge was surprised that Belli and Monzione didn't have any evidence or expert testimony about how the industry's warm-and-fuzzy advertising contradicted the health warnings that the cigarette packages carried. There was also nothing to show that Galbraith had ever seen or relied on cigarette advertisements.

"That's the kind of testimony I think was missing in this trial," Dodds later explained. "It would be very, very effective. Then you could no longer argue, 'Look, we told you right on the package.' The plaintiff could say, 'Yeah, but look what you did to hook everybody and to hook me.' I think that could overcome the problem that the plaintiffs' lawyers think that they have to get somebody who has smoked a long time. If they got somebody who was thirty years old with lung cancer who said, 'Yeah, but I saw those pretty pictures and everybody dancing through the fields,' I think that would be very effective to a jury."

Lacking such expert testimony, the plaintiffs couldn't show the effect of such mind-molding advertising. That, in turn, obliterated the possibility of making a successful failure-to-warn claim, even though Dodds thought such a claim would have been the strongest part of Belli's case and had ruled, as Judge Sarokin previously had in *Cipollone,* that such a claim wasn't preempted by the federal cigarette labeling law.

The conventional wisdom among other plaintiffs' lawyers was that the cigarette companies were controlling the pace of their pretrial motions so that the weakest cases came to trial first. But although *Galbraith* was the first to reach trial, it didn't follow that the cigarette lawyers hadn't fully prepared their case. They had, instead, been using *Galbraith* as a teacher would use a laboratory. They were dissecting this $2 million defense for the benefit of every other lawyer who would have to try such a case if the pace of cigarette litigation quickened. Eight lawyers sat at the defense table or directly behind it. In the courtroom audience, thirty-two other tobacco lawyers watched the proceedings.

The defense lawyers spared no expense. They rented condominiums for the lawyers and support staff and flew in public-relations people to deal with reporters. A copy of each day's trial transcript was flown to R. J. Reynolds' headquarters every night on a private corporate jet.

In the weeks before the trial, Reynolds' lawyers even called in their own psychological consultants, from a Los Angeles company called Litigation Sciences, Inc., to help run mock trials so that the lawyers would know how prospective jurors were going to react to the case. Litigation Sciences had first gained notoriety nine years earlier, when it was hired by the New York defense lawyers for IBM to secretly recruit a "shadow jury" that would help the lawyers gauge reactions of the real jurors during an important trial. The shadow jurors were supposed to sit unobtrusively in the courtroom audience, but before long people became curious about the cluster of observers who were always being hurriedly ushered in or out of the courtroom in synch with the real jury! In any event, even though the judge directed a verdict for IBM before the case ever went to the jury, the trial in *California Computer Products v. IBM* put Litigation Sciences on the map.

In *Galbraith v. R. J. Reynolds*, the consultants paid the participants to fill out an eight-page questionnaire that listed the same questions a real prospective juror would be asked by the lawyers and the judge during *voir dire*—such items as their age and salary and whether anyone in their family had ever had lung cancer. Then, twelve "jurors" were put into a mock courtroom, along with a judge, a court reporter, and two attorneys who questioned them more intensively on their attitudes about smoking. Finally, the mock jurors were shown a videotape of some staged testimony. They saw a bereaved widow talk about her husband's lung cancer, and then they watched as the two lawyers presented their closing arguments on tape for forty-five minutes each.

While the jurors deliberated, they were videotaped from behind a one-way mirror. The mock jurors were told to decide three things: whether the cigarette makers had been negligent in selling their product; whether cigarettes had a design defect that rendered them unsafe, a strict-liability issue; and whether the industry were liable for failure to warn people about the dangers of smoking. When the time finally came to cast ballots, the mock jurors found in favor of the industry on each question: eleven-to-one on the first issue and nine-to-three on the last two.

In California civil cases, a majority of nine votes or more wins a case.

Prospects were looking good for R. J. Reynolds.

"Some of the things we went over Friday, I think we should go over again," the judge told the lawyers for both sides when they assembled in his courtroom on Tuesday, November 12, 1985. The jury hadn't even been selected yet. This was a final meeting with the parties, before the trial began in earnest the following Monday.

"It is very clear that this case is going to generate a great deal of outside interest other than in the courtroom," Dodds went on. "I will expect the demeanor in the courtroom to be such that it's very clear that it's a professional activity we are involved in.

"If it looks to me as if, for any reason, any party is playing to other than the trier of fact or the legal-decision maker, myself, I will call the people down and inform them right on the spot without any question about it. . . . So, let's put it this way: If any remarks are made outside the courtroom that will somehow prejudice this case and end up causing a mistrial, I want it known from the start by all parties that that will be a real expensive proposition for whoever causes it, because I assume the causing party will pay all of the expenses involved in that mistrial."

That admonition notwithstanding, Monzione was glad about this meeting with the judge, because it gave him a chance to request permission to add more experts to his list of witnesses. R. J. Reynolds' lawyers opposed his motion, saying they hadn't been given a chance to take depositions from the new experts. And Dodds wasn't happy about the request, either, chastising Monzione for rushing the case to trial so quickly that he ran out of time for depositions.

"I even invited you to put off the trial date," the judge said sternly. "Mr. Monzione said, 'Let's not put off the trial date. Let's go forward.' I remember your language as something very close to that. You pushed real hard to get to trial. When you do that, you take certain risks. . . . You ran out of time. I was sure that was going to happen from the start."

Next, Dodds laid down some ground rules for the *voir dire* examination of the jury that would be taking place the following week. He admonished the lawyers not to argue the case, "but to discover whether there is any bias or prejudice on the part of the prospective juror. . . . I do not expect an attempt by any counsel to precondition, argue the case. Yet, at the same time, I want to make it clear that counsel will have fairly free reign with regard to questions that don't necessarily relate to the case and the facts of the case, but to the feelings—beliefs of the prospective jurors." Each of the lawyers would be asking his own questions of the people in the jury pool. The judge would be questioning them, too.

Monzione offered a motion to preclude any mention of John Galbraith's visits to a psychologist. Dodds asked F. John Nyhan, one of Reynolds' lead lawyers, whether he intended to mention Galbraith's psychological history in his opening statement. "What is this relevant to?"

"It's relevant to plaintiffs' claim that decedent was addicted to cigarette smoking, your honor," Nyhan replied. "They've put it in issue. . . . Plaintiffs have attempted to portray cigarette smoking as the cause of all the problems Mr. Galbraith suffered. We contend that his health problems were a result of a number of different influences in his life, including his family genetic background, his occupational situation, the stresses at work, the stresses in the family life." Nyhan said all these things together "contributed to the total impact on his physical system."

"The psychiatrist, it's not relevant," the judge finally ruled after more banter between the lawyers. Chalk one up for Monzione.

Now Nyhan had some motions for the judge. He wanted to prohibit any mention of cigarette advertising, since there was no allegation in this case that Galbraith had relied on any ads to start or continue smoking. Dodds gave him that, an important win for the defense.

Nyhan also wanted a ruling that expressly precluded Belli from making inflammatory remarks about the huge size and financial resources of R. J. Reynolds, or about what Belli had previously characterized as malicious conduct by Reynolds.

"This is why I mentioned earlier my comments about mistrials," Dodds answered. "Mr. Belli is here. I read a letter that he wrote to one of the prospective witnesses, somehow indicating that perhaps a whole lot of people were involved in keeping this trial from going forward, including a judge. I don't know what judge Mr. Belli was referring to. I would certainly hope it wasn't this Court." In the sometimes-strange jargon of jurists, the words *court* and *judge* often were synonymous.

"I don't expect counsel to agree with any decision I make. I have no problem with that whatsoever, on any side," Dodds continued. "If you want to comment on that, I am not particularly bothered by that. If you comment on any implication that it was done with bad faith or some kind of conspiracy, I know I'll be real unhappy. I assume you don't intend to go into any of those areas, Mr. Monzione?"

"None of us do," Belli answered, without waiting for Monzione. "If your honor wants me, I will go explicitly into what happened on the prior occasions—"

Dodds: "I don't really care what happened."

Belli: "—of what the tobacco companies did in—"

Dodds: "I don't care what happened before. I am only involved from here on out."

Belli: "I have no intention of doing anything to reflect upon this Court."

Dodds: "Thank you, Mr. Belli."

Sixteen jurors and alternates would be chosen. All sixteen would listen to the trial. Then, at the start of deliberations, they would draw straws to select the twelve who would actually go into the jury room for deliberations. It was a system designed to keep all sixteen attentive during the trial testimony, and to provide a cushion in the event some jurors dropped out during what was expected to be a two-month trial.

Dodds thought it would take two full weeks for all sides to agree on the panel of sixteen jurors and alternates, but Thomas Workman, Nyhan's fifty-eight-year-old senior partner, thought they'd get a jury in a day or two, and Belli thought they'd have a jury by the afternoon of Monday, November 18, the very first day of trial. In fact, Workman's estimate turned out to be the best: The jurors were all in place by Wednesday afternoon.

But not without some fireworks among Belli, the judge, and the Reynolds lawyers.

In open court, Belli told the judge he wanted to reopen questioning of one juror. When Dodds asked him what he wanted to question her about, Belli replied, "The stepped-up advertising campaign," for it was Belli's contention that the cigarette industry was trying to subtly target its freedom-of-choice advertisements to coincide with the Galbraith trial. Dodds, however, had already warned all the lawyers, and Belli in particular, not to so much as mention the word *advertising*, and Workman was at once on his feet, in full view of the jury:

"I object to that, your honor! That is contempt of this Court!"

Dodds immediately summoned all the lawyers into his chambers adjacent to the courtroom.

There were two trials going on—one in public, another carefully shielded from the jurors and the courtroom audience. The judge used frequent conferences like this one, held either at the far side of his bench or in his chambers adjacent to the courtroom, to referee evidentiary disputes and to make comments that might prejudice the jurors if they heard them. A sidebar conference inside the courtroom looked like a football huddle, with the lawyers and the courtroom stenographer drawn tightly around the judge, their discussion audible only as a murmur. In chambers, tensions and voices could rise.

"Mr. Belli, I instructed you not to say anything about advertising under any circumstances. You have specifically, as far as I am concerned, willfully violated the Court's order. I have no idea why you did that. I cannot understand."

"May I explain?" Belli tried to cut in.

"You can when I get done!"

Workman: "For the record, I want to cite Mr. Belli for misconduct of counsel and an attempt to prejudice the jury."

Dodds: "Your conduct is contemptuous of this Court. The Court will make a decision at the end of this case whether we will have a contempt hearing."

Belli: "Let me say this—"

Dodds: "I am not going to—I want you now to know that—"

Belli: "I must put this on the record."

Dodds: "I am going to finish my statement. You're not going to interrupt me."

Belli: "Don't yell at me! Is it something you have against me?"

Dodds: "I am going to finish my sentence and you'll not interrupt me! If you do, you'll spend the rest of the time in the hall, with counsel who knows how to act [staying] in here."

Belli: "I resent that."

Dodds: "You can resent it if you like. If you desire to proceed in this court, you'll follow the rules of this Court. . . . You're going to play by my rules in court."

"Just so the record is completely clear," Belli said the next day, "may we put on the record at this point that I . . . believe—and I am positive and I swear under oath!—that we cannot get a fair trial before this Court. I think it's been evidenced with the threatening to me, and out-and-out pounding on the table by the judge. We cannot get a fair trial."

"You've made your record," Dodds replied evenly. "Let's proceed."

Of the sixteen jurors who were finally seated amid this pandemonium, only two were smokers, and that was a revealing indication of what the Reynolds lawyers had learned during their mock trials. The best jurors, from the defense standpoint, seemed to be those who were independent enough to have made the decision *not* to smoke. They'd truly exercised their freedom to choose, and they had no grounds to resent the cigarette companies for hooking them on a bad habit, as smokers might. Belli was willing to take the nonsmokers, too, but for a different reason: The nonsmokers presumably had good reasons for not smoking, and there was at least a fair chance those reasons were related to the health hazards.

"Are we ready to proceed with opening statements?" a more subdued Dodds asked the following morning. Every seat in the courtroom, more than 100 in all, was filled.

Belli, his trademark red-silk handkerchief flowing from his breast pocket, would go first, for it is the prerogative of the plaintiff to open and close the trial. The reason is simple enough: It's the plaintiff who has the burden of proof.

In the opening statement, a lawyer for each side introduces himself and tells the jury what he intends to prove. He's not supposed to argue his case—that is left for the closing argument—and he's not even supposed to disparage the other side's case. That's something for the closing argument, too.

"I have waited a long time to make this opening statement," Belli began, "but now it's going to be much more brief than I had intended." Belli was subdued, too, because much of the evidence he had intended to bring up—advertisements, the Surgeon General's Reports—had been excluded by Judge Dodds' rulings during the prior three days.

"It's a straight shot now at Reynolds," Belli continued, "whether their brand is carcinogenic, whether it exacerbates, aggravates or causes—"

Workman knew what he was about to hear: The "C" word. At once, he was on his feet. "I think he's arguing, your honor."

"I will allow counsel to make a few preliminary comments."

"—whether it causes *cancer* of the lung," Belli picked up again, "exacerbates, aggravates *cancer* of the lung, or emphysema or cardiac disability."

Belli's case was straightforward. He said he was going to show that cigarettes cause cancer, and that R. J. Reynolds failed to warn people of that danger adequately.

He talked about how John Galbraith first started smoking Camels, at age fifteen, when "he saw a moving picture where Paul Henreid and Bette Davis lit each other's cigarettes."

And Belli directly confronted the freedom-of-choice theme he knew would be central to R. J. Reynolds' defense. "He took the nasal tubes out of his nose so he could smoke a cigarette," Belli said. "This is just shortly before he died. If you have an addiction, you've *lost* your opportunity of freedom of choice, because you can't stop that which you are addicted to."

Now, it was Workman's turn, and he went directly to what Monzione already knew was a fatal flaw in the plaintiff's case.

"There is no evidence," Workman intoned, "that any disease associated with cigarette smoking was a cause of Mr. Galbraith's death.

"Dr. George Fisher, the primary treating physician for Mr. Galbraith's severe lung conditions during the last few years of his life, has already testified on deposition that Mr. Galbraith did not die of cancer." Monzione had been waiting for that.

Galbraith's own doctor, Workman told the jurors, thought other diseases caused Galbraith's death—diseases such as tuberculosis and pulmonary fibrosis that couldn't possibly be related to smoking, diseases that had prematurely killed each of Galbraith's parents, and both of his brothers. John Galbraith, after all, had lived to be a few days short of seventy. His mother had died at forty-nine, his father at sixty-four, and his two brothers at thirty-nine and fifty-two.

Moreover, Workman told the jurors, Galbraith had other habits that jeopardized his health. He drank up to twenty cups of coffee a day, and he regularly consumed as much as a six-pack of beer a day. He enjoyed fatty, greasy foods like hamburgers, steaks, pizzas, and hero sandwiches.

"Notwithstanding the diet," Workman went on, "Mr. Galbraith never had a weight problem because three-fourths of his stomach had been removed back in 1951 because of an ulcer not associated, the evidence will show, with cigarette smoking.

"The evidence will show John Galbraith smoked because he chose to smoke. And, in the words of his widow on deposition, he really enjoyed smoking. To him, the evidence will show, there must have been a benefit.

"As to the addiction claim, we will simply state at this point that the same statistics that are relied upon by Mr. Belli also show that 35 million Americans have been able to quit smoking in the past several years.

"We will show you, as to Mr. Galbraith himself, evidence that, when he made up his mind to, he was able to quit smoking and he did quit smoking."

Finally, Workman presented Reynolds' side of the scientific debate. He said 90 percent of smokers *never* get lung cancer, and that the number of nonsmokers who get it is rising. He said that nicotine isn't the only substance that causes cancer to develop on the skin of rats— that putting tomato juice or dimes on a rat's skin produces cancer, too.

"Statistics," Workman concluded, "don't prove cause. The United States government has not banned cigarettes. . . . The burden of proving the cause of Mr. Galbraith's death is not on my client."

On the following Monday, November 25, Monzione was back in front of Dodds.

"I was defamed in front of the press and members of the public by Mr. Workman, who said I should be disbarred. That is defamation per se in my profession," Monzione complained.

"Bring it up in your new lawsuit," Dodds shot back.

Monzione and Belli were sharing responsibility for their witnesses, with Monzione taking the more difficult task of questioning the medical and scientific experts. Belli would take the first witness that day, though, Galbraith's widow, Elayne. Belli wanted her to go first so he could establish in the minds of the jurors who her husband was: how the two of them met, where they lived, where he worked, what brands of cigarettes he smoked and where he bought them. She had some photographs of her husband in his later years and Belli showed them to the jury, too.

"After John passed away," Belli asked her, "did the question of whether there should be an autopsy come up or not?" Better to get this out in the open now, because his opponents would surely bring it up if Belli didn't.

"No."

"Did you think of getting an autopsy?"

"No."

Belli wanted to know whether Elayne and John had ever discussed anything about his smoking.

"He told me," she replied, "that he was sorry that he had ever started smoking; that he felt that he had been fooled by the tobacco companies and everything that he had read; and that he wished he had believed the federal government."

Now it was Workman's turn to cross-examine Elayne Galbraith. His cross-examination would have to be limited to subjects that Belli had opened up in his direct examination, but, unlike Belli, Workman would have the latitude to ask argumentative or leading questions in his efforts to point up flaws in her testimony. But Elayne Galbraith didn't turn out to be a very cooperative witness.

"Did Dr. Fisher tell you what caused your husband's death?"

"Well, his heart stopped."

The next witness belonged to Monzione. Dr. Michael B. Shimkin was a cancer specialist at the University of California at San Diego Medical School, and it was up to him to establish for the record that smoking could cause the type of lung cancer that Galbraith contracted. Shimkin had been studying lung cancers for forty years, and Monzione questioned him in painstaking detail about the scientific evidence he had collected. That was to pave the way for the payoff question, the point he really wanted to burn into the jury's mind.

"Doctor," Monzione began, "I want you to assume that we have a person who has smoked over forty cigarettes a day for many years, and he develops a squamous cell cancer of the lung. Do you have an opinion as to the cause of that cancer under those circumstances?"

"Yes, I do."

"What is your opinion?"

"Chances are, if not a hundred percent, certainly very high that this was caused by smoking."

"Doctor, are you receiving any fee for your time in this case from the plaintiffs or their attorneys?"

"No," Shimkin replied, "I am not."

"Why is it, Doctor, that you haven't charged a fee in this case for your time?"

"Well, I've dealt with this topic for—"

Robert Weber, another one of the lawyers representing Reynolds, immediately cut in.

"Objection, your honor! Completely irrelevant to any issue before the court!"

"Overruled," Dodds replied firmly. "If it was the other way around, you would be entitled to bring this out. If he is contributing his time and efforts it is equally so."

Monzione began again. "Do you remember the question, Doctor?"

Now Shimkin became the embodiment of the absentminded professor. "About what?"

"Why it is that you're not charging a fee in this case?"

"I feel that it is very important to really tell the American people, through legal channels as well as scientific channels, of the horrible health hazard that smoking, particularly of cigarettes, represents to this country's citizens."

"Thank you, Doctor. No further questions at this time."

Monzione would try to move Fisher, Galbraith's lung doctor, on and off the stand quickly. Reynolds' lawyers would no doubt work him over, and there was nothing Monzione could do about that. The testimony of Fisher was going to be crucial to both sides.

It was clear, from Fisher's answers to Monzione's questions, that Galbraith suffered from many maladies—including a bad back and ulcers—that had no connection to cigarettes. Some of those maladies had, indeed, been listed by Fisher on Galbraith's death certificate. But Fisher had also listed lung cancer and emphysema as two other causes of Galbraith's death, and now Monzione was going for his payoff questions.

"Dr. Fisher," Monzione began, "this is Exhibit Number 40, in evidence. I will ask you, for the jury, to identify that document if you would, please."

"This is the certificate of death for John Galbraith."

"I believe that is your signature at the bottom of the certificate, is that correct, Doctor?"

"Yes, it is."

"Do you have an opinion, Doctor, whether Mr. Galbraith's emphysema was a substantial contributing factor in causing Mr. Galbraith's death?"

"My opinion is that it did."

"Doctor, do you have an opinion whether Mr. Galbraith's lung cancer was a substantial contributing factor in causing Mr. Galbraith's death?"

"My opinion is that it was a significant contributing factor."

"Do you have an opinion as to what caused Mr. Galbraith's lung cancer?"

"Yes, I do."

"What is your opinion?"

"My opinion is that it was caused by his smoking."

"No further questions at this time, your honor. Thank you."

Nyhan was going to take the cross-examination of Fisher. To impeach Fisher, Nyhan would use the doctor's prior deposition answers, the answers that had already proved so nettlesome to Monzione and

Belli. And Nyhan would also hammer away at the fact that an autopsy wasn't performed.

Now, on cross-examination, Fisher seemed to equivocate once again about how much the cancer and emphysema contributed to Galbraith's death.

"Doctor," Nyhan asked, "isn't it also your opinion that Mr. Galbraith's cancer, that you believed he had in 1979, had nothing to do with his death?"

Fisher: "My feeling is that the treatment that we gave him for his cancer—irradiation—contributed to his death because it aggravated his pulmonary fibrosis. I don't believe the cancer itself caused his death or made a significant contribution."

So now Fisher was saying that the *radiation treatment*, and not the cancer itself, was what shortened Galbraith's life.

"Doctor," Nyhan hammered away insistently, "you know of no evidence to say that there was any squamous carcinoma present at the time of Mr. Galbraith's death, do you?"

"No, I do not," Fisher replied, but then he waffled *again*, saying that he had "some question" about whether the cancer might have recurred "just prior to his death."

Nyhan had been waiting for that. He and Monzione walked to the bench and held a whispered conference with Dodds.

"What I want to do," Nyhan told the judge, "is impeach him with his testimony that flatly contradicted his deposition testimony." In a critical blow to the plaintiffs, Dodds gave Nyhan permission to read Fisher's earlier deposition testimony to the jury.

When Monzione called Dr. Raymond Yesner as his final witness on the afternoon of Monday, December 9, his purpose was to knot together all the skeins of testimony that were before the jury. There had been witnesses who spoke of John Galbraith the man, and other witnesses who'd discussed the abstractions of smoking and cancer. But here was an eminent Yale Medical School pathologist, the world's leading expert on the very type of cancer that Galbraith was said to have had. It would be up to Yesner to convince the jury that Galbraith did, in fact, have smoking-induced lung cancer.

Yesner calmly said what Monzione knew he would say: that Galbraith did, indeed, have many things wrong with his heart and lungs, "and he had a carcinoma. All of these things are sufficient to cause the demise of a patient."

"Now, Doctor, do you have an opinion as to whether Mr. Galbraith's cigarette smoking and the illnesses caused by it contributed substantially in causing his death?"

"Yes, it's my belief that it did."

But Nyhan brought out, on cross-examination, that Monzione had consulted Yesner only after another doctor had reviewed Galbraith's case and found that John Galbraith wasn't suffering from cancer at all, but, rather, from a virus he picked up that caused a rare type of benign lung lesion called a papilloma.

In fact, that was going to be a linchpin of Reynolds' case. The cigarette industry lawyers weren't going to deny that there was *something* very wrong with Galbraith's lung. They were simply going to say that it was a viral papilloma, not cancer, and that, without an autopsy, nobody would ever really be able to prove otherwise.

The defense's first witness, James W. Rush, had been John Galbraith's supervisor when Galbraith worked as an office manager for the Occidental Life Insurance Company.

Galbraith, Rush said, had stopped smoking in late 1959, after he had a huge, noncancerous cyst removed from one of his lungs. But he'd also missed a lot of work as a result of that lung surgery, and Rush felt the absences had affected Galbraith's performance. Rush spoke to him about his "sub-par" work in August 1960, and that was when Galbraith's willpower broke down.

"During that conversation, which lasted an hour and a half to maybe two hours, Mr. Galbraith bummed two or three cigarettes from me. . . . The next morning, he arrived at work with a pack of cigarettes, showed them to me, and informed me that I was the cause of him going back on cigarettes."

The implication Reynolds wanted to leave with the jury was that Galbraith wasn't really addicted to cigarettes if he could stop smoking altogether for the better part of a year.

Dr. Roger Bick was an oncologist, or cancer specialist, from Bakersfield, California. He'd reviewed Galbraith's medical records for the cigarette company, and, not surprisingly, he'd formed a contrary opinion about Galbraith's death. "The patient basically died peacefully during his sleep," Bick testified the following Wednesday morning, December 11. "The most likely cause of death was a heart attack or coronary artery clot. . . . I can't find any evidence in the medical records that there was any cancer in him at the time he died." Bick also didn't think the radiation treatments had shortened Galbraith's life at all.

Now it was Monzione's turn to draw some blood on cross-examination.

"Do you have any aversion to cigarette smoking?"

"In general, no," Bick replied.

"I have asked specifically," Monzione persisted. "Do you have any aversion?"

"On occasion, specifically, yes, I do."

A damaging admission.

"Why is that, sir?" Monzione went on.

"Some particular patients that I see, I feel should not be smoking, or should decrease their smoking, so I tell them."

"On what grounds would you instruct a patient not to smoke?"

"Let's say a severe asthmatic, a patient with severe chronic obstructive pulmonary disease."

That was precisely the kind of patient Galbraith was. "Those people shouldn't be smoking?"

"Either that or—I have to look at my patients realistically. If I don't think they are going to absolutely not smoke, I won't tell them absolutely not to smoke because I know I am wasting my breath and will antagonize the patient. I will tell them to cut it in half. I have to live in a world of realism. . . ."

"What are your experiences with patients who smoke?"

"Well," Bick began, "smoking is an identified risk factor with certain pulmonary diseases; and, until we know what that means, it seems logical to try to reduce those risk factors."

"What pulmonary diseases are you talking about?"

"Smoking is an identified risk factor for chronic obstructive pulmonary disease."

"Is that emphysema, Doctor?" Monzione already knew the answer. He was playing this one for the jury.

"Yes."

"What else?"

"Carcinoma of the lung, or lung cancer."

Monzione brought out a few other points. Bick had been doing research for the industry-funded Council for Tobacco Research. And he was also being paid $250 an hour for his consultation and testimony in the case.

Reynolds' star witness appeared in court late the following afternoon.

Arthur Furst was a Stanford University–educated toxicologist, a scientist who studied the adverse effects of chemicals on living systems. Even though he was retired, by his own admission he was "busier now than ever," and much of his time was spent as a consultant to the cigarette industry.

Furst had the distinction of being a scientist who would state categorically that smoking had *not* been proved to cause lung cancer. He was so well known as a protobacco witness that, as a joke, the newsletter *Tobacco on Trial*, published by the Tobacco Products Liability Project at Northeastern University Law School, started the Arthur Furst Award in honor of the professor "who discovered that tobacco does not cause cancer." Furst had done a lot of research on smoking, all right—much of it paid for in full or in part by the industry-funded Council for Tobacco Research, and all of it at least twenty years old!

In his research during the 1960s, Furst studied the effects of cigarette smoke on the lungs by using mice, because their lungs have a cell structure similar to that of humans. He forced the mice to smoke the human equivalent of fifty packs a day. And he never found a single case of lung cancer.

"Doctor," asked Reynolds lawyer Weber, "do you have an opinion, based upon your years of research in this area, based upon the experiments you yourself have conducted, and based upon the reading you've done in the international literature in the many years since that time, as to whether or not it has been proven that smoking causes cancer in humans?"

"Do I have an opinion? Yes, I do."

"Can you state it, sir?"

"On the basis of my own research over many years, and based on all the papers I have read and the people I have talked to, I have come to the conclusion that it's not been proven that cigarette smoke causes cancer."

Belli took the cross-examination. He wanted to bring out the fact that Furst had been conducting industry-sponsored research. And he wanted Furst to acknowledge that, although smoking might not be a *cause* of cancer, it certainly was what scientists called a "risk factor."

"It's a possible [risk] factor," Furst agreed.

"Could it get up to being 'probably' in some cases?"

"In some cases, it may be probably, yes. But we'll have to know the specifics—"

"Wait a minute," Belli broke in. "Could we have the reporter read that back, please?" Belli had a clever way of flagging something he *absolutely* wanted the jury to remember: He'd bring the proceedings to a dead halt and ask the court reporter to read aloud the witness' answer. The judge had caught on, and he'd been waiting for the opportunity to chastise the King of Torts in front of the jury.

"I have noticed that you have a tendency to ask for the answer back when you like the answer," Dodds cut in. "I don't—"

Belli: "I resent that, your honor!"

Dodds: "You can resent it all you like."

Belli: "I resent that. If you want a doctor's certificate I have lost my hearing aid, I will get it."

Dodds: "I am aware of that, but I have also noticed the timing. I suspect—"

Belli: "The record will show I haven't been. I resent that!"

Dodds: "The record will show that you resent it."

Belli: "This has been continuous from the first day! I have tried to be a gentleman and competent lawyer. I have done everything I can. I couldn't do anything more."

Dodds: "It *has* been continuous. Each and every time you asked for the answer, it was when you liked the answer and wanted it repeated."

Belli asked Furst whether it might just be that the mice didn't get cancer, despite their seemingly prodigious consumption of cigarette smoke, because "mice didn't like to smoke." Amid chuckles from the audience, Belli had to insist, "I am very serious."

"Well," Furst deadpanned, "somebody said mice held their breath."

Belli was incredulous. "Are you being serious, too? Did you say mice held their breath?"

"One person," Furst responded, "said the reason you didn't get cancer is because mice would hold their breath when they were in the presence of cigarette smoke. [After that], we definitely proved that mice did inhale the material."

Furst had spent almost all day Friday on the witness stand, but now the end of his testimony was drawing near. So, too, was the conclusion of Reynolds' case. The cigarette industry lawyers were going to put on another witness the following Monday who would testify that Galbraith died not of cancer, but of heart disease and that, given his medical history, Galbraith had actually lived beyond his normal life expectancy. One final witness, an R. J. Reynolds employee, would testify that the company put warning labels on every cigarette package.

Dodds dismissed the jury for the weekend, then told the lawyers to go into the anteroom to his office. Belli was going to get another tongue-lashing for his read-the-answer-back-to-me ploy. "I think the only way to get your attention is to call you down in front of the jury," Dodds told him. "You certainly could care less what I think. I am aware of that. That doesn't matter. I hope you care what the jury thinks. We will start on Monday at nine o'clock. We'll follow the rules or we'll have some problems." Abruptly, Dodds turned and walked away, leaving a forlorn Belli standing there.

"It's my understanding you have a witness on rebuttal you wish to call?" The judge wasn't so much asking Belli as telling everybody else in the room.

"Very short," Belli replied. "Mrs. Galbraith, your honor."

She walked back to the front of the courtroom and took the stand.

"Just a few questions, Mrs. Galbraith. Was Mark ever an alcoholic?"

Elayne Galbraith was stunned. Mark was her son. Belli couldn't even keep that straight. "You mean John?"

"John, I'm sorry."

"Not to my knowledge, he wasn't."

Belli was trying to dilute the effect of some of the things the Reynolds people would surely raise again in their closing argument. They'd raised the alcoholism issue before. They would also keep hammering on the lack of an autopsy.

"There was no autopsy performed on your husband?"

"Objection!" Workman yelled at once. "Leading."

"Sustained," Dodds said. "It suggests an answer."

"Did he have an autopsy?" Belli began again.

"No."

"Why didn't you have an autopsy? Did the family talk about it?"

"Yes, and—well, just Mark and I, the night he died. But John and I had talked about it, and he asked that he not have his teeth in, or his glasses on. He asked not to have the casket opened. He didn't want the children to see him after he died. And he said that he felt he suffered enough—"

Elayne Galbraith started to sob. Workman was trying vainly to get the judge's attention so he could register another hearsay objection.

"—and he didn't want any more done to his body. He'd been sick for so long." Now Elayne Galbraith was racked with sobs. Even Monzione, sitting at the counsel table, felt that he was about to cry.

Workman would be foolish to cross-examine this witness. "No questions, your honor."

Monzione had one more rebuttal witness. He had flown Yesner all the way back from Yale to take issue with the defense theory that Galbraith had a wartlike papilloma virus in his lung, rather than a cancerous tumor.

But on cross-examination, Nyhan landed some blows when he made Yesner admit that, no, Yesner wasn't familiar with some of the recent scientific literature on papilloma viruses, and, no he wasn't a member of the international association that deals with the subject of the human papilloma virus.

"It's outside your area of expertise?"

"Yes, it is," Yesner conceded.

"I want to make clear there will be no appeals to prejudice," Dodds admonished the lawyers in his office right before closing arguments were to begin.

"There will be no mention of big corporations. There will be no mention of lots of counsel. There will be no mention of lots of money by the defense or wealth of any kind, no appeals to sympathy by anybody."

Belli would make the first closing argument. Workman would follow for R. J. Reynolds. Then, since the burden of proof rested with the plaintiffs, Monzione would be allowed a rebuttal.

Belli's was a rambling, folksy stem-winder of a speech. He was turned out in a gray silk-lined suit, and he had the usual red silk handkerchief in his breast pocket. He told the jury that even he, the King of Torts himself, didn't think the case was worth a million dollars, and that it might not even be worth a third of that. Just give me *something* to prove a point, he seemed to be saying.

Alternately strutting, gesturing and pounding the table, Belli appealed to the jurors to think of John Galbraith as a real person, not just as a cause celebre. "Do you remember when I stood up here five weeks ago?" he asked the jury. "Do you remember I said that the man that is before you in spirit is a flesh and blood person; he's an ordinary person?

"You don't pick your clients. But if we could pick a client, we couldn't have picked someone more academically pertinent to this case, because everything he had—all of his emphysema, all of his lung diseases, all the rest of those things—were either caused by smoking or exacerbated by smoking.

"We've got to show to you that smoking of this product is deleterious, to which something now has been added that I present to a jury: First, they catch you and hold you. Then, when you're addicted, you're killed.

"That is strong language. Cancer is a euphonious, gentle sort of a word, but not when you know what it is, not when you see it, not what this man had. If he knew what it was doing to him, really knew, or if he weren't addicted, this man wouldn't have smoked."

Now it was up to Workman to close the case for R. J. Reynolds. "This case is relatively simple," he said. "The plaintiffs have not shown by a preponderance of the evidence that cigarette smoking was a cause of John Galbraith's death eight days before his seventieth birthday. . . . The evidence shows only that Mr. Galbraith died of diseases totally unrelated to cigarette smoking; and that, even if you believe cancer caused"—Workman stumbled; he hadn't meant to say that— "was *somehow involved* in his death, that cancer was cured by the radiation treatment. . . .

"There is no evidence that John Galbraith was addicted to smoking. The evidence only shows that John Galbraith was aware of health hazards associated with smoking. There is no evidence anyone forced him to smoke. The evidence only shows that he freely chose to do so because he liked the taste of it and loved to smoke. That was his right to do in our free society."

Workman had found some fissures in Belli's case, and he kept gouging away at them, widening them more and more. He reminded the jury that even Dr. Fisher, Galbraith's personal physician, didn't think Galbraith had lung cancer when he died. He said Galbraith took off his oxygen mask to sneak a smoke in the final days of his life because "he enjoyed it."

"They didn't even bother to have an autopsy," Workman went on. "You can't blame that on Mrs. Galbraith, but you can sure blame it on their lawyers, because if anyone—if anyone knows the importance of proof in a court of law, it should be Melvin Belli and his young associate, Paul Monzione."

Inside the jury room, the jurors put all their names into a box and pulled out the name of Stacy Proft, a twenty-three-year-old legal secretary. She would be their foreman. Proft had gone into the jury room prepared to vote for Galbraith, but now, as she listened for the first time to her fellow jurors—they had been admonished not to discuss the case among themselves until their deliberations began—Proft began to see the flaws in Belli's case.

The jury's concerns came down to the same two points that the Reynolds lawyers had been pounding away at all during the trial: the lack of an autopsy and the confusion of Dr. Fisher over just what killed Galbraith.

Monzione felt certain he'd lost the case. He was expecting a unanimous defense verdict, and he wasn't sure the jury would stay out for even an hour. So he was surprised when, during the jury's first full day of deliberations on Friday, December 20, they sent out a question to the judge. They wanted Fisher's testimony read back to them again.

That heartened Monzione. He thought it showed that they were locked in serious deliberations. If it had been an open-and-shut case, after all, the jury would have voted once and then been done with it.

In the jury room, though, the consensus was that Belli and Monzione hadn't proved their case because Galbraith had too many other things wrong with him. The jurors only wanted to hear Fisher's deposition testimony once more because they thought it would validate their own misgivings about the medical evidence.

Robert Camp, a thirty-year-old drug store manager who didn't smoke, was one of those who thought the Fisher testimony sealed the case for Reynolds. He looked at the evidence and said, "that doesn't show me that he died from smoking; he died of poor health!" William Stathapoulos, a thirty-seven-year-old computer programmer, who said, "I'd rather be healthy than smoke cigarettes," also was against Galbraith. He had "the little fear that if I voted yes for the plaintiffs, the floodgates would open and you'll have cases of people suing the sugar companies just because this guy got diabetes because he's got so much sugar. So that kind of nagging fear played in the back of my mind."

Monzione blamed Fisher. "It was ill-fated from the start," he said afterward. "You take your case, you put your money into it, your life into it, all this time and energy, and you've got one witness making one sentence, one statement, and the whole thing boiled down to that!"

Monday morning, two days before Christmas and one and a half days after they'd begun their deliberations, the jury returned to the courtroom with a nine-to-three verdict for R. J. Reynolds. If there was any surprise to the verdict at all, it wasn't that Reynolds won—even the plaintiff's lawyers felt in their gut that they had lost—but, rather, that Belli and Monzione had come *within one vote* of a hung jury. The cigarette company had to get at least nine votes to win. That was the law. And that was all Reynolds got—exactly the outcome presaged by the vote at the mock trial months earlier.

The clear inference was that in a stronger case, with a plaintiff whose health history wasn't so confounding, Reynolds might well have lost.

"So they just slipped by," Monzione said later. "They just barely pulled themselves out of that case. We kept a jury out for its third day and it came back nine-to-three against us on a case that, if they had come back in the first twenty minutes with a unanimous verdict for the defendant, would not have surprised me. We did not spend anywhere near the money that the tobacco company did in preparing for the trial. That tells me that the tobacco companies had better watch out because what it comes down to is the jury. Common people applying common sense."

The relieved Reynolds lawyers arranged a lunch for themselves and all the jurors at the nearby University Club. There was a self-serving reason for the lawyers' solicitude. A strange courtship was about to begin between those lawyers and the jurors, because the cigarette people wanted to know as much as possible about what had gone through the minds of the jurors as they listened to the evidence and deliberated. Later on, the Reynolds lawyers would be inviting the jurors into their offices, one at a time, to be interviewed by the psychological consultants who had been running the mock trials and doing the rest of the jury research. The psychologists wanted to know about how the jurors interacted with one another, whom they liked the most, who talked the most, and what they thought of the Reynolds lawyers. This wasn't just a trial, after all; it was a legal laboratory, and the cigarette companies wanted to discover all they could from it.

Outside the courtroom, Belli held his own impromptu news conference. It was vintage Belli, full of blame-placing and bluster and profanity. He blamed Dodds—"the worst judge I've seen in fifty years" —for the loss and vowed to appeal. "I'll come back and try it again," the aged lawyer said. "I don't give up. These bastards [the cigarette companies] are wrong and they're hypocrites. I've got a few dollars to spend and I will, until I catch them."

But Belli had no choice but to give up because, even in victory, Reynolds kept up its scorched-earth defense. Because it won the case, the cigarette company was entitled to reimbursement for $39,000 in court costs, costs that would have to be paid by the Galbraith family out of John's life-insurance money. And Reynolds was, indeed, pressing its claim against the Galbraiths. "A sleazy, greedy thing to do,"

Monzione termed it. "I called them and said, 'If you eat this $39,000, we'll drop the appeal.'" And Reynolds went for the bargain.

So did the stock market. When the Galbraith verdict was announced, R. J. Reynolds' stock immediately rose 5.6 percent at the news.

"It wasn't just good news," *Business Week* wrote; "it was prime-time, stock-price-jump, 'we-told-you-so' news. And what made it even sweeter for the cigarette companies was that one of the big losers was lawyer Melvin Belli."

The tobacco industry had kept its record unblemished ever since. Ten days before the *Galbraith* verdict, a Tennessee judge had dismissed in midtrial another case against R. J. Reynolds. The following June, the six-person Oklahoma City jury in *Marsee v. U.S. Tobacco* had unanimously found after only six hours' deliberations that there wasn't sufficient proof to link nineteen-year-old Sean Marsee's death from tongue cancer to his use of U.S. Tobacco Company's Copenhagen snuff.

That was it. Not only had there not been any big victories for the plaintiffs, but not a single tobacco liability case had even come to trial for a year and a half thereafter. It was hard to decide which was worse: outright losses or the delaying tactics that had stopped whatever momentum the plaintiffs' lawyers once had.

By the end of 1987, though, two new cases were approaching trial, and those who had followed this nascent litigation industry—not just the tobacco industry lawyers, but the stock analysts and everybody else who had some money on the line—were showing great interest in each.

Edell's case was going to come to trial in February of the following year, and the reason for the interest in his *Cipollone* lawsuit was obvious: Edell was going to be the first to use the tobacco companies' heretofore secret documents to prove his case. The more than 100,000 documents Edell had collected as he trolled through the companies' files were still under a protective order, but once the trial began, the best of them would be entered into evidence, and then, once they had been made public, any other plaintiff's lawyer could use them in a case, too. Edell's discovery documents would undoubtedly cause great trouble for the defendants in other cases.

There was obvious benefit to other antitobacco lawyers in what Edell was doing, but no one was pinning great hopes on the beleaguered plaintiff's team of Edell and Walters. Instead, the case that had all the sex appeal—the one that would be featured on "60 Minutes" on the eve of trial—originated a world away from Newark, in Lexington, Mississippi.

Nathan Horton smoked Pall Malls for thirty-seven years, until he died of lung cancer in 1987 at the age of fifty. Represented by a local man named Don Barrett, Horton's wife and son, Ella Mae and Nathan Randall Horton, were suing the American Tobacco Company, and if there were those who saw a chance for a plaintiff's victory in *Horton v. American Tobacco,* their optimism seemed wholly justified.

Horton appeared to be a stronger case than *Cipollone* on every count: An autopsy that clearly showed the link to lung cancer had been conducted on Horton; Rose Cipollone didn't have an autopsy. More importantly, the Mississippi courts had never ruled on issues such as risk-utility or the adequacy of federally mandated warnings, so, unlike the *Cipollone* lawyers, Barrett would have the full range of recovery theories available to him. That was crucial. Barrett also wasn't going to face the same calibre of legal talent as had the other plaintiffs' lawyers. In the *Horton* case, American Tobacco's New York lawyers from the esteemed firm of Chadbourne & Parke were lying low—their pin-striped presence would be a lot more obvious in the hamlet of Lexington than in a city like Newark. American Tobacco's defense was being handled by a couple of local lawyers who were real friendly with their neighbor, Barrett.

Holmes County, where the *Horton* trial would take place in a redbrick courthouse that was built in 1894 and occupied the center of Lexington's town square, was a place that was predominantly poor and black, which meant the average juror would be, too. That was considered a plus for Horton, who was, after all, black and not particularly well off himself.

But the biggest boost came from the way the Mississippi law itself was written. The poorest state in the Union was also one of only ten states that put an extraordinarily permissive spin on personal-injury cases: Even a plaintiff who was 99 percent at fault could recover against a defendant, as long as the plaintiff could prove that the defendant was 1 percent culpable. Mississippi's was a "pure" comparative-fault law, and that meant that even if the jury thought Nathan Horton was almost totally to blame for the smoking habit that caused his cancer, the jurors could still assess damages against American Tobacco. In almost all of the other forty states, including New Jersey, where Rose Cipollone's case was going to be tried, a plaintiff couldn't recover damages unless the defendants were more than 50 percent responsible.

Edell was only too well aware of the long odds against him as he flew to Boston on Saturday, December 5, for a mock trial of his own case.

The tobacco companies weren't the only ones who could afford to do dry runs of their cases. Daynard, the antismoking zealot who ran the Tobacco Products Liability Project from his office at the Northeastern University Law School, offered the use of the law school's mock courtroom for the run-through and split with Edell the $5,000 bill from the company they hired to recruit the jurors, a Boston jury-research company aptly called Trial Run, Inc.

The plan was to present the case simultaneously to two different "juries," each of which would then deliberate separately and come up with a verdict. The Saturday trial would also be recorded and shown on videotape to four more groups on two nights the following week, six mock juries in all, each with nine paid participants who represented a specific demographic group. Using a common jury-research technique that elicited reactions of clusters of people from specific demographic groups, untainted by those from another, one jury was composed of older people and another of young people. Still another had highly educated jurors, while its counterpart group had just the reverse. And, of course, one jury had no smokers, and the other had nobody who *wasn't* a smoker. The jurors were going to listen to Edell and a lawyer playing the role of the defense, and then they were going to discuss the case and vote while others watched. The demographic groups who identified most strongly with Edell and his case would be targeted for the real jury when it was chosen early the following year.

But when Daynard and an associate, David Gidmark, arrived at the law school that Saturday, what they saw was a trial lawyer who seemed ill prepared for the task ahead. Edell's opening statement to the first two panels was flat and unemotional, with none of the fire they'd come to expect from the volatile Edell. His performance was so bad the first day that he cut a whole new videotape that night, to be shown to the remaining four groups of jurors the following week.

Even so, Edell and his client didn't get very far with the mock jurors. During their deliberations, the jurors were asked three questions: Do you believe smoking can cause cancer? What percentage of fault should be allocated to the cigarette companies? What percentage to the smoker? The result wasn't encouraging. Smokers were the worst jurors of all, from the plaintiff's standpoint; they ascribed 90 percent of the fault to Rose Cipollone. The best jurors were blacks and people who were very well educated—but, even then, both groups still thought Rose Cipollone was 60 percent to blame for her cancer.

"Very rough," Gidmark observed. Edell just wasn't, in Gidmark's view, a very "appealing" lawyer to the juries: He didn't convey the pathos of Rose Cipollone's case. The jurors also didn't seem to react well to the *Cipollone* deposition when it was read to them; Edell was encouraged to shorten that part of his case. Gidmark, who followed each case and liked to quote odds at the start of a trial—his own version of the morning line—handicapped this one at four-to-one against Edell—which was just fine with Edell, because he had been following his own agenda during the mock trials.

The young lawyer was innately mistrustful of his opponents, so much so that he sometimes suspected the journalists who interviewed him of being paid agents of the tobacco companies. But his paranoia was running so deep by now that he assumed the companies would have informers among the mock jurors, too. If they're going to report back to the cigarette makers, Edell thought, let their information be *wrong.* He would make sure of that by putting on the worst case imaginable, so that the shadow jurors would lull the tobacco lawyers into thinking they were going up against a real patsy. And that's what he did.

Daynard thought the Horton case was a two-to-one shot, and Gidmark quoted it at three-to-one before the trial began. But as the trial got under way both thought American Tobacco was clearly in trouble. Maybe it was wishful thinking, but Barrett's evidence of all the seemingly bad stuff that went into cigarettes appeared to have the other side alarmed. Barrett's strategy was to put the cigarettes themselves on trial—to tell the jurors that anybody who thought cigarettes were just pure tobacco wrapped in pure paper was dead wrong; that they were really an "adulterated, contaminated bunch of junk" that, unknown to anybody but the tobacco companies, contained such elements as the pesticide DDVP and radioactive polonium 210.

Gidmark, an amiable Canadian who was awed by the different world he found in Mississippi, walked down to the town's only barbershop, as good a place as any to gauge the average man's reaction to what was going on in the courtroom.

"The tobacco company'll win it," one customer told him. "No one forced the man to smoke. No one twisted the man's arm. And the company has all the money to beat it. The company will win. On appeal. The Barretts'll win here, but the company will win it on appeal."

How would he vote if he were on the jury, Gidmark asked him.

"It's hard to say, ya know. Everybody knows that tobacco ain't good for a man. But there's this pesticide stuff. I had just put some pesticide on a cotton field of mine once and my dog ran through it. He died right away. This pesticide is something else again."

But, as frequently happened in such highly publicized cases, what the jurors heard in the courtroom was different from what the outside world, its information flowing through the selective filter of the news media, *thought* the jurors were hearing. It took less than a month for both sides in *Horton v. American Tobacco* to make their case, and it took only two more days after that for the twelve-person jury to become so hopelessly deadlocked that the faction favoring Horton wouldn't even speak to those who sided with American Tobacco. There was no way the jury was going to produce a verdict.

What was worse, from the plaintiffs' side, was the deadlocked vote: seven-to-five *against* Horton. It mattered hardly at all that Barrett later found out that one of the local "jury consultants," a cotton farmer, hired by American Tobacco had spoken with at least three jurors during the trial. As it turned out, two of the three who were purportedly tampered with voted against American Tobacco.

For any cigarette company determined to preserve its record of never having paid or been assessed even one dollar in damages in a cigarette-liability trial, there were, of course, two ways to win: by an outright verdict for the defense or by a mistrial, as had happened here. The plaintiff had the burden of proof, and if he missed by even a single vote the cigarette companies could put another notch in their gun.

The judge in *Horton,* Gray Evans, declared the mistrial at 5 P.M. on Friday, January 29. But, even with a mistrial, Barrett had come closer than any other lawyer to getting a verdict against one of the cigarette companies. *Horton* was the first case in which the verdict wasn't, simply, "not guilty."

And Edell was on deck. The case of *Cipollone v. Liggett Group, Philip Morris, and Loews Theatres* was going to begin the following Monday.

The courtroom where the *Cipollone* case would be tried, Courtroom 5, on the third floor of the main Post Office Building in downtown Newark, looked as if it had been built on a Hollywood set and transported to the most incongruous surroundings imaginable.

Newark itself was a giant combat zone of a city, a big, gutted hulk whose main arteries were clogged with discount stores and boarded-up buildings. The money had moved out and opportunists had come in.

But the third floor of the old federal building was a genteel throwback to the days when courtrooms were built to look the way they ought to, all dressed up with ornate columns and marble. The big granite building had been laid out in 1933, and its Depression-era, WPA-style architecture had worn well in the ensuing decades. A long hall spanned the third floor and big double doors opened to different courtrooms on both sides. You walked down the tile floor in that cavernous hall with a clack-clack-clack that echoed from one end to the other. Benches along the wall were for sneaking a quick smoke or having a whispered conference. Whispers. Always whispers. Maybe it was reverence for the place or maybe it was just nerves, but everything was *sotto voce,* on a need-to-hear basis.

In the center of the hall, beneath soaring skylights, was a statue of

Justice, cleanly done in the art deco style of the period. You could stand outside Courtroom 5, at the far end of that long hall, and see her, arms raised and palms turned upward, beckoning through the smoky haze that caught the sunlight filtering through from above.

The courtroom of Judge Hadden Lee Sarokin was carefully finished in finely carved oak, all varnished and polished. Oak leaves were carved into the cornices, and the plaster detailing in the gilded ceiling was accentuated by hues of yellow, green, lavender and gold. Heavy blue curtains hung around three windows on the left-hand wall, and there were oscillating fans bolted to the paneling on both sides. It was hard to envision needing them in February, but it was a fair bet they would be used before the end of Edell's trial.

Sarokin's courtroom seated seventy-five people on fifteen oak pews. There was room for two counsel tables, the closest one to the jury belonging, as always, to the plaintiffs. The jury sat off to the audience's right on twelve chairs. The witness box, adjacent to the bench, was right between the jury and the judge. Anybody who sat there was no more than a few feet from either one.

It was a courtroom built for the kind of intimate theatre that a good trial always was: no bad seats, only hot ones.

And one of the hottest of all was reserved for Sarokin himself, a judge with decidedly liberal proclivities who had nonetheless managed to frustrate both the plaintiffs, with his decisions taking away their risk-utility and post-1966 failure-to-warn claims, as well as the cigarette companies, who claimed Sarokin was biased and had unsuccessfully sought to have him removed from the case.

At age fifty-nine, Sarokin was lithe of body and wit, a trim, balding man with a fringe of whitish hair and round-framed, tortoise-shell glasses that hovered lightly around his eyes. Sarokin had graduated from Dartmouth in 1950 and had gone on to Harvard Law School, marching quite literally, even then, to a different beat—he'd worked his way through Harvard playing the drums in Boston jazz clubs. Sarokin had been a friend of the basketball star Bill Bradley since he'd done a house closing for Bradley in the early 1970s, and when Bradley ran for the Senate in 1978 Sarokin was his finance chairman. Bradley returned the favor the following year, seeing to Sarokin's presidential nomination for a lifelong appointment to the federal bench in Newark.

In the courtroom that was to be Sarokin's hung the portraits of four former district court judges. Sarokin requested that one more portrait be hung, that of liberal U.S. Supreme Court Justice William J. Brennan, one of New Jersey's own. Appropriately, the Brennan portrait was hung to Sarokin's *left*.

When Sarokin listed the opinions he was proudest of, they were invariably ones that seemed to fly in the face of established legal convention, and that, often as not, had later been reversed by higher courts. Opinions of a liberal mind, most would have called them, and the description certainly was apt. There was the case in which Sarokin invalidated the traditional labor-union rule of last-hired, first-fired, because, he said, it discriminated against minorities and women, an opinion he was later forced to take back after a conflicting ruling by the U.S. Supreme Court. It was also Sarokin who had overturned the triple-murder conviction of Rubin (Hurricane) Carter after the boxer had been imprisoned for nineteen years. Sarokin ruled that the jury verdict against Carter had been "infected" by racial bias and that the prosecution had withheld evidence that could have aided the defense.

Sarokin also considered as one of his finest his decision against the tobacco companies in the *Cipollone* case, holding that the federally mandated warning on cigarette packages and advertising didn't protect tobacco companies from negligence suits like Edell's. But everybody knew what had happened to that one. Ordered by the U.S. Court of Appeals for the Third Circuit to do so, Sarokin had reversed field and issued a new opinion that eviscerated Edell & Co. If Sarokin sometimes gave the impression of being a partisan for the plaintiff, he was also demonstrably capable of laying waste to the most vital parts of Edell's case.

"Mr. Edell?"

Sarokin beckoned to the young lawyer who was now the Great White Hope for all the tobacco plaintiffs. After four and a half years of dogged preparation, Edell was about to deliver the most important opening statement he would probably ever make.

The courtroom's fifteen oak pews were mostly filled with tobacco industry lawyers who would all but take over the place for the months to come, and people were lined up several deep all along the court-room walls. Edell and Walters sat at their counsel table, and Tony Cipollone sat behind them, all alone, nearer the jury. Six lawyers sat at the defense counsel tables pushed together into an L on the far left side of the courtroom, but there were scores more cigarette lawyers in the audience, not just from the three law firms from New York, Kansas City and Washington representing Liggett, Philip Morris and Lorillard, but also from their local counsel—court rules required that a New Jersey lawyer represent each defendant as well.

As had been the case in *Galbraith,* other potential tobacco defendants who thought they had something to learn were using *Cipollone* as a laboratory, too. Lawyers from Jones, Day, Reavis & Pogue in Cleveland, and Paul, Weiss, Rifkind, Wharton & Garrison and Chadbourne & Parke in New York were there as well, representing R. J. Reynolds, Brown & Williamson and American Tobacco, respectively. They were going to show up day after day for as long as the trial lasted, assiduously taking notes and billing their clients for every single hour. Murray Bring, the former Arnold & Porter partner who now was the general counsel of Philip Morris, sat in the courtroom each day, as did Arthur Stevens, the general counsel of Lorillard. Everybody knew everybody else. This was a big party for the observers, one of those rare opportunities to revel in their work for Big Tobacco instead of apologizing for it. Then there were the hangers-on: public relations types for the tobacco companies, and the press, scribblers and sketch artists mostly—no cameras in the courtroom here—who got the two pews closest to the jury.

"Mr. Edell?"

Edell walked up to the lectern. Even though, by tradition, he was going to speak first, he knew he had to be better than the lawyers who would follow him. Intimidation by excellence. And Edell had a strategy for it.

He would memorize his entire opening statement. Speak to the jury for two hours, without notes.

"If it please the Court, counsel, members of the jury, good morning." The obligatory greeting.

"My name is Marc Edell. I am an attorney, and I represent Rose Cipollone, who is no longer with us, and Antonio Cipollone, sitting over here.

"I'm sure, when you heard that this case was about a lady who smoked cigarettes and died of lung cancer, you may have scratched your head and said, Why is she in court?

"Well, we are going to tell you why she is in court, because it is not that simple.

"This case is about a lot more, as you are going to see. You will be the first people to see. You are going to be the first people ever, outside of the private doors and offices of the tobacco industry, to find out the truth about what has happened. Not yesterday, not 1988, 1987, 1986 or 1984—not what we know *now* about cigarette smoking and health, but we are going to go all the way back to 1923, because that is when it begins."

Edell was laying the groundwork for all the documents he was going to introduce. Because the tobacco companies had obtained a protective order on everything they'd turned over to Edell, only he and a few of his associates knew, until this moment, just how explosive those documents were. What Edell had found, and what he was going to tell the jury about on this very first day of trial, were scores of documents going back more than sixty years that showed the two faces of the cigarette industry.

Putting the documents into evidence wasn't just a crucial part of his strategy; it was also what made his case different from every other cigarette-liability lawsuit that had ever been filed by any other lawyer. Without the careful groundwork that Edell had laid through his years of document analysis, a lawyer was in the uncomfortable position of being forced to prove to a jury, as Belli had tried and failed to do, not only that smoking caused cancer, but also that smoking-induced cancer was the cause of the plaintiff's death. What happened in such a case was that the plaintiff and his conduct became the main issue of the trial.

Having studied the *Galbraith* case, Edell knew that he had to make the cigarette companies' conduct the focal point of the trial, and he could do that by using the documents to show that they engaged in what amounted to a conspiracy to mislead the public about the dangers of smoking. He wouldn't have to put on a strictly medical case. Instead, he would use the heretofore-secret documents to prove that the cigarette companies knew much more about the dangers of smoking than they ever told the public, and that by being untruthful they

induced Rose Cipollone to take up a dangerous habit. Whether she
had the kind of cancer that could be linked to smoking would still be
an issue, of course. But corporate conspiracy and misconduct would
be the emphases of his plea for punitive damages against the cigarette
makers. It would be weeks before he ever put on a single witness to
testify about Rose.

"This case is about an industry that decided not to study their
product, not to research, not to test," Edell continued now.

"This case is about an industry that not only didn't warn, not only
didn't test, but you are going to see this case is about an industry that
misled Rose Cipollone and the others of her generation that started
smoking cigarettes.

"This case is about an industry that worse than not warning, worse
than not testing, went ahead and suppressed important information,
suppressed information that would have helped scientists and medical
doctors, that would have provided information so that Rose Cipollone, like everybody else, could expect to make a free choice.

"That is right. A free choice. Because we believe in free choice.
But free choice is nothing unless it's an informed choice!"

Edell had studied the *Galbraith* transcript, and he thus anticipated
that "freedom of choice" would be a major defense argument. His
opponents were going to say that people who smoked had all the
information they needed, and that they chose to smoke because they
liked it. Nobody had ever been able to induce a jury to decide otherwise. But Edell was going to turn that "freedom of choice" logic
around and aim it against the tobacco companies. The documents, he
said, would prove that smokers like Rose Cipollone had really been
deceived into making the wrong "choice."

Edell also believed that jurors wanted to see a good fight, wanted to
see blood. And he was going to spill some.

"This case is about an industry not having warned, not having
tested, suppressed information, misled Rose Cipollone and others,
that turns around and says: Mrs. Cipollone, if you trusted us, if you
thought we would warn, and if you thought we would test, and if you
believed our statements in the press, if you believed our advertisements, if you were *stupid* enough to believe us, then you deserve what
you get!"

Edell was rocking along now, driven by pure emotion. "Thank God for adrenal glands," he would later say.

"I know that is a strong statement, but let me tell you we spent four and a half years gathering together the information from their secret files, taking depositions." Edell digressed briefly to patiently explain what a deposition was, then he fired himself up again: "We spent four and a half years looking through their files pursuant to court orders, taking their depositions of the chief executive officers. We know the truth! You will see the truth and you will see that this is an industry that sacrificed the lives of people like Rose Cipollone for one thing: Money. Dollars.

"They'll talk about personal responsibility during the course of this trial"—that was another tobacco industry argument, another spin on free choice—"and everybody has personal responsibility. The executives that ran these companies have personal responsibility. The corporations have personal responsibility. *You* are going to decide whose responsibility it was."

It was bombastic, it was great theatre, and, more than anything else, it was effective.

Edell intended to take the initiative at the very outset by delivering what amounted to a *closing* argument—a recitation of all his evidence, all his witnesses, and repeated slams at all the arguments he expected the companies to use. "Your opening statement should be your summation, if you can get away with it," Edell would say afterward. "This was just as close as I could get."

Edell walked the jury through the stages of Rose's early smoking: Chesterfields from 1942 to 1958, then L&M until 1968. Both of those brands were made by Liggett, and because she smoked them before the federally mandated warnings appeared in 1966, Liggett was still liable for the pre-1966 failure-to-warn counts while the other two defendants—Philip Morris, whose Virginia Slims and Parliaments she smoked from 1968 through 1974, and Lorillard, whose True brand she smoked from 1974 until 1982—were not.

Edell had also obtained evidence that he thought showed that the companies could have made a safer cigarette, one that didn't cause cancer, but that they decided not to because of fear that making it would be an admission that their earlier products hadn't been safe.

The young lawyer told the jurors the significance of the year 1923

that he'd earlier mentioned. That was the earliest year in which he'd
found allusions to the connection between smoking and cancer in the
scientific literature—"literature that would have put manufacturers
on notice that they should have tested and researched their product."

Document by document, Edell took the jurors up a verbal time
line. "Well, we move up to 1953." That was when a scientist was first
able to paint a cigarette-smoke condensate on the backs of mice and
produce tumors. Publicly, the cigarette companies kept right on denying that their product caused cancer. But privately, Edell said, the
documents he had found "talk about continuing public relations research, not scientific research. Public relations research!"

When Liggett finally did its own in-house mouse-painting studies,
it confirmed what the 1953 study had found.

"Did they tell anybody about it? No. Why didn't they tell anybody? Why didn't they publish this information? They didn't do it
because they were afraid, just like about the safer cigarette, they were
afraid if they published this information, if they made it available,
they would lose sales and it would expose them to liability suits for all
the years that they have sold the product knowing that it caused
cancer, and they didn't do anything about it." Even after the industry
formed its own Council for Tobacco Research, to award research
grants for the study of the link between smoking and disease, the
people who attended the grant-giving meetings were, in Edell's
words, "lawyers, lawyers, lawyers, lawyers, lawyers, not even in-
house lawyers—they had their litigation counsel present!

"You know what? They knew that their program was working.
They knew they were convincing people that cigarette smoking really
hadn't been proven to be the cause of disease. They knew Rose
Cipollone and others like her trusted them. Believed them. . . .

"For nearly thirty years this industry has employed a single strategy, to defend itself, on three major fronts: litigation, politics, and
public opinions. Not health. Not the welfare of the customers.

"What have they done? Created doubt about the health charge,
without actually denying it. 'It hasn't been proven.' Does that have a
familiar ring? That has been their campaign. . . .

"I wouldn't be surprised if they talk to you about social acceptabil-
ity, not directly, but I wouldn't be surprised if you hear in this case
from their very mouth how much a part of America tobacco is. It's

part of America because they *designed* it that way, because they advertised their product and people didn't know about the hazards.
. . . And then, in the early 1950s when cigarette smoking and health appeared in the press, they start saying, 'Chesterfield,' the cigarette that Rose Cipollone smoked, 'is best for you. We've done studies to see what the scientists really think about this.' First to present scientific evidence: Ed Sullivan. He died of lung cancer. Arthur Godfrey, same endorsement, he died of lung cancer. 'No effect to nose, throat and accessory organs.' Here it is! 'First such report ever published about any cigarette.' That's a pretty bold statement."

As an indication of just how thorough he'd been, Edell had located the doctor Liggett relied on in making that 1952 claim about Chesterfield. In a deposition, the doctor told Edell he didn't agree with the claim.

"Members of the jury," Edell intoned more reverently now, signaling that he was about to finish, "freedom of choice is a very, very important part of our lives. It is one of the basic things that make America great. We don't argue that. You will hear a lot about freedom of choice in this case.

"Rose Cipollone made a free choice. You will hear that Rose Cipollone made a free choice and she chose to believe the tobacco companies. She chose to believe if there was really something wrong, they would have told her. She chose to believe they would have researched. She chose to believe in the people that sold her a product for thirty-eight years."

But those same people were now insisting, Edell argued, that "because Rose Cipollone was dumb enough to believe us, if she was stupid enough to take our words at face value—that if our product caused cancer, we wouldn't sell it; that it has not been proven—then she deserves what she gets! It's her personal responsibility.

"Members of the jury, this case is about freedom of choice. Freedom of choice that *they* made." Edell motioned toward the defense table. "*They* had a choice whether to warn Rose Cipollone and millions of other people. . . . *They* made their free choice because *they* knew all the facts, unlike Rose Cipollone."

Every word dripped with bitterness. Edell, the smallest man among all the lawyers at those counsel tables, was the giant now as he stood before the jury. Nobody could take that away from him. He was

landing hard blows on the other side, preempting their best arguments and paying them back for all the trouble they'd shoveled his
way during the long march into this courtroom. Edell was practiced
enough to keep his cool, but this was personal, you bet it was, and
Edell meant to beat them. Right here.

He walked over and pointed to the rail that separated the jurors
from the rest of the courtroom.

"Members of the jury, this box, this box that surrounds you is
impenetrable. Their money, their influences can't reach you there. We
are confident that once you hear all of the evidence, once you see
information that no one has ever seen before, once you understand
the full story, you will come back with a verdict for Rose Cipollone."

Peter Bleakley, the main lawyer for Philip Morris, had been sitting
there at the defense table, doing a slow burn along with all the other
lawyers at what he viewed as the improper tactics of Edell. The judge
had extracted a promise from both sides not to object to the other's
opening statement. Fair enough, Bleakley thought. But Edell had
given a *closing* argument, not an opening statement, and turnabout
was fair play now. The judge had also asked the defense lawyers not
to douse the jury with too heavy a dose of mom, apple pie and the
American flag in their own opening statements—that was invariably
what happened whenever the "freedom of choice" argument was fully
unfurled—but Bleakley was damned if he'd be bound by that promise
any longer.

Instead, he opened with his own patriotic tribute to Philip Morris
—"not just a cigarette company," but one that marketed Miller Lite
beer ("advertised on television by Rodney Dangerfield and his
friends") and Maxwell House coffee and Jell-O. "You've seen Bill
Cosby advertise Jell-O on TV," Bleakley veritably implored as he
tried to find his common ground with the twelve jurors who were
sitting before him. (Only six would actually deliberate; they would be
chosen by lot at the end of the trial.)

It wasn't just Philip Morris that he saluted. Almost as if he were
consciously following the script that had just been laid out for him by
Edell, Bleakley went on to suggest that there was something admira-
ble, even true-blue American, about cigarettes and tobacco. He in-

voked the names of people like Columbus, Pershing, Franklin Roosevelt, MacArthur and Eisenhower, the latter of whom, Bleakley solemnly noted, "smoked cigarettes while he planned the Allied invasion of North Africa during 1941." That's what he said.

Bleakley, a curly haired, bespectacled fifty-one-year-old from the Washington firm of Arnold & Porter, brought a brooding intensity into the courtroom, and if he stayed in such excellent shape that he looked a good ten years younger than his actual age, perhaps it was because he'd literally sweated the years off through the anxious figeting and pacing that became his trademark at the trial.

The abrasive Bleakley didn't care who he insulted. He made it no secret during the frequent sidebar conferences that he thought Sarokin favored Edell, telling Sarokin at one point that the judge was "making the assumption, as you have done repeatedly, that whatever Mr. Edell asserts is fact." As for Edell, Bleakley pointedly told him he ought to "examine the texts and the cases on how to conduct cross-examination." The Arnold & Porter lawyer obviously thought he had a thing or two to teach the young lawyer from West Orange, New Jersey. And the judge, too, for that matter.

Bleakley at ease in the courtroom was Bleakley perched on a window sill or Bleakley arrogantly stalking the courtroom's perimeter while court was in session, brow furrowed and left hand grasping his chin. Murray Bring, the Philip Morris general counsel who was Bleakley's former law partner, sat in the courtroom audience right behind him, occasionally passing notes up to Bleakley or signaling to him like some limpid third-base coach. "These are his boys," Edell said of Bring's Arnold & Porter team at the counsel table.

The problem Bleakley had with the case was the one every other tobacco industry lawyer had, too. He couldn't come right out and say that smoking was unhealthy, but he had to put on enough evidence to make it clear that anyone who smoked had plenty of warning about its evil effects. How to do that? Put the warnings in somebody else's mouth. "Remember King James?" Bleakley now asked the jurors. "He was responsible for the King James version of the Bible." Well, King James had banned smoking as "dangerous to the lungs" more than three hundred years ago in England. Why, the Puritans had banned smoking, too, and the Sultan of Turkey once made it punishable by death. Somebody had even run for president in the 1920s on an antismoking platform.

Rose Cipollone knew the risk, too, Bleakley continued. She'd remembered during her deposition, he told the jurors, that cigarettes were called " 'coffin nails' or 'cancer sticks.' . . . And what you will learn in this case is that she knew all the time she smoked there was a risk involved in smoking. That is the issue."

Donald Cohn, fifty-eight years old, was from the Park Avenue firm of Webster & Sheffield. He was credentialed, of course: Princeton, Yale Law, a fellow of the American College of Trial Lawyers. He had been representing Liggett for nearly thirty years, long enough to have also defended his client during the earlier wave of cigarette-liability lawsuits, too.

Edell knew only too well the outcome of Cohn's 1969 trial for Liggett. The five-week federal trial in Detroit had produced a verdict for Liggett—and such scathing judicial criticism of Liggett's "sophisticated and calculated" evasiveness, if not outright misconduct, that the judge in the case said he would have granted a new trial if the plaintiff's five-man Saginaw, Michigan, law firm could have afforded it. It couldn't. That was the problem every plaintiff's lawyer, even Belli, inevitably faced whenever one of them tangled with a cigarette company.

Portly and balding and a little more rumpled than his compatriots, Cohn wore half-glasses that rode low on the bridge of his nose. There was an air about Cohn that rubbed Edell the wrong way, and he wondered whether the jury felt it, too. Cohn had this way of rocking on his heels and flashing big, toothy grins toward the jury box when Cohn wanted them to think he'd just scored a point. What really grated with Edell was that Cohn usually hadn't scored a damn thing! Sometimes, Cohn would shuffle over to the box and stand alongside the jurors as he made his points, almost as if he intended to climb over the rail and sit right in there with them. It was as if Cohn thought that his ear-to-ear version of a big-timer's rapport with the jury was all it would take to win this case.

"These lawyers are the best," Edell would say later on during the trial, as his animus for Cohn deepened. "But Cohn is a schmuck. If I lose, he's the one guy I'll feel bad about losing to."

Cohn opened with one of the most specious arguments of all: that

Liggett couldn't possibly be blamed for Rose Cipollone's death because she was still perfectly healthy in 1968, when she stopped smoking Liggett products and switched to a new brand. If she became sick
from cigarettes, he was saying, it was on somebody else's watch. His
argument totally ignored cancer's long incubation time.

When it came time to rebut Edell's contention that Liggett could
have marketed a safer cigarette, Cohn had an equally facile reply:
The safer cigarette, which would have used heavy metals in the filter
tip to remove carcinogens, couldn't have been brought to market
before 1981 because the necessary testing wouldn't have been done
before then, "when Mrs. Cipollone was [already] ill. So, in the last
analysis, it's all irrelevant."

As an indication of just how closely the cigarette companies
worked together, the Kansas City, Missouri, law firm of Shook, Hardy
& Bacon not only represented Lorillard but also shared the representation of Philip Morris with Arnold & Porter. Robert Northrip, a
husky, slow-moving forty-eight-year-old man who spoke in a soft Missouri drawl, was the chief of the Kansas City firm's trial team, and he
had been given the responsibility for staging the companies' medical
defense against Edell's claims. That was a crucial role, because even
if Edell could prove everything he said he could about corporate
misconduct and conspiracy, all that mattered not a whit if Northrip
could prove that Cipollone hadn't had smoking-related cancer. Northrip's part of the case was the safety valve by which all the defendants could still escape liability.

And the unassuming, impassive Northrip proved to be just the
right man for the task. Anyone who didn't take him seriously at the
start of the trial would certainly see him by the end of it as the living
embodiment of the name of his birthplace: Sleeper, Missouri.

Northrip had obviously mastered the medical complexities of the
case, and what he now did in his opening statement was to walk the
jury through a scenario that made it seem at least plausible that Rose
Cipollone's cancer wasn't related to smoking at all.

Whereas Edell maintained that Cipollone had small-cell carcinoma
of the type definitely associated with smoking, Northrip claimed she
had atypical carcinoma, which, he said, wasn't associated with smoking.

Northrip had a few things going for his argument. The pathologist who first diagnosed her cancer, Sheldon Sommers, had called it atypical. Further, atypical cancers grew slowly; the average survival time for a patient following diagnosis was two to four years; quick-growing small-cell cancers usually killed the patient within a year. Rose Cipollone lived more than three years after her cancer was discovered.

The Kansas City lawyer also used the flip side of the argument made earlier by Cohn. Whereas Cohn had said that Liggett wasn't culpable because Cipollone hadn't become ill while she was smoking Liggett's brands, now Northrip said Lorillard shouldn't be liable, either, because Cipollone should have stopped smoking when the warnings first appeared on cigarette packages in 1966, while she was still smoking the Liggett brands that Cohn claimed hadn't hurt her, either. "When a woman stops smoking for fifteen years," he insisted, "her statistical risk of getting lung cancer is no greater than that of a nonsmoker." That, Northrip said, was what Edell's own experts' testimony would confirm. The buck-passing that was going on was phenomenal.

With the opening statements completed and the jury dismissed for the day, Sarokin asked the lawyers who'd remained at their counsel tables whether they wished to object to anything that they'd heard in the opening statements. He had specifically asked them not to interfere with the opening statements while they were in progress.

Edell now immediately stood up and raised a series of seemingly petty objections about Bleakley's opening. The strident Bleakley had obviously annoyed Edell with his repeated prediction that Edell wouldn't be able to meet his burden of proof, and with his contention that if warnings had been necessary earlier than 1966 the federal government would have required them. He also was irritated by Northrip's comment that if Cipollone had stopped smoking she wouldn't have gotten cancer.

When Bleakley stood up to defend himself, he got help from Cohn. "That was a closing Mr. Edell gave, more than an opening"—well, Cohn had seen it for what Edell wanted it to be—"and there didn't seem to be much point in objecting. We had the opportunity to meet it in our openings."

Straight off, Edell had given Bleakley a taste of just how contentious he could be, and Bleakley indicated that he was going to reply in kind. He started ticking off in a stacatto baritone his own nitpicks about Edell's opening, "some of which I don't think I would have bothered with." Bleakley finally got to the last one on his list:

"I might add that the claim that Arthur Godfrey died of lung cancer is factually inaccurate. Arthur Godfrey had lung cancer when he was forty-three years old, lived for thirty years thereafter and died of a stroke.

"I'm not objecting to that, your honor— "

Sarokin: "All right."

"—just pointing out a factual inaccuracy."

It was going to be that kind of trial. "If this case turns on how Arthur Godfrey dies—" Sarokin's comment trailed off. He didn't need to finish it.

Edell was going to spend a full week on his first witness, Dr. Jeffrey Harris, a professor at the Harvard Medical School and the Massachusetts Institute of Technology. Harris, forty years old, had gone through mountains of company documents and old medical-journal articles, many written even before he'd been born, to establish the crucial first part of Edell's case: the scope of the tobacco companies' early knowledge about the hazards of smoking.

In legal parlance, Harris' testimony pertained to what was called the medical and scientific state-of-the-art about smoking. To establish that, Harris had logged all the early journal articles into a computer data base, so that they constituted a chronology of what the cigarette companies *should have* known, and when they *should have* known it. Harris had listed 100 important medical-journal articles that appeared between 1923 and 1954 and that linked cigarettes to health dangers.

The first time Edell's paralegal assistant, Nelson Thayer, saw Harris' list, he started laughing: The printout was a twenty-foot-long scroll that, Thayer predicted, would shock both the jury and the cigarette companies when they saw its full length.

The young paralegal was reminded of the scene in the movie *Blazing Saddles* when the swaggering new black sheriff addressed his all-white constituents. "Excuse me while I whip this out," began the sheriff amid swoons all around, and then he reached down into his pants to produce: the text of his first speech. Every time Edell asked Thayer for a citation from Harris' scroll, the paralegal replied in a basso profundo voice: "Excuse me while I whip this out!" He envisioned Edell surprising the cigarette lawyers with the scroll, just as actor Cleavon Little had in the movie. Thayer and Harris started calling the twenty-foot-long scroll "Blazing Saddles," and before long, Edell and everybody else on the plaintiff's team was jokingly calling it that, too.

Harris' testimony was important in another way, too. By reviewing the internal corporate documents that Edell had subpoenaed, Harris could also testify as to *what* the companies actually knew, and *when* they knew it. Juxtaposed against Blazing Saddles, the evidence of the companies' actual knowledge about the hazards of smoking was compelling.

Harris testified, for instance, that two years after the seminal 1953 mouse-painting studies conducted by Dr. Ernest Wynder, Liggett secretly hired the consulting company of Arthur D. Little, Inc., to see whether it could replicate Wynder's results with four of Liggett's own brands, including both Chesterfields and L&Ms, the two Liggett brands that Cipollone smoked. Even though the consultant's tests did, indeed, replicate the results, Little didn't report the results for another seven years, and, when it finally did so, neither Liggett nor the tested brands was identified.

"I would have recommended . . . immediate publication" of the test results, Harris testified. He also brought out another document that showed the two faces that the cigarette makers were putting on the medical case against smoking: a memo from someone at Arthur D. Little to Liggett which flatly stated: "There are biologically active materials present in cigarette tobacco. These are a) cancer-causing [and] b) cancer promoting." The rigorous discovery conducted by Edell had yielded quite a few such gems. In the process, Edell had turned the tables on the tobacco companies by being the first lawyer to ruthlessly dig up dirt against them. Always in the past, it had been the other way around.

Edell used the second week of the trial to make his case about the safer cigarette. Edell's alternative-safer-design claim was based on the theory that Liggett scientists had invented a cigarette that used heavy metals to filter out cancerous substances, but that Liggett hadn't marketed the safer cigarette for fear that doing so would acknowledge the hazards in earlier cigarettes.

His star witness for this part of the case was Dr. James Mold, a Liggett scientist and assistant research director for twenty-nine years who'd had his deposition taken by Edell and the defense lawyers the month before at the county courthouse in Durham, North Carolina. Durham was Mold's hometown, and it was also the location of Liggett's headquarters.

Edell had videotaped the entire Mold deposition, so that what the jury would see beginning on February 11 and continuing into the following week was a witness testifying before them on two television monitors. The lawyers had already agreed on what would be shown and what would be left out, and the videotape had been edited accordingly.

Mold's testimony was damaging, too. Edell first asked him about the Arthur D. Little research that Harris had told the jury about the week before:

"Did Liggett advise its consumers, the people who they were selling their cigarettes to, that they were able to get tumors as a result of applying this smoke condensate on the backs of mice?"

"Not to my knowledge."

"Do you know why they didn't inform their consumers, sir?"

"I wouldn't have any basis for that," Mold replied.

"When did you first realize that there were, in fact, [cancer] promoters and carcinogens in smoke condensate?"

"Probably in the early sixties or late fifties."

"Did you publish this information, sir?"

"No, we did not."

The lawyers from Webster & Sheffield had met with Mold on three different occasions to coach him on answering Edell's questions, and those sessions had produced a witness who volunteered little information and answered the questions as cryptically as possible. But no amount of coaching could erase the fact that the heavy-metal filter invented by Mold, which used palladium to neutralize the carcinogenic effect of cigarette tars, had lowered the incidence of tumors in mouse skin-painting tests by 89 to 100 percent, more information that Edell had first gleaned from the smoking-gun documents. Worse from Liggett's standpoint was the fate that had befallen the safer cigarette. Although Liggett had patented it in 1977, the company hadn't marketed the cigarette and had even prevented Mold from publishing his findings about it.

There was, Mold testified, "continual footdragging by the Legal Department. Whenever any problem came up in the project, the Legal Department would pounce upon that in an attempt to kill the project, and this happened time and time again. So, at this point in time, when they say, 'Well, you can't publish a paper,' we didn't ask why. We knew why."

"You ultimately did, however, produce a cigarette that you thought would be beneficial to smokers, isn't that right?" Edell asked. Every lawyer present objected to the leading question, but Mold responded anyway.

"We produced a cigarette which was, we felt, commercially acceptable. . . . We felt that the cigarette was certainly in the direction of one containing less hazardous materials."

"Well, Doctor, was it your opinion that it was a safer product for human beings to smoke?"

"We could only conclude that if it had removed a number of the materials or lessened some of them that had been pointed to as hazards, that it would be safer, yes."

"Are you still of the opinion, sir, that you did develop a safer product to smoke?"

"With whatever tests we could perform, it should have been safer, yes."

"Safer for human beings to smoke?" Edell wanted to make absolutely sure the jury got it.

"Right. Right."

"Did Liggett ever tell the public it had developed a safer cigarette?"

"I'm sure they didn't characterize it as a safer cigarette. That was never talked [about] in those terms."

There was a certain irony to Liggett's conduct during those early days, when the industry's advertisements assured a concerned public that cigarettes were "Just What the Doctor Ordered" and showed the brain machine, called the "Acuray," that assured a safe cigarette. It was obvious, by the evidence Edell had discovered in the company's files, that Liggett had done the right thing by testing and trying to find a safer cigarette. Liggett had even stayed out of the weak, industry-sponsored Council for Tobacco Research, except for the years 1964 through 1968, so as to pursue its own ambitious research. In short, the company had done what it should have done, but instead of publicizing its findings it had hidden them behind a curtain of puffery, making health claims about cigarettes that its officers knew, or clearly should have known, were false.

As always happened in trials like this, there were two parallel proceedings going on in Sarokin's courtroom, one for the jury's consumption and another behind the scenes. It was the latter, carried out in whispered sidebars when the jury was present and sometimes in heated exchanges when they weren't, that often settled crucial evidentiary and procedural questions.

"Counsel, remain," Sarokin demanded after Edell had finished playing the Mold deposition to the jury on Wednesday, February 17. "I want to ask a question."

Sarokin still had much of the trial lawyer in him, and he had already shown himself to be a blistering questioner when he thought a witness was being evasive. Now, Sarokin wanted to quarrel about an objection that Liggett had made to the Mold testimony: "Just for clarification, and I obviously didn't want to do this in the presence of the jury, do the defendants contend in this litigation what is asserted here on page thirty-three under 'Mold redirect,' namely, that, in reference to the mice experiments, that 'said experiments prove nothing about the possible effects of smoking on humans. The industry has maintained that such a link has not been established.'? Is that a contention in this trial?"

Cohn proffered a reply. "The contention, your honor, is that animal experiments cannot be extrapolated to man, and—"

Sarokin shot back: "What about the patent application? What's the significance of presenting for—as an invention the fact that they rely upon mice studies? I assume you don't expect to sell these cigarettes to mice."

"No, your honor," Cohn politely replied.

There were nervous giggles from the cigarette people in the audience. Cindy Walters turned to her left and looked at Edell, a slight smile tracing her lips. Sarokin was trying to tie the bumbling Cohn into knots on this one, and despite all his efforts to the contrary it appeared that Cohn was going to aid Sarokin in the task. His vulnerability was part of the classic dilemma of trying to deny that smoking caused cancer while saying that smokers assumed a known risk.

Cohn was trying to persuade Sarokin that even though Liggett didn't believe that the mouse studies proved anything at all, it nonetheless assigned Mold to replicate the Wynder study and saw good reason to cite the absence of tumors in mouse studies later on in its patent application for the heavy-metal filter.

"In other words," Cohn tried to argue, "they are in the classic situation: damned if they do and they're damned if they don't. What my client determined to do was to say, We'd rather take the risk of being damned for doing something than for doing nothing. That's what they did and, sure enough, it happened. They did a lot of good work—"

Sarokin cut him off. "Does it seem to suggest that if the mouse— the mice studies are beneficial, that you rely on them but if they're negative, you reject them?"

"No, that's not the case at all."

"Tell me," Sarokin continued, suppressing a facetious grin, "in the application for a patent then, why you would rely upon them, the mice studies, to support the patent application if it had no relation to humans?"

Cohn jabbered on. He was saying now that the mouse studies were being used in the patent application to show that what Edell was calling the safer cigarette was just "different. That doesn't mean it's healthier or safer; it is different."

Sarokin: "All right. So, in answer to my question, what you're saying is you still maintain that, as stated here, that such experiments proved nothing about the possible effects of smoking on humans. That's going to be the position the defendants take in this case?"

Bleakley popped to his feet like a suddenly uncoiled spring. He was better than any of his colleagues at summoning indignation from his vast resources of bile, and now his anger was manifest.

"That's *not* the position of the defendants in this case!" Bleakley shouted back at the judge, leaving Cohn nonplussed and rendering him silent. Cohn raised his right hand like a policeman motioning traffic to stop, but the obviously agitated Bleakley charged ahead. "The position of the defendants in this case is that the plaintiff will not prove by a preponderance of the evidence that she became ill and died as a result of smoking the defendant's cigarettes."

The louder Bleakley got, the more perfectly parsed his sentences became.

"I'm not going to fall into the trap that the plaintiff is constantly trying to make us fall into of defending the issue of whether mice skin-painting experiments prove or don't prove the issue in this case!" At least Edell was getting that theory across. Maybe the jury had caught on, too. "We're not going to argue to the jury that cigarette smoking doesn't cause lung cancer. We didn't argue that in the opening. We're not arguing it today and we're not going to argue it to the jury in closing and it's not the issue in this case. The issue in this case is whether the plaintiff suffered and died from lung cancer as a result of smoking defendant's cigarettes. Now—"

"Do you mean," Sarokin challenged Bleakley, "it will not be disputed in this case that cigarette smoking causes lung cancer?" Amplified by the only microphone in the courtroom, his voice resonated throughout the chamber.

"No, that is not the position. It is our position, and we will continue to argue, that the evidence does not prove that cigarette smoking causes lung cancer, first—"

"I thought you just said it *wouldn't* be disputed," Sarokin shot back, and Bleakley just as quickly corrected the record.

It was obvious that Edell wasn't the only person who was frustrated by the obviously contradictory positions taken by the cigarette manufacturers. Bleakley and his compatriots were telling the judge that they were entitled to interpret the evidence however it suited them at the moment—on one hand, they could say the risk from smoking was nonexistent, and, on the other, that people who smoked assumed a known risk. They could do that. It might not make sense, but it was the way the legal process worked.

"More people who smoke get lung cancer than who don't smoke," a defiant Bleakley told Sarokin. "We're going to have that evidence paraded before this jury for a long, long time. We're going to hear evidence before this jury that Mrs. Cipollone heard that evidence.

"You bet I'm going to take the position that I am entitled to argue that Mrs. Cipollone was aware of that evidence, and you bet I'm going to argue that her awareness is an appropriate defense for us in this case!"

Sarokin: "Even though you contend, or may contend, that the risk was nonexistent?"

Bleakley momentarily stumbled and then firmly replied, "Yes. The answer to that question is yes. I would take that position. You bet."

Sarokin was a partisan, too. The judge knew how to make it clear that he couldn't believe what he was hearing.

When the trial began, Sarokin had offered to let both sides use as a storage room the small anteroom, normally the judge's robing room, that was set off to the side of the courtroom. The defense lawyers chose to store their trial records and exhibits at another downtown office, which meant that Edell and Walters and their paralegal Thayer had taken over the robing room by default. With acoustical ceilings falling down and papers strewn everywhere, the ten-by-twelve-foot room was where the three took their breaks, charted their strategy, ate the turkey-and-swiss-on-rye sandwiches one of them carried back each day at lunch time from a little shop around the corner called Sandwichtown. A filing cabinet maintained by Thayer contained all the "Blazing Saddles" documents, their name and exact location stored in the memory of the only data bank Edell's firm could afford: Thayer himself.

Over the usual from Sandwichtown, Thayer was preparing Edell for the afternoon's reading of two depositions, those of Milton Harrington, the former chief executive officer of Liggett, and Kinsley vanR. Dey, Liggett's current president and CEO. Depositions were read into evidence when witnesses were from outside the state or were otherwise beyond the subpoena authority of the court, as was the case with Dey; or, where the witness was dead. Harrington was dead. Since Edell hadn't videotaped the depositions, an actor would sit in the box and play the role of each witness, reading the actual replies to each of Edell's questions. It had the same weight as live testimony.

"Where's the good stuff?" Edell demanded with an impish grin as he saw Thayer examine one of the corporate documents that would shortly be introduced.

Thayer proudly read aloud a passage from one of the documents that showed the industry was more concerned about public relations than about doing good research: " 'We must look for the opportunity to influence the media, et cetera.' I think that shows some pretty good CIA-type activities."

Milton Harrington had gone to work for Liggett at age twenty-six as a factory manager, after graduating from Duke and playing minor-league baseball for two years. It was the start of a career that would span thirty-nine years and take him far from the warehouse floor to a nine-year stint in the CEO's office.

Harrington's deposition answers, which were read to the jury by a young, bearded actor and lawyer named George Gorchala, were incredible for the stonewalling they demonstrated by the company's most senior officers. If there were a problem with cigarettes, Liggett's top people clearly didn't want to know about it.

"When you joined Liggett on a full-time basis in 1934, did you receive any information concerning smoking and health?"

"No."

"Did you ever receive any information from Liggett concerning cigarette smoking and health?"

"No. I mean, I didn't receive any letters or word or anything from the officials of the company about smoking and health."

"Did you ever hear that cigarette smoking might be harmful to your health?"

"The first real time that I heard that was after the Surgeon General's committee report that said that it might be harmful to your health."

"So the first time that you—"

"First time I paid any attention to it, anyway. I didn't believe it then."

Harrington told Edell it never occurred to him that a warning label should be placed on cigarette packages. "I didn't think it was necessary."

Why not? Edell wanted to know.

"Just because."

"Because why?"

"No reason for it."

"No reason for placing a caution label on packages of cigarettes regarding the potential health hazards relating to it?"

"Not in my opinion."

"Upon what facts did you base that opinion?"

"None. Just my thoughts."

Harrington was unreconstructed in his loathing for the intereference of government warning regulations and do-gooders like Edell. "We didn't care to warn the public about anything. We just had to put that warning on [in 1966]," he told the young lawyer. "It wasn't because we liked to. It was just something we had to do. We weren't interested in warning the public about something."

Edell had divided his case into discrete sections: an overview of what the companies knew and when they knew it was provided by his first expert, Harris; then the evidence on alternative safer design and Liggett's efforts to cover up its safer cigarette. During that same phase, the jury heard witnesses and saw documents revealing that the tobacco companies were frequently more concerned about preserving their public relations image than about conducting serious research into the perils of smoking.

A new phase of Edell's case was going to begin on Monday, February 29. That was when Darnell, who was being allowed to participate in a limited way in the Cipollone case despite the tobacco industry's success at having him disqualified from new cases, was going to start presenting evidence on the addictive nature of cigarettes.

Darnell's first addiction witness, former Philip Morris chairman Joseph F. Cullman III, had already been on the stand three days. Now, on the fourth, Darnell questioned the dapper executive about a 1980 document from the Philip Morris files that said nicotine had "powerful" effects on the body and "may be the most important component of cigarette smoke." The company scientist's memo also said: "Nicotine and an understanding of its properties are important to the continued well being of our cigarette business since [it]has been cited often as 'the reason for smoking.' "

Yes, Cullman acknowledged, nicotine was a drug. But, well prepared by a consultant who'd told him just how to dress and sit and speak to the jury, the executive told Darnell that his company was selling cigarettes, not nicotine—a product, not a drug. And Cullman said Philip Morris was "delighted to bring tar and nicotine levels down." No, Cullman suavely testified with a charm that could talk the socks right off a rooster, Philip Morris didn't think it was necessary to have some minimum level of nicotine in its cigarettes.

Disqualified from future cases and deprived of fees for his further work in this one, a discouraged Darnell had stayed away from the courtroom until now. He didn't have the rhythm of the place, and, interrogating Cullman woodenly from a script, he didn't seem able to follow Cullman's feints to his questions. Instead of asking a follow-up question, Darnell would stand there, appearing not to know where to go next. Then he'd just proceed down to the next question on his list.

Edell and Walters were aghast. Darnell's nervous tic had become so pronounced that the jurors were becoming noticeably uncomfortable.

"We're losing it. Right here, we're losing all the ground we've gained," Walters said. "The jurors have daggers in their eyes."

"This is painful," Edell agreed.

Edell didn't want to be the one to tell Darnell just how badly he was doing. But Walters, a former New Jersey probation officer who, at age thirty-eight, was well into her second career, was unfettered by the kind of frat-brother bond that Edell and Darnell had. After Darnell had spent one more day in a tortured examination of their next witness, a crucial one on the issue of addiction, Walters walked up to Darnell and said, gently but firmly, "I think the jury is attached to Marc. It would be better if Marc went back to them." That was it. Darnell got the message and rarely returned to the courtroom after that.

Each morning as the jurors filed in, Tony Cipollone, a small man with a hopeful air about him, would slip up to the front of the courtroom and quietly assume his regular seat, slightly to Edell's right, against the rail separating the audience from the lawyers. Whenever the jurors filed back out, he would repeat the procedure in reverse, walking silently to the back bench in the courtroom and sitting down beside his second wife, Doris. The two of them commuted an hour and a half each way, every day, from their retirement home in Leisure Village near Lakehurst, New Jersey. They kept to themselves, sitting quietly on the benches in the hallway outside the courtroom before court began in the morning; walking incongruously up and down the hallway, back and forth past Lady Justice, during the breaks, speaking to no one. Tony Cipollone favored sweater vests rather than sport coats or suits, and he wore his bright blue one frequently. It stood out against the sea of dark suits in the audience behind him.

When he talked to Edell, Tony Cipollone, more so than his new wife, was usually upbeat, optimistic. We're winning, he'd say. It's going great. Cindy Walters had that same sense of confidence and tried to keep Edell pumped up. But Edell was the jaded one, the guy who swallowed his nervous energy and lost ten pounds during the first month of the case, the guy who dared not look beyond the current witness for fear of what he would find.

"I look at every defense witness as the most important witness," Edell explained. "I say to myself, 'If I don't *get* that witness, I'll *lose* the case.' I don't look ahead. I don't have a good sense of whether we're winning or losing." In the early days, as he was putting on his own case, Edell felt confident, well prepared. But Edell didn't have enough time to prepare each night for the cross-examination that would come the following day. The defense lawyers used a platoon system—one group would handle the courtroom chores while another huddled away from court, getting ready for a later witness. But Edell didn't have a back-up platoon to call in. He was outnumbered at least thirty-two-to-three by the lawyers and paralegals spending full time in the courtroom for the other side. What was amazing was that Edell was able to mount any effective cross-examination at all, forced, as he was, to hurriedly prepare at the counsel table or during evenings at home.

Edell could feel the trial taking its toll. "I'm getting more and more frustrated," he complained as the litigation went into its third month and he found himself hopelessly outnumbered by the cigarette defense lawyers who threw witness after witness at him as they put on their case. Sarokin had issued a ruling two weeks earlier that effectively gutted much of Edell's case, and the Cipollone team had experienced a real letdown, made worse by the fact that they'd been given a long-scheduled one-week break that only allowed Edell and Walters more time to brood about the ruling.

At the conclusion of the plaintiff's case, it was customary for the defendant to ask the judge for a directed verdict of acquittal. The request asked the judge to rule, in effect, that the plaintiffs had put on such a weak case that the defendants shouldn't even have to reply to it. It was a boilerplate motion, and it was also one that was usually denied because the federal rules required evidence to be viewed most favorably to the party *not* making the request. In this case, it meant that Sarokin had to give Edell every benefit of the doubt in weighing whether to rule against him.

Even so, the judge stunned Edell and Walters by totally throwing out their safer-cigarette claim—one they'd spent weeks of court time painstakingly trying to prove—saying that there was no evidence that Rose Cipollone would have smoked the safer cigarette even if it had been put on the market. Sarokin also granted directed verdicts for Philip Morris and Lorillard on the breach-of-warranty and pre-1966 failure-to-warn counts, because Cipollone hadn't smoked their cigarettes until *after* 1966, when the federal labeling law started protecting them from such claims.

That left Liggett, whose cigarettes Cipollone had smoked before the federal warnings began, hanging out with much more potential exposure to damages than the other two defendants. It also left all three defendants still facing Edell's conspiracy allegations and the threat of punitive damages. Sarokin expressly left those in the case, issuing a tart thirty-three-page opinion on April 21 that said the jurors could reasonably conclude that Edell had proved the major part of his case.

It was the kind of opinion the irrepressible Sarokin was known for, an activist's unbridled comment on the evidence he had been silently watching amassed.

"The evidence presented also permits the jury to find a tobacco industry conspiracy, vast in its scope, devious in its purpose and devastating in its results," Sarokin wrote. "The jury may reasonably conclude that defendants were members of and engaged in that conspiracy with full knowledge and disregard for the illness and death it would cause, and that Mrs. Cipollone was merely one of its victims.

. . . If the jury accepts the plaintiff's version of the facts as to the conduct of the defendants, it is difficult to envision a more compelling case for an award of punitive damages."

Once again, Sarokin had aimed his harshest words at the cigarette makers but saved most of the body blows for Edell and Walters. With Sarokin's directed-verdict ruling, there was almost nothing left of Edell's original case. Moreover, now the cigarette companies were asking for a mistrial on the ground that Edell's evidence about the safer cigarette—evidence that even Sarokin agreed hadn't met Edell's burden of proof—had poisoned the trial. Sarokin denied the motion and sent everybody off on the long-scheduled week of vacation. Walters felt refreshed, but Edell considered the time off "a waste. Broke my stride."

Edell likened his long struggle against the cigarette lawyers to a marathon. "When you start the case you're like a trained marathon runner. But you get to the start and then they take away your shoes. Then you start running and they break your arm. You keep going and then they cut off one of your legs. Still, you keep running."

Wednesday, March 23. Seven weeks into the trial, Edell's final witness in the causation phase of the trial was completing his testimony. After that, the plaintiff's team would bring up Rose Cipollone's family —Tony Cipollone's testimony about his wife's dying in his arms would clearly be the most moving—and then Edell was going to rest.

Leonard Schuman, a professor at the University of Minnesota School of Public Health, was the only witness who'd also been a member of the Surgeon General's committee that produced the landmark 1964 report on the dangers of smoking. He'd never testified in court before. White-haired and jowly, sporting a pencil-thin moustache and wearing horn-rimmed glasses, Schuman was the quintessential professor, patiently lecturing the lawyers in a fatherly tone on the etiology, the *cause*, of lung cancer, and, even more important from Edell's standpoint, on the scientific and medical state-of-the-art in the 1940s, when Rose Cipollone was taking up the habit and when Schuman was a young researcher. Edell was trying to use Schuman to show the jurors that, long before even the mouse-painting experiments, respected researchers were raising serious questions about the health effects of cigarette smoking.

And the tobacco industry lawyers were doing their best to bloody Edell's witness before the jury.

Schuman was vulnerable on the issue of the 1940s state-of-the-art, because he had only recently finished his schooling then and he obviously hadn't personally conducted any of the applicable research at that time. Edell had used his direct questioning of Schuman to try to bring out that Schuman hadn't just read the early articles that he was referring to in his testimony, but that he had also discussed the 1940s state-of-the-art with one of the most respected researchers of that period, a chest surgeon named Alton Ochsner. Ochsner and Schuman had served together on the Surgeon General's committee that produced the 1964 report.

Over Edell's heated objections, Bleakley was using his cross-examination to try to show, as he explained to the judge, that "this man did nothing in the way of his own research to reach these opinions, that what he did is he simply read Jeffrey Harris' report and adopted it. . . . He doesn't know what he's talking about when we go back to the thirties and forties."

Bleakley walked to the lectern, leaving it exactly where Edell had placed it, ten feet from the witness stand. But Bleakley rarely questioned a witness very long from there. He was a pacer, a lawyer most at home questioning a witness while he walked between lectern and counsel table and witness box.

"You said you talked to Dr. Ochsner, who was one of those doing research in the thirties and forties. When did you talk to him?"

"As I said, I don't recall. It was after the Surgeon General's report had been released."

"Did you talk to Dr. Ochsner about what he thought the state-of-the-art was in the thirties and forties?"

"Wasn't put that way. No."

"Do you know what Dr. Ochsner thought about the state of the art in the thirties and forties?"

"Well, he was—he remained convinced that his impressions at the time were correct. That subsequent events had proved him correct, even though his impressions were clinical observations."

"Is it your testimony that Dr. Ochsner's impressions in the forties were that cigarette smoking had been proven to be an etiological factor in causation of lung cancer?"

"I do not recall his using the word 'proven.' . . . He felt convinced that because virtually every case of lung cancer that he operated on had been in heavy smokers, that that was responsible for the lung cancer."

Having nailed down Schuman's version of events, Bleakley now wanted to show Schuman some documents, documents that clearly seemed to raise questions about Schuman's story. Bleakley turned and walked back to his counsel table, picked up two medical-journal articles, and, arms folded across his chest, wheeled back toward Schuman, who by now was so dry-mouthed that he had to ask Bleakley to pour him some water.

The two journal articles which were written by Ochsner, one in 1946 and the second, coauthored by Dr. Michael DeBakey, in 1947, both contained statements that seemed to clearly contradict what Schuman had just said about Ochsner's position on the link between smoking and lung cancer. Bleakley read the sections aloud and handed the entire articles to Schuman. "No factor was found which might bear a significant relationship to the recurrence of the disease," one said. "Occupation and smoking . . . were found to have no special significance," said the second.

It was a damaging cross-examination from the defense team's most fearsome lawyer, but Schuman kept insisting that the quotes were being taken out of context and that Ochsner couldn't possibly have meant what this sounded like. Bleakley kept hammering back, forcing Schuman to admit that, at least in those two articles, Ochsner hadn't described a connection between smoking and cancer.

"Your testimony was that Dr. Ochsner thought in the 1940s that smoking was an etiological factor?" Bleakley asked Schuman again.

"That is what he expressed to me in the sixties at the time of that meeting."

"But you know now that isn't what he said in the article he wrote in '46?"

"But I insist that there seems to be an inherent contradiction here."

One of the forty-four tobacco people in the audience flashed a thumbs-up sign to John Scanlon, the New York public-relations guru who specialized in handling the press at big, splashy trials like this one. Scanlon was a roguish man, short and burly with curly salt-and-pepper hair, a florid face and a white beard. Splayed out across one of the rear pews, half listening to the proceedings, he was also the only person who refused to stand, as ordered by the bailiff, when the jury entered or left the courtroom.

It was Scanlon who'd handled the media at the 1985 libel trial of *Westmoreland v. CBS*, and he'd perfected the art of litigation PR in the process. Scanlon and his five aides ran a positive-spin machine, feeding reporters whatever transcripts and story ideas favored the defense. And they seemed to be enjoying this witness.

True, it wasn't going well for Schuman. Edell beckoned to his paralegal, Thayer, who walked over and crouched down alongside the plaintiff's table so he could hear Edell's whispered instruction. "Run back there and get Blazing Saddles," Edell told him. "Look up all the other articles by Ochsner and bring me any that contradict the ones Bleakley has."

Bleakley was still going at it. "Did you know," he asked, "that researchers back in the 1930s were able to produce tumors on the backs of laboratory animals by painting destructive distillates of a lot of things other than tobacco?"

"No, I was not. I don't recall being aware of that."

"Did you know that they produced tumors, for example, by painting destructive distillates of coffee on the backs of animals?"

"No."

"Or tea?"

"No."

"Or human skin?"

"No."

"I have no further questions." Bleakley had given the courtroom a textbook lesson on the art of cross-examination, moving in quickly on Schuman and finishing him off strongly. The courtroom was awash in smiles and nods from the tobacco people.

But by the time Northrip and Cohn had finished their cross-examination of Schuman, Thayer had found the Blazing Saddles articles that Edell wanted, and Edell walked back to the witness box with renewed confidence.

"Mr. Bleakley didn't provide you with copies of other papers written by Dr. Ochsner and others in which he expressed other opinions, did he, sir?"

"No, he did not."

Edell now proceeded to bring out that Bleakley had conveniently passed over a 1939 article by Ochsner that said, "inhaled smoke . . . undoubtedly" was a source of chronic bronchial irritation, an important article because it showed that Ochsner had made up his mind long before he wrote the articles Bleakley had cited.

Bleakley had also conveniently left out a 1945 article in which Ochsner stated that "the increased incidence of lung cancer is due to the increased incidence of smoking," as well as a 1952 article— important because it showed that Ochsner's position had been consistent over the years—that said, "it appears, without a doubt, that inhalation of cigarette smoke exerts a carcinogenic effect upon bronchial mucosa, and it can be predicted that if cigarette smoking continues at the present rate or if it increases as it has in the past, the future incidence of bronchogenic carcinoma will be many times that of other cancers of the body." There was even another 1947 article by Ochsner and DeBakey, but this one, just like all the others, characterized the increase in bronchogenic carcinoma as "probably due to the carcinogenic effect of cigarette smoking."

"Did he read you that?"

"No. He did not."

If Edell's redirect examination was devastating in its own right, it also had far exceeded the bounds of permissible questioning, because the kind of leading questions he was asking were only permitted during a cross-examination. Edell had been reading from journal articles, making speeches rather than asking questions; Schuman was just replying yes or no. But Edell guessed, correctly, that Bleakley wasn't going to object. "When you put it up another lawyer's ass and he knows you did that to him, he's afraid to object because it draws more attention to what's being done."

"We made out okay—this time," Thayer said with a grin once Edell had finished.

Scanlon walked up to the front of the courtroom and pulled aside one of the regular reporters so he could put the industry spin on the morning's events.

Edell ambled over, too, and leaned over the rail. "What?" Edell said with mock surprise to a nonplussed Scanlon. "You're not *sleep-ing?* I thought you had narcolepsy!" Scanlon had been dozing in the courtroom the day before.

Edell turned to the reporter. "That's how he can make those outrageous statements to you! He sleeps through all the testimony, then he comes up and says to you: 'Lemme tell ya what happened today.'" Edell spun around and walked away, a big smile painted across his face.

By now, there was nothing particularly mysterious about the case the cigarette companies would present. The strategy was to deny the connection between smoking and cancer; assert that Rose Cipollone nonetheless freely assumed a known risk; and, if both of those gambits failed, deny that her particular cancer was in any way related to smoking.

They intended to trot out all the usual suspects, including Arthur Furst, the Stanford University toxicologist who'd been testifying for the industry since 1960 that an association between smoking and cancer hasn't been proved, but who hadn't published an article on smoking and lung cancer in twenty years.

The defense also brought in a University of Michigan marketing professor who testified that the $250,000 an hour spent by the tobacco industry on cigarette advertising had "relatively small or no impact" on a person's decision to take up the habit. And they presented a University of Connecticut economics professor who'd been charged with gathering together anything and everything he could find in Rose Cipollone's "information environment" that related to the hazards of smoking. He said the books, magazines, newspapers and television shows she saw abounded with dire warnings about smoking. But Edell was able to bring out on cross-examination that the ratio of cigarette advertising to all advertising in those media was much greater than the ratio of smoking and health news to all stories. In other words, Edell's cross-examination revealed, the prosmoking advertisements overwhelmed whatever antismoking information Rose Cipollone saw.

For Edell, though, the most problematic part of the defense presentation was going to be the medical evidence about Rose Cipollone's fatal cancer. The link between small-cell lung cancer and smoking was clear, but the tobacco lawyers insisted Rose had atypical carcinoma, a very rare variety that wasn't so clearly linked to smoking.

What made Edell's task infinitely more difficult was that the pathologist who first diagnosed Cipollone's cancer as an atypical carcinoma was, quite literally, in the hip pocket of the tobacco industry, having gone to work as the $150,000-a-year research director of the Council for Tobacco Research (CTR) just one week after he made the diagnosis at New York's Lenox Hill Hospital.

Sheldon C. Sommers had remained in that tobacco industry job until the end of 1987, and even now he was still a consultant to the CTR and a valued expert in Big Tobacco's stable of witnesses. Sommers had been consulted in the *Galbraith* case, too, although he'd never been called as a witness at the trial.

With every motive to skew his testimony to favor his employer, the seventy-one-year-old Sommers was going to get up on the stand on April 19 and repeat his firm belief that Rose Cipollone didn't have smoking-related cancer, testimony contradicted by every other pathologist and treating physician who had seen the tissue in 1983, during her final operation for removal of a cancerous adrenal gland.

Edell and Walters were going to double-team Sommers, with Edell first cross-examining the doctor on his work for the industry-funded Council for Tobacco Research and Walters questioning him closely on his specific diagnosis of Rose Cipollone's cancer. It was going to be the most tense cross-examination Edell would confront, for the elderly Sommers was nonetheless a cagey, well-schooled witness who had testified many times before, and he was going to volunteer absolutely nothing to Edell. Sommers was determined to make Edell work hard to earn any admissions from him.

"You told us yesterday that you believe that cigarette smoking is a risk factor. Is that correct?" Edell was laying the groundwork for showing the jury just how far out of the mainstream of medicine this doctor was.

"I agree that it is a risk factor," Sommers replied.

"Does that mean it's a possible cause of lung cancer?"

"Yes."

"But it hasn't been proven that it *is* a cause of lung cancer; is that your testimony?"

"I consider it has not been proved."

"Do you know of any research organization of scientists that have considered the issue of cigarette smoking and lung cancer and have taken the stand that it hasn't been proven, other than the Council for Tobacco Research?"

Edell knew the answer to that question already. He'd had a paralegal contact every scientific organization to verify their positions on the connection between smoking and lung cancer, and he'd listed all the responses on a huge chart that he could drag into the courtroom and place on an easel in front of the jury. On one side were scores of organizations that considered smoking to be the principal cause of lung cancer. On the other side was one name: the Council for Tobacco Research.

Sommers tried not to step into Edell's trap. He quibbled with the characterization of CTR as a "scientific" organization. It was a "funding organization," Sommers contended, one that just doled out research grants. Besides, the doctor went on, what group of scientists *wouldn't* be expected to call smoking dangerous? It was like saying that driving faster than fifty-five miles an hour was hazardous. Big deal.

"Dr. Sommers, we're not talking about automobiles here. We're talking about cigarettes and lung cancer, with all due respect."

Now Edell asked his question again. And, again, Sommers refused to answer. This time, he snapped his own lawyerlike objection from the witness box: "All right. Answered."

Now Sarokin told Sommers to answer.

"Already answered."

Edell asked the question a third time. And a fourth. Finally, Sommers yielded. He didn't know of any organizations that didn't think the link between smoking and cancer had already been proved.

Hasn't the federal government also concluded that cigarette smoking is the major cause of lung cancer in the United States? Edell asked.

"The Surgeon General so claims," the crusty doctor replied. "It just doesn't have any acceptable scientific basis. . . . I know the Surgeon General holds these opinions. He is a pediatric surgeon."

Sommers had a one-word description for all those things that the Surgeon General had been saying about cigarettes: "Sad."

But Edell wanted to push Sommers further. The doctor had already acknowledged, after all, that smoking was a possible cause of lung cancer. So Edell was going to surprise Sommers by asking him to quantify that risk factor for the jury.

Edell walked over to a large white pad on an easel propped in front of the jury. Carefully, he used a felt marking pen to draw a horizontal line across the big sheet of paper. On the left end of the line, Edell drew a hash mark and wrote above it, "No Evidence." Then he put a second mark on the right-hand side and wrote, "Proven."

"I'd like you to come down for a second, if you would, sir."

Sommers stepped out of the box and joined Edell in front of the easel.

Make your mark, Edell instructed: "Where on this evidential line does your opinion fall, in terms of possibilities? Is it right over here, over here, over here, over here?" Edell pointed to different spots on the line. He wanted Sommers to make a mark that represented the weight of the evidence about smoking's relationship to lung cancer. "Where is it on this line, sir?"

Sommers resisted. But Edell kept coming back at him. Sommers had, after all, weighed all the medical evidence in coming to his opinion that a connection hadn't been proved, right? Well, Edell demanded, there must be *some* evidence on the other side. "We know we're past No Evidence? Is that right?"

"There is clearly evidence," Sommers grudgingly conceded.

Edell smiled a little bit inside. Now he was getting somewhere.

Sommers finally said he could provide the estimate that Edell wanted if someone would give him a pencil and paper and a few minutes to make some calculations. Sarokin called a twenty-minute recess and told Sommers to do his figuring in the back row of the courtroom.

Edell was pleased. But this was definitely not what the defense lawyers had in mind. Keeping the causation issue as cloudy as possible was a major defense strategy in this trial, and the suddenly compliant Sommers was about to blow it.

Out of the jury's earshot, Edell asked for an assurance that none of the defense lawyers would say anything to Sommers until he'd finished his calculations. He didn't want any defense signals sent to the doctor.

"I won't talk to them," Sommers volunteered.

But the defense lawyers walked all over Sommers' line. And two of them, Cohn and Patrick Sirridge, the latter a lawyer from Northrip's firm, were so angry about what they thought was Edell's badgering of Sommers that they said they wouldn't voluntarily accede to Edell's request. They wanted to be able to talk to their man. It was tough lawyering with a hollow threat, though, because Sarokin could have the final word by simply entering an order on the spot prohibiting all the defense lawyers from talking to Sommers. And that's exactly what he did.

Sommers was going to return to the easel to make his mark, but not before another acrimonious sidebar in which the defense lawyers made one more effort to halt Edell's efforts. Bleakley accused Edell of "trying to demonstrate how clever he is at trying to tie up the witness."

Sommers, Edell retorted, was "not a newcomer to this courtroom. I think he is purposefully taking advantage of his age and going through theatrics that are unnecessary and inappropriate and he knows it and is taking advantage of it."

Sarokin: "Let's get going."

This time, it all fell into place for Edell. He posed his question again, and Sommers walked to the easel to assign probabilities to the link between cancer and four different types of lung cancer: small-cell cancer, the type everyone but Sommers said Rose Cipollone had, 45 to 55 percent; adenocarcinoma, 20 percent; squamous cell carcinoma, 25 percent; and large-cell undifferentiated cancer, nearly none.

The percentages were clearly shaded to favor the tobacco industry. But, even so, no representative of Big Tobacco had ever so directly acknowledged the relationship between smoking and lung cancer— indeed, Sommers himself had called the cause of lung cancer "a biological mystery" in his own 1982 testimony before Congress. In a grueling cross-examination that had taken nearly the entire day, Edell had wrung a damaging admission from a key industry scientist. It would be hard for the tobacco lawyers to use Sommers in any future case.

Tuesday, May 10. Sarokin's directed-verdict order of a few weeks before had gutted much of Edell's case against Philip Morris and Lorillard, the two companies whose cigarettes Rose Cipollone didn't use until after the federally mandated warnings began. Liggett had the most at risk now.

But fraud and conspiracy counts still survived against all three cigarette companies, and Edell had found enough incriminating material in the companies' files to cause serious problems for the only in-house scientist who was still around from the industry's glory days.

Alexander Spears, a frail man whose colorful outfit, a yellow button-down shirt and red tie, meshed incongruously with his silver wire-rimmed eyeglasses and close-cropped fringe of white hair, was Lorillard's research director. He was a scientist, surely, but he was also a man who appeared to never forget who his employer was. The company line was that the link between lung cancer and smoking wasn't proved.

"You either conclude that it is or is not [proved]," Spears testified with the kind of stupefying nonchalance that marked all the tobacco industry witnesses. "It is not a probability or possibility. I mean, *everything* is a possibility, obviously."

In March of 1980, Spears' counterpart at Philip Morris had forwarded to Spears some Philip Morris recommendations for industry research. Edell had the document. Now, he flashed it onto a screen for all the jurors to read:

"Subjects to be avoided by industry-funded research:

"—Developing new tests for carcinogenicity;

"—Avoiding any attempt to relate human disease to smoking;

"—Avoiding any research which involves experiments which require large doses of carcinogens to show additive effect of smoking."

Spears was a well-prepared witness, replying to Edell's angry questions in a monotone and yielding nothing to his adversary. Even when confronted with this document, as he now was, Spears denied the public relations emphasis of the industry-sponsored research he and his counterpart at Philip Morris supported through the Council for Tobacco Research.

"Isn't it a fact," Edell intoned, "that the industry used research from the Council for Tobacco Research for public relations purposes?"

"Well," Spears replied slowly, "I think most of the documents that came out of CTR were scientific documents, along with their annual reports."

"Isn't it correct, sir," Edell demanded again, "that CTR and the research funded by CTR was used by the industry for public relations purposes?"

"I am trying to think of some documents or some instance of that," Spears answered flatly, "and I don't come up with any."

Edell had begun his setup of this amnesic witness. The sting was to come.

"Let us look at *your* document," Edell shot back. He pulled out a confidential 1974 memorandum Spears himself had written to Lorillard's chief executive and read from it: " 'Historically, the joint industry-funded smoking and health research programs have not been selected against specific scientific goals, but rather for various purposes such as public relations, political relations, position for litigations, et cetera.'

"Remember discussing that?"

"Yes," Spears answered, a little more subdued now.

"This doesn't refresh your memory that the research funded by the Council for Tobacco Research was used for public relations purposes by the tobacco industry?" Edell was doing absolutely nothing to restrain his incredulity.

Spears kept trying to dodge the obvious implications of what he'd written: that the supposedly independent, scientific arm of the tobacco industry was really nothing more than a trade association.

"In fact, sir, you recommended that the Council for Tobacco Research be combined with the Tobacco Institute!" The latter was, indeed, the industry's lobbying and public relations arm.

"I don't remember recommending it," Spears replied impassively. Funny how you could forget things like that.

"Look at page four!" Edell barked again. "Maybe I took it out of context. See where it says, 'It is suggested that CTR be combined with the Tobacco Institute . . .'?"

Spears insisted he was only looking back then for a way to use the

Tobacco Institute to prevent duplication of research, "and to make sure that all of the appropriate research areas were being covered."

But that wasn't what his memo said. Show me where it says that, Edell commanded. "Show me!"

Spears looked at the document again. "I don't see it," he finally admitted. "But I sure spent a lot of time discussing it."

Edell turned his back to Spears in disgust and walked back to his counsel table. "I spent a lot of time looking for it, too," he muttered loudly, "and it is *not* here!"

"Objection!" Bleakley thundered, jumping to his feet.

"Sustained," Sarokin sighed. "Sustained." Edell thought the judge was becoming noticeably more tired as the trial wore on.

Edell didn't care about Bleakley's melodramatic objection. There were some things a lawyer said for the jury's benefit, with full knowledge that the other side would object. That was how the game was played.

Closing arguments would begin on Wednesday afternoon, June 1, exactly four months after the trial began. By New Jersey law, the defendants would speak first. That was unusual. So, too, was another New Jersey rule that prohibited Edell from pleading for any specific amount in damages.

Liggett had the most at risk because Rose Cipollone had smoked only Liggett brands before the advent of the federally mandated warnings, warnings that insulated the other companies from much of the liability to which Liggett was still exposed.

The tobacco lawyers agreed that Cohn, Liggett's lawyer, would go first. On a sweltering day thick with humidity and the foreboding of an afternoon thunderstorm, partisans from both sides were lined up three deep against the walls of the courtroom, just as they would be on every succeeding day until the case went to the jury.

"If you believe the testimony of Rose Cipollone and her family—that she smoked cigarettes because she wanted to, because she liked to; that she didn't want to stop smoking cigarettes, even though she knew the risks and the dangers associated with the cigarettes, which she knew from before she started to smoke—if you believe that testimony, I believe you should return a verdict for Liggett & Myers Tobacco Company."

Cohn was relying on the tried-and-true argument that had won the day for R. J. Reynolds in the *Galbraith* trial. He was going to spend three hours railing at the jury about the dead woman and her smoking habit, but freedom of choice was what his argument came down to: Rose Cipollone's decision to take a risk.

Edell was the lawyer who always brought up the old cigarette advertisements, the ones that featured Peggy Lee saying Chesterfield was "best for you" and Rosalind Russell and Barbara Stanwyck, telling smokers that L&M was "just what the doctor ordered." Edell wants you to believe those ads tricked Rose Cipollone into smoking, Cohn told the jurors. But, Cohn insisted, health claims like that couldn't possibly have had any effect on Rose; if they had, he asked, then why didn't she smoke Camels, which ran an ad in 1947 saying " 'More doctors smoke Camels than any other cigarette. Your 'T-Zone' will tell you. T for Taste. T for Throat.'

"Did Mrs. Cipollone smoke Camels because of this ad? No! She went back to Chesterfields because she *liked* them."

Anyway, Cohn said in one of several inadvertent puns, advertising like that was just "puffing."

Cohn's summation sounded more like that of a schoolboy debater than the Park Avenue lawyer that he was. It was a melange of rhetoric and tortured logic, as when he told the jurors that regardless of what variety of lung cancer Rose Cipollone had in 1981, "it couldn't have been there very long [and] the plaintiff has no claim in this case for anything that happened after 1966, fifteen years earlier." Cohn just totally ignored the decades-long gestation period that deadly cancer can have; totally ignored the cumulative effect of the 370,000 cigarettes that Rose Cipollone smoked in her lifetime.

Then there was Cohn's answer to the failure-to-warn count, which the judge had dismissed as to Philip Morris and Lorillard but which still was pending against Liggett. "It would have made absolutely no difference to Rose Cipollone," Cohn insisted. How could he be so sure of that? Because Rose Cipollone kept right on smoking when Liggett started putting the federal warning on its cigarette packs in 1966.

The jury could take its pick from Cohn's menu of defenses: that

Rose Cipollone's cancer wasn't caused by smoking or that she should have known better than to keep smoking. "If you light something up and smoke comes out of it and you breathe it into your lungs, how can it *not* be harmful?" he told them, paraphrasing one of Edell's experts. "Anybody who smokes knows that." Everybody has some bad habits, Cohn rambled on. "Different strokes for different folks."

"Sorry this took so long," Cohn apologized to the jury when he was all done. "It is a four-and-a-half-month trial. As you can see, I am just full of it in more ways than one, probably." No telling whether the jury could see that or not. "My work is now over. I'm going to go home and take a few belts tonight."

Just as Cohn finished, the sound of a thunderclap boomed through the courtroom. The threatened storm had arrived. "I hope that's not a comment on the length of your summation," Sarokin chided Cohn.

Edell had named three tobacco-company defendants because he had no legal choice but to do so. But in doing that, he had given the companies a chance to triple-team him, to play three-on-one in the courtroom. That was obvious now in the way the defense lawyers split up the closing argument chores. Cohn, going first, had been the bad guy, making the time-worn but effective argument that Rose Cipollone should have known better than to believe the puffery of the industry's claims about cigarettes. Northrip, the Lorillard lawyer who had taken the lead whenever sophisticated medical evidence was at issue, would follow Cohn's visceral plea with his own cerebral one. His presentation would be a very clear, emphatic explanation of how Rose Cipollone couldn't possibly have had the kind of lung cancer that was related to smoking. The jurors were being given a choice. They could accept the logic of Cohn's argument or of Northrip's. Either way, they'd find against the Cipollones.

"If there is thunder today," Sarokin said amid laughter all around as Northrip walked to the podium the next morning, "you will surely know it is a message."

Northrip plunged right into the medical evidence, telling the jurors what they'd already heard for weeks as the defendants put on their case: that there was, at best, a difference of opinion about the kind of cancer Rose Cipollone had. Sheldon Sommers, the pathologist who became the research director of the Council for Tobacco Research just a week after Cipollone's first operation, had diagnosed it as atypical carcinoma. So had some of the other pathologists during her first course of treatment at Lenox Hill Hospital, although, by June of 1982, all the pathologists except Sommers seemed to be in agreement that she had smoking-related small-cell carcinoma.

But Northrip's objective was to perpetuate the controversy in the collective mind of the jury. If he could show that there was still a question about her cancer even after the middle of 1982, that might be enough to muddy the water for the plaintiffs. Northrip's ace in the hole was an entry in a 1983 preoperative report made by another surgeon. That report still referred to atypical cancer and didn't mention small-cell carcinoma. Who knew why? Northrip asked. The plaintiffs hadn't called that surgeon as a witness.

Northrip also wasn't going to sit down without hammering home the industry's favorite argument about free choice. Rose Cipollone, Northrip said, had a right to take whatever risks she wanted to. He recalled Edell's opening line four months earlier, "that the defendants' position would be, if you are dumb enough to believe that, you deserve what you get.

"Well, that is not our position. It never has been, and Mr. Edell was wrong to say it.

"Our position is this: When someone is bright, well-read, independent, and strong-willed, like Rose Cipollone; when someone has heard about the risks of smoking, like Rose Cipollone; when someone believes that cigarette smoking causes lung cancer, as Rose Cipollone believed; when someone enjoys smoking, as Rose Cipollone did; when somebody smokes of their own free will, as Rose Cipollone did; then it is our position that that is her decision to make, and that we shouldn't second guess her. Not me, not Mr. Edell, not Mr. Cipollone."

As the last defense lawyer to address the jury that Thursday afternoon, Bleakley launched what amounted to a third prong of the cigarette companies' pincer attack against Edell. Bleakley's strategy was to cite the inconsistencies among Edell's own experts to undermine Rose Cipollone's case. More subdued now than he had been throughout the trial, a toned-down Bleakley walked right up to the jury box and got as close as he could to the finders of fact in his case.

People don't start smoking because of advertising, Bleakley told them. "Remember Jerome Jaffee, the plaintiff's addiction expert?" he asked. "Mr. Darnell spent an hour qualifying Dr. Jerome Jaffee as an expert psychiatrist. The first question he asked Dr. Jaffee substantively after he established his qualifications was, Dr. Jaffee, why do people smoke? The answer he gave: They begin in adolescence and do it because of peer pressure, because it makes them look more grown-up, because people have described that they are trying to anticipate adulthood, because they want to seem more sophisticated.

"It wasn't just Dr. Jaffee who said that. Mrs. Cipollone said that. Remember when Dr. Jaffee interviewed Mrs. Cipollone, he had her fill out a questionnaire in which he asked her a bunch of questions about her smoking. One of those was, What one reason explains best why you started smoking cigarettes? Rose Cipollone checked D, To act or feel more like an adult."

The thing about comments like that was that they ignored the whole point of what Edell had been trying to prove. If the advertising message was a subliminal one, as Edell contended, everything Bleakley was saying could be true and Edell could *still* attribute smokers' underlying motivations to advertising. He had to hope that the jury could see through the superficial appeal of Bleakley's logic.

Bleakley criticized first one and then another of the plaintiff's experts. Jeffrey Harris, the forty-year-old academic and the author of the Blazing Saddles bibliography, had only "hindsight" in analyzing the state of the medical art during the 1930s and 1940s, Bleakley asserted. "He used hindsight, attributed significance to these articles that medical science did not attribute to them when they were published. . . .

"And what did Dr. Schuman, who lived during that time, say?" Schuman was another of Edell's experts. "He said when he was in medical school in 1940, they never told him there was evidence cigarette smoking caused lung cancer. He testified when he was an intern in Chicago in '41 treating cancer patients, no one told him cigarette smoking might cause cancer and he didn't think so. . . . Finally, he testified [that] in 1962, after twenty years as a specialist in public health and preventive medicine, Dr. Schuman was invited to join the Surgeon General's Advisory Committee because he didn't have a position on whether cigarette smoking caused lung cancer!"

Bleakley did have a position, though. "We know," he said firmly, "that the maximum risk for someone who smokes their entire life is only 5 percent." Rose Cipollone made her own decision to take that twenty-to-one shot, Bleakley concluded. "She made her own personal assessment of the risks and she made a decision to continue to smoke. She made that decision. . . . It doesn't entitle Mr. Cipollone to recover money."

Edell and Walters went back that afternoon to Edell's house, where they were going to prepare for Edell's closing argument. It was going to be delivered the following morning, a Friday.

Ever since the start of the trial, Edell had felt that the hardest part of his job was going to be getting around everybody's preconceived notions of the hazards of smoking. It was easy for the cigarette industry lawyers to say Rose Cipollone was on notice right from the start, but society's *present* knowledge of the hazard was so much more sophisticated than it was two or more decades ago. "Trying to get by that predisposition to believe that what we know *now* was what we knew *then,*" Edell mused. "Trying to wipe the slate clean. That's the hardest hurdle to get over." Walters had always worried most about the medical evidence, but maybe that was just because the medical part of the case was her principal responsibility. "They have a tremendous ability to muck it up, so that everything looks like a blur of confusion to the jury," Walters complained. And that was exactly what was happening at the end of this trial.

Pondering the Thursday summations at his home that evening, Edell felt now that he'd lost ground. What hurt them most, Edell thought, was Northrip's compelling analysis of the medical evidence. Walters had been the chief lawyer on that part of the case. Again and again, he and Walters went over the ways they could rebut Northrip, but it posed too many problems for Edell. He wanted to memorize his entire closing argument, just as he had his opening statement. But there was just no way he could find the ammunition to use against Northrip and memorize it all in one night. Bernadette Lyons, Walters' legal assistant, had been standing by at home, awaiting a summons to return to the office once Edell and Walters had decided what documents they would need copied or made into slides for the next morning's presentation. But when Lyons' telephone rang at eleven o'clock that night, it was Walters calling to tell her not to bother returning. Edell wasn't ready. He'd already phoned Sarokin earlier that night to tell the judge he couldn't go on in the morning.

The fifty people standing in a knot outside the courtroom at 8:30 the following morning didn't know that, of course; nor did the more than one hundred people, most of them cigarette lawyers and assorted hangers on, who crowded into the courtroom when the doors were opened at nine o'clock. Murray Bring, Philip Morris' general counsel, stayed out in the hall, puffing on a cigarette as he talked confidentially to Bleakley and his defense team. Cohn and his Liggett cronies sat on another bench outside the courtroom; they didn't have to worry about staking out a seat in the audience, either.

A little after nine o'clock, Sarokin summoned all the lawyers into his chambers. "So, Mr. Edell?"

Edell called it "the most difficult thing I had to do during the course of this trial, to come here and tell everybody we are not prepared to close today." But that's what he had to do now that logic had taken over from ego.

The defense lawyers opposed any delay, with Bleakley acting as the de facto spokesman for the group. If Edell didn't make his closing argument on Friday and went on Monday, instead, that would mean Cohn's close would be a week old by the time the case finally went to the jury. Bleakley's and Northrip's would be almost as stale.

Forget it, Bleakley told the judge. Edell was scheduled to go on. It was up to Sarokin to make him do it.

"It's like a pack of wolves that are smelling blood, and I can see the eyes glaring down at me in the middle of the wolf pack with my foot up in the air," Edell replied. "I cannot sum up today. You know, quite frankly, I am prepared to be sent to jail if you order me to sum up today."

Cohn was playing his usual role. "If you can't stand the heat," he said to Edell, "you get out of the kitchen."

Sarokin ordered everybody out of his office and wrote out his decision on individual sheets of a yellow lined legal pad. At 10:50, he walked into the courtroom, took his seat at the bench, and started reading out his reprieve of Edell: The plaintiff's lawyer would be allowed to give his closing argument on Monday, June 6. But each defendant's lawyer would get an extraordinary opportunity to rebut Edell's summation immediately, so as to offset the advantage Edell was getting by being given extra time. After everybody had spoken, Edell would get one last, half-hour shot at the jury. All this would be done on Monday, and on Tuesday, June 7, the jury would begin its deliberations.

"This is being turned into a circus!" Bleakley raved at Sarokin when the judge had finished reading aloud his order.

The tobacco lawyers had used their closing arguments to do just what Edell and Walters had been predicting all along. The companies didn't have to prove anything; all they had to do was to cast a fog of doubt over the jury.

"What you have heard continually throughout this trial is what the tobacco industry is best at," Edell said when he propped up his outline on the lectern and stood before the jury on that first Monday morning in June. "A strategy that they devised over the last thirty, forty years. A strategy of creating doubt, and they are very, very good at it. It took us five years before we stepped into this courtroom on February first, to sort out the truth, to gather the evidence, so we could show to you what the industry was all about."

Edell was going to spend three and a half hours telling the jury one last time about all the documents he'd previously brought out— "their own internal documents" that proved the companies hadn't done anything to tell the public the truth about the hazards of smoking.

"Members of the jury," Edell said respectfully, the defendants' counsel in this case have come into this courtroom and told you that the reason they didn't warn about it, the reason they didn't tell Rose Cipollone and everybody else was because everybody knew. *Everybody knew.* Everybody always knew about the health hazards. That is why we didn't warn.

"Think: Does that make sense? . . . Do you want to know the truth of the matter? That is nothing more than a fabricated legal defense. You know how we know? Because we asked the corporate executives, Why didn't you warn?"

Edell reminded the jurors of what the former CEO of Liggett, Milton Harrington, had said. "We didn't care to warn the public about anything."

The Cipollone lawyer talked next about Joseph Cullman, the chairman emeritus of Philip Morris. "Very smooth. Very polished. Very sophisticated man. Probably one of the greatest marketing men the tobacco industry has ever known. He is the one who created the Marlboro Man."

Cullman was also a liar, Edell told them. "Nice gentleman, hand-some-looking man," but a liar nonetheless because he said "we didn't warn because the Federal Trade Commission wouldn't let us."

"An outright lie," Edell said again. It was strong stuff, but that's what it was going to take to win this case.

Edell told the jurors to examine the Big Tobacco statement that "Everybody knew." Did they? He reminded them of Milton Harring-ton, who'd joined Liggett in 1934. Harrington said he hadn't heard that cigarettes might be harmful until 1964, when the Surgeon General's Report came out. Edell read from Harrington's testimony:

"Had you received any information concerning cigarette smoking and health prior to that time, sir?

"Answer: No.

"But Rose Cipollone knew, all their customers knew, and that is why we didn't warn!" Edell let his sarcasm fill the courtroom.

He also tried to transport the jury back to the time when Rose Cipollone first started smoking, because Edell had believed all along that in order to win he had to put the jury in a frame of mind to be able to visualize the early culture of smoking: not what people know today, but what they thought back then. Edell got out a 1959 Roper Poll secretly done for Philip Morris. Eleven percent of the respondents said that smoking was the most dangerous risk they were exposed to, "just slightly edging out climbing in and out of the bathtub. Is that an appreciation of the nature and extent of the hazards of cigarette smoking?"

Edell moved from the companies' failure to warn to the conspiracy in which he claimed they'd engaged.

"Judge Sarokin will tell you that we can prove the conspiracy both by direct evidence and by circumstantial evidence.

"What does that mean?

"Well, direct evidence is easy. I mean, you are going to *see* the documents. You have seen them before. . . .

"Circumstantial evidence, every one of the tobacco companies didn't warn before 1954. Every one of the tobacco companies didn't conduct research before 1954. Is it a coincidence?

"Every one of the tobacco companies maintains it hasn't been proven. Coincidence?

"Every one of them says advertising doesn't have an impact, yet they advertise to neutralize the effect of information concerning the hazards of cigarette smoking. Those are all coincidences?

"All of them failed to publish their research results. A coincidence?

"Well, it could be a coincidence or it could be circumstantial evidence, supported by the direct evidence of the conspiracy."

Edell said it was a conspiracy that had changed over time. Prior to 1954, it was "keep your mouth shut, don't say anything, don't do any research. Don't know and you don't have to do anything.

"From 1954 onward, don't warn. Don't do any in-house research. Don't do any research that will really get to the bottom of cigarette smoking and health, and always say it hasn't been proven."

Edell next played a snippet of videotape from his deposition of James Mold, Liggett's assistant research director who invented the safer cigarette. That claim was out of the case now, but Mold's testimony was still useful because it also struck at the heart of the industry's defense. Mold said, point-blank, that Liggett didn't warn consumers even after its own secret research showed that mice developed cancer after exposure to cigarette smoke condensate.

Edell's closing argument was, in fact, about as close to a multimedia extravaganza as Edell could get in the courtroom. He not only played the Mold video deposition but also showed early Liggett advertisements that appeared on television and even read from the 1952 scripts of the "Arthur Godfrey Show" to show that Liggett was making explicit health claims about its cigarettes. The law called that an express warranty, and Edell's case against Liggett (but not the other defendants) was still alive on that count.

The causation issue was one in which Edell could also use his biting wit against the lawyers who had advanced an array of contradictory arguments during the trial.

"First they say it hasn't been proven—cigarette smoking doesn't cause lung cancer. Second, they say, even if it does, Rose Cipollone didn't smoke enough. Third, even if she smoked enough, it couldn't have been from the years that she smoked their cigarettes. Remember Liggett saying it wasn't pre-'66, it was *post*-'66? Finally, they say even if it could be the cigarettes she smoked during those years, she had the wrong kind of cancer! Is that how we deal with everyday life? Either cigarette smoking causes lung cancer, or it doesn't! . . . Every major health organization. Remember that chart? Every major health organization concerned with people's welfare has concluded that cigarette smoking is the major cause of lung cancer, heart disease and all other diseases, both those organizations in the United States and those organizations in other parts of the world.

"There is only one group that has considered the issue of cigarette smoking and health and it has come out the other way—and they are sitting on the other side of the room." Edell gestured toward the retinue of cigarette lawyers behind him.

"Another mere coincidence."

Despite having been so concerned the Friday before about his ability to rebut Northrip's medical summation, Edell now seemed content to let Northrip's statement speak for itself. The industry pathologist Sommers, Edell told the jury, was the odd man out, but what did that really matter, anyway?

"It doesn't make a difference for them because they say cigarette smoking doesn't cause lung cancer." It was a deft lunge back at the defendants. "If it doesn't make a difference, it doesn't make a difference whether it's an atypical or small-cell. But, no, they want to hedge their bets. They say there is an association between cigarette smoking and small cell but *no* association between cigarette smoking and atypical carcinoid. That is the only reason we spent weeks and weeks going over the medical issue. . . .

"You have to remember," Edell intoned, "that Rose was a human being. She wasn't a time line. She wasn't in bits and pieces of a deposition. She was a real person. She was a real person that was eaten up very slowly over a long period of time by a horrible disease; a horrible disease caused by cigarette smoking; a disease that she was never warned about by the defendants."

Edell reached all the way back to his opening statement to give the jury the same exhortation that he had delivered to them then.

"You have the power to regulate one of the most powerful industries in the world. In this courtroom, there are no deals. There are no compromises. There is no political influence, no political promises. Just the truth. . . .

"The bottom line is very simple: You can do one of two things with your verdict in this case. You can tell the tobacco industry it is okay to withhold information. It is okay to distort information. It is okay to mislead people. It is okay to lie to people. It's okay. Tomorrow, business as usual.

"Or, you, as the first jury ever to see the internal workings of this industry, can say, That's it! We've had enough! That this is not acceptable behavior by any industry, and you can put a stop to it in this case!

"All we ask is that when you return a verdict in this case, you return a verdict that won't demean the life of Rose Cipollone, and the courage that she had to bring this lawsuit."

The six jurors who would actually deliberate consisted of a thirty-five-year-old male smoker; three ex-smokers, a man and a woman who were both sixty-four years old and another man who was fifty-two; and two women, aged fifty-two and fifty-six, who said they had never smoked. All were members of the white middle class who came from suburbs adjoining Newark, probably a plus for the defense. But all of them except the young smoker were old enough to identify with Rose Cipollone, who'd died when she was fifty-eight. And they were also of an age to remember the golden age of cigarette advertising. That helped Edell.

As the jury began its deliberations, both sides hunkered down in different parts of the courtroom to await the outcome. Edell and Walters cut the tension by playing backgammon at their counsel table. The defense lawyers played double solitaire and bridge.

But inside the jury room, the six jurors immediately took a vote and found they were divided four-to-two for the defendants on all counts. Firmly in the defense corner were the three women (a housewife, a factory worker, and a food laboratory researcher), and the only smoker. But Edell luckily also had two pro-plaintiff stalwarts in the jury room. Those other male jurors, a county loan adviser and an engineer for a utilities company, were insistent throughout the four days of deliberations that some damages, maybe even as much as $5 million, had to be awarded.

The pro-defense jurors were unrelenting in their view that Rose

Cipollone's cancer was her own fault; they bought the cigarette industry's argument about free choice, and they were well enough entrenched to threaten to call the deliberations off and send a note to the judge telling him there was a hung jury. But the two-man minority ultimately brokered a compromise. Rose would get nothing, a concession to the majority. But Tony, her husband, would be given a nominal amount because, even by the lights of the pro-defense jurors, Liggett's advertisements had been misleading.

When the jury brought in its verdict at five o'clock on the afternoon of Monday, June 13, Edell and Tony Cipollone began to brace themselves for a total loss as, one by one, the jury's findings were read out to the courtroom.

The jury had been given its own set of twenty questions, called *interrogatories*, to guide its deliberations. Now, as Edell heard the jury's replies, it appeared that he had lost:

Has the plaintiff proven fraud by Liggett, Philip Morris, or Lorillard? No. No. No.

Was there a conspiracy among the three companies? No.

Should Liggett have warned consumers prior to 1966 about the dangers of smoking? Yes. Maybe that presaged a win for Edell.

Was the failure to warn a proximate cause of Rose Cipollone's smoking, and, if it was, did smoking cause her lung cancer? Yes. Yes.

What was Rose Cipollone's percentage of responsibility for her injuries? Eighty percent. Not enough to collect a dime from the companies under New Jersey's comparative-fault law.

The jury, in other words, thought that Edell had proved his breach-of-warranty case against Liggett, but, even so, it had found that Rose Cipollone wasn't entitled to any damages, a peculiar finding, one that couldn't easily be explained in any way except one: another goose egg for Edell.

Finally, on the fourth-to-the-last question, with his hopes for victory all but collapsed, Edell heard what he'd been lusting for: a breach-of-warranty verdict against Liggett in favor of Tony Cipollone. It was almost as if Edell had foretold the future months earlier when he spoke of beating the one lawyer he considered a "schmuck." Cohn and his team from Webster & Sheffield *had* been beaten.

The jury's verdict in favor of Tony Cipollone was for $400,000, an amount trivial in all but what it represented to those who had tried for more than three decades to beat Big Tobacco. So what if the judgment couldn't possibly pay back Edell and his law firm for the millions that had already been advanced on the case? So what? It was still sweet revenge for two men who'd stuck with the case for their own private reasons.

Rose's estate hadn't received one penny in damages, and no punitive damages had been voted, either. But Tony Cipollone, the silent man who'd spent every day of the trial sitting alone behind Edell, had won his case.

And so, at last, had Edell.

Hit-Man Lawyer:
Stephen D. Susman and
the Notorious
Hunt Brothers

Lawyers are basically not very well paid people, given the hours we work, the blood, sweat and tears we put in and the educational background we have. Compared to investment bankers or business executives, basically, as a group we aren't that well paid.

STEPHEN D. SUSMAN
Annual compensation:
at least $1 million

Nelson Bunker Hunt, the scion of an extraordinarily rich family, scanned the Dallas horizon. From his twenty-fourth-floor office in the downtown building he and his brothers named Thanksgiving Tower, he looked out on the big new skyscrapers rising up to pierce the thick Texas haze.

"I haven't had a chance to appreciate the view," he chuckled. "I always thought those buildings were obstructing my view. When we first moved in three and a half years ago, that one wasn't there"—he pointed to one of the towers which, like his own, sprouted during the flush times—"and that one wasn't there."

Next door stood the new Allied Bank Building, a gleaming green-glass edifice that looked like a giant crystal bookend. "It's now owned by Manufacturers Hanover," Bunker Hunt continued. "They foreclosed on it for $214 million. Bought it in at auction." What he didn't say, because it wasn't necessary, because everybody in Dallas already knew, was that the same fate was awaiting Thanksgiving Tower and just about everything else owned by the sixty-one-year-old Bunker and his younger brothers Herbert, fifty-eight, and Lamar, fifty-five.

Beneath Dallas' gleaming new skyline in 1987 there was enough vacant office space to fill a seventy-two-story building nineteen times over. Hard times in the oil patch meant trouble for all of Texas. But nowhere was the thud of the Texas economy hitting bottom heard more loudly than in the House of Hunt.

It once was the richest in the world, girdling not just Dallas but the entire globe with holdings in oil, silver, real estate, sugar and race horses. For a time, in the 1970s, Bunker was the world's richest man, worth $16 billion. He made and lost more money in the Libyan oil fields and in the commodities markets during the previous two decades than his legendary daddy scored in a lifetime. And, despite oil's fall, he and his five brothers and sisters were still among the world's superrich. They still had interests in more than 200 trust funds, corporations and partnerships. "I'm still eating three squares a day," the irrepressible Bunker chortled.

In many ways, the Hunt brothers were carrying on as usual, exploring for oil in ventures from South Texas to Africa. Bunker kept a close eye on his successful thoroughbred stables, Herbert oversaw his vast real estate holdings, and Lamar made frequent trips to Kansas City, where his professional football team, the Chiefs, was based. Lamar also owned a professional tennis circuit, as well as mining and underground storage facilities and amusement parks called Worlds of Fun and Oceans of Fun.

But these were tough times for Texas and for the Hunt brothers, who in many ways embodied the broad, rough-and-ready image of the Lone Star State. Politically conservative, personally low-key and amiable, they always displayed a typically Texan fondness for size—big deals, big risks, big payoffs. "There is something about being a Hunt," observed the Dallas author and historian A. C. Greene. "You're never rich enough."

But now it was the Hunts' losses that were larger than life. After almost cornering the silver market in the late 1970s, the brothers took a thumping in the early 1980s when prices for the metal plummeted. Then oil prices nosedived, and matters went from bad to awful. The Hunts, whose assets had a liquidation value of $1.48 billion, owed their collective creditors $2.43 billion.

This meant that the three Hunt brothers, and their thirteen sons and daughters, the ultimate beneficiaries of the fortune that H. L. Hunt placed in trust for Bunker, Herbert and Lamar, were facing the loss of virtually all of their wealth.

The empire that oil built was under siege, and the brothers were playing out a litigation gambit in their desperation bid to save it.

As Bunker Hunt gazed out the window that steamy summer afternoon, the Hunts were battling to prevent twenty-two banks from foreclosing on their property to satisfy a $1.5 billion debt. In Lamar Hunt's words, losing "would be a very dramatic end result." But that was a classic understatement from the sportsman-brother who knew his odds as well as anyone.

Still, they'd managed to hang on by cleverly using the courts to protect their prized assets, placing both the family-owned oil company and a huge trust fund in bankruptcy and filing a gigantic lending-fraud lawsuit against their banks to keep them on the defensive.

Their lawsuit was the ultimate in audacity, claiming, as it did, that the banks weren't entitled to have any more money repaid to them because the banks should never have lent any money to such bad risks as the Hunts in the first place! And yet it said something about the Hunts, and the legal system, that such a lawsuit had to be taken seriously.

In the oil patch, a new drilling project is called a "play." It's a term of Texas endearment, a good ol' boy's way of saying that finding oil isn't as exciting as prospecting for it: putting millions at risk and savoring the thrill of the drill.

And their lawsuit was a typically Hunt-sized play—big, brash and ballsy.

It also was the perfect strategy for troubled debtors like the Hunts, for it played right into the weakness of a legal system that can be rendered impotent by the legal equivalent of a dirty tricks campaign. The Hunts almost surely had an unwinnable case, and yet that didn't matter. Their objective was to use the legal system *against itself,* making matters so contentious that their creditors would lose the will and the financial wherewithal to continue going after them.

The brothers didn't have to win their longshot case. All they needed was to hold their banks at bay until either oil prices rebounded or the Hunts made a billion-dollar oil strike somewhere.

That was why they were spending much of what remained of their liquid assets on a two-pronged hedge to save themselves. Their first gambit was the lawsuit being handled by a group of young Houston lawyers who were outnumbered as much as fifty-to-one by bank lawyers on the other side. The lawsuit, which by now had already been pending a year and wasn't scheduled to go to trial for at least another year, sought at least $1.5 billion in damages against such institutions as Citibank, Manufacturers Hanover, and Bankers Trust.

A year into the litigation, legal fees already totaled $50 million for the banks, and they had been running as high as $6 million a month.

The theory of the case was that the banks had a secret agenda to bankrupt the Hunts and then take over their business at fire-sale prices.

But the real purpose of the lawsuit and a companion bankruptcy proceeding was to hold off the banks while the brothers got ready for their ultimate gamble: Against strenuous opposition from their creditors, the Hunts were about to start drilling in the Gulf of Mexico's Green Canyon in search of that big oil strike they needed if they were ever going to rebuild their fortune.

And that was just fine with their chief trial lawyer of the moment, Stephen D. Susman.

Susman was the heir to a ruggedly independent style of Texas justice that had turned the likes of "Racehorse" Haynes and Joe Jamail into modern day legal legends. When the big Texas deals went down, it was the lawyers like them who profited. But in the hardscrabble Texas economic landscape of the late 1980s, it was Susman who'd become a corporate hit man, working the courts, awaiting the kill. A company hired Susman when it was out of options and some dirty business needed to be done: Collect a debt. Eliminate a competitor. Enforce a contract. Call Susman.

The Hunts were paying four different law firms—Susman's and three bankruptcy specialists—more than $1 million a month. And just like any other deadbeats, the Hunts had to give Susman cash in advance, $400,000 a month.

The Hunts paid well but they were demanding clients and they wanted to be able to confer with their lawyers on a moment's notice. There was a cramped little suite of offices just down the hall from the brothers' Hunt Energy offices in Thanksgiving Tower, and any law firm that took their case had to relocate there for the duration. Somebody observed that the brothers changed lawyers almost as often as they changed shirts, but when they tried on Susman they finally found a lawyer who fit. The forty-six-year-old Houstonian could relate to these gamble-it-all Dallas mavericks because he was one, too. Eschewing the big Houston law firms he'd once been part of, Susman had made the big money early by gambling his reputation and his own money on chancy plaintiffs' cases that few lawyers would touch. He knew what the Green Canyon play was all about.

The brothers, after all, were wildcatters. "These people are gamblers," he said. "If you're a gambler, you don't have to be very smart. You take your shot. I mean, it doesn't matter what's on the contract. If you hit, man, everybody's going to be happy! A contract's put together for a disaster, and gamblers aren't thinking about disasters. They're thinking about the *hit*. Green Canyon is their Great White Hope. They view it as their saviour."

H. L. Hunt bequeathed his boys the blood of a gambler—the old man was a professional poker player nicknamed "Arizona Slim" before he ever hit it big in the oil field—and, thanks to Susman, H.L.'s sons were still in the game. They still controlled their empire.

You had to go to Dallas to understand this dynastic battle: this hugely rich, intensely secretive family taking on the bankers who'd once fawned over them in what had become an embarrassing spectacle for both sides. And it was in Dallas that a writer could get an unprecedented view, during this period of great turmoil for the family, of the Hunts and their world—following them around, sitting in on business meetings, living with them. Their lawyer convinced the Hunts that their lawsuits necessitated this extraordinary cooperation. As complex as their legal case was, Susman reminded them, if it went to a jury it would probably hinge on whether three fabulously rich men could persuade their fellow Texans of something that almost no one believed: that Bunker, Herbert and Lamar were just plain folks who got in over their heads.

H.L. Hunt sired fifteen children in three different families before his death in 1974. Along with their two sisters, Margaret Hunt Hill, seventy-one, and Caroline Rose Hunt, sixty-four, and a mentally impaired brother, Haroldson Lafayette III (Hassie), sixty-nine, Bunker, Herbert and Lamar were from what Dallas referred to as H.L.'s "first family," by his marriage to a young Arkansas schoolteacher named Lyda Bunker. After Lyda died in 1955, H.L. married Ruth Ray of Shreveport. By the time of their marriage in 1957, the former Hunt Oil secretary had already given birth to four of H.L.'s children. The elder Hunt also had an alliance with a Florida woman, Frania Tye, who said they were married. After his death it was revealed that there were four children from that relationship.

Despite the "first-family" appellation, Dallas had always regarded the brothers warily, in part, no doubt, because that was how the brothers wanted it. Like their father, they'd cultivated a collective image as amiable tightwads, driving old cars, flying coach class, making their high-priced out-of-town lawyers double up in cramped, Hunt-owned apartments downtown. Yet there were also trappings of wealth—all three brothers and their children lived in mansions in the exclusive suburbs of University Park and Highland Park—and a sharpness to their business dealings that the brothers masked by keeping their own families close and others at a distance. "I don't consider myself to be any genius, businesswise," said Lamar, the easygoing younger brother who spent the least time in the family business and who was also the only one of the three who hadn't brought his adult sons into it. (Lamar Jr. played the flute with the Kansas City Symphony Orchestra, and Clark, a recent college graduate, was an investment banking trainee in New York.) "I'm fairly boring, fairly average. Probably a lot of people think of us as eccentric, but most people think everybody from Texas is eccentric." Lamar Hunt wasn't as close to Herbert and Bunker as the two were to each other, but he stuck by them.

If Lamar's real passion was the Chiefs football team, Bunker's was his thoroughbred horses. He owned more than 500 of them. His overall breeding operations, which included Bluegrass Farm Stable in Lexington, Kentucky, led the nation in money earned. And his 2,000-acre Circle T ranch in Westlake, near the Dallas–Fort Worth airport, was itself worth many millions: IBM was building a major office complex next door, a freeway was coming, and the industrialist H. Ross Perot had purchased land on the other side. "Wish all my investments were doing that well," Bunker said with a grin.

Herbert, the middle Hunt brother, diversified into shopping centers, office buildings and a Phoenix resort called Arrowhead, all in longtime partnership with his friend Paul Stephens, who oversaw the Arizona enterprise.

For such a secretive family, this federal case forced a change. Every aspect of the Hunts' lives and business operations was examined in microscopic detail by lawyers and reporters alike. But friends stuck by them. At a Friday night party at Herbert's house, an informal, catered affair for friends complete with a one-man poolside band, valet parking and a serving staff of six, guests would nod knowingly at the whispered comments about their friends' latest legal peccadilloes. Yes, they had seen the stories. And with that the subject would be deftly changed.

There were pride and ego and, of course, plenty of money wrapped up in these huge lawsuits. "But it's the final battle that counts," Herbert Hunt said with conviction, and to win that one he had to win over a city that had always viewed the two older brothers as renegades and the sportsman Lamar as their agreeable protege.

"Herbert and Bunker are as much a mystery to Dallas as they are to the rest of the country," said A. C. Greene. "People who deal with them see a pair of guys who're shufflin' and grinnin' and diggin' their toes deeper and deeper into the horse manure, and they don't realize until later that they've been good ol' boyed to death! Herbert and Bunker aren't going to win the Nobel prize, but they aren't dumb, either. They've fought an awful lot of battles with an awful lot of smart people, and they've won most of them. I'd put 'em up against any of those highly touted entrepreneurs, Lee Iacocca or anybody else. They'd hold their own, no question."

But it was more than a billionaire's desire for privacy that underlay their secrecy. Ironically, what seemed to propel Herbert and Bunker into the kind of situations that jeopardized what they had was an innate fear of *losing* what they had. Certainly, that was what led them into serious legal trouble in 1973, when the two were indicted in federal court for wiretapping and bugging some former employees they thought had cheated them, and for obstructing justice by trying to cover up what they had done.

There was a lesson in that criminal case for those who underestimated the Hunts now: They became the ultimate pragmatists in order to win their case. The ultraconservative Bunker—he had been on the John Birch Society national council and was a $484,000 financial angel of Oliver North's covert fund for the Nicaraguan Contras— hired a civil liberties lawyer who had previously represented black militant H. Rap Brown. They consulted with a public relations firm to burnish their image, and they told a tale of woe to a sympathetic Texas jury that acquitted them.

Quite clearly, they were holding their own now against the banks. "We're bloody but unbowed!" Bunker exulted. "I am not losing any sleep over how the banks perceive me. I don't know what they think of me, I don't care, and I'm not worried about it. I'm not sensitive to publicity. After forty or fifty years of reading semiunfavorable articles about myself, I really got other things to worry about. I'm not trying to run for political office. I'm not trying to be popular. I'm not trying to win any goodwill contests. I just do the best I can."

"We're still in business," Herbert said, a hint of defensiveness in his voice. True enough, their empire was broke. And yet they had used the legal system to strategic advantage. Their business went on. And in a community as hard hit as Dallas had been by the fall in energy prices, there were those who wanted nothing more than to see these three brothers outduel their pin-striped bankers.

Susman was about to begin a six-month sabbatical when the Hunts asked him to take their case. With their younger of two children having just gone off to Yale, Karen and Steve Susman were going to take the trip of a lifetime, a sporting venture around the world. "We were gonna jog the Great Wall for a month, dive the Barrier Reef for a month, ski for a month, sail for a month in Sardinia, one month in the ideal place where we've always wanted to be, for six months. And that is our plan, as soon as this case is over." Problem was, Susman had no idea when that would be. "It could be a month, could be a year, could be three years from now. It's a case where you never can tell when it's going to be over." He thought about buying a car and a house to make his stint in Dallas easier, but then he thought, "as soon as I do that, this case will end—which I guess would be a good reason to do it!"

The fact was, Susman needed a rest, "because I don't know whether I can keep up this pace very much longer. You get tired. So much to do, you get exhausted. That's why I want to take a sabbatical, get a fresh breath. I just think I've created a monster for myself. I've gotta keep running at a fast pace to keep ahead of the younger lawyers." That drive to compete, even against his alter egos within the firm, kept Susman going during a year when he tried back-to-back cases and was preparing for the Hunt trial to come.

This hawk-nosed, bullet-headed man with a body builder's physique jogged every morning for exercise and chain-smoked big fat Nat Sherman Canary Island cigars, but his real love was scuba diving, the reason why his law firm had its annual retreats in places like Cozumel, Mexico, where the diving is fine. He was also an intense man who didn't relax easily, a seven-day-a-week workaholic who racked up 3,000 billable hours a year. (In most law firms, the target for a productive partner would be around 1,800 hours.) His normal fee was $400 an hour, but he charged the Hunts $600 an hour—a 50 percent premium for the aggravation of moving half his thriving practice to Dallas. He even demanded that the Hunts hire his lawyer-wife, too, and, good family men that the Hunt brothers were, they readily complied. But even then, the couple wasn't thrilled with the change.

"I finally got my house in River Oaks," his wife said when she saw the two-bedroom apartment they'd be sharing downtown with an assortment of her husband's partners who were rotating through on the assignment, "and now look where I'm living: in a railroad station!"

Susman molded his law firm in his own image: young and aggressive. The average age of the twenty-two lawyers at Susman, Godfrey & McGowan was thirty-seven years, not much older than the founding partner everybody called "Dad." Susman's flippant nickname for seemingly all twenty-eight of the firm's other lawyers and legal assistants was "Babes," as in, "See ya, Babes," or "What's happenin', Babes?" That's the way they all talked. And yet the youth and informality of the office belied the pressure to produce. It was palpable even on a Sunday at midday, when fully half the lawyers at the firm were in their offices, along with Susman, who was wearing a knit T-shirt, khaki shorts, and penny loafers sans socks, a weekend uniform that was as much a Susman trademark as his suspenders and broad-brimmed Panama hat were during the week.

His partners and associates were preparing for the trials or depositions that are the litigator's lot. They were also earning a great deal of money at a very early age, through a compensation system that directed the law firm's loot right back to the lawyer who either brought in the business or did the work.

"We're set up differently from most law firms," Susman explained. "I made a decision, when I set up the firm, that we were going to have a meritocracy. One of the reasons I went out on my own was, I wanted an opportunity, as a young man, at age thirty-five, to make money in my late thirties and my forties, rather than wait until I was in my late fifties and sixties, which is the way the income is distributed at a big firm. We don't have a pyramid structure, with a lot of associates coming in at the bottom to produce profits for the partners at the top." That's the way the big firms work. The young lawyers bring in the money, but the older ones spend it.

"The difference here is the way the money's distributed. You make the money when you're most productive, not when you have the most gray hair. And so it's a firm for vigorous, young, energetic workaholics. It's not a firm for people who want security, a way to retire on the job.

"Litigation gets down, ultimately, to being pretty much a lone wolf kind of deal. You're dealing with people with big egos. We don't want to do anything other than litigation. It's something we understand. It's something we know about, and it gives us a great deal in common. When people have a lot in common, they stick together."

Susman earned at least a million dollars a year, with no apologies. "There's no favoritism," he said. "The numbers come out where the numbers are." The partnership track was so flexible—in contrast to that of the big legal institutions—that Susman, Godfrey lawyer Parker Folse III made the grade in just one year, at age thirty-one, on the strength of his trial work in a year-long Los Angeles antitrust case. A young partner like Bill White, who hadn't yet turned thirty-five, could easily make half a million dollars a year. "It's every young lawyer's dream—earning lots of money and handling big cases," said partner Kenneth McNeil, a forty-four-year-old, second-career lawyer who'd been a university professor before going to law school just a few years ago.

What a Susman, Godfrey partner earned depended on how many hours he billed and how much business he brought in. Partners' "draws," or base salaries, were paid out of the first $3 million in profits, a target the firm always expected to reach. Draws averaged $270,000. But as gross revenue climbed—it rose by $2 million, to $9 million a year, even before the Hunts became clients—the excess profits were divided on the basis of performance. "You eat what you kill," a first-year associate there once said. At the end of the year, all the fees generated by a partner—whether through business he brought in, his own work or the work of associates he supervised—were totaled up, then divided in half. The amount above his base-salary draw was the partner's bonus for the year.

"The basic notion," said Susman, "is that the partner takes out of the law firm what he's responsible for producing. We look at a computer printout of all the fees he receives from his efforts. Fifty percent is overhead. He should get the other 50 percent."

When Susman started out, he did so as a plaintiffs' lawyer, working for a contingent fee. But prosperity changed that. Now, his firm represented plaintiffs only about 40 percent of the time and devoted an even smaller percentage to contingent-fee work. During the Hunt litigation, the firm decided not to take any new contingent cases at all, because of the fear that open-ended commitments to new contingency cases would divert resources from the Hunts. "We don't want every little dog and cat," Susman said.

Some firms have become enormously enriched by the contingent fee, but those usually are the ones banging out lots of personal-injury settlements and rarely taking such a case to trial. Over time, the courts establish a market rate for injuries, and the insurance companies who settle those cases know what they're worth. If a lawyer can get his one-third cut without going into the courtroom, that's what he does. But the commercial-litigation firms like Susman's don't do assembly-line settlements. Each case is different, each is complex, and each is usually far from being a cinch to win. So, not only did Susman deemphasize contingent-fee cases, he also became a no-nonsense businessman when it came to his fees. He required a security deposit, enough to cover three or four months' worth of bills, on every case his firm took. It stayed in the bank until the case was finished, whereupon the client got it back, as long as he'd stayed current on his bills. Even contingent-fee plaintiffs had to put up an earnest-money deposit of $15,000 to $20,000—something almost unheard-of elsewhere. Susman justified it because, by the time a contingent-plaintiff's case was over, the law firm would probably have invested much more in it than that, and "we want to make damn sure you have an investment in that lawsuit, too.

"I preach this to the firm: We're professionals but we also run a business," Susman said. "It's a business in which we all own an interest. We've gotta operate it in a businesslike fashion. We're a small firm. And while we've done wonderfully well in three years, as quickly as everything came to us, everything can go. We are not a big, major institution with a lot of depth, either in our finances or our client base. All of our clients are, by and large, one-shot clients. They come to us once. You may never see them again. We just do litigation. And while we have one or two clients that we've done repeated lawsuits for, you could name on one hand the clients we can expect repeat business from. Our clients may never have the same problem again.

"The only way you can attract clients on that basis is to keep winning lawsuits. If you begin losing lawsuits, word gets out just as quickly that you're a loser as it got out that you were a winner."

Susman stopped and wondered aloud about the Hunt case. The worse the Texas economy got, the better things seemed to go for his firm, because people wanted to win in court what they'd lost in the marketplace. The Hunts were no different. And although Susman had his worries about their case, he rationalized them away.

"I'm worried about losing *every* case I'm in," he said. "Every case I'm in, I have sleepless nights about losing. And why do I work until twelve o'clock at night, or one o'clock, and on weekends? Because I don't want that to happen. And I just feel that another little effort on my part, a little extra, will be the difference between winning and losing a case.

"That's what motivates me."

How the House of Hunt became imperiled is a fascinating tale told in more than a million pages of documents and depositions produced in the maze of federal lawsuits, countersuits, and bankruptcy proceedings that accompanied the brothers' downfall.

It is also the story of brash entrepreneurs who belong to another time and place. "There's something about being a Hunt," said A. C. Greene, the Dallas author and historian. "You're never rich enough. It's kind of like a disease. The old man had it. He called it success. And the brothers thought they could do what he did. But the times were against them. They tried to play robber baron in an era when you just can't get away with it."

Despite all the problems brought on by the drop in oil prices, the decline of the House of Hunt had its origins in another precious commodity: silver.

Bunker, Herbert and Lamar first began investing in it in 1973. Bunker was flush with cash from his Libyan oil operations that had just been nationalized. Herbert had read a book entitled *Silver Profits in the Seventies,* and in it he found what he thought was a strategy for the rough times ahead. Buying silver would give the brothers a precious-metal hedge against the inflation that was eating away at the dollar's value, "deteriorating the value of the assets," in Lamar's words. Private citizens couldn't buy gold then. Silver would do.

As investigations by Congress and the Commodities Futures Trading Commission later established, the brothers literally bought tons of the stuff, paying for it in cash and shipping the silver, on planes guarded by their own gun-toting ranch hands, to vaults in Switzerland. Though the brothers deny it to this day, the authorities contended the Hunts were illegally acting together to try to corner the silver market, an incredible scheme that would have allowed them to monetize the metal and issue silver-backed bonds.

For a time, the Hunts' ploy was phenomenally successful. From a price of $1.94 an ounce in 1973, the metal soared to $50.35 an ounce in January 1980 at the end of the brothers' buying spree.

When it reached that peak, alarmed commodities exchanges, trying to get control over the markets, changed their rules so as to prevent the Hunts from doing anything other than *selling* their silver. With no buyers, the per-ounce price of silver fell precipitously.

Bunker had borrowed $654 million to finance his silver buys, and Herbert had loans totaling another $498 million. Lamar, as ever going his separate way, hadn't bought that much, but together the brothers were in debt to the tune of $1.3 billion on an investment that now was worth much less than that. Worse, they'd contracted to buy another $665 million worth of silver, and they didn't have the cash to make good on their commitment.

Fearing that a Hunt default would reverberate throughout Wall Street, then–Federal Reserve Chairman Paul A. Volcker prodded the Hunts' creditors to renegotiate the brothers' loans. New terms were worked out to give the brothers a longer payback period, so that they could sell off their silver when the price was more favorable. They also had to agree not to speculate in the commodity markets for the whole term of the loan, until 1990.

The Volcker-instigated loan was a turning point. It relieved the brothers' immediate liquidity crisis, but it created a long-term problem for the entire Hunt family because the consortium of banks, led by Morgan Guaranty and Los Angeles–based Interfirst, wanted new, more secure collateral, not just from the brothers, but from the rest of the family, too.

The family's most valuable unencumbered asset was Placid Oil Company, then a hugely profitable production company that H. L. Hunt had founded in the 1930s and placed in trust for the future generations of his family. The banks wanted Placid to underwrite the brothers' debt. To lock the family company in, the banks loaned the $1.3 billion directly to Placid, which then *reloaned* the money to the three Hunts after Placid's independent trustees made them put up a raft of personal assets as additional collateral, right down to Lamar's gold Rolex.

Placid's note seemed good as gold. Had it not been privately held, Placid Oil would have been in the top tier of the Fortune 500; its assets in the oil-hungry economy of the early 1980s were worth at least $2.2 billion, nearly twice what the banks were owed. And Placid held title to many of the original East Texas oil fields that were the core of the old man's fortune.

But by making Placid responsible for repaying the silver debt, the banks, in effect, put every family member at risk. That was because Placid belonged in equal shares to the six trust estates H.L. had established for each of his children and their offspring. Placid was an asset to be passed on from one Hunt generation to the next, providing investment income to everybody along the way.

Through Placid's involvement, the trusts of Margaret, Caroline, and Hassie had thus been transformed from innocent bystanders to vulnerable partners in the soured silver operation. Then the oil market started to soften. This meant the Hunt family now had a new worry: If Placid couldn't keep up its payments to the banks, the financial institutions could take over Placid and still try to collect from the personal assets of each brother, sister and child in the family, on the theory that they were all alter egos of Placid.

Seeking to prevent that, an anxious family divided its assets in 1983, with the trusts of Herbert, Lamar and Bunker getting Placid—and its attendant silver debt—and the trusts of the sisters and Hassie taking other valuable real estate and oil and gas leases. The Placid loan was refinanced for $1 billion, with Bankers Trust and Texas-based Republic Bank coming in as the lead banks. The idea was to make only Herbert, Bunker and Lamar responsible for repaying the Placid loan.

This was the first time that the sisters had stood apart from their brothers, told them, in effect, that they couldn't count on being bailed out by the rest of the family anymore. Even after that, when the banks foreclosed on some property owned by the Bunker and Lamar trusts, it was their sister, Margaret, whose trust bought the land at auction to keep it in the family. But the rift, coupled with the ensuing financial success of the Hunt sisters, left some bruised egos among two generations of Hunt men.

With her husband, Albert G. Hill, Margaret oversaw her own oil investments and managed the posh Garden of the Gods Club in Colorado Springs. Caroline was an enormously successful businesswoman. She owned an investment company, office buildings and a string of elegant hotels, including the Mansion on Turtle Creek, one of the most fashionable in Dallas, and the Bel Air in Los Angeles.

As the brothers scrambled, you could hear the mixture of jealousy and envy that constituted sibling rivalry, Texas-style.

"Only thing I can remember my father telling me *not* to do is this: Don't have anything to do with hotels," Bunker said in an obvious reference to his sisters. "He said the first guy always lost it all and had to sell at a loss to a second guy, and the second guy would sooner or later have to sell out, too, and only when the third guy bought the hotel would the price be down to where it ought to be."

Herbert, embarrassed at how Bunker's envy had bubbled over, quickly changed the subject. "He told me never to be a director of a bank!"

Bunker: "He had a brother that was. Brother got into trouble."

Herbert saw one of Caroline's elegant hotels on his drive home one day and ruefully remembered what Bunker said about avoiding them. "My sister wouldn't like that."

Even as the family divided its holdings in 1983, the three brothers were busy on another front. They were the sole partners in one of the world's biggest oil drilling companies, Penrod Drilling Company, and during the boom days in the oil patch Penrod expanded quickly on borrowed money. The partnership borrowed $700 million in 1980 to build new drilling rigs. But two years later, with the market already starting to soften, Penrod realized it was overextended and asked for a renegotiation of that loan, too. It took time, but a new deal was finally cut in 1984, with the banks, this time led by Manufacturers Hanover, asking for another $200 million worth of collateral. Herbert's trust had $100 million worth of real estate that hadn't already been mortgaged to Placid, and the banks finally settled for that.

What happened next was what the Hunt brothers' lawsuits with the banks were all about: Depending on who did the talking, the Hunt brothers either jumped, or were pushed by the banks, into the financial quagmire that bankrupted them.

No one disputed that the oil business went into a depression that took the Hunt companies with it. There was also no doubt that the two Hunt businesses were deeply in debt and, by mid-1985, on the verge of defaulting on the $1.5 billion they collectively owed their banks. Moreover, three of the brothers' sugar companies had just filed for bankruptcy protection after losing additional millions in another oil-drilling scheme, so the banks were already wary. So was Herbert. Paranoid to the point of believing that the banks were engineering the Hunts' fall, he started taping his telephone calls with the bankers.

Desperately seeking to avoid default, Placid began trying in April 1985 to raise money by selling some of its oil properties in the Dutch North Sea. Amoco was interested, but before the parties could come to terms word apparently leaked out to Amoco that this was a distress sale, and Amoco's bid came in unacceptably low. According to the Hunt's lawsuit, the leaks came from one or more of the Placid lenders who wanted to sabotage the sale and take over Placid's assets themselves. Susman, going further, said flatly that he had evidence the leak came from Bankers Trust, one of Placid's lead banks.

In late 1985, Placid thought it had put together a favorable refinancing package, only to have that fall apart, too. The Hunts' lawsuit claimed their bankers gave the prospective new lenders "detrimental false information." Susman claimed at least one of the banks put out the word that "the Hunts don't pay their debts. You shouldn't get involved." Negotiations to work something out with the existing lenders bogged down as well.

As Herbert explained it, "virtually every loan document of any significance that I've ever entered into, at one time or another, has been redone. That's just standard procedure. You put together a loan document and, a year or two down the way, it's going to be redone." But the banks that had in the past been so obliging to the Hunts now were uncooperative. There would be no more refinancings. The banks claimed the Hunts had simply become bad risks. But the brothers contended that the banks wanted them to fail.

"They made no bones about it," Herbert Hunt explained. "They said, 'If Placid can't pay, get it from some other member of the Hunt family. Get it from your sisters. Go get it from somebody else.'

"Essentially, the same thing happened with Penrod. They said, 'Go get it from the partners. If you can't get it from the partners, get it from somewhere else.' I'd say, 'Well, my sisters are not obligated to pay.' They'd say, 'We don't care. Just get the money from somewhere.' They've taken the position that they're going to get paid by somebody, regardless of whether they're on the note or not. They perceive, frankly, that there's much more assets, in the way of cash-paying ability, than is really there. If oil was 30 bucks a barrel, they'd probably be right. But at $15 or $18, they're not right.

"There's no way that the banks are going to prove that my sisters and my kids and my personal account is responsible for Placid's debt, or is responsible for Penrod's debt. That's like saying you own a share of General Motors, so you have to come in and take care of their problems. That's essentially the position the banks are taking."

With default all but inevitable, the Placid bankers met with the Hunts on March 6, 1986, and urged a liquidation of the oil company's now-greatly-diminished assets. When Placid resisted, Bankers Trust declared it had the authority to veto any future drilling project that couldn't guarantee a payback in two years. That would push Placid even closer to the brink.

When it came to Penrod, however, at least some of the lenders had something different in mind. On January 30, 1986, they held a meeting with the Hunts in Dallas to reveal a bank-sponsored plan for creating a huge international oil-drilling cartel. This was important, because if one big entity controlled most drilling rigs, it could set prices as it wished. The cartel could push drilling rates high enough that companies like Penrod could staunch their losses. And, of course, the banks would start getting paid again.

Under the plan, drawn up by an officer of Houston's First City National Bank and endorsed by Chemical Bank's managing director for international banking, the banks themselves would get an ownership interest in the cartel, thus profiting along with their borrowers as drilling rates were pushed up. Drillers who joined the cartel would get preferential work-outs of their debt and wouldn't risk foreclosure.

On March 14, Chemical Bank's officer made one final, elliptical effort to persuade the Hunts to join the drilling cartel: "I have visited with most of the key banking players and outlined generally the proprietary concept which we presented to you," he wrote. "They are uniformly interested and excited about it. If you haven't had the opportunity to confirm for yourself that it accomplishes what we described, I urge you to do so." The banker was closing hard. "You have an opportunity to not only survive," he told the Penrod partners, "but to do so as the strongest player in the market."

On March 27, Placid failed to make a scheduled principal payment and thus defaulted on its loan. The debt then stood at $705,050,450.72. On May 27, Penrod failed to make a scheduled interest payment, thus defaulting on its remaining debt of $714,210,338.21. Interest started piling up on the loans at the rate of more than $400,000 a day.

An atmosphere of mistrust now pervaded relations between the Hunts and their bankers. Herbert, particularly, worried that the rest of the family was going to be drawn into the legal problem because of the "alter ego" theory. Discussions to work out new payback arrangements were still being held, but both sides were far apart. The main sticking point was that the Hunts wanted to keep enough cash freed up for their big oil exploration gamble in the Green Canyon. This was important both to Placid, which owned the leases, and to Penrod, which would get the contract to do the drilling for its sister company. The banks thought the plan was a loser, just one more way for the Hunts to deplete their assets.

"The banks took the position, 'Hey, just shut it all down,' explained Herbert. " 'Just produce your reserves and we're gonna get paid regardless of what happens to the price of oil, even at $10 or $12 a barrel.' In effect, the banks said, 'Liquidate the company.' "

Throughout this period, the Hunts' negotiations with the banks had been handled by Alan Miller, a partner in the respected New York law firm of Weil, Gotshal & Manges. But now, fearful of being sued by the banks in New York, a venue they deemed would be hostile to a trio of buccaneering Texans, the Hunt brothers started laying plans for a lawsuit of their own.

Without telling Miller, one of the brothers contacted a Boston litigator, Stephen Gordon. In the arcane world of bankruptcy law, Gordon's firm, McCabe/Gordon, was a high flier. The firm liked to set itself apart, beginning with its posh State Street offices high above Boston Harbor and the trendy slash in its name. Partners Gordon and Edwin McCabe styled their twenty-nine-lawyer firm as an elite strike force, available for litigation anywhere in the country.

In the three years since its founding, McCabe/Gordon had gained a reputation as a "kamikaze" law firm: one that would push the limits of legality when it came to suing banks and filing for bankruptcy, even if it meant, as it twice had, that McCabe/Gordon would be reprimanded by judges for unethical conduct. Banks rightly feared McCabe/Gordon, but they also distrusted the lawyers. Played by the official rules, litigation still is a gentlemanly pursuit. But McCabe/Gordon stretched the rules and occasionally broke them.

On April 30, Gordon met in Dallas at the Adolphus Hotel with the Hunts and the group shook hands on a plan to start drawing up a lawsuit. But it wasn't until nearly a full month more had passed that Herbert Hunt informed Weil, Gotshal's Miller that Gordon had joined their legal team. Miller wasn't any happier about Gordon's arrival on the scene than the bank's lawyers were, and within a month after that —on the day that Gordon left a phone message at Miller's office telling him the Hunts were filing their lawsuit against the banks— Weil, Gotshal resigned the account.

The lawsuit alleged that the banks used their lending power to try to take over the Hunts' assets, and it sought an astonishing $3.6 billion in damages. A second lawsuit, filed afterward and then folded into the first one, alleged an antitrust conspiracy among the banks to cartelize the world drilling market. It asked for an even more incredible $10.2 billion in damages. The banks countersued to collect on the loans, and the brothers' siblings jumped into the litigation to protect their own fortunes.

A few courts had endorsed the Hunts' legal theory, known as *lender liability,* but this case applied it on a mammoth scale. Whatever the outcome, the Hunts were writing a whole new chapter on the emerging legal doctrine, under which banks are accused of defrauding borrowers by making loans that the banks know can't possibly be repaid and then driving the borrower into bankruptcy so the bank can take the collateral. The banks had no choice but to take the Hunts' case seriously, because in the months following its filing there were two $60 million lender liability jury verdicts, the largest amounts ever awarded in such cases. Those other judgments couldn't compare to what the Hunts were asking for, but that was just because no private citizens had ever borrowed as much as the Hunts!

As it turned out, filing the lawsuits was the high-water mark of McCabe/Gordon's representation of the Hunt brothers. With both the federal trial judge, Barefoot Sanders, and the bank lawyers watchful of and wary of McCabe/Gordon's every move, the firm seemingly achieved the near-impossible feat of putting the brothers at even more of a disadvantage against the banks. McCabe/Gordon lost every legal battle.

When in July 1986 the banks started to foreclose on the Hunt property that had been posted as collateral for the Placid and Penrod loans, Gordon marched into court with more than 600 pages of affidavits and pleadings. On August 27, Judge Sanders ruled against him. Two days later, Gordon placed Placid Oil and a related entity into Chapter 11 bankruptcy proceedings in New Orleans, thereby blatantly disregarding Sanders' order requiring that all legal proceedings relating to the Hunts be filed in Dallas. Sanders initiated a contempt proceeding against McCabe/Gordon and a few days later ordered the bankruptcies sent back to Dallas. The mercurial Bunker Hunt, meanwhile, turned once again to Philip Hirschkop, the lawyer who'd once represented black militant H. Rap Brown, and whose credentials on the radical Left were as impeccable as Bunker's were on the ultra-Right. Hirschkop's assignment was to dig up some dirt on Sanders that would get him thrown off the Hunt case. Bunker believed Sanders had a liberal bias against the conservative Hunts. Hirschkop cooked up some flimsy conflict-of-interest charges and filed a motion seeking Sanders' replacement. But that motion was denied, too.

McCabe/Gordon, meanwhile, had serious problems of its own. For one thing, it now represented a whole slew of Hunt entities in a variety of proceedings, and the bank lawyers accused the Boston firm of having a conflict of interest. The conflict arose because another one of the brothers' partnerships was owed over $677,000 by the bankrupt Placid Oil. This meant that McCabe/Gordon was representing both a creditor and a debtor in the very same bankruptcy proceeding. Facing certain disqualification, the law firm resigned from the bankruptcy case on October 10.

McCabe/Gordon also faced a court-ordered return of $695,264 in fees it had received from Placid and the Hunts. At the start of the case, McCabe/Gordon had received at least $1.8 million, perhaps much more, as a retainer. But there was no written fee agreement, just the handshake between Gordon and the Hunts that previous April. On its own, McCabe/Gordon allocated $1 million of the Hunt-paid retainer to the bankruptcy action, keeping $800,000 for itself and sending another $200,000 to the New Orleans law firm that briefly served as its local counsel. At the least, there was an appearance that McCabe/Gordon had played fast and loose with the Hunts' money. But since legal fees in a bankruptcy case have to be approved by the court, the bank lawyers saw their opening. In their own feat of kamikaze lawyering, the bank lawyers summoned Gordon to an eighth-floor conference room at Baker & Botts in Dallas, put him under oath, and took *his* deposition in an attempt to prove improper conduct and thus force McCabe/Gordon to return the money it had received from the Hunts.

"I want to make sure everybody here understands what this is about: Who is going to end up with the money—Mr. Gordon, or Placid?" Baker & Botts' J. Michael Baldwin began when the Bostonian showed up that Wednesday for the March 11, 1987, grilling by Baldwin and nine other bank lawyers.

It was a session in which all the enmity between Gordon and his foes spilled out, with Gordon calling the bank lawyers' marathon questioning "a tag team match." Morning wore deeply into afternoon as the lawyers beat away at him, probing into every aspect of his failed relationship with the Hunts. "Rat-killing questions," Gordon's own legal mouthpiece branded them, because everybody sounded more like predators than lawyers. Gordon finally announced he was keeping his 5:20 P.M. reservation on the last direct flight back to Boston. "I don't think it's proper to keep this witness hostage," Gordon's lawyer proclaimed with whatever certitude he could still muster.

In April 1987, after months of contention that included the acrimonious all-day deposition of Gordon by the banks' lawyers, bankruptcy Judge Harold C. Abramson ruled not only that McCabe/Gordon's fee applications "contained material misrepresentations," but that all hourly rates charged by the firm were "excessive" and that the firm's final fee application "contained duplicative and vague entries and was poorly presented." The bank lawyers had, indeed, scored a hit on their kamikaze foes. The amount the judge ordered returned represented almost the entire amount McCabe/Gordon earned for its unauthorized bankruptcy work.

The Boston lawyers appealed, but a victory couldn't possibly inure to the benefit of their firm: Two weeks after Abramson's ruling on the fees, in May 1987, McCabe/Gordon announced it was going out of business, itself a victim of the litigation it had started.

"This was exactly the risk we perceived," McCabe said then. "The worst we feared, happened. We were betting all our resources, our entire firm, on one case. The ideal law firm has a variety of clients, so it's not rising or falling on a single case. We had a lot of other business, too, but we couldn't adequately service it. And potential new clients looked elsewhere." The Boston firm had twenty-five of its twenty-nine lawyers working full- or part-time on the case, from the same office later occupied by Susman's firm in Thanksgiving Tower just down the hall from the Hunts. Travel expenses alone totaled as much as $68,000 a month. When McCabe/Gordon lost the account, its lawyers scrambled for new business but didn't find enough. A consultant recommended wholesale firings—sixteen lawyers remained at the end—but they weren't sufficient, either.

"They're a long way from Texas," a laconic Bunker said after the brothers fired them. "They perhaps didn't fit into the local conditions here."

"Get involved in a New York lawsuit, you need a New York lawyer," Herbert added with the seeming ingenuousness that marked everything he said. "If you're involved in a lawsuit in Texas, you need a Texas law firm. For sure."

Said Susman: "The banks want to make an example of McCabe/Gordon. They get a free shot at a law firm that's broken up and won't do a good job of defending itself. If they thought it would benefit them to turn on us, they would."

Abramson's May 1987 ruling on the legal fees was the final blow to McCabe/Gordon, but, as early as the previous November, Herbert Hunt, mistrustful and ready to switch lawyers for the third time in just seven months, had once against started telephoning prospective new law firms. Chicago's Kirkland & Ellis was approached, as was Minneapolis' Robins, Zelle, Larson & Kaplan, the firm that was already trying to outrun Coale in the Bhopal chase. Both Kirkland & Ellis and Robins, Zelle were known as outstanding litigation firms, but both had also done legal work for some of the bank defendants in the Hunt litigation, and thus both were precluded from taking the case by legal conflict-of-interest rules.

Finally, the Hunts turned to Susman's Houston firm, interviewing

Susman on November 13 in Dallas and offering him the job a month later.

As a young lawyer from an obscure Houston firm a decade ago, Steve Susman earned a giant-killer's reputation—and a $7,350,000 fee—as the lead attorney in a price-fixing class action that returned $366 million, plus another $219 million in interest, to the purchasers of cardboard folding cartons. It was largely on the basis of that reputation that he established his own law firm specializing in complex commercial litigation, and he was already earning his coveted $1 million a year when the Hunts found him.

Although Susman charged the Hunts $600 an hour—twice the McCabe/Gordon fee the bankruptcy judge branded excessive—he got away with it by cleverly writing off the premium fees to the plethora of nonbankrupt companies and partnerships that the Hunt brothers still controlled and that were beyond the bankruptcy court's jurisdiction. The brothers' maze of business entities was so bewildering that the bank lawyers couldn't find the source of the extra fees.

Susman avoided some of McCabe/Gordon's other mistakes, too. Unlike his Boston predecessors, he committed only seven of his firm's twenty-two lawyers to the case. Eight other lawyers, rounding out the Hunt litigation team, were hired on a contract basis for only as long as the litigation lasted.

The Hunts finally professed to have found an alter ego in the cigar-smoking Susman. He was a Yale man, true enough, but he also was a University of Texas Law School graduate, a Texan who spoke, with a drawl, the lingua franca of both sides. During twenty-one days of depositions of Herbert Hunt, it was Susman who relieved both the monotony and the tension with adroit wisecracks that seemed to leave the defense lawyers at a loss.

Better than that, though, after getting rid of McCabe/Gordon the Hunts began winning. Susman defeated the banks' attempt to collect the Hunt's $1.5 billion debt prior to a final resolution of the case, and Henry W. Simon, who was handling Placid Oil's bankruptcy proceedings, got a ruling permitting the brothers to go ahead with the Green Canyon oil-drilling project.

The Hunts, using an untested technology, were scheduled to begin operations in Gulf water deeper than anyone had ever drilled in before.

The risk was obvious. One of the brothers' own employees had even testified that if Placid had the benefit of hindsight on the project, "we probably wouldn't have gone forward." Although preliminary drilling of six wells indicated that three of the six would produce oil and gas, there had been many technical problems, not the least of which was determining how to bring to the surface what might be down there. No existing rig could work so far offshore, so the brothers had to design their own at a Brownsville drydock. And when the deep water prevented ships from laying the last 10 miles of their underwater pipeline, the Hunts had to fashion another ingenious solution: They rented the entire island of Matagorda in the Gulf and welded the 10 miles of pipe into a single piece on the beach. From there, it was to be dragged 585 miles to the Green Canyon along a 1,000-foot-wide path on the Gulf floor.

For a $4.5 million premium, Lloyd's of London was insuring the finished contraption against a breakdown in its first year, but nobody guaranteed how much oil the Green Canyon project would ever produce.

"What bottlenecks do we have? What might delay us?" Herbert asked Phil Clarke, Placid's vice president for operations, one day in Clarke's office.

"Maybe a hurricane," Clarke replied.

"Isn't going to be one," Herbert said emphatically. Clearly, there was no arguing the point, but puzzlement weighed heavily on others in the room. Herbert sensed it, too. "I've consulted my long-range weather guru," he explained, completely serious as knowing smiles broke out all around. "He's looked at the jet stream and the sun spots, and he says no hurricanes in the Gulf this year."

The banks opposed the project, declaring that if the Hunts had any cash they ought to be repaying their loans, not gambling on such a risky venture.

But the brothers replied that since most of the money to bankroll Green Canyon was coming from outside investors, the brothers (and their banks) wouldn't be much worse off, if the project failed, than they already were. A big strike, on the other hand, would make everybody healthy.

"It's important because it's the major asset that the companies have that can produce some positive income stream," said Lamar. "It definitely is helpful in us being able to show a positive way to get out."

"Seems like to me," added Bunker, "here we are, we've raised the financing from outside parties. There'll be substantial income from it, and at no cost to the banks. I would think they'd think that was wonderful. And I think they're really not very sincere about wanting to see us do well, because otherwise they wouldn't oppose it. I guess maybe their strategy is just to fight us and cause us as much trouble as they can. Maybe that's the ordinary bank strategy. But I think that just helps prove our case: that they're trying to give us a hard time."

"Where's Bunker?" Herbert wanted to know. In the Hunt Energy offices, two geologists who worked for the family were waiting to present the seismic evidence on some new oil and gas "plays" the Hunts were considering, but the rumpled and rotund Bunker—the older brother who played Oscar to Herbert's fastidious Felix—had not yet ambled in. Herbert peered again out the conference room door. "Where's Houston?" he said this time, and soon learned that Bunker's son, who was also supposed to hear this presentation, was attending his wife's tenth high-school reunion in Tulsa. "Doug saw this yesterday," Herbert muttered to himself as he mentally checked off still another of the third-generation Hunt oilmen—Doug is Herbert's oldest son—who would be given a chance to buy into this project. Herbert's two other sons, Bruce and David, were part of the family business, too, and it was Bruce who uncovered this prospective deal in the South Texas fields below San Antonio. The timing was important, and the risk was apparent. Energy prices had finally stabilized, and the Hunts were betting they'd bottomed out. But to capitalize on that bet they had to start drilling now, with prices still in the trough, so they'd have something to sell on the upturn.

If the family made this deal, exigencies of the bankruptcy proceedings dictated that the Hunt elders not participate. Their cash was tied up by the banks. Nevertheless, it was clear that Bunker's reaction to the deal would carry great weight. "He's the big picture guy," another Hunt geologist told me. "Herbert tends to the details."

"Let me explain what we've got here, Bunker," Herbert began upon his brother's arrival. "This is mainly a gas play." He sat at the twelve-foot-long table in the stark twenty-fourth-floor room and explained the underground formations as chief geologist Bertram Hayes-Davis pointed to the formations on wall-mounted seismic maps. Bunker said nothing, seemingly uninterested, arms drooping alongside his chair, then interrupted: "How deep a well do you need?"

Bruce: "Fifteen thousand feet."

Bunker: "How much does that cost?"

Bruce: "$2.2 million dry, $3 million complete. Shell had a shot at this already, and it didn't produce. It's not a sure thing."

Bunker: "Looks like a pretty decent prospect."

Herbert: "Okay, give him the numbers."

Hayes-Davis believed they might have to drill six wells before finding anything, and that, in itself, would cost an estimated $14 million. The potential revenue would be $150 million at today's prices, but production expenses would also be high, leaving a profit of only $29 million. Hearing this, the family seemed more attracted to a second field nearby. This one, encompassing 2,400 acres, was four times larger than the first. Exploratory wells would have to be deeper, and thus more expensive to drill—$25 million in total—but with lower anticipated production costs the potential return on their investment could be as much as $125 million.

They leaned toward making a bid for drilling rights to this parcel, but it would be a tricky negotiation. Two major oil concerns also were snooping around the property, and, as big as the Hunts still were, they were also wildcatters with less bargaining leverage than the majors they sold to. Amoco "owes Bruce a favor" because the son passed along a tip about another oil field, Herbert said. "They'd be a good partner. Why doesn't Bruce see if they want to make a deal?"

Bruce, sensitive enough about being the son that he called his father "Herbert" in the office, concurred. "I'm afraid if we don't contact 'em and they want this, they'll blow us out of the water."

The wealth represented around this conference table was immense, but the truly striking aspect was the informality of the decision making. Although the brothers and their sons had adjoining offices, each man ran what amounted to a separate business entity, an empire within the empire. Each had his own account and made his own decisions about how to spend the money in it. Once a month, everyone sat down together for a business meeting and all the accounts were charged their pro rata share of the Hunt Energy Company overhead.

With millions of dollars needed for a drilling investment, each brother or child had the option of participating. If there weren't sufficient Hunt family partners for a particular deal, that wasn't a deterrent; wealthy partners could still be easily found. "Whoever has the cash and the appetite," in Bruce's words. In the big Green Canyon project, for instance, there were several outsiders putting up big money.

"They're sort of born into it," Herbert later said of the Hunt children, "because they have investments of their own that were made for them when they were young." The Lennox corporate headquarters in Dallas, for example, was owned jointly by Herbert's son, Doug, and the son of Paul Stephens, Herbert's longtime partner in many other real estate ventures. Yet Bunker and Herbert took obvious pride in the fact that their sons were with them. A few times a week, the Hunt men put on their suit coats—no matter what the summer heat—and the gaggle of fathers and sons walked the few blocks to the Dallas Petroleum Club for lunch. Lately, only a few tables were ever occupied—"couple of years ago, every table'd be full," a chagrined Herbert said. There was friendly banter about a thousand-dollar-a-pound dieting bet between Bruce and Herbert, and there was serious discussion about the prospects for the Hunts' soon-to-begin $20 million drilling effort in Zambia. Bunker thought the landlocked African nation was one of the final petroleum frontiers, and he wasn't deterred by the fact that the nearest producing oil well was 1,700 miles away.

Sounds like a gamble, somebody told Bunker.

"It's only gambling when you don't know your odds," Bunker replied. "If the seven of us were playing poker, one or two guys would win all the money every time. Same guys. That's because poker's a game of skill. Just like this is." It was a working lunch. Everybody went through the buffet line, everybody ordered iced tea, and everybody picked up the obligatory toothpick on his way out the door.

The family was close, "but everybody is free to do his own thing now," Herbert said. "If you want to go on your own way or pack it all in, go ahead."

In that way, the legendary H. L. Hunt's influence abided, for that was how he raised his sons. "He wasn't a fellow to force his views," Bunker explained. "Even when you asked his opinion, he'd tell you to figure it out for yourself. He didn't encourage going to school, or, if you went, what to study." Bunker never got beyond the first year of college. Herbert and Lamar both finished (at Washington & Lee and SMU, respectively), but, Herbert recalled, "I can remember coming home and telling him I wanted to quit. He said, Fine, do what you want. I didn't ask Mother because I knew what she would have said. She'd have insisted I stay. That was the schoolteacher in her. I know Bunker thinks our mother was a much stronger influence, but the kind of independence my father gave me is a strong influence itself."

Ironically, the independent spirit that H. L. imparted to succeeding generations of the Hunts probably kept the family business together. It's usually hard for a big, monolithic family corporation to survive the strains that come from the competing interests of third- and fourth-generation shareholders who don't share the vision of the founders. The Hunt brothers and their children didn't face that problem because their interests were already widely scattered, with family assets divided among hundreds of separate trusts funds, corporations, and partnerships.

Entwined within this hard-to-untangle knot of business interests, the three brothers of H. L. Hunt's first family still owned free and clear an estimated $450 million worth of personal property that the banks and the IRS (which had its own lawsuit against the brothers pending) might, or might not, be able to get their hands on. That was one of the many issues to be resolved in the pending lawsuits.

On a Saturday morning, Herbert got up at dawn and put on a T-shirt that said "War Games," the name of one of several movies he bankrolled a few years ago when times were better.

In a weekly ritual, he went for a twenty-mile bicycle ride that took him all over North Dallas. Sometimes Herbert pedaled over to one of his shopping centers and rode his bike all around. "You see all kinds of things on a bike you'd never notice otherwise." He'd put on 20 pounds with the strain of the litigation, and although his ample frame and square jaw helped him carry the extra weight reasonably well, "now I'm too heavy to jog, so I have to do this instead." The five foot ten Bunker, same height as his brother, had a weight problem, too, and he tipped the scales at close to 300 pounds before checking into California's Pritikin Institute, a pricey fat farm where he shed 80 pounds (mostly regained now) and made friends with John Ehrlichman, who was also there.

Five miles from home, Herbert's rear tire blew out. He telephoned his wife of thirty-six years, Nancy: "Mom, come and get me!" When she arrived, he threw his bike into the trunk, slid behind the wheel of her Cadillac, and immediately started driving the wrong way down a one-way street. "Dad! Dad!" his wife yelled from the back seat. Unfazed, Herbert whipped the sedan around and headed for home.

Lamar was in Kansas City, checking on his Chiefs. Bunker had flown off to California's Del Mar race track to watch one of his horses run. Although this was a weekend, Herbert tended to his business. He wanted to look over some commercial real estate he owned north of town. Herbert's Promenade Center in Richardson occupied acres of valuable land at a key intersection, but the center itself was decrepit and poorly maintained, the victim of his lack of cash for improvements and the economic decline that had forced many merchants out of business. Sporting sleek lizard-skin cowboy boots and a hand-tooled leather belt with a fancy silver-and-turquoise buckle that said, "Hunt Energy. Herbert," he went off to meet son-in-law Al Allred, the manager of the family's real estate company. Over lunch at an almost-deserted Mexican restaurant, there was talk of finding developers for a major new regional shopping center on Hunt property in Phoenix. Herbert was curious about one prospective developer.

"What's the story with him. Mafia?"

Allred: "He's outta Philadelphia, a little shady. Maybe. Who knows?"

Farther out, in Plano, the various Hunt partnerships and trust estates owned vast amounts of raw land, commercial property and warehouses. The Hunts once owned 5,000 acres here, bought for as little as $146 an acre. It was worth $300,000 an acre now, but nothing was selling and the buildings and warehouses were mostly vacant. Another major Dallas developer, Trammell Crow, had big interests in Plano and owned much of what the Hunts didn't. "Over there," said Allred, pointing to a building as they drove past it. "Trammell Crow had a tenant in that building paying $4 a foot. We offered him $3 a foot, and Crow bid $2 a foot to keep him." The irony wasn't lost on either man. Herbert's daughter, Barbara—Allred's sister-in-law—just happened to be married to Trammell C. Crow, son of the Dallas real estate magnate and a partner in his father's business.

They drove through what was to have been a townhouse complex. But bad times hit before the townhouses were built, and the only things finished were the streets. One of them was called Profit Drive. H.L. believed six-letter words starting with *P* were lucky.

His sons did, too.

As Herbert put it, "Everybody has luck one day and not the next."

Part of what Susman still had to overcome in this case was the perception of the Hunts as bad-boy brothers asking the courts to do what the rest of their family had done before: bail them out of trouble. "My biggest problem in this case is, I represent the Hunts," he said. "How can the richest people in the world be victims? How can the richest people in the world be unsophisticated? It just doesn't make sense. How can they have been taken advantage of by the banks? Shit, they're almost as big as the banks! Everyone perceives that the banks can beat up on the little guy. There's a lot of sympathy there. But who would have sympathy for the *Hunts?* What people don't realize is that they were just as desperate for money as the little guy.

"Everyone assumes that the Hunts are sophisticated businessmen. They are not. They aren't rubes and hayseeds, and maybe they don't fall off the turnip truck, but unlike other wealthy families—the Basses in Fort Worth and others—who have gone out and found top executives, paid them a half a million dollars a year and given them a piece of the business, there is no one you will meet around here who you will be impressed with, who is a financial genius and whiz, who would have gone far on his own."

That would be Susman's strategy at trial: portraying the Hunts as hapless Joes who needed protection from the banks. Not surprisingly, Susman still viewed that as a tough gambit to pull off—given the publicity a loss would have, he almost did not take the case for that reason—but he sure did believe in the strategy. If the Hunts were gamblers waiting for the next card, so was Susman.

"There's an economic reason for people filing a lawsuit," Susman told me. "You know, people say, 'The Hunts are trying to delay paying the money. The Hunts don't want to pay the money.' I'll stipulate that! Sure, they don't want to pay! The question is, Do they have a good legal and factual basis for not paying? It's also a question of, What will be left for them if they pay?"

Steve Susman was as much a misfit in the Texas bar as the Hunt brothers were in their own community. Among the white-shirted, risk-averse lawyers in the big firms of Houston, Susman was clearly a renegade, and he relished that role. In his own way, he was a gambler, too, and when he was starting out on his own as a young Houston lawyer he'd taken out a $400,000 loan to fund the only case his law firm had, a class action that took five years to complete. He'd literally bet his entire fledgling firm on that one case, and if he had lost it he'd have been in no better position to pay off that loan than the Hunts were to pay off theirs.

Susman understood the Hunts because he understood what it meant to buck the odds. His father, a former *Yale Law Journal* editor and a respected Houston lawyer, died when young Steve was eight. With her own law degree from the University of Texas, his mother then went back into practice, and she made it clear to her sons that law should be their career path, too. Steve and his younger brother, Tom, both went to Yale, then both returned home to the University of Texas for law school.

Steve was the classic overachiever, editing the law review, graduating first in his class with the highest grade-point average in the school's history, clerking for Judge John R. Brown of the Fifth Circuit and then heading to Washington to clerk for Justice Hugo Black during the Supreme Court's 1966–67 term. He toyed with the notion of staying in Washington when his clerkship ended. After all, a fellow Texan, Lyndon Johnson, was in the White House and "there were Texans all over town." But Susman went home instead, to become the first Jewish lawyer in Houston's powerhouse firm of Fulbright & Jaworski.

There, he quickly gained a reputation as a bright, brash associate who lunged after the big, glamorous cases rather than earning out his indenture the way other Fulbright & Jaworski associates did, handling countless little cases in the rural Texas courthouses to prime them for the big time.

"He wanted to work on nothing but the big cases and to travel to exciting places," one Fulbright & Jaworski partner said of him. "After all, staying at the Pierre is a whole lot better than staying at the Three Palms Hotel in Angleton or the Oasis in Bay City."

Susman was possessed of such confidence in his own skills and disdain for his own firm's little conventions that the partners took it for arrogance, a lack of "team spirit." He arranged trips to rattlesnake roundups in Sweetwater, Texas, and organized parties to professional wrestling bouts. He entered a crawfish-eating contest in Louisiana and, as the "Earl of Oregano," took a team to the annual chili cook-off in Terlingua, Texas. But the stunt that was to earn him the lasting enmity of some of his fellow Fulbright & Jaworski partners was his sponsorship of a bartender friend of his, Carter Townley, for an associate's position at the firm.

Townley was just a high-school graduate, but Susman phonied up some hot-sounding credentials for him—membership in the "Order of the Wig and Gavel," the "Riley L. Finsterbach Moot Court Excellence Award," appropriately turgid law review articles and a clerkship with a nonexistent judge. Word was floated that local rival Baker & Botts was also after Townley. Sure enough, Susman's unsuspecting partners offered Townley a job, and then Susman rubbed their noses in their mistake by revealing his ruse at a firm party.

It said something about Susman that in spite of his wayward ways he made partner at the staid firm in just six years. But it also said something that he left what should have been a life estate just two years later, in 1975.

The bureaucracy of a big firm wasn't any match for the ego of an ambitious young lawyer like Susman, and he'd known that on the day he made partner, when he gave the news to his wife. Karen Susman was a petite woman. Steve met her while he was in law school. She had been an undergraduate at the university, a finalist in the University of Texas Bluebonnet Belle competition. "I remember racing home to tell my wife that I had made partner," Susman recalled. "She asked how many others made it, and I said, 'Eleven.' She wasn't very impressed. And I asked myself what had really changed. Now I was a junior partner. So what?"

Dissatisfied by big-firm life and still seeking a place that would accommodate his independent spirit, Susman decided to try academia. He took a leave of absence from Fulbright & Jaworski in 1975 and got a job teaching antitrust law at the University of Texas, but that wasn't satisfying, either. To Susman, money was a way of keeping score, and his $25,000-a-year law-school salary wasn't enough. Almost as soon as he started teaching, he changed his mind again and decided he wanted to resume practicing law. But now the doors were closed to him at Fulbright & Jaworski. It's one thing to mock your fellow partners, but it's quite another to kiss them off altogether, and that's what Susman had done just two years after they anointed him. From here on out, he'd have to make it on his own. Putting the best light on a bad situation, the young lawyer professed not to care that he'd been shunned by his own partners.

Besides, he said, "I was tired of doing the same old thing. I wanted to roll the dice for a lot of money, to pass my contemporaries, to go on the offensive."

Susman started looking around for a lucrative niche in the Houston legal market, and he thought the big money might lay in plaintiffs' antitrust class action work. Houston didn't have any lawyers specializing in that; when it came to the arcane but lucrative practice of antitrust, Houston was a defense lawyer's town.

Class actions—in which thousands of plaintiffs can be represented in a single lawsuit—had taken on an important function in the legal system. Without them, big corporations could overcharge people a few dollars here and a few dollars there, secure in the knowledge that nobody would bother to file a suit since the cost of litigation would far exceed the amount recovered. The class action concept made these cases worthwhile.

It also made them attractive to lawyers who sought out such cases and paid hundreds of thousands of dollars worth of expenses on behalf of clients they'd never met, gambling that they'd win the case and be rewarded by the court with a huge fee. The losers got nothing for what could be years of work, but the prospect of a multimillion-dollar fee made it worth the lawyer's risk. When the publication *Class Action Reports* added it all up a few years ago, it found that lawyers had received almost 14 percent of the $1.25 *billion* recovered in 135 antitrust and securities class actions litigated or settled in the past decade.

The antitrust class actions Susman wanted to bring would be aimed at companies that got together to fix prices. Price fixing occurs when two or more competitors *explicitly* agree to charge the same price for their product. The law says that's wrong because it makes customers pay more than they should. The economic basis of the antitrust laws is simple: When price fixing stops, prices drop and buyers benefit. The lawyer's job in such a case is to prove how much everybody was overcharged by the price fixing. Those who've been gouged are entitled to recover from the price fixers three times the amount they were overcharged.

From the lawyers' standpoint, maybe the best thing about class actions was that judges didn't like to try them. The lawsuits can be so complicated that settlements aren't just welcomed, they're encouraged by an overburdened judiciary. And a settlement can produce a generous fee for the plaintiffs' lawyers without the risk and hard work of a trial.

But any notion of Susman's that he had discovered a legal goldmine was soon replaced by the realization that others had found this mother lode much earlier. There was already a well-established plaintiffs' antitrust class action bar, comprising lawyers in Philadelphia and Chicago. (New York and Washington was where the antitrust defense lawyers were). This tight group controlled every major class action. Susman was an outsider once again.

Undaunted, Susman started looking around for another partnership to join, one small enough to showcase his considerable talent and desperate enough for it to let him have the leeway he couldn't get at Fulbright & Jaworski.

In September 1975, having just begun his search for a new law firm, Susman ran into fellow lawyer Sidney Ravkind in a local barber shop. He told Ravkind his story, and, in what would begin an amazing run of good fortune, Ravkind encouraged Susman to consider joining his law firm.

Ravkind's firm, Mandell & Wright, was an outsider in the Houston legal community, too, a law firm that made its money from personal injury litigation but that much earlier had earned its reputation as a haven for gadfly Herman Wright, a lawyer for all sorts of unpopular left-wing causes in Texas, and a candidate for governor of Texas in 1948 on the Progressive Labor ticket. Unlike Houston's establishment firms in those days, Mandell & Wright was also willing to take cases on a contingent-fee basis, under which its lawyers were paid a share, usually a third, of the money they won for their client. That landed the firm in hot water, too: In 1957, Messrs. Mandell and Wright had been suspended from practice for several months for allegedly soliciting clients.

"The old, stodgy Houston lawyers sitting around playing dominoes at the country club say, 'Mandell & Wright, shit, they're ambulance chasers,' " Susman remarked. But that bad-boy reputation had an allure for Susman.

Now all he needed was a big case.

But clients weren't exactly rushing through his door. In fact, he was picking up what little work he could get as an antitrust-law consultant to other lawyers who *did* have cases.

In the fall of 1976, Susman got a telephone call from a friend and former client, Victor Samuels. Samuels was a sales manager for the Houston Corrugated Box Company, a small maker of corrugated boxes, and he'd received a subpoena to appear before a federal grand jury investigating price fixing among corrugated box makers. The grand jury was meeting right there, in Houston. Would Susman represent him?

"Come on in," Susman told him. "And bring the subpoena with you."

As Susman waited for Samuels, he pondered this turn of events. "Samuels probably isn't a target of the investigation," Susman thought, "so he won't need me for long. If I represent Samuels I'll make, maximum, maybe $5,000. But I'll also be disqualified" from ever representing a private plaintiff who might later on sue Houston Corrugated or any other box maker for the same practices the grand jury was then investigating. That's what the conflict-of-interest rules were there for.

So when his friend Samuels arrived, Susman told him to find another lawyer. Then he used the visit as a chance to find out as much as he could about the grand jury investigation.

"I'd heard rumors about that grand jury," Susman said. "But when I saw that subpoena, then I *knew.*"

"Vic," Susman told him, "once you've been to the grand jury, I'd appreciate it if you come back to tell me what they asked you." Samuels said he would.

Susman and another young Mandell & Wright lawyer, Gary Mc-Gowan, met with Samuels on March 2, 1977, soon after his visit to the grand jury, and he gave the two lawyers the information they needed, the same information he'd given the grand jury.

"Hell, yeah!" Samuels told them about his competitors in the corrugated-box business, "they've *all* been fixing prices." Susman had checked out an encyclopedia of trade associations from the library, and, in Susman's office, Samuels went down Susman's list of Fiber Box Association members and told the duo which of the big corrugated box makers he thought were fixing prices.

Now Susman knew enough to file a lawsuit. The important aspect of Samuels' information was that it gave Susman a rock-solid basis for rebutting any defense claim that he lacked probable cause for such a lawsuit. Under Rule 11 of the Federal Rules of Civil Procedure, a lawyer has to be able to show that his lawsuit is based on facts, not guesswork, and a Rule 11 motion would be one of the first documents a defendant would file. "With Samuels' notes in my file, I knew I wouldn't have a Rule 11 problem," Susman said.

There was just one problem: Susman had a case but he still needed to find, as a client, a box buyer who'd been overcharged by the price fixing.

What makes class actions different from every other type of plaintiffs' litigation is that the lawyer usually has the case *before* he gets the client. It's a classic case of lawyers chasing clients, and anxious lawyers have been known to pay hard cash to prospective plaintiffs to entice them.

The reason is that when a big case comes along—and the corrugated-box investigation certainly qualified—many separate class actions are likely to be filed, each with its own cast of lawyers and representative plaintiffs. Sooner or later, the multiple actions have to be merged into a single big lawsuit. Once that happens, the court appoints a steering committee of the plaintiffs' lawyers to oversee the case. The committee parcels out work assignments and otherwise runs things. So, to a lawyer, getting onto that committee is vitally important.

When the case is finally litigated or settled, every lawyer submits his time sheets to the judge, who then pays the lawyers out of the pool of money available for the plaintiffs. The lawyers' straight hourly rate is called the *lodestar,* but if the judge thinks the lawyers produced an exceptionally good result, he can pay them more by applying a *multiplier* to the lodestar.

Just as for mass disaster lawyers, the name of the game here is control: getting on the steering committee and getting work from the committee are key elements in the class action lawyers' legal strategy, because they need to put in their hours in order to get a share of the judgment when the case is over. Moreover, the lawyer who files his case *first* has a strategic advantage. The presiding judge might perceive the lawyers who filed later to be copycats, and he might be more likely to reward the first lawyer with a choice position on the steering committee.

All this was on Susman's mind as he pondered his next move. "I wanted to be the first," he recalls. "I didn't want some turkey to beat me."

McGowan had a lawyer friend in Austin named Bill Kemp, and, for a piece of the action, Kemp thought he could help. He had a client, Adams Extract Company, that spent $7,000 a year on corrugated boxes to ship its vanilla extract. Kemp delivered the client, and on March 21, 1977, Susman filed his class action in Houston federal court on behalf of Adams Extract and all others similarly situated.

He hadn't been quite fast enough, though. Another lawyer had also heard of the grand jury investigation, inferred that price fixing had been going on in the industry, and filed a similar case in Chicago on behalf of a furniture maker and a golf supply company. The rest of the class action bar weighed in thereafter with cases of their own. All told, during the ensuing six months thirty-seven more class actions were filed in seven judicial districts across the country.

Importantly, the deans of class action litigation, Harold Kohn of Philadelphia and Perry Goldberg and Granvil Specks of Chicago, had filed cases of their own, but not in Houston, because they had no intention of letting Susman play a meaningful role in the case. They wanted the cases consolidated in Chicago, a venue they knew and were comfortable with because they'd already prosecuted some class actions there.

"Many of these people were known for bringing class actions based on what they would read in the newspaper, and settling the class actions," remembered Bill White, then a young lawyer working with Susman on the corrugated-box litigation. "By and large the plaintiffs' class action bar was not comprised of people who were good trial lawyers. Some people had developed a skill for finding roles to play in large cases. And other people had developed a skill for politically organizing the plaintiffs' bar in a way that would put themselves in an advantageous position." In other words, there was, and is, a you-scratch-my-back-and-I'll-scratch-yours mentality in the plaintiffs'-class-action bar. The class-action power brokers who got onto a steering committee always remembered their friends when they doled out the work.

Clearly, a solution was going to be brokered between these two competing groups, too, but how much leverage did Susman really have? "We were *virgins*," he said now. "We had *never* been involved in one of these major class actions. We had nothing to trade. No prior alliances. *Nothing*."

What Susman did have going for him was this: Among all the competing factions, he was the only lawyer with an office in Houston. And since the grand jury investigation was taking place there, a good argument could be made that a local lawyer ought to be in charge of the class action.

Since a judicial panel was going to meet in November 1977 to decide where to consolidate all the cases, Susman flew to Chicago to meet with Goldberg. He wanted to defuse the argument so a united front could be presented to the judges, who usually rubber-stamp the recommendation in such circumstances. But Goldberg would have none of it. He was set on a trial in Chicago, with him as chairman of the steering committee. If Susman would go along, Goldberg told him, he would reward him for his acquiescence with choice assignments. But if Susman refused, Goldberg would ruin his future in the plaintiffs' antitrust bar.

Susman agonized over the threat for weeks. "I knew that I had good arguments for trial in Houston, but was my position worth the risk to my career?" he asked himself. "Goldberg and Specks wield a lot of power, and they're so creepy and snaky." Ultimately, he decided to take his shot at the judicial panel, telling the judges on September 30 during arguments in Boston that the case belonged in Houston because the government's criminal investigation already was taking place there. The Specks-Goldberg faction made the argument that the case belonged in Chicago because an analogous price-fixing case, against the makers of folding cartons, already was pending in the same court. But it was clear that Susman had impressed the panel with his argument, and next it was the Chicago faction that made the entreaties. Specks called, offering to make his peace with Susman by proposing Susman as his cochairman of the steering committee. Then Kohn called, asking Susman to be his liaison counsel in Houston. Susman turned them down. He wanted to own this case *himself,* and he would soon get the chance. On November 29, 1977, the special judicial panel consolidated all the cases and sent them to Houston. And, on December 5, all the plaintiffs' lawyers met again in Houston to elect their thirteen-member steering committee for the case.

Susman's side had already met, separately, in Houston on November 28. Realizing they had enough votes to control the committee no matter what the outcome on venue the following day, they held a straw vote for their seven members and came up with Susman as chairman. With him were six allies: Vance Opperman, whose family owned a big chunk of West Publishing Company, the big legal publisher in St. Paul; Philadelphia's Allen Black, who had left the Kohn firm and now was an outsider; Lowell Sachnoff, a Chicago lawyer who had spurned the rest of the Chicago faction to side with Susman; Jack Corinblit of Los Angeles; Seymour Kurland of Philadelphia; and Joseph Tydings, a Washington lawyer and former U.S. senator from Maryland.

The December 5 meeting at the Houston Club was so raucous that the forty warring lawyers couldn't even agree on how the votes would be tallied. Three systems of secret balloting had to be used: "one lawyer, one vote," weighted toward the firms that had sent many lawyers to the meeting; "one case, one vote"; and "one plaintiff, one vote." There were Houston, Philadelphia, and Chicago factions—"Just like a bunch of Mafia dons," Susman thought—and the powers from each warring faction caucused in different corners of the room before every key vote. No matter which balloting method the lawyers used, though, Susman kept winning. He'd impressed the lawyers by his leadership during the divisive battle over venue. And there were many who resented the tactics used by the Chicago faction that wanted to control the case.

In a gesture of magnanimity, the seven elected members of the Houston faction chose just one more local lawyer, Charles D. Kipple, and then allowed the Chicago faction to designate five additional members of the steering committee. The Chicagoans chose Specks and James Sloan, both of Chicago; Kenton Granger of Kansas City; Jack Chestnut of Minneapolis; and Jerry Cohen of Washington, one of Kohn's partners. But the eight-to-five split guaranteed Susman control of the litigation, and, it would turn out, a fair-sized headache from the outfoxed Chicagoans who couldn't abide the power this young upstart now possessed.

To get the steering committee organized and keep it running, each law firm was assessed a pro rata share of expenses. Each lawyer paid for his own travel, Xeroxing, postage, and related costs. But the lawyers had a common fund to pay for such expenses as a document depository to hold the 2 million documents produced in the case, transcripts, mailings to class members, and expert witness fees. All told, the plaintiffs' counsel paid $1.4 million in assessments. Of that, $126,000 was paid by Susman's firm.

With that much of their own money going out, the lawyers understandably wanted to keep the case moving along. Their first objective was to have the class certified—in other words, to persuade the Houston judge, John Singleton, to agree that the plaintiffs had a valid case to take to trial. Such a certification of the class—by no means a certainty, despite the fact that, by now, the government had produced scores of indictments from its own investigation—would be the main inducement to settlement. Defendants occupied with the criminal case, which would go to trial quickly, could ignore Susman's civil lawsuit until he had the class certified.

On the other hand, a criminal conviction would be powerful evidence for a civil trial, and *that* was an incentive for a company to settle *early*. Susman was hoping for an ice-breaker settlement like that, and he didn't have to wait long. On February 1, 1978, just five days after the criminal indictment was handed up, a lawyer for the St. Regis Paper Company approached Susman and suggested that St. Regis, which hadn't even been indicted in the criminal case, was willing to discuss a settlement.

The anomaly of *joint and several liability* in the antitrust law gave a company like St. Regis a strong incentive to extricate itself from the case. Two or more companies found liable for antitrust damages are treated the same way a husband and wife would be if they failed to pay their taxes: If one can't pay, the other must, no matter what the relative guilt of the parties. In the corrugated-box case, this meant that a company had an incentive to settle early, paying as little as it could get away with and leaving the rest of the defendants on the hook for the remainder of the damages.

Susman's settlement strategy would play on that. Companies would pay on the basis of their own market-share percentage of the total nationwide sales of corrugated boxes and sheets, but those settling early would get a big break. The longer a company waited before settling, the higher the price per point would go.

St. Regis had come through the door first, offering $428,000 per point, or $1.7 million overall, even though it had escaped unscathed from the two-year federal criminal investigation. That offer was accepted; if an unindicted company would pay that amount, it would show all the defendants just how strong a case Susman had!

It wasn't long after that when Susman had breakfast with the lawyer for the Mead Corporation at the Whitehall Hotel in Houston. Mead's lawyer was Harold Baker, of the respected Washington law firm of Howrey & Simon. Baker wanted to know what it would take to settle the case, and Susman suggested a number: $1 million a point.

Baker laughed at Susman's suggestion. "You've got to be kidding," he said, "the class hasn't even been certified yet! You don't have a case!"

Susman sat there stone-faced. "Okay, Harold," he replied, "if that's the way you want it."

That would have been a bargain for Mead, because soon thereafter the steering committee decided to place a much higher value on its settlements. Estimating that the overcharges due to price fixing might be as high as $350 million, the lawyers established what amounted to a rate card for early settlements. Indicted defendants would pay $3 million a point; unindicted coconspirators, $2 million. And companies that hadn't been indicted at all would get off with $1 million a point. Moreover, the plaintiffs decided to lay their strategy out on the table for the defendants, hoping to encourage them to come forward quickly and to quash any efforts they might make toward a no-settlement policy of solidarity.

Susman also wanted another settlement to break the ice, though, and so the committee decided to accept one settlement from an indicted defendant at the $1 million-a-point level. Susman thought a settlement like that wouldn't go unnoticed by Judge Singleton, who was considering the class certification motion. That a defendant represented by competent and prominent counsel elected to pay Susman and his men millions of dollars in advance of any ruling on the certification motion would be evidence that the defendants felt the plaintiffs would ultimately be certified and prove their case.

International Paper Company thus became Susman's next settlement target. The company had already made settlement overtures, although only at about half what Susman would be asking for. With International Paper's 8.3 percent share of the market, a $1 million-a-point settlement would raise the precertification pot to over $10 million. Furthermore, the company's lawyer, Henry King, of New York's Davis, Polk & Wardwell, appeared to be someone Singleton respected.

Susman got his settlement on August 11, along with an agreement that the International Paper Company, a felony indictee and therefore one of the most culpable price fixers, would provide the plaintiffs with documents from its files that would help the class make its case against the others. The next month, Singleton certified the class.

Susman's case was moving, and the steering committee raised its rate card again, this time to $5 million a point for felony indictees and $3 million for everyone else. But now there were some new problems. True, more defendants were offering to settle, but none wanted to pay more than the $1 million a point that International Paper had paid. It was clear that Susman's divide-and-conquer strategy was failing. He received letters from three defendants—Owens-Illinois Inc., Continental Group, and Weyerhaeuser Company—that read almost alike and held fast to the $1 million-a-point offer. Then he learned that Leroy Jeffers, a crusty senior partner from Vinson & Elkins, the Houston firm where John Connally also practiced, was proposing a group settlement using the International Paper formula. There was going to be an off-the-record conference with the judge to explore Jeffers' group settlement proposal just one week later.

Defendant solidarity was just what Susman wanted to prevent. He needed to break the settlement logjam, and now he saw his chance as he received a telephone call from a lawyer from Union Camp Corporation, an unindicted defendant. The Union Camp lawyer was asking for the $1 million-a-point benchmark, too. But Union Camp hadn't been indicted, and a settlement with Union Camp at the lower level would actually *strengthen* Susman's hand in bargaining with the others who were more culpable. If Union Camp wanted to settle for $1 million, Susman told the lawyer, there was a chance to work something out. But Susman would have to work quickly, for the conference requested by Jeffers was imminent. Susman and some of his fellow lawyers met over the next three days with Union Camp's principal pretrial attorney. Using the government's grand-jury and trial documents, the plaintiffs' team showed him that, although unindicted, Union Camp certainly wasn't without blame. The result: a $2 million-a-point settlement, with an *unindicted* defendant, that would be a model for others to follow.

On December 13, 1978, Jeffers was in Singleton's chambers, speaking on behalf of the indicted defendants. What was fair for International Paper was fair for the rest of the indicted defendants, Jeffers said. They wanted to negotiate as a group, and they weren't going to pay more than $1 million a point. When it came time for Susman to speak, he stunned Jeffers by revealing that he'd just concluded a settlement with an *unindicted* defendant *at $2 million per point.* Jeffers was beaten, and he knew it. Soon, many of the remaining thirty-three defendants would literally be lined up outside Susman's office, "like customers at a butcher shop," Susman would gleefully say, to preserve their place in the settlement line.

Jeffers had painted himself and the hold-out defendants into a corner. He'd led them to believe that his Houston hometown would be prodefendant. Indeed, the defendants had been so certain that Houston would let them down easy that they'd appeared in court *on Susman's side* when the renegade plaintiffs tried to have the cases transferred to Chicago. But now the cost of holding out looked very high, indeed. And Jeffers thought Susman was bent on making him look like a fool.

Now, it was Jeffers who began putting the heavy hand on Susman, a man roughly half Jeffers' age and a lawyer with none of Jeffers' clout in Houston. Enraged by the off-the-record conference in Singleton's chambers, Jeffers went to Susman's office and threatened him. "Steve," he said, "you have a living to make in this community after this case is over. A lot can be done for you by Houston firms. They can refer business to you. Don't rub our noses in this shit!"

Inside, Susman was shaking. "I was just a *kid.*" But he gazed back evenly and replied: "Do what you have to do, Mr. Jeffers." The conversation had its effect, though. From that point on, Susman believed it was strategically important to settle quickly with the defendants who had Houston lawyers, even if it meant giving in on the amount of money the plaintiffs received. If any defendant went to trial, Susman wanted the home field advantage with the jury. He didn't want to face another Houston lawyer on the other side.

Immediately after the off-the-record conference with Singleton, Susman returned to his office for a meeting requested by the lawyers for two unindicted companies, Container Corporation of America and Champion International. They said they spoke for *all* the unindicted companies, and they made the same announcement as Jeffers had that morning: All the unindicted companies, they said, were going to stand firm and negotiate as a single group. They would pay, as a group, $27 million, no more. That was less, per point, than the $2 million per point that Union Camp had already accepted.

Susman was facing another settlement impasse, and, just as he had with the indicted defendants Jeffers spoke for, he needed to formulate a stratagem for breaking their unanimity. Caucusing with his other steering committee members, Susman suggested they assign a settlement dollar number to each unindicted defendant on the basis of what the plaintiffs' lawyers believed to be their relative culpability in the price-fixing scheme. Then, Susman said, the plaintiffs should make the fact of what they'd just done well known to the defendants, without giving them the actual numbers.

The defendant-by-defendant settlement numbers ranged from $2 million to $4 million per point. But, Susman told the defense lawyers, as long as they insisted on negotiating as a group the plaintiffs would only give them their overall settlement demand of $60 million from the unindicted companies. He also told them that, as before, early settlers would get discounts over later ones.

Susman reckoned—correctly, it turned out—that each defendant would believe it had been ranked at the low end, and that it could get a better deal by negotiating separately than by paying the flat rate in a group settlement. The next day, December 14, four of the unindicted companies separately negotiated settlements at $2 million per point. The resolve of the unindicted companies had been broken. In the ten days prior to Christmas of 1978, the three conference rooms in Susman's law firm were constantly filled with defense lawyers. Subgroups of the plaintiffs' lawyers would be negotiating with each defendant, with Susman's lawyers constantly running back and forth from the law firm's offices on the twenty-first floor of a Houston office tower to the document depository three floors below so they could retrieve crucial hot documents that demonstrated both the strength of the plaintiffs' case and the appropriateness of the defendants' rank in terms of culpability. Susman shuttled from room to room like a maitre d' checking on his guests.

There was an important reason to keep the settlement fever burning. The federal government's criminal trial would start soon after the beginning of the new year, and Susman wanted to bank as much settlement money as possible before that. If the government lost its case, he would lose his settlement leverage. The companies had an incentive to settle before the criminal trial, too, because during it a lot of incriminating evidence would start to emerge.

Meanwhile, other problems were still unfolding. Undeterred by his poor showing before Judge Singleton, Jeffers was still pushing for a group settlement for the indicted defendants. And Susman had lost control of some of his own people. The Chicago faction was still making trouble for him. Sloan and Specks, two of his steering committee members, had refused to sign the Union Camp settlement, and now they were objecting to *every* settlement being negotiated. They stopped attending steering committee meetings and instead attacked their cocounsel at every opportunity.

"These attorneys," Susman would later write of Sloan and Specks in a court filing, "objected to preliminary approval of the settlements, attacked the class notice, objected to final approval, appealed the judgments of final approval to the Fifth Circuit, attacked the District Court's additional findings entered on remand at the trial court level and before the Fifth Circuit, and one of them recently petitioned the Supreme Court for a writ of certiorari in a continuing effort to upset the settlements. Other than that, they did not raise any trouble about the settlements."

Susman's settlement committee had hired two economists, Richard Hoyt of Minneapolis and Jeffrey Harrison of the University of Houston, the latter of whom was also an attorney, to estimate the total damages caused by the price fixing. They told the lawyers at the start of the new year that corrugated-box prices during the four years preceding the lawsuit had probably been inflated by about 4 percent, about $490 million during that short span of time.

The plaintiffs' lawyers wanted to use those numbers to arrive at a total-recovery target for their case. They decided they could realistically expect to get another $150 million from the eight holdout indicted defendants, bringing the total settlement pot to $363 million. With interest, that would rise, in two more years, to $440 million. But there was nothing scientific about their calculations. They were simply pushing for what they thought they could get.

Their objective was to divide and conquer the eight holdouts Jeffers was leading, and that meant using the same strategy that had been so effective on the unindicted defendants. When Jeffers visited on January 9—less than a week before the criminal trial was to begin —Susman told him the indicted defendants had been ranked, on the basis of culpability, from $4.5 million to $6.5 million per point, but that as long as Jeffers' defendants were negotiating as a group, they would be given only the package settlement price demand. Another meeting was held the next day, and, the day after that, the group effort of the indicted defendants collapsed as lawyers for Owens-Illinois Inc. and Olinkraft called to make their separate peace, for $6 million a point each. Then, with pretrial proceedings and jury selection already under way in the criminal case, Susman brought in still another indicted defendant, Continental Group, at $6.5 million a point, along with three other companies that had been charged by the government with misdemeanors—St. Joe Paper, Stone Container, and Inland Container—at $4.75 million per point. When the criminal trial began in earnest on January 22, 1979, Susman and his plaintiffs' lawyers had $298 million in settlements in eight Houston banks, earning interest. Almost overnight, he became one of the state's largest depositors.

Almost everyone had settled with the government, too. Only Mead Corporation and Continental Group, and seven of their executives, were going to trial in the criminal case. Susman sent lawyers into Singleton's courtroom to watch, but what they reported was not encouraging. The inexperienced government lawyers were using economists and other experts to prove the price-fixing conspiracy, but all their fancy graphs and theorems couldn't overcome the fact that the government didn't have a single live witness who had smoking-gun proof of a conspiracy. The defense counsel were demolishing the credibility of the government's witnesses. The case finally went to the jury on April 27, and the jury took just three hours of deliberations to acquit every defendant. Later, when Susman interviewed the jurors, some said they were ready to acquit even before the defense put on its case. By not producing any live victims, the government had lost.

This was awful news for Susman and his lawyers. There were still many holdout defendants. This meant that they probably *wouldn't* settle. It also jeopardized the nearly $300 million the lawyers already had in the bank, because now the push to overturn the settlements was coming from *two* sides, the disgruntled Chicagoans and the companies who already had settled and now understandably believed they had given up too easily. Susman knew that if his earlier settlements were set aside, he could never duplicate his success again.

It was clear that Mead, at least, intended to make Susman prove his case in court, just as it had forced the government's hand earlier. "Millions for defense and not one cent for settlement" was how Susman wryly described it at the time.

Susman could use the formal pretrial investigative phase of the lawsuit, the *discovery*, in various ways to get the proof he would need at the Mead trial. One way was to take the sworn testimony of a potential witness, a *deposition*, before trial. Another was to ask for answers to written questions, called *interrogatories*. And, because there had been a prior criminal case, Susman had still a third way of getting his proof, because he had a court order that let him see some of the grand jury testimony that had been taken as the government prepared its case.

But the people whom Susman questioned during discovery were not always very helpful. They did, after all, have a Fifth Amendment right to remain silent, and so many of the box-making officials—160 in all—took the Fifth that Susman started deposing them by telephone, rather than wasting the expense of sending a lawyer to a deposition only to have him return empty-handed. All told, the plaintiffs took 400 depositions from mid-1979 to mid-1980, 150 of those by telephone. Because many witnesses had taken the Fifth Amendment, Judge Singleton was going to allow Susman to tell the jury about it. The law didn't let the court draw any inferences about guilt or innocence from the invoking of the Fifth Amendment in a criminal case. But, in a civil case, the court was allowed to view "adversely" a witness' exercise of his constitutional right to remain silent. Because it was a sensitive legal issue, though, any revelation about the use of the Fifth Amendment would be followed by a strong cautionary instruction from the judge. Invoking the Fifth Amendment was a constitutional right, after all. It would be up to Susman to somehow weave the inference of guilt, from so many Fifth Amendment takers, into his case. The jurors needed to conclude, by themselves, that people invoked the Fifth Amendment because they were guilty. If Susman said that, it would cause a mistrial.

Susman put together a team of five young lawyers who would spend the next six months cloistered in the plaintiffs' eighteenth-floor document room preparing for the trial against Mead. The idea was that those five greenhorns would comb through the 2 million subpoenaed documents and depositions, gathering the proof that would eventually be put into evidence by Susman and his team of older, more experienced lawyers.

On April 2, 1980, Susman summoned to Houston the six lawyers who would be spending the next five months of their lives trying the case with him. Kent Granger traveled down from Kansas City to take charge of the trial office that was set up in the document depository. Jerry Cohen, a bleary-eyed, rumpled bear of an attorney, arrived from Washington. Also on the trial team were Allen Black and Laddie Montague of Philadelphia, Vance Opperman of St. Paul, and Charles Kipple of Houston. There also would be nine paralegals and another seven full-time and nine part-time attorneys working behind the scenes for the plaintiffs, fetching documents, interviewing and preparing witnesses, writing briefs and doing all the other things that needed to be done during the trial.

"There's winning," Steve Susman intoned. "And there's losing."

Susman was describing what made a trial lawyer different from the rest of the nearly 700,000 lawyers in this country. "When you do deals, when you write wills, you aren't winning and losing. You're finishing jobs. But there's no sense of victory, or defeat, that you get in trial work. It's part of the competition. The game. That's it. It's the battle, the confrontation with the other lawyers in court, coming out ahead. I get off on that battle. I love it."

Winning.

"You have to have the physical stamina to work eighteen hours during a trial and then get four or five hours of sleep, week after week. You have to perform publicly before a jury. You're always on the line, you're always out front, you're always performing.

"There are people who don't want to put themselves in that position," people who aren't possessed of Steve Susman's supreme self-confidence. "You can make a fool of yourself. You can lose.

"What you have to remember," Susman said, "is that trial law is a spectator sport. What you really want to do is give a performance, and you have to do it in such a way that the jury *understands.* The jury must know when you land a blow on the other guy. So the key is, how do you articulate to the jury, 'I'm gonna knock this guy out,' and then, after you've done it, announce, 'I just knocked him out!'

"It's the way you question a witness on cross-examination. The way you lead up to it. The way you modulate your voice. The way you approach the witness, and the way you ask a leading question, looking at the jury so they understand you're about to ask a really important question. The way you repeat the answer."

There was the time in 1986, for instance, that Susman was representing a small company accused of having sold defective oil-well casing to a driller. Susman was bearing down on the plaintiff's key witness during cross-examination. The questions were coming one after another. Bam. Bam. Bam. Then the knockout punch, when Susman confronted the witness with his own earlier statement that the casing was good. The witness paused, then said: "Steve, may I take a break and talk to my lawyer?" Susman knew right then that he had the case won. The jury knew it, too. They returned a $4.1 million verdict for his client three weeks later.

That same year, Susman represented the *Arkansas Gazette* in an antitrust suit against the rival *Arkansas Democrat*. The *Gazette* was accusing the *Democrat* of trying to run it out of business. Before the trial, Susman had taken the deposition of the *Democrat*'s publisher, Walter Hussman, Jr., and he had seemed, to Susman, to be a man who didn't even know what was happening in the business he owned. But by the time Hussman got to the courtroom, he was a different witness. "They had cleaned up his act," Susman recalled.

Susman, prepared to cross-examine a bumbler, found himself confronting, instead, a publisher who clearly impressed the jury. Susman kept on, but Hussman never lost his composure. He was in control. Susman wasn't.

"When I finished, I knew I had taken some blows," Susman recalled. "By that, I mean, I didn't *destroy* him. Because cross-examination allows the witness to keep talking to the jury, and, unless you're using it to destroy the witness, you might as well not cross-examine him, because he's establishing more rapport with the jury, demonstrating he's an honest guy, he's responsive, and all that stuff.

"I was prepared, in my mind, to examine a witness who was going to bumble around. And he didn't. I just should have sat down. Finally, I did, but it wasn't soon enough.

"When the guy's landing blows on you, the key there is, *not* to show it," Susman explained. "The biggest problem most lawyers have during a trial is, how to sit there stone-faced. How not to show you're hurt, when you've just been *gutted.* It's real tough. Because this is the amazing thing: Most of what the jury picks up is what people are *doing.* Not what they're saying. Only a small part is picked up through the spoken word. They're bombarded with words, too many words for them to understand."

Susman knew these things because he spent a great deal of time interviewing the very juries that judged him. Lawyers are free to do that once a trial has ended. Usually, it's done immediately after the trial, before the jurors have gone their separate ways. But Susman often went further, inviting them to his office and paying them to critique his effort.

He has changed his style as a result. "They expect lawyers to be combative. They expect fights! That keeps them awake. They love it! At one time in my career, I thought it was better to be a real gentleman. Then you talk to the jury after a case and they say, 'We didn't get enough fireworks. You weren't forceful enough.' "

Susman was trying to be, in his words, "more folksy" now with jurors. He talked to them more, didn't try to wow them so much with splashy graphics and charts. That's because, in the oil-well-casing trial, the jurors he interviewed told him afterward that he'd been too overbearing on the opposing lawyer, Ed Junell of Houston. Junell played up his underdog role to the jury, and Susman thought it was "the most effective thing that lawyer did during his closing argument. He said, 'Mr. Susman is so fast, he's like a railroad train. He gives you so much information and goes so fast, I can't keep up with him. I can't jump on that train.'

"I try to be less cerebral, more folksy. Look around the country. You won't find very many good trial lawyers who have been editors of law review, clerks to justices of the Supreme Court. Why? Because usually the guy who makes the good trial lawyer is at the bottom of his class in law school. He does everything nonintellectually. It's all on instinct. Joe Jamail is the perfect example," Susman said, referring to the legendary Houston lawyer who represented the Pennzoil Company in its record $10.53 billion judgment against Texaco. As a law student at the University of Houston, Jamail flunked a class on torts, the branch of law dealing with wrongful acts. "He's a wonderful jury lawyer. But there ain't a thing intellectual or scholarly about what he says. Last time he's read any law, God only knows if there *is* a last time! Joe has a wonderful way with people. People skills. But you'd *never* hire him to argue an appeal. They didn't let him go near the Texas Court of Appeals. Even though Joe is a big [campaign] contributor to those judges."

And that was how Susman, with the ego characteristic of any successful trial lawyer, differentiated himself from the pack. He wasn't another Jamail, wasn't even particularly friendly or approachable, if the truth be told. As Susman saw it, he didn't need to be. He was a thinking man's trial lawyer: an *intellectual.* In his own mind, he stood apart because he could take on the cases that required more than just a smile and a shoeshine to win; cases that, in Susman's view, maybe no other lawyer could win.

"Look at the guys who are great personal injury lawyers, the guys who are great criminal defense lawyers. It's easy! The criminal lawyers are dealing with witnesses you can just murder! They're dealing with prosecutors on the other side who are inexperienced. If you can't practice law and make money, you go to the prosecutor's office.

"With the personal injury lawyers, usually, it's a question of how much: A guy gets his arm blown off, he's gonna win! It's just a question of, is he gonna win $2 million or $15 million. And so it always sounds like a great victory.

"But in our cases, it's not always clear who got hurt and who didn't get hurt. You're dealing with wonderful lawyers on the other side, and with witnesses, most of them, who have a master's degree, or a law degree. You're cross-examining people who are twice as smart as you are! It's very, very difficult to land what you'd consider an absolute knock-out blow."

On Monday morning, June 10, 1980, Steve Susman walked up to the jury that had just been selected for the trial against Mead. (There were two other corporate defendants who would soon settle, leaving the Dayton, Ohio, giant to go it alone.) Susman held before them a corrugated box.

"A couple of weeks ago—I guess it was a couple of weeks ago—when you were here and selected as jurors, Judge Singleton showed you a corrugated box, a little like this, but probably smaller. And he told you that these corrugated boxes come in all sizes, shapes, and colors. And they certainly do. And you will see a lot of them before this trial is over."

Indeed. And the jurors also would be hearing a lot about one of the most esoteric areas of law in modern jurisprudence: antitrust. Right from the outset, Susman had to bring this case down from the rarefied heights of the antitrust theoreticians and economists to a level that the average man could understand.

Susman told the jurors that he was going to be presenting a complicated case, one encompassing fifteen years of time, during which $60 billion worth of containers were sold to 200,000 purchasers (the class members) by thirty-three different companies. But he had a simple way for them to look at all the evidence: What the corrugated companies had done was to confer among themselves before they set their prices. It was just like "the fellow who takes his car to a body shop" to get an estimate on repair work. "You want a second estimate, so you drive across town to another body shop and ask for a second estimate," except what the second shop does is to call the first one "and asks what that body shop quoted you in the estimate.

"Now, I suspect that if that ever happened to you, you would suspect that you did not get the benefits of free and open price competition. I suspect further that it wouldn't give you much comfort if, after you caught the two body shops talking about the prices they were going to charge you, they both said, 'Well, we didn't have any agreement on what the price was going to be. We didn't fix the price.' "

That was how Susman wanted the jurors to view the antitrust laws: not as a bunch of technical rules that were a nuisance to businesses, but, instead, as "the bill of rights of the free enterprise system." Texans were an independent, outspoken bunch, and Susman tried to appeal to their free-spiritedness when he said that the people who passed the Sherman Act "thought that economic freedom and independence was as important to our economic system as it was to our political system."

Susman's two-and-a-half-hour opening statement, a carefully scripted-out set piece, led the jurors through an analysis of law and corporate conduct that added up to guilt by analogy. The defendants had "tampered" with prices, and that was like tampering with "the nervous system of the free enterprise system." They'd committed their crimes not in some smoke-filled room, not through contracts and blood oaths, but, rather, by a tacit understanding that had simply evolved—"a little more like embezzlement than a bank robbery. The victim is not hit all of a sudden. It goes on slowly, gradually, over a period of years."

The Mead lawyers didn't like Susman's analogies, and they rose in objection every time he used them: "Your honor, we have wandered off into argument again. We are going to have to object every time he does it. He is talking about bank robberies. He's lost his theory."

The judge admonished Susman, but the young Texan kept to his script. It was working.

The victim was the average man, Susman told them, and the average man was "the last one to know he's been the victim of secret understandings, meetings, phone calls that went on for many years behind his back. It's a little like the nuclear kind of disaster that almost happened at Three Mile Island."

Another objection. "Are we going to try the Three Mile Island case or this case?"

And so it went. Susman told the jurors his case was going to involve mainly circumstantial evidence, a perfectly acceptable way for him to prove his case. "It is a conspiracy case. Conspirators do not conspire in public. They do not keep notes. They do not announce to the world what they're doing. It is like—I'm sure you remember the story of Robinson Crusoe, who saw footprints on the sand and concluded there must be someone else on the island without seeing the other person. That is circumstantial evidence, the footprints. We are going to be able to show you some footprints in this case. Some are very deep, many are shallow, and many have been just covered up by the people who made them."

Harold Baker was a highly skilled antitrust defense lawyer from the brass-knuckles litigation firm of Howrey & Simon in Washington, and he tried to take the offensive away from Susman, attacking the number of lawyers Susman had on the case—"believe it or not, over 100"—and battering away at what he, and, privately, Susman as well, saw as the weakest part of the plaintiffs' case: the absence of real, live victims. That was the strategy Mead's lawyers had used to sink the government's criminal case, and Baker, who'd been living with the case since the government first began its grand jury investigation in 1975, was certainly going to use the gambit again.

"He says, 'I can't prove my case through my clients,' " Baker said, mocking his young rival. "I don't know how in the world one proves their case if they don't prove it through their clients, but I will make you one small promise: We will put some of those 200,000 clients on the witness stand to prove we didn't do it. Neither footprints nor buzz words and especially footprints in the sand on Fantasy Island can be the basis of a finding of a mutual agreement [to fix prices]."

Mead had a lot riding on Baker's ability to get it off the hook.

Under the antitrust laws, a defendant who lost at trial was liable for *three times* the actual damages, not only for its own antitrust violations but for those of all companies found to be its coconspirators. Mead was the last holdout, and with a guilty verdict it would be left holding the bag for every one of its thirty-five alleged coconspirators. Susman was, after all, putting on evidence of an industrywide conspiracy, and although everybody else had already settled, it didn't follow that the jurors wouldn't find that the trebled damages far exceeded even the large settlement fund that Susman already had in the bank. Hoyt, one of Susman's economic experts, had recalculated the overcharges in the corrugated carton industry, and he now estimated that they had exceeded $997 million during 1974 through 1976 alone, a mere fraction of the twelve years that the evidence covered. Trebled, that meant Mead was looking at a potential payout of something like $2.6 billion just for those three years!

But Baker wanted such stupendous amounts to be seen by the jurors as nothing more than the product of some economist's fanciful theory. He kept banging away at the absence of real victims who could put a price tag on what the price fixing really cost them.

The buyers of boxes, Baker said, were even bigger and more powerful than Mead. "All of the giants of American industry," he correctly pointed out: IBM, R. J. Reynolds, General Foods, Procter & Gamble. "They're members of the class, believe it or not. . . . You fool somebody like that and keep them in the dark for twenty-five years?" No way.

Susman's first witness was Grover Daly. He'd worked in the corrugated-box business for twenty years and had used the industry as the subject for his Ph.D. dissertation. Daly gave the jurors a three-day oral history of the esoterica of the billion-dollar business of boxes, explaining the whole process of how a tree becomes a container, and how the peculiar structure of the big industry had led to divisive competition that could only be staunched by the kind of price fixing that the company executives had engaged in.

Susman and his cohorts had conducted what they'd called a Witness Interview Program, quietly calling around in search of price-fixing participants who might have been overlooked by the feds. Incredibly, they'd struck gold more than once. Susman's second trial witness was an industry executive named Norman Lacey who'd neither appeared before the criminal grand jury nor been named during the criminal trial. Now, he appeared in the courtroom to lend credence to Susman's tale of a conspiracy: Lacey described how industry executives swapped price information over the phone and agreed not to undercut each other's prices.

Witnesses like Lacey had been hard for Susman to find, because, as in any other industry, particularly one as close as this one, the corrugated-box executives were a clubby group who protected each other and had no incentive to help a hired gun blast apart their good thing. Susman always had to be wary, even of industry witnesses who professed to be cooperating. When Susman's people interviewed one out-of-town executive, Don Gamblin, who was going to testify for Susman the following morning, he told them he was planning to visit the Mead lawyers as soon as he left Susman's place. Gamblin's direct testimony was going to be powerful. But Susman fretted that Mead could work with Gamblin to lay a trap for him on cross-examination. On the night before Gamblin's testimony was to begin, "bad vibes" finally got the best of Susman. He dropped Gamblin as a witness.

But Susman's informal interviewing had produced an even more potent witness in Ralph Redmond, who took the stand for the first three days of the trial's second week. Redmond had been fired by Mead in 1972. According to Redmond, the dismissal was based on his refusal to go along with the price fixing. The government could have used Redmond to its advantage, but he had never seen a courtroom until Susman discovered him. Mead claimed Redmond, who'd worked for Mead from 1954 until his firing from his position as a regional sales manager in 1972, was just a bad employee who got what he deserved and now was carrying out a vendetta against his old company. But Redmond's testimony was potentially damaging enough for Baker to have acknowledged it in his opening statement.

Redmond told a tale of palace intrigue within Mead—of meetings with a company antitrust lawyer who really didn't seem to want to know about the price fixing that Redmond told him about; of private sessions with Mead lawyers in which sales executives lied, with a wink and a nod, about the common practices that everybody knew were illegal; of secret price information shared between competitors via the telephone and pieces of scratch paper.

Redmond testified about how he had told a Mead in-house lawyer, in the presence of Redmond's own boss, Robert Neff, that Neff had been fixing prices. Neff had dropped his head to the table then and muttered, "Oh, Ralph, oh, Ralph," several times.

A little while later, Neff asked Redmond to raise his bid on a big order at Kimberly-Clark Corporation, ostensibly at the customer's request. Redmond thought it preposterous that a customer would ask for *higher* prices; he assumed the request was really coming from a Mead competitor who was part of the price-fixing scheme.

Redmond kept the bid where it was and called Mead's antitrust counsel, Jon Sebaly. But lawyer Sebaly, Redmond testified, was in on the conspiracy, too.

"I said I had just received a phone call from Bob Neff that he wanted me to pull his prices at Kimberly-Clark, and he said, 'Yes, I'm aware of it. Kimberly-Clark.'

"And I said, 'How's that?'

"And he said, 'Well,' he said, 'you really should pull those prices.'

"And I said, 'Why is that, Jon?'

"He said, 'Because that particular order,' or 'that particular business, requires a special grade of linerboard which we cannot get.'

"And I said, 'Jon, that's not so. I researched this just before I quoted it, and that board's available.'

"He said, 'That board's not available.' "

An incredulous Redmond once again dialed the Mead employee who allocated the linerboard, "just to confirm that the asked-for impregnated linerboard was available. And he assured me that it was."

Reliving his firing now, Redmond started quivering with emotion. He still couldn't believe how he'd been railroaded out of his job while Bob Neff, who was sitting right there, watching intently from the trial audience, had been promoted to president of the whole division.

Redmond recalled the moment he realized that everybody was in on the conspiracy, and he put his head down on the rail and started sobbing softly.

"And I knew I was dead. You know, I didn't stand a chance of remaining with the company."

Susman kept up a stoic demeanor, but he was warming up inside.

Redmond's testimony was potent stuff, made all the more so by Harold Baker's inept cross-examination of Susman's star witness. For a day and a half, the defense lawyer unsuccessfully tried to shake Redmond's story, alternately arguing with him and berating him. But about the only admission that Baker could wring from Redmond on cross-examination was that Redmond saw himself as a good guy vastly outnumbered by the crooks all around him, hardly something that would go down well for Mead with the jury.

"I knew that I was doing things that were going to lead to my dismissal, absolutely," Redmond told Baker from the witness stand.

"You know," Redmond intoned, "I guess you might—I don't know if this is a good analogy or not, but if you had Eliot Ness working amongst you and you were in the Mafia, you'd get rid of Eliot Ness."

Baker tried to counterpunch. "Is that the way you consider yourself, Eliot Ness?" But all that question did was give Redmond an even bigger opening.

"Yes, I did. I did."

"Among the Mafia?"

"Among the guys who were violating the company policy, yes."

The Mead lawyer simply couldn't beat Redmond down. Even Judge Singleton, ordinarily a patient man, got tired of it.

"I realize that it is important to the defendants to attack the credibility of Mr. Redmond," he told Baker the next morning as the cross-examination wore on, "but I think your cross-examination is getting rather tedious—"

Baker: "I've only got forty-five minutes or less."

"—and really not too productive this morning," Singleton went on, ignoring Baker's entreaty. Singleton had dismissed the jurors for the rest of the morning, so he could be blunt with the defense lawyer without worrying about influencing the jurors. "It is going into matters that the court cannot see are relevant except in a test of his credibility. And I think we ought to move along."

"I am, your honor." Baker tried again. "And I state very candidly exactly where I am going, so the court understands the relevance of it: He was a failure. A business failure. It will be our—"

"Your position—" Ah, how well Singleton knew these defense tactics.

"—position," Baker sputtered.

"I have already gathered that," Singleton said impatiently.

"And I think that we can pretty well prove that. And then I am going to sit down."

Singleton: "Well, I'm just saying I think—not commenting about whether—but I think you've gone along about as far as you ought to go."

Baker: "Have I reached the point where you will give them [the jurors] an instruction that he's not credible?"

Now Susman plunged in with his rapier wit: "The plaintiffs suggest you not rush Mr. Baker. We're enjoying it."

Susman and the rest of his trial team also enjoyed it when the Mead defense blundered into another trap that had been laid for them. Mindful of the government's defeat after its failure to present victims of the price fixing, Susman found some corporate purchasing agents who agreed to testify. Problem was, there was no way for those purchasers to know whether prices had been fixed or not. Baker knew that, too, so Susman expected him to open his cross-examination with a gloating question like "So, Mr. Purchaser, how can you be so sure that prices were fixed?"

There's an old saying in the legal profession: Never ask a question if you don't know the answer. Lawyers are forever arguing over its validity, but one thing was sure in this trial: Baker shouldn't have asked that predictable question, because Susman's purchasing-agent witness was ready with an answer that finally let Susman get his point across about all the Fifth Amendment taking that had been going on.

What evidence do you have that prices were being fixed? Baker asked.

Well, the witness replied, all I know is that a whole lot of people were taking the Fifth Amendment in this case, and if that's not evidence that *something* fishy was going on I don't know what is!

Baker sat down.

It had been the hottest summer Houston had ever had, and the jury had been hearing evidence all during June, July and August. Now, just after nine o'clock on Wednesday, September 10, the case was finally over and the day-long closing arguments were to begin.

Susman went first. He had the burden of proof in the case, so he would have not just a two-hour closing argument but a one-hour rebuttal as well.

Susman's closing argument was aimed squarely at the credibility of Mead's witnesses: "Of the twenty-three current and nine former Mead employees implicated in pricing communications, Mead called only three witnesses to this stand to look you in the eye, to tell you what they did, good or bad, to appear before you in flesh and blood, so that you could hear them, you could see them, you could judge their credibility." Instead, Susman argued, the company presented witnesses who hadn't been involved in pricing decisions at all. In other words, the people Mead put on the stand were "clean enough to get up on this witness stand and look you in the eye and tell you what they did and did not do" because they really had nothing to do with the case.

Mead's lawyers had also promised to produce as a live witness its own chairman of the board, Susman went on, but the board chairman hadn't been called for the same reason most of the rest of Mead's price fixers hadn't been called: "He, too, doesn't want to have to explain the failure, the utter failure, of Mead's antitrust compliance policy and program." Although Mead had promised to let the jury eyeball its employees from top to bottom, "Mead delivered all bottom. And no top."

Susman also threw cold water on Mead's assertion that its antitrust compliance program had been working well by using the Mead lawyer's own notes, which Baker had made in 1975 after the grand jury investigation began but which hadn't been turned over to Susman until midway through the trial.

"Well, I don't need to dwell long on that one," Susman drawled in a way that only made his sarcasm more obvious. "Maybe Mead didn't think the judge would require Mr. Baker to turn over to us his one-on-one interview notes, because those notes, standing alone, indicate that 29 percent of those folks who had pricing authority in '75 had violated the compliance policy!" Susman said an even greater number, 39 percent, had admitted such antitrust violations to the grand jury. "Now, that hardly sounds like substantial compliance to me. That sounds like the kind of exaggeration we've come to expect from the Mead Corporation."

Susman was trying to tell the jury, in so many words, that his nemesis hadn't told the whole story in the courtroom. Mead hadn't produced all the witnesses it said it would, and it hadn't, until it was forced to by the judge way into the game, turned over the evidence of antitrust violations that its own lawyer had collected. And yet, Susman said with the kind of good-ol'-boy impishness he was so effective at, the boys from Dayton wanted the jury to believe that there was simply no way that prices could have been fixed.

"When a company comes into court and says it's impossible, you need to consider whether it's exaggerating, overstating, giving the impression of certainty where none exists. When a witness or a company answers a question with an unequivocal 'You betcha!' it is important to call his bet, to make him disclose his hand. Are all of his cards on the table, or is something up his sleeve? Has he been bluffing?"

There was no question about Susman's view on that.

His experts estimated that the average overcharge as a result of the price-fixing conspiracy was 19.3 percent, but since the smallest overcharge by any of the companies was estimated to be 7.7 percent, that was what Susman wanted the jury to hold Mead accountable for.

"Mead, even if you return the verdict I request, will be able to keep over half, over half of its ill-gotten gains. Even if you return a verdict for 7.7 percent, it is the 200,000 corrugated purchasers, not Mead, that are once again leaving money on the table.

"Ladies and gentlemen, I'm not one of those lawyers that, in their closing argument, pound the podium, slam down books, jump up on the table, wave the flag. I have not attempted to appeal to your prejudices or emotions by ranting and raving about the free enterprise system, or consumer rip-offs, or inflation, or how collusive activities affect and cause inflation. . . . You know, sometimes still waters run deep. Lawyers who represent the plaintiffs in this lawsuit desperately want you to return a verdict in favor of those 200,000 American businesses. And we think that you will do that if you follow conscientiously Judge Singleton's instructions, and review carefully what you have seen and heard in this lawsuit.

"But equally important, however you return your verdict, we want you to leave this courthouse saying that those lawyers representing the plaintiffs, those lawyers leveled with us, they were candid with us, they did not try to cover up or hide any weaknesses in their case.

They respected our intelligence to understand a complex contest and to see through efforts to confuse, cover up and obscure.

"Thank you for your attention."

Baker's closing argument had to be good, because even at 7.7 percent the overcharges Susman was alleging totaled $4.8 *billion.* Trebled, that was $14.4 billion, and Mead was going to be on the hook for almost all of it if the jurors found the company guilty.

"We have called their bluff," Baker began in an obvious reference to Susman and his trial team. "And here we are." This was only the second time in history that an antitrust class action had actually gone to a jury.

The essence of Baker's closing argument was that Susman couldn't possibly have proved his case because the way the box industry operated made a nationwide conspiracy impossible. There were many little plants making strictly local sales; that was antithetical to a big, national price-rigging scheme. Further, Baker contended, everybody's market share was low (Mead had 2 1/2 percent) and profits were actually dropping during the years in question, hardly what would have been expected during the heyday of a $4.8 billion rip-off. (Low profits, Susman would correctly reply on rebuttal, certainly weren't a defense to price-fixing charges.)

Baker had nothing but contempt for the economist who'd calculated the overcharges to be $4.8 billion. "He said, 'I've got a magic machine. I've got a formula. I've got a magic computer, and it spits that out!' It tells me there was collusion. I don't need a jury! It tells me there was collusion, and I haven't heard one word, and then it tells me how much they were overcharged. Every one of them. . . . But, of course, he told you in no uncertain terms that he did not care about the evidence. He didn't give a hoot, because he had a magic mathematical formula! It was a conspiracy formula built into that magic computer. Rather astounding, isn't it? Especially when you're talking about 8 percent of $60 billion—$4.8 billion. Do you know how many zeros that is? Don't even have room for the cents."

The jury gave Baker his answer three days later, on Friday the thirteenth, when it finally returned a verdict in favor of Susman and his team, a verdict affirming that Mead had been a member of the price-fixing conspiracy in the corrugated industry that continued for at least twelve years; that nineteen other manufacturers had also participated in it; that the conspiracy had damaged box purchasers throughout the country; and that overcharges had been at least 5 percent.

Susman's victory was astounding, considering that the government had lost the criminal case against the same defendant. And, although Susman couldn't know it yet, Mead would earn still another victory from a jury when its third corrugated-carton price-fixing case went to trial later. In other words, the only trial Mead *didn't* win was Susman's.

It was time for the blow-out of Susman's life. He and fifteen other lawyers from the trial team drove out to Gilley's, fifteen miles outside Houston in the shit-kickin' town of Pasadena, and whooped it up that Friday night. That was the night that his ungainly cigar-smoking cocounsel, Jerry Cohen, leaped astride the mechanical bull *and stayed on* as it leaped and lurched. "That sunovabitch!" Susman yelled with glee. This was truly a day for miracles.

And Susman would be looking for more before he was through, because Mead had no intention of paying the billions of dollars that would no doubt be assessed against it once a separate damage-setting hearing was concluded.

Instead, the big paper company hired a slew of big-name lobbyists to win in Congress what it had lost before the jury.

Griffin Bell and Benjamin Civiletti were former attorneys general of the United States, and Irving Shapiro was the former chief executive of DuPont. Together, they and their law firms were paid $800,000 to lobby for something that was euphemistically called the Antitrust Equal Enforcement Act. Actually, the legislation was really designed to eviscerate the mammoth verdict that was rightfully Susman's, and it was going to do that by eliminating the common-law antitrust doctrine of joint-and-several liability.

Baker hadn't been kidding when he told the jury that Mead had called Susman's bluff. The problem was, Mead lost everything that it had so brazenly shoved into the pot.

Mead was, after all, the holdout company, and it thus had to pay any damages that exceeded what Susman already had in his settlement fund. The bill Shapiro and Bell and Civiletti were peddling all around Capitol Hill was designed to save the company's ass by retroactively rewriting the law. Instead of being liable for 100 percent of the unpaid damages, Mead would be on the hook for just 2.5 percent, a proportion no greater than its own market share. The real kicker, though, was that Mead would be able to sue to recover the other 97.5 percent of the unpaid damages from all of the companies that had already settled with Susman. A lawsuit like that would nullify all the settlements and send Susman home without any of the millions of dollars he stood to collect as the victorious lead counsel for the class.

There was a certain logic to making every company pay its fair share of damages. That might well have been fairer than letting a culprit settle, as many of the box makers had, for a fraction of the actual damages while a less culpable holdout ran the risk of holding the bag for a much greater amount later on. But Susman, who now was being forced into some high-pressure lobbying of his own in an effort to defeat Mead's retroactive bill, was concerned about losing all the settlement funds he'd worked years to amass.

Mead had found a way to use its political clout to double what already were stratospheric stakes. And now it was Susman who was whipped. He took his billions of dollars in chips and cashed them in with Mead for a mere $45 million, the settlement amount Susman finally agreed to accept in exchange for Mead dropping its ruinous proposed legislation. The deal was a good one for Susman only in that it protected all his other settlements and ended all the litigation, but even in defeat Mead twisted him hard, insisting that its paltry settlement be dribbled out to the class over a ten-year-period that stretched well into the 1990s.

That wasn't to say that Susman hadn't also done some sharp dealing, too, by the time he and his partners collected their nearly $8 million share of the corrugated-box fees. Nobody, after all, had ever accused Susman of being anything other than a young man in a hurry to make big money, and his phenomenal courtroom victory against Mead had heightened those aspirations, to a point where he could start fighting with his partners about a fee that hadn't yet been, and might never be, paid. Almost immediately after that fateful Friday the thirteenth, Susman and his litigation group at Mandell & Wright started arguing with the rest of the firm's partners over how the anticipated corrugated-box fees would be divided, and within three months Susman's group walked out and founded Susman, Godfrey & McGowan.

Before they left, though, Susman and his cohorts told the rest of the Madell & Wright partners that they thought their total fee would be in the $3 million range, and they cut a deal whereby their old partners would get one half of the corrugated-box fee, up to a limit of $1.5 million.

When the fee awards finally came out, anybody who could add and subtract knew that Susman & Co. had just received a $5 million windfall.

Such was the luck of wildcatters.

When the Hunts went looking for a law firm that would stop at nothing to beat the banks, they sought advice from a fellow Texan who wrote the book on kamikaze law: Jack Stanley of Houston.

As a New England gasoline-station mogul turned oil refiner, Stanley built a company called GHR Energy Corporation that virtually nosedived into bankruptcy court in 1983. Stanley's company had been there before, under a different name, from 1975 until 1980. Stephen Gordon represented Stanley then, and he collected $3 million for his work. But when Stanley's company went into bankruptcy the second time, Gordon was disqualified from working on it. A federal district judge in Houston, where the GHR bankruptcy was transferred, ruled that Gordon had violated three canons of the lawyer's Code of Professional Responsibility by hiring as a McCabe/Gordon associate a former employee of a GHR creditor, and by allowing two McCabe/Gordon lawyers to serve as GHR officers.

To fight the disqualification, Gordon hired Susman's law firm. Even though Gordon didn't beat the legal rap, it gave Stanley a chance to see both young firms in action. He recommended McCabe/Gordon to his friends, the Hunts. And when he needed a lawyer to file a $600 million lawsuit for him in Houston, Stanley, whose lawsuits were nurturing a whole generation of kamikaze lawyers, turned to Susman.

The lawsuit Susman got was called a "take-or-pay" case. In it, the Stanley-owned TransAmerican Natural Gas Corporation sued the El Paso Natural Gas Company for allegedly reneging on a natural-gas purchase contract that was supposed to run through 1996. Stanley claimed El Paso had to pay him for the gas even if it didn't need it or use it.

The lawsuit was one of many Stanley filed in his attempt to resuscitate his oil and gas business amid the hardships caused by the severe drop in oil prices. His strategy in each case was to exhaust the will and the financial resources of the opposition by making the legal proceedings as contentious as possible. Any lawsuit filed against him was met with a torrent of cross-claims, exactly as it was when El Paso, unwilling to pay the above-market rates for TransAmerican's gas, asked a state court to nullify its contract with TransAmerican. Stanley's legal targets were usually his creditors, and Stanley was so successful at using lawsuits to hold them at bay that, by 1987, he had been running his thriving energy business under bankruptcy-court protection for nine of the prior twelve years.

The Hunts admired what their fellow Texan had done to hold off his creditors. They wanted that kind of representation for themselves, too. So, by the middle of 1987, Susman was deeply enmeshed in lawsuits for both Stanley and the Hunts.

It was a hectic time. Stanley's take-or-pay case came to trial in Houston just as the pretrial maneuvering in the Hunt case reached a crescendo. Susman was in court five days a week for Stanley. He shuttled to Dallas on weekends when he had to and tried to keep in touch with his lawyers there by phone. Meanwhile, the Hunts and their bankers were locked in a war of attrition. Platoons of lawyers had examined and indexed over a million documents. Bunker, Herbert and Herbert's son Bruce had collectively spent months in depositions, being quizzed by the bank's lawyers. Bunker was so short of cash he even decided to sell for $50 million his most prized asset, his stable of 570 thoroughbred horses. "Hard times come knocking on your door," Bunker said, "and they did mine."

Susman, still hungering for his sabbatical, was drained. "The thing I dislike most about trial work is the pretrial discovery. It's laborious, tedious," he complained. "I'd like to spend all of my time in the courtroom. But here I am, stuck on a big discovery machine, as a manager of a bunch of lawyers. It's not as fun as having your own case in court, appearing before the jury every day, arguing, saying your own thing."

From the outset, Susman hadn't been at all sure he even wanted the Hunt case. After an unbroken string of courtroom victories beginning in 1976, he'd lost four important cases in a row between 1984 and 1986. His two back-to-back wins later that year had been his first since 1983.

"When I got this case, I said, 'Well, how much should they pay me to handle another losing case? This is a losing case. A bullshit case. A desperate move. The case has a lot of visibility, but a *loss* is going to be very visible, too. And do I want to take a visible, losing case? *A dead-certain loser?*' "

Susman did what he had always done in situations like this. He psyched himself up for the fight ahead. He talked to the Hunts, looked at their documents and then literally persuaded himself that their case had merit. A $1 million advance payment by the Hunts didn't hurt, either. Susman would go along with the theory fashioned by McCabe/Gordon: that even though the Hunts still had the banks' money, the brothers shouldn't have to give it back because they'd been defrauded.

Bank lawyers denigrated the theory. "Isn't that the silliest thing you've ever heard?" observed R. Paul Wickes, a Dallas attorney for First Republic Bank, a major Hunt lender. "The Hunts say the banks tricked them. The Hunts say the banks knew their business better than they did themselves. It makes no sense. Why would a bank knowingly loan money to somebody who couldn't pay it back? The banks don't want oil and gas properties."

The litigation was taking its toll on the banks, too. "We're not afraid of a Dallas jury," another lawyer for one of the banks told me at midyear. "We're very confident going forward. This isn't a case of average guys going up against giant corporations. The Hunts are infamous. They are in a parity situation with the banks. And if we go to trial everything's going to come out. If you look at the history of the demise of the Hunt family fortune, they've always maintained that every one of their problems was caused by someone else. It's always somebody else's fault. But a jury is going to see whose fault it really is. When the whole picture is painted, these guys aren't going to get sympathy from the average man. The shameful thing is that it's taking us so long to get there. We've spent well over $50 million in legal fees and we're no closer to a resolution now than we were fourteen months ago. It's been such a terrible waste of time and money."

The statement reflected the banks' growing frustration with the

Hunts' staying power in the litigation. "People are frustrated because it's been going on a long time," another bank lawyer told me. "We're tired. It's a lot of work. There are two big loans that aren't producing. You've got Susman willing to blather on for the record, and, unlike Susman, the banks take with some seriousness the proposition that you respond in court, not in the newspapers. And the fundamental strategy of the other side is to delay."

But shortly thereafter, an unforseen turn of events caused the advantage to change again. When McCabe/Gordon still had the case, the Hunts had tried, unsuccessfully, to have Sanders thrown off the case, ostensibly because of a conflict of interest, but, in reality, because Bunker thought he was too liberal. Susman had spent months trying to dissuade the Hunts, and he had finally patched things up with the judge. But then one of the Hunts' lenders merged with a bank that Sanders owned stock in, and Sanders promptly took himself off the case.

With Sanders off the lender-liability case and Judge A. Joe Fish newly assigned to it, the banks renewed their efforts to obtain a summary judgment to collect on their loans, a motion that Sanders had already denied. Granting it would mean sudden death for the Hunts' empire. Over Susman's objection, Fish agreed to consider the motion anew.

During a status conference before Fish not long after that, Susman was forced to concede in open court what the banks had been saying all along: Susman couldn't prove a key contention that the banks harmed the Hunts by conspiring to monopolize the offshore drilling rig business.

Even as Susman dropped the antitrust allegation from his complaint, the new judge voiced skepticism about the loan-fraud allegation that remained.

"Although this case involves a lot of money and a lot of paper, it's basically a suit on a note," Fish lectured Susman. "It's a collection case. . . . You mean the days are past when a lender can say you owe me a hundred dollars which you promised to pay me today, and I haven't been paid, and I am going to court. Those days are gone? A lender has the obligation to say if you can't pay today, can you pay me tomorrow or next week?"

What was supposed to be a fifteen-minute introductory meeting between Fish and the lawyers had turned into a three-hour debacle for Susman. The new judge was virtually arguing the banks' case for them!

Susman: "The banks recognized that [the Penrod] loan would be in default as soon as the signatures were affixed to the credit agreement."

Fish: "What's their motive in doing that? I don't understand why a bank would want to make a loan that was going to be in default before the ink was dry!"

Susman was shaken. "The newspapers will report that the hearing went poorly for us," he grumbled afterward. "If this was before Sanders, it'd be a shoo-in. We're rearguing the same thing. But Fish might undo what Sanders did." Susman was so disconsolate that he didn't even give a report to his clients, who had waited for him back at their office.

The bank lawyers were elated. "You didn't come away with the feeling that the judge thought much of the Hunts' claim," one said.

Meanwhile, Abramson, the bankruptcy judge, was also turning up the heat on the brothers. An activist who believed in moving cases swiftly along, Abramson was pressing for a settlement. He summoned the brothers and their bankers to a closed-door meeting on September 22, from which litigators would be excluded.

During a hearing the month before, the brothers' bankruptcy lawyer, Henry W. Simon, Jr., had told Abramson, "I have considerable confidence that something will happen before September 22." Simon was saying, in so many words, that he thought the brothers would put an offer on the table.

Privately, Simon was putting great pressure on them to do that. Publicly, Abramson was doing the same. And still more pressure was coming from Fish, who might well gut the Hunts' entire case by granting the banks' summary judgment motion.

First Boston Corporation, the big New York investment banker, was already working behind the scenes to help the brothers and their lawyers put a market value on their assets, so they'd know what they had at risk. Now Simon, working with the energy specialists at First Boston, had concocted a gambit to pressure his own clients to make some tangible move toward settling the case before the crucial September 22 conference with Abramson. The plan was deceptively simple: First Boston, working on its own, would devise a sell-off plan. The First Boston plan would require the Hunts to break up Placid and Penrod and sell off enough of the parts to raise the $1.5 billion they owed the banks. That would pave the way for a global settlement of all the pending bankruptcy and legal proceedings.

But it was a seat-of-the-pants idea. No one, least of all First Boston, knew whether the properties would even fetch that much. And no one had even talked to the Hunts about it. That would be done on the following Tuesday, the day after Labor Day. But since the First Boston people assumed they'd come up with *something*, they started calling the Hunts' banks and invited them to a settlement presentation scheduled for September 8, the Thursday after Labor Day.

After First Boston's calls to the banks, word of the possible settlement had circulated with ferocity. Even Simon had been on the phone with reporters, explaining what was going down.

Unaccountably, though, not even Herbert, the brother most involved in day-to-day operations, had been told. Even Simon failed to tell the brothers of his behind-the-scenes maneuvering. They learned of it, along with the rest of Dallas, the next morning in a Dallas *Morning News* banner-headline story. Herbert was furious with the leaks, furious at seeing his picture in the newspaper alongside another bad-news story. When the First Boston people arrived at his office Tuesday morning, he told them to cancel the Thursday meeting with the banks. Under no circumstances, Herbert fumed, would the brothers ever give up control of their empire.

But the conference with Abramson still loomed. The bankruptcy judge might start pushing his own solutions on the brothers if he thought they weren't even trying to settle, Simon told Herbert. Reschedule the meeting with the banks, Simon counseled.

Herbert Hunt already knew what kind of a day it was going to be when he was pulled over by a Dallas policeman the following Wednesday, September 16, on his way in to work. Herbert got a ticket for driving with an expired inspection sticker on the 1972 Mercedes he affectionately called "Ol' Blue." Later that afternoon, Herbert, Bunker, and Lamar walked the few blocks over to the Sheraton Dallas Hotel and sat down in the front row of the hotel's seminar theatre. Their demeanor was serious, verging on grim. They said nothing. And they shook hands with no one. They simply sat and listened, along with the bank lawyers who'd been summoned there, as a First Boston official gave a status report on how much Placid and Penrod were worth. The banks were surprised that there was no settlement offer, but they should have known the Hunts couldn't abide that. This was just their way of saving face, of telling the banks *something* while telling them absolutely nothing.

Sure enough, deceit was the way of the Hunts. The only thing their high-priced hired guns did was make the sharp dealers look more respectable.

Caveat Emptor:
Philip Corboy and the
Malpractice Case of
Karsten v. McCray

I have what jurors want. They want charisma. They want
a fight in the courtroom. They don't want placidity. They
don't want a one-dimensional lawsuit. They came here for
a show! And they want to do what's right.

PHILIP H. CORBOY

The city of Chicago carried a horde of big-shot
lawyers astride its broad shoulders, but Philip Corboy topped them
all. Nobody at the bar surpassed the white-haired wizard when it
came to capitalizing on tragedy.

Corboy earned millions of dollars a year representing clients in
personal-injury lawsuits, but instead of shrouding such good fortune
he virtually trumpeted it in a profession in which megaverdicts meant
megabusiness. If your injury was bad enough and the defendant big
enough, Corboy was yours for a third of the recovery, plus expenses.
He'd just earned a twenty-thousand-dollar fee for four hours' work
settling a case, and he made no apologies for his hourly rate of five
thousand dollars. "You and I could have the same case," he boomed,
"and I'm gonna get the client more. And that's why I'm entitled to
that contingent fee."

Automobile accidents, unsafe products, workplace accidents, plane
crashes and medical malpractice were the sordid stuff of Corboy's

lucrative practice, and in a career that spanned a third of a century he had redefined the art of personal-injury law, taking each desperate case of human suffering and molding it into a commodity marketable to any jury in Cook County.

He packaged his cases for the juries, because, as he put it, "trial lawyers are people persuaders. They are marketers." Corboy knew how to sell a case to a jury. Often as not, a Corboy trial meant market research, lifelike models, day-in-the-life films and snazzy charts: a little razmatazz for the hoi polloi.

"It's show business! Absolutely! No question about it!" Corboy exulted. "Yeah! The great trial lawyers of this country are pseudo-celebrities!" Corboy fancied himself a pin-striped warrior against the establishment, a guy who looked like a corporate president, but who still felt inside like a scrappy Irish kid spoiling for a fight.

"I'm antiestablishment, but I'm *accepted* by the establishment," Corboy said in a voice that still carried the lingering traces of the brogue of his far North Side Irish neighborhood.

"When the head of Montgomery Ward gets hurt, who's he gonna hire? Yet, when the head of Montgomery Ward finds out I've sued Marshall Field's and finds out I've gotten a million-dollar award, he thinks that's a travesty! He thinks it's terrible!

"If Iacocca gets hurt and he's hurt in the city of Chicago and he talks around and finds out who the best lawyer in the city of Chicago is, he'll be happy to hire me. Particularly if he finds out that I've knocked off Ford and knocked off General Motors. But if he reads in the paper tomorrow, before he's my client, that I got a big verdict against Ford, he's affronted, isn't he? He's terrified that it's going to affect his part of the establishment. But, when he gets hurt, who's he gonna hire?"

Even by his own lights, Corboy was a rogue, a rascal on death's stage, and in his own complicated way it was a role he savored for the acceptance it finally brought to the neglected Irish kid who still brooded within him. "I want to be loved. I want to be stroked. I want to be accepted," said the policeman's son who even now acknowledged he was battling his own family's "outcast mentality."

"I tweak the nose of the very establishment that embraces me when they need me! It's fun. I'm immune—there's nothing they can do to me! What can they do to me? My refuge is the jury. That's where I'm safe! Whatever battle I have to fight, no matter who my foe is, is right over in that courthouse." Corboy nodded toward the Cook County Courthouse that loomed like a dull brown hulk diagonally across from his own office. "And that's where I can hold my own."

He was in his element practicing this kind of law, a "swell"— Corboy's Irish slang for fat cat—who could have his wealth and still see himself as a rebel. "I'm antiauthoritarian and antiestablishment. I'm a hybrid, really, because the people in the establishment are quick to hire me whenever they need me.

"They *trust* me. Because they, too, like what they regard as the *best.* They, themselves, are *entitled* to me. In their minds, that's how they think. It's complicated, isn't it?

"I enjoy not having to be part of the establishment. But, certainly, I enjoy the benefits of it. It's fun tweaking them! I can say to them: 'When you need me, I'm here—and I'll be GLAD to help you, even though you're the first to criticize me.' "

The law firm of Corboy & Demetrio ran like a well-oiled machine, every part in place and working flawlessly. Pending cases were tracked by a $250,000 IBM System 36 computer specially modified for the firm's needs. Lawyers worked on the platoon system, each specializing in certain types of cases and each backed up by an alter-ego legal assistant.

The firm did no hourly work at all. In Corboy & Demetrio's world, that was small-time. It was the contingent fee that gave the firm all its economic incentives, and other lawyers marveled at the money Corboy & Demetrio could afford to spend in its quest for a superior result. Corboy's firm, for instance, almost always did sophisticated market research before a big trial to determine what kinds of jurors would be best. "I can't afford it, even when I know he's doing it," lamented one of the city's finest defense lawyers, an occasional Corboy foe. "What account would I bill it against? There's so much competition among the defense law firms for insurance company business that I've already discounted my rate to $150 an hour for major clients. If I start charging them more, I'll lose the business." Corboy didn't have to worry about that. No client would chastise him. He could spend the money and take it out of the recovery.

"Competence. Excellence. Constant striving for excellent execution of my responsibilities." Corboy's litany made you want to stand up and salute. "We just don't consciously do anything that is not the extra yard."

And yet, even though it churned out big settlements and verdicts with such apparent efficiency, there was also a familial air to the place. It was a haven for the Irish and the Catholic, for people, like Corboy, whose blood was red instead of blue. Thomas Demetrio, Corboy's forty-one-year-old partner, was like a son to the elder Corboy, and except for a one-year judicial clerkship he'd been working for the law firm ever since he graduated from law school. But Corboy had known him long before that, because Demetrio's father operated the restaurant in Corboy's office building.

Corboy's oldest son, thirty-eight-year-old Phil Jr., nicknamed "Flip," also was an associate at the firm. So was Demetrio's younger brother, Michael. The office manager was named O'Keefe, and a whole family of Rooneys—five in all—also worked as drivers and support staff. When somebody needed a messenger, a cry went up: "Get me a Rooney!" Almost half the office's twelve lawyers had attended Catholic universities—Corboy and Demetrio both went to Notre Dame—and a quarter went to law school at Corboy's alma mater, downtown Chicago's Loyola University.

Associates started at a $40,000 annual salary, but they could earn $250,000 a year or more along with special presents from the master like a new BMW or all-expenses-paid vacations to anywhere in the world. Corboy, in fact, genuinely liked his people. He called young Bruce Pfaff, the only Ivy Leaguer in the bunch, "Mr. Cool." Cyril McIlhargie, the firm's malpractice specialist out of Bad Axe, Michigan, was "Mr. Doctor." And Orvin Kacprzyk, the law firm's newest associate, was "the Polish Prince."

But Corboy was the rainmaker among them all, the master business-getter at his twelve-lawyer firm. The Corboy reputation was what lured so much business through the door, as many as fifty prospective new cases a week. And it was this astounding demand for its services that allowed the law firm to carefully select the two or three new cases it took each week. The firm's success was self-perpetuating, because by being so selective the Corboy firm could take only those cases in which the defendant was so well-insured, and the injury so grievous, that a big settlement or jury verdict was all but assured.

By 1985, that penchant for skimming off only the best cases had stretched Corboy's winning streak in the courtroom to seventeen years, a streak that was helping the law firm of Corboy & Demetrio to produce verdicts and settlements of $46 million a year and contingent fees of more than $13 million. Corboy alone was taking more than $3 million a year out of the business, and it was buying him the accouterments of the superrich: a chauffeur-driven Cadillac, a $2 million foundation that bore his name, and a $1 million-dollar forty-sixth-floor apartment in the Water Tower building next door to the Ritz Carlton Hotel. He was, as usual, among the "swells." Oprah Winfrey lived there. So did actress Barbara Eden and a slew of business executives. It was a long way from Corboy's boyhood in the Irish neighborhood of Chicago's Rogers Park.

Corboy, sixty years old then and going through a messy divorce, had knocked out some walls and turned the place into a chrome-and-glass bachelor pad with a Matt Helm–style bedroom, a giant Jacuzzi ("Don't ask me how many people it'll fit!"), and a commanding view of Lake Shore Drive and Lake Michigan. As a boy, Corboy had worn hand-me-downs from his cousin, but now, in the cedar-lined walk-in closet in his bedroom, there hung ten silk bathrobes, thirty-six fine shirts, and dozens of custom-tailored suits. This man on a perpetual diet—he carried 168 pounds on his five foot eight frame—kept no food in his kitchen. If Corboy wanted something, he called room service at the Ritz. And he had no booze, either, having foresworn the stuff in 1977. "It figured if you were an Irishman and you hadn't drunk enough by the age of fifty, there was no hope for you!"

This was where Corboy cloistered himself as he prepared for a trial, with boxes full of files spread out across his living room floor.

At Corboy & Demetrio, perhaps 10 percent of the cases went to trial, against a nationwide average of just 3 or 4 percent. The higher ratio at Corboy's firm was related to the gravity of the cases accepted: They were rarely routine, and insurance companies were always more likely to bridle at the size of the settlement demands Corboy and his people made.

Corboy seldom became deeply enmeshed in a case until he was certain it was going to trial. It took years for a case to wend its way through the Circuit Court of Cook County. Associates and legal assistants were more than competent to attend depositions and push the paper that precursed a trial.

When a trial was a certainty, though, Corboy became the firm's designated hitter. Alone or with the associate who had been honchoing the case in the years since it had come to the firm, he sat at the Louis XIV campaign desk in his living room, reading the entire file of depositions and motions and investigative reports until he was totally immersed in the case. Messengers ferried files to and from his nearby office. If Corboy needed something, a Rooney was standing by. Corboy likened the whole process to "taking a tremendously satisfying bath. You become an expert in many details, in a small portion of a large discipline. And when it's over, the bathtub is emptied."

There were good reasons, of course, why Corboy & Demetrio turned down so many potential new cases. "Insurance plays a role," Tom Demetrio explained. "If we know that the defendant isn't insured, we're not going to take that case because there's not much we can do to help them, and we tell them so." That was the main reason for a turn down, but there could be others: "If he has filed fourteen other lawsuits, we're not going to get involved with that person. He's too litigious. We want to like our clients, because we know, ultimately, that twelve people are going to have to like our client in order to give him full compensation."

Likewise, Corboy & Demetrio had no qualms about dropping a client if an anticipated deep pocket didn't materialize. "We won't stay on that case," Demetrio explained. "If, despite whatever professional talent we have, it's not going to create a corpus [fund for paying damages], we'll get out."

Corboy shrugged his shoulders. Sure, it was an imperfect system. "Well, it's a very imperfect world."

Even though the law firm turned down many more cases than it accepted, the ratio of refusals was by far the highest on malpractice cases. Of every twenty prospective malpractice cases, eighteen were turned down outright by a legal assistant, without even conferring with one of the lawyers. On average, of the two that survived the initial screen, one would be accepted, the other rejected.

Simply put, the lawyers took so few malpractice cases because the odds were against them. Amid all the furor over malpractice insurance premiums and the liability crisis, the trial system's bias in favor of doctors had been ignored. But it was clearly there: When cases went all the way to trial, four out of five verdicts favored the doctor. A countervailing consideration, though, was that malpractice cases also were the ones producing some of the *biggest* verdicts when the plaintiff won.

So Corboy and his lawyers had to do their own cost-benefit analysis when they decided whether to take a malpractice case, balancing the risk of losing—and getting not a penny in fees—against the potential big payday.

"You have to work your ass off on all malpractice cases," Corboy lamented. "There's no such thing as an easy one. Where are the biggest verdicts today? In malpractice cases! And the lawyer has to break his neck to win 'em.

"Why do we turn most of them down? Because mostly there's no negligence. Or, there's no damage. Or, there's neither. Or, we have a conflict." Corboy wouldn't sue a doctor who had ever helped his firm or testified on some other client's behalf. "We regard it as professionally uncosmetic, discourteous, to sue the doctors who helped us with another client."

But when the malpractice case of Joan Karsten had come into the office six years earlier, Corboy decided to put his money on it.

Edward Karsten and his wife lived outside Chicago in the booming, upper-middle-class county of DuPage. He was a Cornell-educated stockbroker; she was a housewife who raised their four children in the quiet community of Glen Ellyn, a vivacious forty-six-year-old known for her fine tennis game.

This much was clear: Joan Karsten had entered the emergency room at Central DuPage Hospital on April 29, 1979, complaining of abdominal pain. Thirty-five hours later, an appendectomy was performed by a board-certified general surgeon who also happened to be a family friend. The surgeon found that the appendix had previously ruptured, and that the area around it had become infected, so, when he removed the appendix, he also drained the abscess. Eight days later, Joan Karsten was discharged from the hospital. Everything seemed to be going fine. But, within four days of her discharge, she experienced bizarre symptoms: Her speech became slurred, her eyes rolled back into her head and she had tremors in her extremities.

Although she was readmitted to the hospital, Karsten fell into a deep coma within five days. Specialists from every branch of medicine were called in, but nobody could understand the problem. When Karsten emerged from the coma six weeks later, she was hopelessly brain-damaged. She was unable to walk independently or to feed herself. Her speech was labored. Around-the-clock nursing care was needed.

At age thirty-three, David Horan was one of the bright young associates in Corboy's office. After graduating from the University of Virginia, he'd continued on to its medical school, graduating in 1978. That was followed by a one-year residency at Washington University in St. Louis. But suing doctors interested Horan more than being one, so he enrolled at the Washington University Law School and earned his law degree in 1983. His stint at what other lawyers admiringly called Corboy U. came after that.

Horan earned $50,000 a year, a piddling sum compared to the check his boss cashed each January 31, when the prior year's books were closed. But Corboy was the rainmaker and Horan the nuts-and-bolts guy, and the roles suited them both. Horan, who had been born the same year that Corboy began his law practice, could afford it. At Corboy U., you served an indenture for the experience.

Since he spoke the languages of medicine and law with equal ease, Horan was the office's in-house malpractice expert. Soon after he arrived at Corboy & Demetrio in 1983, he was given the Karsten case to evaluate.

By then, the case already had a checkered provenance. The lawyer originally hired by Edward Karsten, Ronald Davis, was going to become a judge. Davis had an office in the same building as Corboy's. Davis needed somebody he could dump the case on, and who better than his friend Phil Corboy? Corboy agreed to take it for the standard lawyer-to-lawyer referral fee. It was the customary Rule of Thirds. Corboy had a one-third contingent interest in whatever recovery he could get for the Karstens; Davis's old firm, in turn, would get a third of whatever Corboy got.

From the start, both sides had been troubled by the absence of any clear-cut, easily explainable reason for Joan Karsten's tragic plight. The defendants could use that confusion to build their case on a theory of plausible denial: Whatever the cause of Karsten's problems, it was something other than medical negligence.

But, as he thumbed through the medical records and the pretrial depositions, Horan theorized that the treating doctor, Robert McCray, *must* have done something wrong. There was simply no other plausible way to explain what had happened—and, of course, no other way to justify a fat recovery against McCray and the other doctors who treated Joan Karsten.

As Horan viewed it, the thirty-five-hour delay between Karsten's hospitalization and the appendectomy was crucial. Horan thought her appendix had burst during that period, spewing fecal material into her abdomen and thus causing an infection. As the infection spread, what had first seemed to be a routine recovery became a worsening condition, until, finally, an infection was raging throughout her body.

McCray had had a chance, during the second hospitalization, to reverse Karsten's downward spiral by finding and draining a second abscess that undoubtedly had formed, Horan speculated. The fact that he hadn't done so had ultimately led to an infectious condition called *sepsis*—literally, blood poisoning—that caused tiny blood clots to block the capillaries leading to the central nervous system. Such a clotting of the capillaries is called *disseminated intravascular coagulation,* or DIC for short. Horan believed the infection-induced DIC had deprived Joan Karsten's brain of oxygen, thereby causing her brain damage.

Horan's theory boiled down to this: McCray waited so long to operate that his patient's appendix burst, causing an infection that led to brain damage.

Even McCray didn't argue with parts of the theory. In fact, by the time of his deposition in 1982 he, too, had come to the conclusion that the ruptured appendix had caused the infection-induced DIC. "Little capillary-sized clots," he lamely explained under questioning. "It would be like a lot of flea bites all over the brain. . . . But, since that's an extremely rare condition, nobody, to my knowledge, has been able to come out flatfootedly and say that she had that condition. We all say that we think she had it. Even if we all agreed that she did have it, then there is the question of how often do you see that following appendicitis? Medicine is like that. Sometimes you get rare things."

That was the thing about McCray: He could bumble around in his own kindly way and come off as a guy you'd cut some slack to, a likeable Joe who meant no harm.

Even if McCray agreed in hindsight with the diagnosis, though, he certainly wasn't taking the blame for Karsten's condition. So the first thing Horan needed was a medical expert who would support his hypothesis.

Horan hadn't been present at McCray's 1982 deposition. In fact, no one from Corboy's firm had, because Davis still had the case then. But as he read through Davis' questions and McCray's answers, Horan now focused on an answer that Davis had either overlooked or ignored:

Q. "Is there any doctor in the field that has written on appendicitis that you consider to be an authority on appendicitis?"

A. "In a general sense, I would say that there are several."

Q. "Could you name one or two?"

A. "I could name one. H. Harlan Stone, I would say."

McCray remembered Stone as having written frequently in the medical journals—249 articles and 6 books, when somebody finally got around to counting. McCray also remembered where Stone had gone to medical school and where he then was teaching: Emory University in Atlanta.

Horan had an idea: If he could persuade this Dr. Stone to testify *against* McCray, it would be devastating to the defense. McCray's own words qualified Stone as the man most fit to judge his work. McCray wouldn't be able to credibly disavow Stone's testimony. Everyone would see that.

Horan walked down the hall into Corboy's corner office and read back to him McCray's description of Stone. This could be their lucky break! Horan had already called Emory and found out that Stone had recently transferred to the University of Maryland Medical School in Baltimore.

"Get out there!" Corboy thundered.

Horan was on a plane to Baltimore the next day.

Stone had never testified for a plaintiff in a malpractice case, but young Horan laid out the facts of Joan Karsten's strange malady and then asked Stone a direct question: "If the medical records support what I've just told you, will you testify for us?"

Stone, a deliberate man who spoke with a resonant Georgia accent, said he'd think it over. Two weeks later, having studied Karsten's file, he telephoned Horan and told him, yes, this was definitely malpractice. Stone would testify.

Horan was elated. Stone's testimony would establish the three building blocks of the malpractice case: the delay in surgery, which led to the burst appendix, which caused the brain-damaging infection. Proving that chain reaction was crucial. All three would have to be present, in that order, for McCray to be guilty of malpractice.

Corboy & Demetrio was pressing the Karstens' case against four separate defendants. McCray, obviously, was the main target, but he only had a $1 million malpractice liability policy, hardly enough to make the case worth Corboy's while. So the lawyers were also suing one of McCray's partners, Dr. Glen Asselmeier, on the ground that Asselmeier hadn't acted quickly enough to readmit Joan Karsten to the hospital when she started having neurological problems after the appendectomy. They were also suing the Glen Ellyn Clinic, in which both Asselmeier and McCray were partners. Asselmeier and the clinic each had another $1 million apiece in malpractice coverage.

But the big tuna in the case was Central DuPage Hospital, which had a $5 million policy. Davis, the lawyer who originally had the case, contended that Central DuPage should also be held liable because the hospital had failed to maintain adequate records by which Karsten's doctors could be kept informed of her deteriorating condition. It was a thin case against Central DuPage, though, and when Corboy got the case he wanted to drop the hospital and concentrate on the doctors and their clinic instead. Nothing doing, Davis' old firm replied. Davis' former partners still had an ownership interest in the case, too, and they wanted to reach the hospital's deep pocket. Corboy grudgingly obliged. But his strategy still was to focus on the defendants he thought were most culpable.

The insurance company hired a lawyer for McCray and the clinic named Roger O'Reilly. He was an experienced trial advocate from Wheaton, Illinois; fifty-one years old, shortish, squat and freckled; with big, bushy eyebrows and red hair going to gray. O'Reilly's style, in conversation or in the courtroom, was a low-key counterpoint to the stentorian Corboy's.

Since Asselmeier was entitled to present his own defense, the insurance company hired a different lawyer, William V. Johnson, for him. Johnson, forty-five, with thinning blond hair, was a strapping, cigar-smoking man from Owensboro, Kentucky, who still spoke in a kind of slow, backwoodsy drawl. His appearance was as disarming as it was disingenuous. Johnson was the skilled senior partner of an insurance defense firm in downtown Chicago, and he had gone up against Corboy in the courtroom the year before. It was a case that both men claimed they had won, a case that guaranteed a grudge rematch between two of Chicago's finest advocates.

In that 1984 case, Corboy represented a promising young DePaul University Law School professor, Randolph Block, who'd been left a quadriplegic after his automobile was struck on a country road by a construction-company pickup truck. The truck's driver was looking at a map instead of the road, and he'd run a stop sign and struck Block's Datsun at forty-five to fifty miles an hour. The truck driver's wife and Block's grandmother had been killed. But Randy Block had suffered, at age twenty-eight, the worst possible injury: He'd been paralyzed from the eyes down. And yet, despite his injury, he had emerged from a six-month coma to become completely aware of everything going on around him.

Johnson hadn't understood how that could be. You could talk to Block and, watching his eyes blink back at you, wonder whether he could comprehend anything at all. So Johnson visited Block in his hospital room one day, to assess the young man's plight for himself.

By then, Block had learned to communicate with people by typing words onto a computer screen using eyebrow movements. They were the only parts of his body he would ever be able to move. Laboriously raising and lowering his eyebrows, Block typed out a message to Johnson: "I.'m. s.o. f.u.c.k.e.d. u.p., I. d.o.n.'t. k.n.o.w. w.h.a.t. t.o. d.o."

Johnson called in Dr. Fred Plum of the Cornell University Medical School, one of the world's leading experts on injuries like Block's. After reading the file, Plum told Johnson: "This is the worst injury known to man." Plum called it "locked-in syndrome," a ghastly injury which leaves the victim in a state of suspended animation, alive and fully aware of everything around him, and yet unable to move.

Johnson and his client certainly didn't want this case to go to trial. So, before trial, Johnson offered Corboy $9 million to settle the case. The settlement would be one of the largest personal-injury awards in the state's history.

Nothing doing, Corboy replied. The white-haired wonder wanted $40 million. And, given the insurance policies in the case, Corboy thought he had a shot at getting that much.

The Block case had the makings of a record verdict, so much so that the *Chicago Daily Law Bulletin,* the legal equivalent of the *Sporting News* for Windy City lawyers, covered the case like a championship bout. The construction company's $100 million liability policy was the prize, and, given that the company's driver was obviously at fault, the only issue was how much of that $100 million insurance policy Block and Corboy were going to get.

And Corboy needed to find out what kinds of jurors were most likely to give him what he wanted.

Three years before the Block case went to trial, Corboy had discovered how he could use sophisticated market research to gain an edge in the courtroom.

His client was an attractive young woman named Marirose Johnson. The five-foot-eight-and-a-half-inch blonde was the most popular girl at Elizabeth Seton High School in South Holland, Illinois, a gymnast and captain of the cheerleaders who was out on a date with a boy when his car was rammed from behind.

Marirose's seventeen-year-old date, Jay Michel, had had a few drinks and was driving her home at two o'clock in the morning when he sideswiped another car on the expressway. Both drivers left their cars in the left-hand fast lane and got out, leaving Marirose alone in Michel's car. Seconds later, a third car came roaring down the fast

lane and plowed into the two parked cars. Marirose was left a quadriplegic.

The accident itself involved a complicated question of liability.
Three cars were involved, and each of them bore some responsibility
for what happened. If it hadn't been for Michel, of course, the second
accident would never have happened. But the driver Michel hit had
failed to move his car over to the shoulder—he was liable for that—
and the third driver had caused the catastrophe by not paying attention to what was happening on the road ahead.

Corboy sued all three drivers—better to do that than leave an
empty chair for everybody else to blame—but, in fact, only one of the
three defendants was his real target. Michel's automobile had $5.5
million worth of insurance. The other two drivers had $35,000 insur-
ance between them.

"Obviously," said Susan Schwartz, then a brand-new associate at
Corboy & Demetrio, "you know who it is that we want to hit. We want
to have the jury render a verdict for a large amount of money against
the seventeen-year-old boy."

To find out which jurors were most likely to award big damages
against the boy, Corboy paid $21,000 to a Chicago market research
company, Leo J. Shapiro and Associates, to survey a cross section of
potential Cook County jurors on their attitudes about the case. The
Shapiro firm used the same kind of demographic-sampling techniques
it would use to determine a consumer's preference for a new brand of
soap powder, interviewing people selected at random and drawing a
careful profile of their attitudes and habits.

The poll-takers showed 713 people a small booklet that contained
six illustrations and a short text that explained what happened that
night to "Sue Carlson" and "Jeff Adams." "As a result of this accident," the booklet explained on the very first page, "Sue is now a
complete quadriplegic; that is, she is paralyzed from the neck down,
has no use of her arms or legs, has tubes connected to her body to
collect bodily waste, has no control over her muscles or body func-
tions, must be fed by others, will never have children. . . . In short,
she must be cared for continuously by other people for the rest of her
life."

The Sue Carlson pictured in the booklet actually was Susan

Schwartz' cousin, but that was all right. The idea was to use the hypotheticals to explain how the accident happened, and then to ask eight pages of questions that would yield a profile of the person most likely to hold a teenage defendant liable for big money damages, the idealized juror for Corboy's side.

A month before the trial was to begin, the researchers reported back to Corboy. They had ranked the Cook County juror pool from 1 to 9, with a 9 the kind of person most likely to find the young man guilty and award $7 million or more in damages, and a 1 the least likely to do so. A juror rated 5 or higher was more likely than not to reach the desired result.

The best jurors in the case were deemed by the computer analysis to be nonwhite female high-school graduates, people who thought Marirose was being cheated of a great life, just as they were. There were also some "secret" questions that Corboy could ask during the *voir dire*, the first phase of a trial in which potential jurors are questioned, ostensibly to determine their objectivity and lack of bias.

Corboy's secret questions of the jurors might make them unwittingly tip their hands. The secret questions seemed innocuous but actually were loaded with hidden meaning. The poll-takers had found, for instance, that people who owned old cars, or who didn't drive at all, were more likely to vote Corboy's way, as were people who were of Irish or Scandinavian descent, or who were Protestant, or who liked to go hunting or camping. By asking prospective jurors about their background or hobbies, Corboy could find out whether they were likely to be his allies in the courtroom.

If, on the other hand, somebody answered yes to the secret question "Do you belong to a labor union," then that person would be a negative juror for the plaintiff. The same went for someone who was a registered Republican or who owned stocks.

The worst jurors, from Corboy's standpoint, also turned out to be nonwhites, but the research suggested they were what some blacks called "Oreos"—black on the outside, white on the inside. The research specifically told Corboy to stay away from nonwhite male college graduates, because they had already attained the good life and probably wouldn't think Marirose could achieve all that they had.

April 30, 1981

From: Leo J. Shapiro and Associates
Re: Damages

The pattern of response suggests that the best juror is one who places high (almost unrealistically high) value on the FUTURE that is lost to the girl.

Good Jurors

People who are young and haven't as yet started their own "future," that is, they are unmarried, renters with incomes under $15 thousand, etc.; look forward to their careers with high expectations. They are good jurors because they see that Sue has lost her opportunity and assign a very high dollar amount to cover this loss. Other jurors who have a not-so-fabulous future themselves, in other words, they are lower income, blue collar, older with families to support, look at the prospect of this lost future for Sue with a great deal of sympathy perhaps because they believe that Sue, like anyone else, could have a great life and perhaps want such a life for their children or feel that they themselves were "cheated" out of such a life.

Not-So-Good Jurors

The other group is one where they themselves and probably their children have successfully made a "good life." They look at Sue's predicament differently, feeling that it is just a matter of putting an appropriate price tag on Sue's loss which in most cases is a lesser price than they would put on their *own life* and their children's. They have made it in life and feel that Sue might not make it as well as they did. Therefore, they feel she should get less than they do. . . . e.g., if they make $50,000 a year . . . mentally they juggle this for a period of say twenty to thirty years, throw in inflation and arrive at a figure of one to three million dollars as what Sue deserves. In other words, their own lives and income are the yardstick for measuring the settlement.

A few weeks after he received that memo, Corboy gave the judge in the case some questions he wanted asked of prospective jurors—ostensibly, to determine whether they might be biased against his client, but really to create a profile of each juror that Corboy could then match up against the research already done by the Leo Shapiro firm. Corboy requested that the judge ask about the jurors' educational backgrounds and occupations, the kind of car they drove and whether they liked to go camping, hunting, or skiing. He touched on everything the market researchers told him to, and, unbeknown to anyone else, what he came up with was a jury that the marketeers had faith in. Including alternates, there were two 9s, two 8s, one 7, eight 6s, and a 4.

Corboy still went on gut instinct when he used some of his peremptory challenges, dismissing one juror solely because the man wore a toupee—a personal dislike of the bushy-haired Corboy—and seating another man, rated a 4, even though the computer profile showed he would vote against the plaintiffs.

Corboy had been trying cases too long not to temper the computer printouts with his own intuition.

"I don't know any lawyers who know how to pick juries," he said. "All a lawyer can do is de-pick. De-select. Use his own peremptory challenges in a very discriminating fashion. So he can get rid of those who look overtly bad and hope that those who are left will be suceptible to his persuasions.

"There are some general rules. What does a person do with most of his or her life? If I were a hangman at Buchenwald, you know what I do with my life. Do I, as a hangman, have much concern for human dignity and life? No! Let's try to translate that. Do cops? No. Do sociologists? Yes.

"Cops don't have that concern for life because they see nothing but rapes, murders, liars and thieves every day of the week! You don't want cops. And you don't want people in the atmosphere where cops are. You wouldn't want a bartender in a cop bar. You wouldn't want a waitress who does nothing but hang out with cops.

"You wouldn't want a lawyer for a variety of reasons. Lawyers are know-it-alls. And every lawyer in the world doesn't think I'm the greatest guy that eats Campbell's soup. Why should I run the risk of having some lawyer who may think he can do it better? Or who has sour grapes? I wouldn't take the chance."

Corboy had even begun using an all-night Flash Cab driver, Ed Mica, as a kind of poor-man's jury consultant. Mica knew all the Chicago neighborhoods so well that, just by looking at a prospective juror's address, he could tell Corboy the resident's probable income, social status, political affiliation and ethnic background, as well as whether the neighborhood were a high-crime area—each answer a bit of information about how the juror might vote in a case.

Mica, sixty-seven, had been moonlighting for Corboy for eight years. He got the assignment when Corboy hopped into his cab at a downtown restaurant late one night and gave Mica an address he thought Mica might not be able to find.

"So I said, 'Sir, just to get the record straight, I'm going to call out the streets one after another, but I'm going to stop when I run out of breath.' " Mica recited them so quickly he could have earned a commendation from Federal Express. "Needless to say, he stopped kidding me," and a week later Corboy called to offer him a job.

Here, in the Marirose Johnson case, all that experience in jury selection would translate into an instinctive decision. The research in the case, after all, told Corboy he should have an all-woman jury. But the 4, Nello Magrini, a sixty-two-year-old blue-collar worker, was of Italian background, and Corboy's gut told him this man would help him. "I looked upon him as a warm-blooded Mediterranean, an Italian, someone who had a zest for life, who had lived and who appreciated life." As it turned out, Corboy's sole deviation from the research was right on the money.

Corboy had been holding out for a settlement that paid him and his client the full value of all the insurance policies in force on each car: $5,535,000. The night before closing arguments in the *Marirose Johnson* case were to begin, the insurance companies offered $4 million, and, when Corboy rejected that, they returned the next morning and met his demands in full, an Illinois record for a traffic accident. That meant there was nothing left for the jury to decide—or was there?

When Corboy told the judge about his then-novel use of market research in jury selection, the judge suggested an experiment: Let the jurors vote on damages anyway, to see whether Corboy's research would have really paid off.

The result: Nello Magrini, the warm-hearted Italian whom Corboy took a chance on, was willing to award the most money: $8 million. Even without hearing Corboy's closing argument, almost everyone else said she would award between $3 million and $5 million—in other words, just about what Corboy finally got in his settlement. Not a bad first effort. Corboy had begun to craft another tool for getting the edge in a big case.

"The jury *voir dire* is the most important part of the lawsuit," he said with a resoluteness that belied his own considerable courtroom talents. "After the jury is picked, the case is over."

Corboy's firm was on a roll. Each year had always been better than the one before, and the several years since the *Marirose Johnson* case had certainly produced their share of million-dollar awards. But even Corboy and his partner Demetrio hadn't expected all the riches they began to realize in 1984.

Tom Demetrio had started things off the year before with a record-setting 1983 victory in the Cook County Circuit Court that hadn't been paid until the defendant's appeals ran out the following year. Demetrio's case involved a young mother whose Datsun had been struck by a semitrailer, killing the mother and her eight-year-old son and rendering her ten-year-old boy a brain-damaged quadriplegic. These were the kinds of cases that were worth the most in the personal-injury trade: It would take millions of dollars to compensate such a horribly injured child for all the pain and suffering he would endure, to say nothing of the special treatment he would require.

Spurning an $8 million settlement offer two months before trial, Demetrio decided to take his chances with a jury instead. Not many lawyers would have done that, but such uncompromising evaluation of cases was the rule at Corboy & Demetrio. The lawyers took no prisoners. Defendants either paid the firm's settlement demand or took their best shot with a jury, a jury which, once again in this case, was going to be chosen with the secret help of a twenty-eight-thou-sand-dollar survey of 1,001 registered voters conducted by Leo J.

Shapiro and Associates, and, of course, with the curbside advice of Ed Mica, the Flash Cab driver.

Two months before the trial, Demetrio knew the kind of jurors he wanted: women who were Democrats, thirty-four years old and younger, high school graduates, married with three or four children, who thought abortion should be illegal. Their children should be involved in sports, and the women should take pride in their homes and their families. The computer tabulation said Demetrio should challenge women aged thirty-five to forty-nine, who were college graduates earning over $40,000, with no children.

When the twelve jurors voted after the three-week trial, they set still another record with their award: $11,876,000, all but $1 million of it for the disabled boy. The trucking company unsuccessfully appealed the verdict, and then, in 1984, it paid Illinois' largest judgment ever: $12 million. Four million dollars, plus $147,877.20 in expenses, went to Corboy & Demetrio. Demetrio's gamble of not accepting the $8 million settlement had produced, for him and Corboy, a 50 percent higher judgment and another $1.4 million in contingent fees.

The Shapiro organization had been doing some jury-selection research for Corboy, too. He was about to take to trial the case of Randy Block, the DePaul law professor who was paralyzed from his eyes downward. Corboy thought the Block case might produce an award even bigger than Demetrio's. He was, after all, demanding $40 million from the insurance company to settle it.

The key to Corboy's strategy was his use of the challenges that were given to him and his opponent, Bill Johnson, to use during the *voir dire* questioning of the jury pool. Roughly translated, the French phrase meant "to say truthfully," legal jargon for the process by which the judge and, sometimes, the lawyers could question jurors under oath about their backgrounds and beliefs.

During the *voir dire*, the lawyers could challenge an unlimited number of prospective jurors "for cause"—that is, because they gave answers that showed a potential bias. But the lawyers also could exclude a limited number of jurors for absolutely no reason at all. These were called *peremptory challenges,* and in the Block trial Johnson and Corboy would each get eight. Corboy's research was designed to help him make the best possible use of his peremptory challenges.

More than anything else, he wanted to use those challenges to exclude potential jurors who would be most ideal to Johnson's side.

What Corboy didn't know, though, was that Johnson was using a jury-selection consultant, too. While Corboy was paying Ed Mica to keep his meter running and the Shapiro firm eighteen thousand dollars for its market research, Johnson had retained a $1,200-a-day husband-and-wife psychologist team from Dubuque, Iowa.

This time, Shapiro's 1-to-9 classification of prospective jurors showed that the best jurors would be members of minority groups who had strong family ties and who voiced strong support for the statement "Life is sacred, no matter what." Women and white, college-educated males about the same age as Randy Block—young men with their life still ahead of them—would also be good, but the worst jurors would be white men over fifty with a college education. Corboy got pretty much the jury he wanted. It had eight men and four women. Five jurors were black. Nine were rated 6 or higher. One of the potential jurors Corboy excluded had a Germanic-sounding name, wore his hair short, and had a thin, wispy moustache which made his face look, in Corboy's words, "pinched." Another of Corboy's peremptories went against a Christian Science practitioner who didn't believe in medical care.

But Johnson also got a jury that suited him and his psychological expert. Thomas Sannito, the consultant hired by Johnson, was basing his decisions on traits and personal appearance. As a defense consultant, Sannito liked jurors who "steepled" their hands together when they answered questions, because, he said, it was evidence of a feeling of superiority that would hurt the plaintiff in the jury room.

Sannito also counseled Johnson to strike "strong" jurors who would most likely influence others during the deliberations. A high-school biology teacher described by Sannito as "a very sweet, warm and understanding person [who] was very bright, and talked very quickly and easily," thus was excluded. She "had big, open blue eyes and big, full lips," Sannito observed. "Her dress was casual but she was daring enough to wear a bright yellow sweater. If you put it all together, you realized she would be a very nice person to know, a very nice lady, very dear and compassionate, but probably would have a great deal of sympathy. She would be extremely dangerous for the defense because she also appeared to be influential and could impose her beliefs on others."

Sannito usually didn't like a juror whose X's in the boxes on the jury questionnaire spilled out over the edges. That, Sannito suspected, indicated a devil-may-care attitude. But he put aside that suspicion for a man with vertical worry lines down the center of his forehead. Those kinds of creases, Sannito believed, indicated an exacting nature—the kind of person who wouldn't throw money around carelessly.

But no matter how much he'd psyched out his jury, this was not the kind of case on which Johnson wanted to go up against Corboy.

There was, after all, no disputing who was to blame. Right after the wreck, the other driver had even emerged from his pickup truck and confessed, "I'm a hundred percent at fault!"

There was also no question about the brilliant career that had once been charted for young Randy Block, an accomplished swimmer on his Princeton University team who'd gone on to become a University of Chicago Law School graduate. With LSAT scores in the ninety-sixth percentile, he'd been an associate at one of the city's best law firms, Reuben & Proctor, and it was likely he would have returned there to make his fortune after teaching a few more years at DePaul.

"One thing we *do* agree on," Corboy once leaned over and cracked to Johnson in the courtroom, "his LSAT scores are higher than yours and mine put together!"

Randy Block's family also had clout in the city. His father, George, was an internationally known surgeon who also was the chief of staff of the University of Chicago's Billings Hospital, and it was there that Randy Block had remained in a coma for six months after the accident.

George Block and Philip Corboy, two men roughly the same age who had each seen much tragedy and personally experienced some of it, too, found an affinity in their private pain. It was George Block who had the final say in whether to take the ever-higher settlement offers that periodically were proffered by the insurance companies, offers that were based on the theory that Randy Block had been so badly injured that he couldn't possibly live more than a few more years, and that his damages for lost wages, pain and suffering, and medical care thus were way out of line with Corboy's stratospheric $40 million demand. But Block demurred. The surgeon-father wanted to keep fighting on behalf of the son he still believed would live to a normal life expectancy.

And Corboy did that. He spent the better part of six months preparing for the trial to come, even going so far as to obtain and study copies of every closing argument Johnson had ever made. Johnson's law firm also learned its painful lessons about the Corboy Method: With the University of Illinois playing in the Rose Bowl on New Year's Day 1984, one of Johnson's young associates, twenty-seven-year-old Pat Morris, threw a big party and invited over another young Illinois alum, Corboy & Demetrio's Terry Lavin. Lavin begged off, and Morris was incredulous. "I can't believe you're gonna turn down this party!" he remembered saying to Lavin. "What's so important that you can't come over?"

"You'll see," Lavin replied. And Morris did. With the trial about to begin, Corboy was anticipating that Johnson wouldn't argue the issue of who was at fault and would, instead, use his opening statement to go directly to the issue of damages. Lavin thus was spending New Year's Day preparing a motion for a directed verdict in favor of Randy Block, a motion in expectation of an argument Johnson hadn't even yet made!

Corboy, of course, had guessed right. So, when Johnson admitted that "my client was 100 percent at fault, or *almost* 100 percent at fault" (a qualifier that momentarily let Johnson slip off the hook), Corboy immediately made his motion and offered Lavin's previously prepared brief arguing that since guilt wasn't any longer an issue Block should get a verdict in his favor.

"Now you know what I was doing," Lavin told Morris impishly.

The central issue in the trial was going to be damages, and that, in turn, depended on how long Randy Block might live. Corboy's medical witnesses claimed Block's life span hadn't been shortened by the accident, but Johnson brought in his expert on "locked-in syndrome," Cornell's Fred Plum, who testified that Randy Block's condition greatly diminished his life expectancy, and that Block had a strong probability of death in two years.

By the morning of Friday, February 3, Corboy and Johnson were nearing the close of their trial across the street from Corboy's office in the municipal building named for Chicago's mythic tough-guy mayor, Richard J. Daley. Plum was in the box, and Corboy was about to begin his usual relentless cross-examination, hammering away in an effort to break down Plum or at least to raise some doubts about his testimony in the jury's collective mind.

Corboy began his cross with the customary pleasantries—"Good morning, Doctor"—as he maneuvered to find his ground.

Plum was a scholar, a professor, and a physician with an active private practice. "You are a very busy man?"

"I think that's fair," Plum replied.

Corboy wanted to know whether Plum believed he had a responsibility to look at his patients, no matter how busy he was.

"Yes, sir."

Corboy shot back: "Did you ever look at John Randolph Block?"

Plum: "No, sir."

Plum was testifying only from what he'd read in Block's medical records. Even though that was common practice for expert witnesses, it still looked bad for Plum. A plus for Corboy.

"By the way," Corboy went on, "this terrible, terrible condition that you find by looking at these records of John Randolph Block, stems from what?"

Plum was playing the absentminded professor now. "Can you help me with, I'm not sure what you are asking. What does his condition stem from?"

Corboy lurched impatiently forward. "Did he fall out of a tree?"

Everybody knew the answer. It was Corboy's way of making the point for the jury that Block was, after all, just an innocent victim. Corboy wanted to put Plum on trial, not Block. And he wanted to do that by taking the rest of the day to painstakingly build his cross-examination around two essential points: that Fred Plum, the defense's own world-renowned expert, considered Block's condition to be the worst known to mankind; and that even Fred Plum couldn't deny that Block might live in this agonizing state until he was an old, old man.

"Mr. Johnson asked you if you coined the phrase 'locked-in syndrome,' do you remember that?"

"Yes."

"Did he ask you anything else about locked-in syndrome?"

Now Johnson was on his feet, objecting. Corboy had to ask his own questions, not make Plum repeat Johnson's.

Corboy began anew. "Have you any idea why he asked you about the term *locked-in syndrome?*"

Johnson objected again, but this time he was overruled.

"I assume," Plum replied, "he was establishing my credentials."

"Okay, okay," Corboy rejoined with evident sarcasm as he continued this desultory line of questioning. "So, your credentials, is that the only reason you are here today with reference to John Randolph Block is to establish your credentials?"

"No. Credentials for understanding the nature of his condition."

"Well," Corboy came back, "what *is* his condition? I guess that's what I'm trying to find out."

"Well," Plum said a little incredulously, "he is locked in."

"Oh, okay," Corboy feigned surprise. "You never told us that before."

Johnson couldn't believe it. "Excuse me, your Honor. If I forgot a question that Mr. Corboy wants me to ask, I will be pleased to ask it. I don't think there is any issue."

The judge told Corboy to get on with it.

"Is John Randolph Block the victim of a symptom which is called locked-in syndrome?"

Yes, Plum finally answered.

Now Corboy could nail down the first of the two points he wanted to drive home to the jurors.

Could Block communicate like an adult? Yes.

And if Block could communicate like an adult, could he also suffer like an adult? Suffering and language were two different things, Plum answered, but, yes, "I assume this man has the capacity to suffer. . . . This is a man who, through his communication devices, expresses deep depression and suffering because of his inability to communicate. I think that is justifiably called agony."

Q. "Can you think of anything worse and still be alive? Can you think of anything worse to a human being than being locked in a locked-in condition, knowing there is a world out there that you cannot comprehend?"

A. "No."

Q. "And this condition of being locked in and knowing there is a world out there, that you are inside of a body of, like in jail, is permanent in this young man's condition, is it not, sir?"

A. "I think so. Yes."

Those were the answers Corboy wanted: There was nothing worse than Block's condition, and it would never change. Such a clear acknowledgment by the defense's main expert wouldn't go unnoticed by the jurors. Now, Corboy was going to spend the rest of the afternoon setting up the doctor for the coup de grace, the last question that he would splatter all over Plum and then walk away.

Corboy handed Plum a copy of an article Plum had coauthored in *The Lancet*, Britain's most respected medical journal.

"I would like this marked as an exhibit, your honor," Corboy said as he handed Plum the article.

Johnson protested. Corboy hadn't previously given his opposing counsel a copy of the article.

"I'm very sorry," Corboy said solicitously. "I apologize. I thought that *you* had given them to *me*. You supplied me with all of Dr. Plum's writings, and I thought that you had one. Excuse me. I apologize."

Johnson bridled. Corboy could kill you with kindness, as he was doing now. Corboy was using his feigned politeness to show the jury that the article he was now showing Plum had actually been *given* to him by Plum. That gave the article an added aura of authority, and it let Corboy take the high road. He was surely going to ask an embarrassing question using a surprise document, but he was just as surely going to deny he'd done anything other than show Plum a document that Plum, himself, had given Corboy in the first place.

Corboy apologized once again to Johnson and then reminded him, "But you did give me all of his writings, and that's how I found out about it."

"Now," Corboy turned back to Plum, "if you'll go to the first page, you'll see your name, will you not, doctor?"

"Yes, sir."

"And right under it it says: 'Fred Plum, New York Hospital, Cornell'?"

"That's right."

"That's *you,* isn't it?" Corboy was circling. Moving in.

"Uh-huh."

"Then does this not say under your headline: 'Patients with severe brain damage due to trauma or ischemia [oxygen deficiency] may now survive indefinitely?' "

"Yes," Plum replied, looking for a way to blunt Corboy's point, "for which I could substitute the term 'now survive for no prescribed nor pre-determined limit.' "

"But you *didn't,* did you, doctor?"

"No, no, but I mean, that's the definition."

"But you didn't, did you, doctor?"

"No."

Corboy bore down harder. "In the first paragraph of that, in the summary of it: 'Patients with severe damage due to trauma or ischemia may now survive indefinitely.' John Randolph Block was a patient with severe brain damage, was he not?"

"Yes."

"It was due to trauma?"

"Yes."

"You started out by telling your readers: 'Patients with severe brain damage due to trauma or ischemia may now survive indefinitely,' did you not, sir?" Corboy was going to make doubly sure the jury didn't forget that sentence.

" '*May* now survive indefinitely,' yes. . . . *May.*"

"And it's not an exact science, medicine, is it?"

"No, sir."

"So when you say he may die in two years, he may live a lot longer than two years?"

Plum didn't answer the question, so Corboy barreled ahead. "But whatever the reason for writing it, you knew that your people in your peer group would read it! And you wrote it at a time, as you know right now, that there are no national statistics with reference to longevity or mortality with reference to the locked-in syndrome, are there, doctor?"

"Not for locked in."

"Thank you, sir, I have no further questions."

Travelers Insurance, the defendant's primary insurance carrier, had already paid Johnson's firm over $150,000. Corboy was out-of-pocket $114,206.91, although he would get all that back, on top of his one-third contingent fee, if he won the case.

Now, just as closing arguments were to begin the following week, Johnson made his last effort to settle the case: $9 million. Corboy talked it over with George Block and gave Johnson his reply: Nothing doing. They'd let the jury decide.

Johnson was resigned to a big judgment, maybe even a record-setter, as the Chicago legal newspapers were predicting. Christ, he even came right out and *told* the jurors to render a verdict against his client. Four million dollars, Johnson told the jury. That's what he said the verdict should be. "I can't believe I'm doing this," he said to himself then. "I never thought I'd stand up before a jury and tell them to find *against* my client for $4 million!"

Privately, though, Johnson had set his own goal for the case. He wanted to keep the jury's verdict below $10 million. Anything under $10 million would be a solid victory as far as Johnson was concerned, particularly since Corboy was asking the jurors for $40 million.

But, once in the jury room, the jurors proved to be just as divided as Corboy and Johnson on how much longer Block would live. That was the only real issue, after all, but Plum's testimony that Randy Block would only hold on a few more years preyed on their minds. The first thing they'd done, after electing a foreman, was to cast secret ballots on how long each juror thought Block would live. It was like "playing God," foreman Robert Stagg said, but they had no choice. The jury's estimate of Randy Block's longevity—five to ten years—was a compromise, and so was the verdict they settled upon soon thereafter: $9,000,332.05.

Johnson was elated. He'd kept the verdict within his own private goal. Johnson considered this a big victory over Chicago's courtroom master—and Corboy evidently did, too. As soon as the wizard heard the verdict, he walked out of the courtroom.

Johnson didn't even appeal. His client wrote out a check almost on the spot, and the Chicago gossips played it as the $3 million windfall it obviously was for the law firm of Corboy & Demetrio: "Band on a Run," ran the jazzy headline in the *Tribune*. "The major leagues of verdicts is still down the street at the Daley Center, as one of the town's all-stars has proved again. Media fixture Phil Corboy may be too high-profile for some tastes, but give him his due and revise the record books. In a period of five weeks, Corboy and partner Thomas Demetrio have snared jury verdicts worth $21 million . . . and last week Corboy won $9 million for a law professor who suffered brain damage in a truck crash. Okay, now roll the cameras."

Corboy saw it differently. It wasn't much of a victory when the jury gave him what the defense was already offering in settlement. But Corboy was also going to have a chance to even the score, because the *Karsten* case would be coming up for trial the following year, with Johnson once again on the other side.

In a real-life scene that could have been scripted for "L.A. Law," the young lawyers of Corboy & Demetrio piled out of their offices up and down the law firm's main corridor in response to a disembodied summons from the office intercom. It was time to assemble for "the call," a daily 4:30 P.M. status conference during which the lawyers discussed their cases, checked deadlines, accepted or rejected new clients, and generally scoped out the next day's work to make sure everything was covered. What started as an efficiency tool had become an integral part of each lawyer's support system.

Todd Smith, at age thirty-eight the firm's senior associate, sat at the head of the table ruthlessly running through a fourteen-page agenda, barking out the names of clients for whom the firm would make court appearances the next day.

"Bradner."

"Got it!" somebody quickly yelled back.

"Cronin."

"Got it. But I could use a back up on that. At 1:30."

"Put me down," a colleague replied. "Low on your list!"

"Martinez?"

"Got it!"

And so it went in a daily check-off for the assembled lawyers of cases on trial, motions due to be filed or answered, depositions to be taken, statutes of limitations about to run out and, finally, new cases to be accepted or rejected.

Smith looked over at Cyril McIlhargie, the firm's medical malpractice ace. "On the White case, Cyril?"

"Rejected."

"And Vlasek is rejected." Smith dispatched one of his own prospective cases with equal efficiency.

The call at Corboy & Demetrio was unique, and its importance was in promoting teamwork and creating a sense of community among the twelve busy lawyers there. It was a time for serious discussion, ribald humor, or just venting of the frustrations of a rough day. The afternoon meeting was also a time when, as Demetrio put it, "everybody helps each other out. Egos are not involved. Somebody's not afraid to say, 'I don't know.' Sometimes, if there's a pretrial settlement conference and one of the lawyers is having trouble determining a reasonable settlement value, we'll discuss the case. Sometimes we bring new clients in. It's a time of day to help each other."

"No time for turf wars," the firm's newest lawyer, Orvin Kacprzyk, said. "We're too busy trying to be the absolute *best.*"

Now Kacprzyk, an engaging guy who wore a punkish flat-top and favored tennis shoes and jeans as his office uniform, cleared his throat and solicitously explained to his colleagues: "I received a call today from Mrs. Ryan, whom we formerly rejected. She was so impressed by the way we rejected her that she wanted us to take a look at her case again."

The woman's husband had been killed in a railroad-yard accident. Corboy & Demetrio had previously rejected the Ryan case because she already had an attorney, but now the woman had fired her first lawyer. The older attorneys sitting around the table peppered Kacprzyk with questions: Was the man a railroad employee? Yes. Who would the third-party defendant be, then, since under the workers' compensation law you couldn't sue your employer? Was a lawsuit ever filed by the first lawyer? What's the statute of limitations? Was there an inquest? Demetrio, standing back against the conference-room wall, weighed the answers and said it didn't sound like much of a case. "I agree," Smith added, "but we probably oughta have her in."

As soon as the call ended, Kacprzyk eagerly headed for the conference-room phone. "Hello, Mrs. Ryan? This is Orvin. . . . Can you come in tomorrow?"

The next afternoon, he eagerly returned with another new case. "T. M. Mandrake is driving northbound on I-55 in Joliet when a southbound automobile crosses the median, gets airborne, and tears off the right side of her car." Kacprzyk described his case with the painstaking precision of a rookie. "All of her passengers are killed, including her sister and two nephews. She has sustained an open compound fracture of her right arm, chipped tooth, multiple lacerations and contusions, and she's seeking our advice.

"Defendant driver is seventeen years old. The car is registered to his father's name. Defendant's insurance company, State Farm, has already tried to contact Miss Mandrake. She knows that her sister's car was insured, but doesn't know the amount of coverage as of yet."

The younger Corboy, Flip, broke in: "What's the question?"

"Shall we see her?" Kacprzyk said meekly, and the room went wild with uproarious laughter all around.

"The CASE-O-METER is at 10!" blurted out forty-four-year-old Kenneth Miller amid still more guffaws. Miller was the firm's oldest, highest-paid associate. He'd earned $250,000—with a new BMW thrown in as a bonus—the year before from his airline-crash cases.

Kacprzyk tried to continue. "She called me last night at home."

"Why weren't you at her house this morning?" Miller asked slyly.

Added Todd Smith: "Get that Firebird fired up, boy!"

Only one lawyer at the firm *didn't* regularly attend the calls: Corboy, the Man himself, was the one who stayed away, and it almost seemed as if his ambivalence about straddling the line between roguishness and respectability had also found its way into his feelings about the firm. To the outside world, he WAS the firm, and he liked being the face man even though it meant that he supervised his domain from an uncomfortable distance. Corboy was complicated like that. He could burst in on the call in progress and stand, shifting from foot to foot, alongside Demetrio, preppy and blond, the boy next door with his surrogate dad. Look up a few minutes later and Corboy had disappeared again. He was hands off and hands on, a product, like so many of us, of his own insecurities.

And it was those insecurities that had motivated Corboy to become one of the nation's finest trial lawyers. He'd chosen personal-injury law because "I genuinely wanted to be financially secure. I wanted it. Needed it. I didn't think in terms of big money. But I wanted to be able to do what *I* wanted to be able to do." He didn't want the life his father had led as a Chicago cop who earned $50 a week and lost the family house in the Depression. Didn't want that even though his younger brother, Daniel, had joined the force, too. "Trial law was a way of getting away from that."

It was also a way of getting the attention and the adulation that he'd been denied by parents who were too busy with each other to do much for their kids. Corboy's mother was ill during his childhood, and she died of nephritis at age forty-one. It was Corboy's uncle, Daniel Harnett, a Roman Catholic priest, who was closest to him. And even though Corboy had received the proper Catholic schooling and some support from his extended family, he was an outsider even in his own home.

He hungered for approval, for some sign that he was doing all right.

"I was not given the attention as a child that, in retrospect, I probably thought I was entitled to," Corboy said, probing thoughtfully for the reasons why he'd strived for recognition in what was already such a high-profile profession. "A shrink would have to determine that." Pause. "My mother was sick when I was a kid. That might have had something to do with it. Most Irish Catholic mothers smother their children with love. I don't think my mother had time for that, because she was ill most of my childhood life. My dad was a policeman who had very little money. He had a lot of problems just paying the medical bills. My clothes always came from my first cousins, and they always went after me to my brother. That might have given me some need for recognition, and some need for stroking and attention."

That self-knowledge had also brought with it the realization that most of his peers weren't all that different. "Very few trial lawyers were born rich," Corboy noted. "Most of the great trial lawyers are people of my ethnicity. Irish. Or Jews. People who have not been

accepted by the establishment. They're outsiders, for the most part."
Just like Corboy was. And is.

What Corboy remembered most about his uncle was how much the priest had taught Corboy about himself. "From the time I was seven years old, I was always treated as an adult. I was trusted as an adult." Corboy remembered how, as a sixteen-year-old, he'd smashed up his uncle's car. Corboy was afraid to drive again, but Uncle Daniel took young Phil out that night and put him behind the wheel of another car, so he could show Phil what he'd done wrong. "My uncle wasn't concerned about the car; he was concerned about *me*. That's why I don't have any concern with material things that are damaged or hurt or stolen. They can be replaced. *People* can't be replaced."

A man who saw grief daily, as Corboy did, already knew that. The cruel irony was that Corboy had to experience the lesson all over again when his youngest son, twelve-year-old Bobby, was killed on a suburban street corner. The youngster was on an errand to buy cookies. He'd just parked his bike when an out-of-control auto jumped the curb and struck him. The seventeen-year-old driver was uninsured. Corboy never sued. Instead, he created a charitable foundation with the $100,000 he collected from his own insurance company. Over the years, he added millions more to the Robert H. Corboy Trust, using the money, among other purposes, to build a moot courtroom for his downtown Chicago law school, Loyola. And when his ex-wife, Doris, became the foundation's trustee he started a new trust, the Philip H. Corboy Foundation, and funded *it* to the tune of a cool $2 million. The new foundation's latest project: to give the Archdiocese of Chicago a million dollars for the inner-city Catholic schools that Corboy himself had attended many years before.

And yet, for all his grieving about the loss of a son, Corboy also protected himself by taking pains to say that he felt no special affinity for his clients as a result. "It had the same effect on me as it would have on any father. It was devastating. It was a terrible, terrible experience. But it had no more effect on me as a person than it would have if I were a bartender. It was a terrible, terrible experience.

"It did not supply me with any asset. Because tragedy is personal. It did not give me any insight into other people's tragedy. I would never call upon it as a resource, or an edge to understand something or somebody. Nor have I consciously done it. Why? Because tragedy is so personal. So different. Every tragedy is different for every person. If nothing else, it taught me that. But I already knew that."

Still, you could hear in Corboy's words the gradual awakening of a man opening himself up to the pain and the insecurity he'd been trying to cheat for so long. Sure, he was fiercely proud of being his own man; he still said he didn't care what most people thought of him. "I'm sure there are a lot of people who wouldn't go to my funeral. A lotta people who'll sorta smile when they read my obituary. Most people are kinda two-faced. You can't go through life, visible, and not have people dislike you." But he also saw his children—his oldest son Flip, a daughter who was an Illinois judge, and two other sons who were, respectively, a doctor and a film-maker—and his law firm as his legacy. Corboy wanted to make some of his other lawyers partners, too, so that the law firm would be self-perpetuating.

"What good's a law firm if you're dead?" Corboy wondered aloud. "My kids and Tom Demetrio are what this whole world's about, as far as I'm concerned. Your children, when it's all over, are all you've got. They're the only thing that counts. All the goddamn money, and all the acclaim, and all the celebrity, and all that, doesn't mean a thing in the end.

"Money comes so easily. At first, it was startling. But, then, you take it for granted. And you wonder: Well, why do some people just keep running for the sole purpose of making *more money?* That's not why I'm working. I think people who retire, die. I want to practice law the way I want. I want to keep pursuing excellence."

Thursday, February 7, 1985. Corboy was already holed up in his Water Tower apartment, preparing for the trial of *Karsten v. McCray* that would begin the following month. Corboy shut himself away before every big trial. By the time opening statements began, Corboy meant to know *more* than the doctors themselves did about Joan Karsten.

But there were still hurdles to overcome. Bill Johnson, Corboy's nemesis from the Randy Block case who now was representing one of Karsten's doctors, and Roger O'Reilly, the lawyer representing the lead defendant, Dr. Robert McCray, were still amassing proof for their theory that Joan Karsten was already very sick when she came in for her appendectomy.

One of the lawyers' theories was that Karsten had a rare, but *dormant,* blood disorder that had somehow been triggered by the stress of the appendectomy, without any fault on anyone's part. O'Reilly and Johnson were going to try to prove that it was this rare condition, known as *thrombotic thrombocytopenia purpura,* or TTP, that caused the tiny blood clots which, in turn, had cut off the oxygen to Joan Karsten's central nervous system and left her severely brain-damaged.

They also had found some medical support for another theory: that Joan Karsten was suffering from some other neurological malady that had long preceded the appendectomy. Karsten's husband had been the first to tell one of McCray's partners about his wife's hospitalization in 1972 for what her doctors then thought might be multiple sclerosis. Tipped off by McCray's partner, the two lawyers found the neurologist who treated Joan Karsten in 1972, and they examined her earlier hospital records. The lawyers discovered that her doctors had been concerned enough then to recommend that Karsten enter the Mayo Clinic for more tests.

The evidence of some preexisting condition was confusing, even contradictory, but it wasn't up to O'Reilly and Johnson to prove conclusively the cause of Karsten's tragedy. All they had to do was to raise some major doubts in the jurors' minds about what really happened. The medical experts they were going to call at trial might just do that.

Just as surely, though, young David Horan was going to do his best to stop them. He was new to this world of high-stakes malpractice cases. But even though there was great distance between Horan and his mentor Corboy, both in age and in experience, Horan was a real go-getter, and his medical degree gave him an advantage in such complicated malpractice cases.

That was why Corboy had sent him out on this particular Thursday morning, a month before trial, to take the deposition of the doctor who both Corboy and Horan thought was going to be the defense's star witness.

A *deposition* is a fact-finding exercise, an examination under oath that lets the other side freely explore the testimony and evidence expected to be presented by a witness at trial. The subject of the deposition is called the *deponent,* and on this particular day the deponent was a fairly accommodating witness named Dr. John M. Shaw. Shaw was an assistant professor of hematology and oncology at the Northwestern University Medical School, and he had given depositions many times before. The defendants were paying him two hundred dollars an hour. What made him that valuable was his experience in treating patients with the rare condition known as TTP, and O'Reilly had already told Horan that Shaw was going to link up the allegedly preexisting TTP in Joan Karsten to the oxygen-deprivation condition, known as DIC, that both sides were pretty sure had caused her brain damage.

Horan dispensed with the usual preliminaries—eliciting the oral resume: age, education, university affiliation, and so forth—and got right to the point: Did Joan Karsten have TTP?

Yes, replied Shaw, and "it may have been as early as 1972." But when Horan tried to pin Shaw down to specifics, Shaw conceded he couldn't really be certain about what had triggered the so-called TTP, or even when she'd contracted the rare disease. "No," he said, "I cannot make the statement with a reasonable degree of medical certainty that she had TTP in 1972." Even Shaw seemed bewildered by the records he'd examined. "If you *don't* evoke TTP," he told Horan late in the day, "you really are at a loss to describe her neurological findings." Shaw also confessed that he hadn't even evaluated the plaintiff's theory, that Karsten had contracted brain-damaging sepsis from her burst appendix because McCray delayed operating. "I am not either an expert in infectious diseases nor do I have claimed to have reviewed every bit of the chart to determine whether she did or did not have [sepsis]," Shaw admitted.

Horan spent most of the day probing and prodding Shaw, testing just how strong a witness he would be for the other side. His conclusion was that Shaw's testimony wouldn't hold up on the stand: too many holes, too much equivocating. And even if Shaw cleaned up his act and became a strong advocate for the defense, Horan and Corboy would be able to impeach his testimony with the very words from his earlier deposition.

Horan went to the apartment and gave Corboy a blow-by-blow account of the deposition. "He backed down!" an elated Horan reported. "Shaw's a weak witness, and without him they don't have a case at all." When Horan told Corboy about Shaw's statement that he couldn't say "with a reasonable degree of medical certainty" whether Joan Karsten had TTP in 1972, Corboy erupted: "That's not close enough! If he gets up there we'll cross him and peel him and chop him up and throw him out to dander!"

That was the arch Corboy reaction, the reflexive comments of a great lawyer who was psyching himself up for the battle ahead. Even his nemesis Johnson marveled at how Corboy did it. "He's got a pile of money, and you're damn right I'm jealous," Johnson said, shaking his head. "He doesn't have to try cases. Yet he gets all geared up for cross-examination like he's a thirty-five-year-old guy! You've got to admire that."

It was just part of the Corboy Method. Like every outstanding trial lawyer, Corboy first had to convince himself, totally and unalterably, that his client was a victim who deserved just compensation. *"You have to work it up.* You have to be thoroughly immersed. It's your job to make sure that the jury believes in you, and that you believe in the case! If you don't believe in the case, you have no business being there, because it's going to come out. The responsibility I have is to supply the finders of fact with the genuine impression that my side of the case is the *right* side of the case, and that my client is *entitled* to compensation in the amount of money that I am seeking. If you have absolute faith in your lawsuit—if you are absolutely and completely aware that this lawsuit deserves the attention of the system, and you handle yourself in a way where you believe that, that fervor comes out! That's charisma." And Corboy had it.

Inside the courtroom, Corboy maneuvered for whatever advantage he could use to take control. The courtroom was the daylight world of lawyers and jurors and witnesses and judge, and Corboy tried to rule it as his own eminent domain. He used little ploys—"credibility devices"—to gain the upper hand, like bringing in his own custom-made highly varnished lectern. His secret worry was that, without it, he'd look like a pipsqueak if he got stuck behind some giant, government-issue courtroom lectern—and that he'd get a verdict befitting such diminutive status.

So concerned was he about presenting the proper image to jurors that for thirty years he'd even refused to let any of his lawyers sit at the counsel table with him. Against what was frequently a phalanx of attorneys from the other side, Corboy was totally alone. "I wanted the jurors to think that I had complete control over the case."

And even though he had recently relaxed that total prohibition, Corboy hadn't lost the egotism that underlay it. He wanted the jury to perceive in him what Corboy called the Three Cs: Competence, Credibility, and Charisma.

"I want them to think I have some X-factor that the other guys don't have. Why? Because I'm the one that'll get their attention! The person in charge of that courtroom is the one who gets the attention! And I want the jurors to know that *I'm* in charge. I'm not the docile little boy that's willing to let everybody else take charge. I'm willing to run that risk."

Corboy needed the whole room to make his points. He didn't so much hold a conversation as usurp it. With his forefinger jabbing the air and his arms painting the empty space to make a point, he'd pace around, then stop momentarily as he shifted from side to side, and finally crawl up on top of a desk or a credenza, dominating the room from the high ground. And Corboy could tear through a quiet conversation or a cross-examination with equal vigor. "I have some attributes which might be alien to professional serenity," Corboy confessed. "I'm a Type Double-A."

But Corboy's pulverizing intensity was a decidedly mixed blessing. Yes, his featherweight's quickness was what made him so formidable. Few besides Corboy could be confronted with a defense-attorney's film of his "vegetable" client's *changing a tire*—and, as Corboy did, win a huge award after slamming the other side for *invasion of privacy*. Then there was the time Corboy presented a witness who testified he'd seen an automobile accident from his hotel-room window. When the defense produced the guest register, it didn't contain the witness' name. Aghast, Corboy quickly conferred with his witness and then returned him to the stand, to reveal that he'd been there with a young woman, under an assumed name that *was* on the register!

Corboy had attacked his own divorce case the same way he ran every other case, fighting every step of the way and turning what began as an amicable split-up into an embarrassing feud that was splashed across the pages of all the Chicago newspapers. He'd done the same thing when the feds caught a crooked judge and then snared a surprised Corboy in their net, too. Corboy had given the judge a check for $1,000, an apparent legal-ethics violation, although Corboy claimed the money was for the judge's mother. Too proud to accept what he called the "Scarlet C, for Censure," that a bar disciplinary panel wanted to carve on his forehead, he turned a matter that would otherwise have been quickly forgotten into an all-out war before the Illinois Supreme Court. He had friends there, justices with whom he'd been generous in his campaign contributions. "This thing's a pimple on my ass," Corboy grumbled. "It's bothering me a lot."

Jurors loved a fight and Corboy certainly gave them that. But Corboy had also seen how he could hurt himself. "You've got to be in charge of the courtroom *without* being in charge of the courtroom," he tried to keep reminding himself. "You can't be dominating to the extent you're *crushing* people. Be in charge, but be the *good guy.*"

This was where the boxing metaphor—the idea of two combatants in the ring, fiercely slugging it out—broke down. A boxer who pummeled his foe could win. But Corboy knew he could lose, or, in the Block case, get less money for himself and his client if the jury felt sorry for somebody Corboy had been pummeling.

"I have a weakness as a cross-examiner: activism. When I'm on a roll, I've got a tendency to brutalize. My business, bottom line, is to win. Sometimes it takes a stiletto rather than a guillotine! I have to be constantly on guard, constantly aware that crucifixion of every witness is not a necessity!"

Corboy was veritably shouting now, and no matter how hackneyed or tortured his metaphors became there was no doubting his sincerity. That was the Method actor in him. "Winning," he intoned in one great, theatrical burst of energy. "Winning isn't everything, it's the ONLY thing! There are no excuses for losing. Every time I've ever had any semblance of failure, I've said to myself, on reflection, 'There are lots of lawyers who could have done better than I. And that's what the client's entitled to get. He's entitled to get the best, and if I can't give it to him I shouldn't be in the case! This is masochism, it's hair shirting, it's self-flagellating! Call it all those things! It IS all those things!"

Corboy was, in a sense, on foreign turf as he stepped inside the quaint county courthouse at 201 Reber Street in Wheaton, Illinois. This was DuPage County, next door to Cook County but also a world apart: affluent, white, suburban, and possessed of the kinds of potential jurors Corboy liked to avoid. Corboy had never before tried a case here. And he hadn't used his vaunted market researchers because he thought word about his big-city methods would travel fast in the county's tight-knit little communities, and Corboy feared a backlash. So he'd relied on his own instincts during the nine days both sides spent questioning prospective jurors. Corboy was looking for women and members of minority groups, compassionate people who he thought would have the most sympathy for an energetic middle-aged woman who'd gone into the hospital with a minor ailment and come out with the mind of a child. But that perfect jury proved hard to find in DuPage County, and Corboy ended up with jurors who represented the area's white, middle-class backbone. There were eight women and four men. No members of minority groups, but he thought the preponderance of women was a plus.

The jury had been selected in the courthouse's main courtroom, a stately forum that Corboy hoped would put the jury in a big-money frame of mind. He needed a push like that, because the juries of DuPage County weren't like those in the downtown courtrooms where Corboy usually played the game. DuPage jurors had only once given a plaintiff more than a million dollars, and even then DuPage's lone $1,250,000 verdict was in an auto-accident case in which fault wasn't an issue.

O'Reilly and Johnson had, in fact, already offered Corboy $1 million to settle this case. It wasn't a bad settlement given the circumstances, but it sure wasn't enough for Corboy. He knew that the defendants, all together, carried $8 million in malpractice insurance. He wanted $3 million, the full limit of coverage for the clinic and its two physicians who treated Joan Karsten.

DuPage's tightfistedness was going to be a decided detriment for Corboy. But, as it turned out, so was the courtroom, because the spacious, ceremonial room was the turf of the senior judge in the county, and on the Monday morning that the trial began she pulled rank on her subordinate judge, Richard A. Lucas, and told him to take his important case with its big-shot lawyers back into his own courtroom, thank you very much.

When Corboy saw the room where he'd be spending the next six weeks, his square jaw collapsed. He was used to working the big rooms. He was a performer. He needed that space. Corboy liked to walk around, but if he took two steps to the right of his table in Lucas' courtroom, Christ, he'd be falling into the jury box!

Corboy walked over to Bill Johnson. They'd had a battle royal in the Block trial, and from his experience against Johnson then Corboy knew that in a room this small he couldn't afford to be so aggressive. The contrast with the laid-back Johnson would just be too great. Even given the bigger downtown courtroom, posttrial interviews of jurors in the Block case had revealed their discomfort with Corboy's combative style when they compared it to Johnson's.

"Johnson," Corboy murmured to his foe, "I'm gonna smile at you all through *this* trial even if it kills me."

Friday, March 8. With the trial slated to begin the following Monday morning, Corboy was asking the judge to withhold from the jury any mention of Karsten's 1972 hospitalization for what her doctors thought then might be multiple sclerosis. "It's so nebulous as to not be able to be hooked up to the present condition," Corboy said. He read aloud the testimony of Dr. Shaw—testimony that Corboy thought proved his case, not theirs—"and I don't know Dr. Shaw but I'm sure he's not going to change his testimony."

Read the whole Shaw deposition, O'Reilly replied, and you'll see that the defense will be able to use Shaw to connect the 1972 hospitalization to the 1979 brain damage. Johnson agreed with his cohort, as would the judge the following Monday.

Corboy was incredulous. His two opponents knew the judge wouldn't be able to go through the whole deposition on such short notice. He thought the two lawyers were playing fast and loose. "Give the court anything he wants," Corboy said with evident sarcasm.

"Sure," the judge said good-naturedly. "I will look at it over the weekend—"

"Give him all 187 depositions if you want," Corboy broke in.

Corboy opened his case on Monday morning, March 11, just short of five years after Joan Karsten had gone into the hospital with appendicitis.

It was a workmanlike opening, full of the medical descriptions and the terminology that the jurors would be hearing throughout the trial, but oddly bereft of much emotion about Joan Karsten's lonely crucible. Corboy became so caught up in describing every little nuance on her medical chart that he didn't bring Joan Karsten's plight alive for the jury. Worse, he made no mention at all of what he knew, from Shaw's deposition and from the hearing before the judge only the previous Friday, would be the main defense contention: that Karsten had had a neurological illness since at least 1972, and that her brain damage thus wasn't any doctor's fault.

Corboy's main contention was that McCray had waited so long to operate that Karsten's appendix had burst while she was in the hospital, thereby setting up the brain-damaging sepsis infection.

But Corboy did anticipate another defense argument, that Karsten's appendix had burst several weeks before McCray ever saw her. That didn't matter, Corboy said, because the standard of care was that McCray should have operated much sooner than he did.

"The evidence will further show," he told them as he finally wrapped up his opening statement, "that one of the defendants in this lawsuit, Dr. Robert McCray, has specifically stated, under oath, that the sepsis came from the ruptured appendix, and that the ruptured appendix caused the sepsis. The question that you will be able to answer will come from the lips of Dr. McCray himself.

"Now, ladies and gentlemen, the multiple organ failure and all the kidney damage, brain damage, of course, came from the sepsis, which came from the rupture, which came from the appendectomy."

It was a lot for the jury to follow, this hip-bone-connected-to-the-thigh-bone kind of opening statement, but Corboy gave it his best shot and sat down. He'd always said opening statements weren't his forte. But he considered himself dynamite on the close.

O'Reilly was up next. He represented McCray, and, standing in the same spot as Corboy had, just five feet away from the jury box, he spoke in a folksy, low-key style that seemed perfectly suited to the intimate courtroom. He introduced himself—"I am Roger O'Reilly, a lawyer from Wheaton"—because, he thought, everybody knew Corboy, "and I thought perhaps you didn't remember who I was." A nice touch.

"And let me just start out by telling you something about this man, whose professional medical conduct you will be called upon to judge in this case."

McCray was a local boy, a DuPage County native who'd gone to college after World War II and who'd been among a group of doctors who founded the local clinic "so that they could take better care of" their neighbors.

O'Reilly went through the same set of facts all over again, patiently explaining to the jury how, despite all the tests and the exploratory operations and all the specialists McCray brought in, nobody, really, could understand what had happened to Joan Karsten. O'Reilly made his client sound like a doctor who was so totally confounded by what he saw before him that he didn't know what to do next; like a pilot who could see that his plane was crashing but who didn't know which switch to throw.

But that impression was all right with O'Reilly if it placed sufficient doubts in the jurors' minds, too, about what had happened to her.

"Throughout the course of that hospital stay," O'Reilly went on in his own undramatic way, "the doctors who cared for her never determined what was the cause, the real cause, of the neurological symptoms.

"Sure, they had a lot of thoughts and a lot of impressions, but nothing where they ever said, 'Hey, we can point to this and that's obviously what's causing this. This is what happened.'"

O'Reilly told them that they were soon going to learn that medical experts sometimes don't agree on anything.

"But it's really only in hindsight, looking back, examining the records"—now he was deftly sliding back into the 1972 hospitalization—"and I am not talking about only the hospitalizations in April, May, June and July of 1979, but also the hospitalization back in August of 1972, do we get some insight as to the most likely or the most probable cause of what occurred to Mrs. Karsten at this time in 1979.

"The evidence in this case will show that back in 1972 Mrs. Karsten was examined by a neurologist, a specialist in abnormalities of the nerves and nervous system, as well as an orthopedic surgeon." O'Reilly told them all about the diagnosis of possible multiple sclerosis, but he said the most likely cause "for all these unusual things and the unfortunate things and tragic things that Mrs. Karsten suffered" was the rare blood disease, TTP. "It has this tendency, this particular disease, to strike, recede, stay in recession for a number of years, and then anything can turn it on again, trigger it, an operation, the stress of an operation, whatever."

Corboy just sat there, boiling away, with Horan and his other young associate who'd also worked on the case, Susan Schwartz.

Johnson represented Dr. Glen Asselmeier, McCray's partner. Asselmeier had been dragged into the litigation because he'd been the first doctor to see Joan Karsten when she began having complications after being sent home from the appendectomy. Asselmeier hadn't wanted to readmit her to the hospital; Joan's husband insisted on it and Asselmeier then relented. Corboy now maintained that Asselmeier's initial reluctance was indicative of the overall level of care at the clinic. That was why Corboy had sued Asselmeier even though Asselmeier had ultimately complied with Ed Karsten's wishes.

From the standpoint of creating another deep pocket, there was good reason to keep Asselmeier in the case. But what Corboy had also unwittingly done was to set up a very effective Mutt-and-Jeff strategy by the other side. O'Reilly and Johnson coordinated their defense. When O'Reilly made an important point to the jury, Johnson could step up next and ram it home again. And, because each man was permitted to cross-examine the other's witnesses, it meant that the lawyers on the defense team could take turns lobbing big, marshmallowlike leading questions to each other's witnesses.

The idea, after all, was to create enough doubt in the jurors' minds that they wouldn't find for the plaintiffs, and if that meant bombarding the jury with a lot of improbable medical and scientific jargon, that was Corboy's problem, not the defendants'.

Johnson finished up by telling the jurors he didn't know the source of Joan Karsten's infection, but that it sure wasn't present when McCray and Asselmeier treated her.

"So, we have an [infection], that's the basis for the case against these doctors, that wasn't there. And that is why you get to all of the initials in the case. Was it TTP? Was it DIC? That is another exotic disease, a tragic disease.

"It's a tragic thing. Not only was TTP considered, but tetanus. . . . It was considered by the plaintiffs' own expert witness as one probable cause of this lady's condition, and the tetanus has nothing to do with surgery."

Tetanus. That was a new one.

Corboy had been at trial for ten days when, on the evening of Wednesday, March 20, he met with three visitors at his apartment.

Harlan Stone, the University of Maryland surgeon who would be Corboy's principal expert witness, was there to go over the testimony he would give beginning the following morning.

Horan, Corboy's malpractice ace, was there to help.

And so was Dr. George Block, the eminent surgeon for whom Corboy had won $9 million the year before.

Block was Corboy's secret adviser on the case, a kitchen-cabinet-of-one who was street-smart about the Corboy Method because he'd endured, along with Corboy, the trial of his own son's case. Now, unknown to the other side, Corboy was relying on George Block for advice on how to try this case. Block not only knew Corboy's style; he also knew Johnson's. And Block could translate convoluted medical jargon into understandable English, no mean task as far as Corboy was concerned.

If, as Corboy later said, Block was concerned about the care Karsten had received, he surely also wanted the satisfaction of seeing Johnson beaten. That night, Block became Corboy's sounding board as the four men sat around Corboy's apartment, first walking Stone through his direct testimony and then prepping him for the thorough going-over he would get on cross-examination.

Corboy couldn't have found a better-qualified expert to call to the stand the next morning. Harry Harlan Stone had performed as many as four thousand appendectomies, and he was also a leading authority on postoperative infections. With his resonant voice deeply etched by its Georgia drawl, Stone commanded every juror's attention.

Corboy stepped him through the testimony they'd discussed the night before. Yes, from studying the hospital records Stone had made a diagnosis of Joan Karsten's condition: "sepsis as a consequence of perforated acute appendicitis," a complication arising directly from the operation McCray had performed. No surprise there. That was consistent with what Corboy had been saying all along, and it was even consistent with the diagnosis that another of McCray's partners had entered on the patient's hospital record.

The next key question was whether McCray had waited too long before operating on Karsten. "[Was] Dr. McCray negligent?"

Yes, Stone boomed back. "He was negligent."

"And, Doctor," Corboy asked as he continued this carefully orchestrated minuet, "upon what do you base that opinion?"

"The standard of care is to observe a patient whom you suspect has acute appendicitis for somewhere on the order of six to eight hours, and at the end of that interval of time, if the patient still persists in pain, to proceed with operation. If the patient is not dramatically improved or the patient has worsened, then one should proceed with operation, essentially never going beyond twelve hours."

Stone had his own theory about what had caused Karsten's permanent brain injury. He told the jurors that there must have been a huge, undiscovered abscess somewhere in Joan Karsten's body. To Stone's way of thinking, McCray should have performed an operation called a *laparotomy* to locate and drain this abscess during Karsten's second hospitalization. Instead, he prescribed an antibiotic therapy that Stone called ineffective.

O'Reilly and Johnson thus had to neutralize on cross-examination Stone's two main points: that Karsten's appendix had burst during the day and a half while McCray was debating whether to operate, and that the doctor had been too knife-shy the second time, too, when he didn't go hunting for the big abscess.

"Dr. Stone, I'm Roger O'Reilly," McCray's lawyer said with his usual diffidence. "I think we met?"

"I recall meeting you," Stone replied warily.

"We took your deposition, Doctor, was it May of 1984?" Still circling. Measuring the distance. Sizing each other up.

"Late spring. I don't remember the exact date."

Joan Karsten had had an upset stomach after eating pizza, a few weeks before her appendectomy. O'Reilly contended that the upset stomach was actually appendicitis, and that Karsten's problems were her own fault because she'd delayed treatment. Early in the questioning, though, Stone told O'Reilly that he "would not put any great credence" on that.

But, O'Reilly persisted, Karsten had suffered such a fierce bout of indigestion that she'd later told a nurse at Central DuPage Hospital how guilty she felt about not seeking medical attention earlier. O'Reilly demanded: "Would that change your opinion?"

"I doubt it."

"Okay. Dr. Stone, you do a great deal of writing, as we have seen on your curriculum vitae, do you not?"

"That's correct."

Well, O'Reilly wondered, would Stone agree with a statement from a 1971 medical journal article that said many people endangered themselves, even put themselves in life-threatening situations, by self-diagnosing appendicitis as indigestion.

Corboy broke in. "Could I have the author, please?"

"You're looking at him," O'Reilly replied, triumphantly nodding toward Stone. He'd uncovered one of Stone's own articles that seemed to directly contradict his indifference to Karsten's earlier abdominal pain, and to suggest that her appendix might have burst weeks earlier. In his own revisionist history of the trial, O'Reilly would later recall the exchange as "one of these unsurpassed delights. . . . I felt a surge of adversarial joy that only a trial lawyer can experience."

But O'Reilly found himself with an even juicier setup about a half-hour later.

"Doctor, you apparently, as I understand your testimony, are under the impression that Joan Karsten had a very large abscess, I believe you said, that was never detected?"

"That's correct."

"Is that your testimony?"

"Yes."

"How large would this abscess have to be, in your opinion?"

"I would think it would be at least a pint size."

O'Reilly held his hands apart. "Are we talking about like this?"

Stone wouldn't bite. "A pint—"

"You show me."

"—you know—what a pint milk bottle looks like, a pint milk carton, about that size."

Aha! That was what O'Reilly wanted to hear. Karsten's hospital charts showed that McCray and the dozen or so consultants he'd called in had been pushing and palpating their patient's abdomen almost continuously since she'd first been brought in. There was no way that all of them would have missed a hard, swollen area the size of, say, a Coke bottle or a milk carton.

O'Reilly and Johnson now had a damaging inconsistency that they could save for their closing argument. They could argue that it was folly for the plaintiff's main expert to accuse a dozen doctors of missing something that big, and why wouldn't the jurors believe them?

But Stone's admission was so blatantly wrong, in the defense lawyers' minds, that when Johnson's turn came the next day he immediately took out after him.

"Do we have a milk carton?" Johnson inquired. "Did anyone think of bringing one of those?"

The answer was no, but Johnson produced a Coke bottle instead. He held it up against a life-size skeletal model he'd brought into the courtroom and incredulously asked Stone how the doctors could have missed something that big.

But Stone had already picked up on his previous mistake, and now the expert reversed field and ran right at Johnson. Stone replied that the sixteen ounces could have been "distributed out" through Joan Karsten's body. "It could be like an extremely long piece of bacon."

"Drink this Coca Cola," Stone told Johnson, "and I would like for you to lie down and see if we can feel this in your abdomen!"

Score one for Stone.

As Corboy saw it, a trial was "a manic-depressive sort of thing. Sometimes you're up, and sometimes you're down. Every trial's like that. It's like quicksilver. Like mercury."

And Corboy was finding out just how low he could get, because the preceding weeks had been going badly. Corboy's out-of-pocket expenses, which he always carefully tallied, had reached $191,018.48, and now the whole bundle was at risk because Johnson and O'Reilly, who'd already billed $275,000.00 on the case themselves, were tearing Corboy apart.

McCray had been called early in the trial as an adverse witness by Corboy, and the local doctor had done an excellent job of defending himself during his three days of testimony. The excitable Corboy was a vivid contrast to the avuncular, low-key McCray, and Corboy had gone after him with a discomfiting intensity.

It infuriated Corboy that McCray seemed to be the very picture of a self-effacing, affable family doctor, an image that was burnished further when, right in the middle of the trial, McCray rendered aid to a seventy-six-year-old woman who'd been struck by a train in front of the courthouse. "The jurors see this humble man," Corboy groused. "He's no more humble than Aristotle!"

When Corboy was finished with McCray, he thought he had "cut him up with impunity," but what he had really done was to establish McCray as the underdog, somebody for the jurors to cheer.

Corboy had done exactly what he knew he had to avoid. "I castrated," he later acknowledged, "when I should have tickled."

Still, Corboy hadn't learned his lesson, for when the defense's main witness took the stand on Friday, March 29, a frustrated Corboy started ripping into him, too.

Dr. Thomas S. Moore, chairman of the Department of Surgery at the county's Elmhurst Memorial Hospital, had been practicing in the area even longer than McCray, and he had performed almost as many appendectomies as Corboy's chief witness, Dr. Stone. But the difference between them was palpable. Whereas Stone was an impressive speaker who held firm positions from which he seldom diverged on the stand, it was hard to pin down Moore on anything. While Moore circled, Corboy chased him for answers that the doctor just wouldn't give—and the frustration showed, as when Corboy tried to drive home the point that McCray, himself, had originally diagnosed his patient as having the septic condition that Corboy now claimed had caused her brain damage. A key objective of the defense was to shrug off that original diagnosis.

"And, Doctor, what was the final diagnosis signed by Dr. McCray on the sheet which is right in front of you?"

"Over here, maybe?" Moore fumbled around.

"On the top sheet of the first one. What does that say? What was Dr. McCray's final diagnosis?"

"All kidding aside," Moore replied, "would you read it? Because you can read his writing. It is difficult for me to read his writing. I will try if you want." Moore studied the document. " 'Sepsis, postappendectomy.' Go ahead. Tell me what it was. I can't read it."

Corboy: "You will agree that that was Dr.—even though it may be hard to read, that that's what he put down, did you not?"

Moore: "I can read the first part of it, and I am sure I can struggle with the rest of it by your reading it to me."

Corboy: " 'From' or 'for', I don't know whether it's 'from' or 'for', 'sepsis postappendectomy for ruptured appendicitis'?"

Moore: "I would think 'from', I don't know. I don't know what it is. 'Ruptured appendicitis', yes."

Corboy now tried to put his line of questioning back on track. "In any event, as an expert in this case and having reviewed the records, you would conclude, would you not, that the final diagnosis written by Dr. McCray was 'sepsis postappendectomy.' And sepsis is what we are talking about, are we not?"

Moore: "That's what *you* were talking about."

The following Monday, Corboy was back in the judge's chambers, arguing out of the jury's hearing about still another witness whom O'Reilly and Johnson were planning to use against him.

Dr. Paul Menet wasn't just another of Karsten's treating physicians. He was also a partner of McCray and Asselmeier, and, after privately conferring with the defense lawyers who represented his clinic and his partners, Menet intended to give testimony that would hurt Corboy's case.

An obviously agitated Corboy wanted Menet kept off the stand. "This witness, your honor, is an attending physician of my client!" The doctor-patient relationship precluded Menet from saying anything without his patient's approval, Corboy maintained. "There is going to be an attempt, apparently successful, to have this doctor change his diagnosis and change his treatment and change everything as to what he found on and after the fourteenth day of May, 1979."

The judge let Menet take the stand anyway to testify that, even though his diagnosis of sepsis in 1979 was the same as Corboy's experts' now, Menet didn't think the sepsis had any connection to Karsten's brain damage.

But if the appendicitis-induced sepsis didn't cause her brain damage, then what did? That was where Shaw, the expert whom O'Reilly and Johnson were saving for the end of the trial, was supposed to come in. Shaw was going to attribute the whole sordid mess to the exotic disease TTP. But O'Reilly and Johnson must have come to realize what Corboy and Horan already knew: that Shaw wasn't going to be a credible witness. If Shaw got up there, Corboy would use Shaw's deposition answers to destroy him. O'Reilly and Johnson decided not to call Shaw to the stand.

Corboy cried foul. The lawyers had specifically mentioned Shaw and his diagnosis of the rare disease TTP in their opening statements. The jury had heard all about the TTP; was *contaminated* by it, even; and now Corboy wasn't going to get his shot at proving Shaw's alleged diagnosis wrong.

An astonished Corboy shifted about restlessly. He'd been jobbed. He felt absolutely certain that his two foes had intended all along to keep Shaw off the stand.

"Excellent lawyering," he said grudgingly. "If they get away with it."

Instead of Shaw, the lawyers brought in Dr. Richard Dominguez, the doctor who'd treated Joan Karsten in 1972, when she'd been hospitalized for weakness in her left arm. O'Reilly had privately spoken to Dominguez, too.

Dominguez had ordered an electromyelogram test then which confirmed the existence of some kind of neurologic abnormality. And, he testified, he was concerned with the possibility that Joan Karsten appeared to be suffering from multiple sclerosis.

An enraged Corboy was back in the judge's chambers again, crossing swords with O'Reilly and demanding a mistrial. "It is a brand-new element in this lawsuit! There has been no diagnosis of multiple sclerosis!"

"I didn't ask for a diagnosis," O'Reilly calmly replied. "You asked on your cross-examination."

"Can I finish?"

"I thought you finished," O'Reilly said coolly. "You stopped talking."

"One at a time," the judge broke in. "He *never* stops talking."

Corboy wanted the last word in this battle of experts. He was going to present a fresh rebuttal witness.

Although the ever-prepared Corboy, anticipating rebuttal, had held three expert witnesses in reserve, when the time finally came he was left with little choice about which of them to use.

One of his three spare experts was a University of Chicago hematologist, a specialist, like the defense expert Shaw, in diseases of the blood. But Shaw had never been called to the stand, so there wasn't anything for Corboy's hematologist to rebut! No sense in calling him.

That left the Corboy side with two general surgeons who, like the experts who'd previously testified, were specialists in treating infectious diseases. But one of the two had another commitment he couldn't break, and that left, by default, Dr. S. Martin Lindenauer.

Lindenauer had come to Corboy along with the case. The University of Michigan professor had been brought in by Davis, the Chicago lawyer who ceded the case to Corboy when he became a judge. Corboy didn't know much about Lindenauer, but he seemed credible enough as Corboy took him across ground that by now was so well traveled. Lindenauer, like all of Corboy's witnesses, held firm to the chain-reaction theory that a botched appendectomy had caused Karsten's sepsis, and, in turn, her brain damage.

"Doctor," O'Reilly said as he began his cross-examination, "let's clear the air a little bit. You have testified before in court, have you not, in medical malpractice cases?"

Yes, said Lindenauer, maybe three or four times. In California, Florida, Missouri, Illinois. Always for the plaintiff.

"Do you work with any lawyer referral services of any kind as far as expert testimony is concerned?"

"No."

O'Reilly asked the same question two more ways, and both times Lindenauer replied, No.

Lindenauer had been asked the same question by O'Reilly at his deposition the year before, and he'd answered no then, too. But O'Reilly knew that Lindenauer's answer then, as now, was a lie— knew it because he'd already checked around in Lindenauer's home- town of Ann Arbor and obtained a copy of a deposition Lindenauer had given five years earlier, in which he admitted to having taken cases from an expert witness referral service.

The best lawyers stay away from expert witnesses who advertise their services, because those witnesses-for-hire have the taint of a hired gun about them. It was a point of pride with Corboy that he didn't use hired guns. But now the chagrined Corboy had to watch as O'Reilly dismembered his last witness. Lindenauer was impeached. The impact of that one lie would carry over to all of Lindenauer's testimony.

O'Reilly kept banging Lindenauer over the head with that 1980 deposition, and the more the doctor tried to weasel out with an "I don't recall" the longer O'Reilly kept reading from it to refresh Lindenauer's recollection. A sorry performance.

"It referred to a referral service, Dr. Lindenauer?"

"Yes," Lindenauer finally confessed, "it does."

"One more nail," Corboy said under his breath.

Corboy considered the closing argument to be his greatest skill. That was where he tied his case together and made his pitch for the big money. Corboy was working, of course, for the Karstens, but he also had an interest to protect: He was riding their case for a contingent fee of one third of the gross, plus reimbursement of expenses that now were closing in on $200,000. Lose it and he'd get nothing but a blemish on his seventeen-year perfect record.

This time the dapper, white-haired lawyer with his elegantly fitted suit lived up to his own expectations. Standing only a few feet from the jury behind his special lectern, he gave a skillful, soulful close that touched on every part of the case, beginning with an apology for being too aggressive and ending with a lesson in economics.

"All you can do in this lawsuit," Corboy intoned, looking first at one juror and then at the next, all twelve of them, "is bring Edward Karsten back to an optimum of what he had before. You might say to yourself, 'How crass can the law be? This white-haired guy is saying, You can bring him back to his optimum by giving him money.' . . .

"You know the life he has. He is not entitled to get some bunch of money and say, 'Here, go have a ball for yourself.' . . . He is not to be given something, a medal. But he is entitled to compensation. Not for showing he is gallant and honorable and decent—because he is supposed to be all those things—but for what he has lost, not what he has to gain."

Corboy arrived at the money part. He always spent a lot of time on that, because he didn't want the jurors to feel guilty about delivering big money, and that was what he was looking for here, a verdict of between $4.5 million and $8 million, four to eight times more than any lawyer had ever received from a DuPage County jury.

The verdict form had a top line for the total and lines underneath for the individual components of the award—disability and disfigurement, pain and suffering, medical expenses, lost wages, and so on.

Don't fill in the top line, Corboy urged them. Don't fill it in.

He wanted them to assign a value to every subcategory first, even if the individual numbers added up to "some large figure." Remember, he said, "I asked [in *voir dire*] if each and every one of you would have any difficulty in signing a verdict for a very large sum of money, even if that large sum of money is in the millions of dollars, and each of you said under oath [that] you would have no such problem."

When O'Reilly's turn before the jury came, he reminded the jurors of another oath they'd taken: to keep sympathy and compassion *out* of their deliberations. O'Reilly said he didn't know what had happened to Karsten—"only God knows"—and he didn't rise to Corboy's bait on damages. "I'm not going to comment in regard to any astronomical figures that Mr. Corboy may ask you to return against me, because the Court also will instruct you that if you decide for Dr. McCray on the issue of liability, you have no occasion to consider that."

Because the burden of proof lay with Corboy, he could use his rebuttal for one final, desperate rejoinder at O'Reilly.

"Well," Corboy said to the jurors, summoning back the words of his foe, "God isn't here. He may be in this room in various forms in a capacity over all of us, but He is only going to give you help in this lawsuit. He is not going to tell you what the diagnosis was."

Jurors can be fickle in the same way that members of any group can be. Some people mix well together; others don't. The difference here was that millions of dollars and a doctor's vindication depended on the group dynamic of people who'd been pushed together and yet who barely knew each other.

The lawyers had been talking to the twelve men and women in that box for six weeks without receiving any hint of what was going on behind the eyes that tracked them from point to point and occasionally nodded off.

Now, they were going to find out.

Corboy, who thought he had won the case, was going to learn just how defective his human radar was.

The first order of business was to elect a foreman, and the group selected a machinery salesman because he seemed to be the best talker.

The next vote that afternoon was to see where everybody stood on the case, and it turned out there wasn't much of a dispute on that, either. The first vote was ten-to-two in favor of the doctors, and even those two jurors quickly moved over to the other side after a little discussion with the others. Everybody thought Corboy was a great orator—one of the jurors paid him the supreme honor of saying he was eloquent enough to be a preacher—but nobody thought he had much of a case.

"It seemed to me," one juror said, "like everything that Corboy got over to the jury, either Johnson or O'Reilly got up and just kind of tore the witness apart."

"You go through the charges and make your decisions," another juror said, "but still, at the end, there are still no answers." All the defense evidence about exotic illnesses and preexisting conditions made it too tough for them to fix the blame on McCray. "The essence of his [Corboy's] argument was that she had had an infection and the doctor had missed it. That is probably the biggest point that there was no ultimate answer for."

When the jury sent word the following day that it had a verdict, Corboy and Horan were packing up back at their hotel in Naperville, and Schwartz was keeping a vigil near the courtroom. A verdict coming that fast was usually a bad sign for the plaintiffs. Arguments over money always took longer, and this deliberation had already been dragged out because the jurors even gave themselves a half-hour cooling-off period, in case anybody wanted to change his mind.

Schwartz telephoned Horan: Verdict's coming in. Get back here.

More bad news: When the jurors filed back in, some of them didn't even look at Ed Karsten and his children who were sitting there in the courtroom.

One of the men, on the other hand, made a special point of staring right at the family, to show that what was about to happen didn't bother him at all.

By the time Corboy and Horan returned to the courtroom the verdict was already in: innocent as to all defendants.

Corboy seemed genuinely astonished, but he tried to stay upbeat as the bad news sank in. "Okay," he said curtly. "We've lost it. Now it's time to fight it on appeal."

After the verdict was in, the judge told the jurors that Corboy and Karsten had turned down the malpractice insurance company's $1 million settlement offer.

"They should have accepted it," one of the jurors said, "because right now, the way this goes, they will probably get nothing, when they could have had a million bucks."

Trouble in Paradise: Rex Carr and the Longest Jury Trial in History— the Toxic-Tort Case of *Kemner v. Monsanto*

A poor trial is better than a good settlement.

—REX CARR

$\mathbb{I}$n the solitude of his makeshift law office two blocks from the St. Clair County Courthouse in Belleville, Illinois, Rex Carr pondered the irony of his success.

"I frequently get more money in settlements than I believe I can get in a trial," he said. "It's asinine, but some insurance companies, they hear my name and they say, 'Pay that sucker what he wants!' They're fools to do that. But they believe in my reputation, and they pay."

Carr had every reason to be boastful. He was, indeed, one of the nation's most successful lawyers specializing in cases involving personal injury and catastrophes. Carr's firm was to downstate Illinois what Corboy's was to Chicago: the best of the breed.

Carr relished the good fight, and the opposition's propensity to settle contradicted his own natural law. Carr still remembered what

Joseph Goldenhersh, a lawyer friend of his from Belleville who'd gone on to become chief justice of the Illinois Supreme Court, once told him about settling cases. "He said that a poor settlement is better than a good trial. Well, my discovery has been just the opposite. A poor trial is *better* than a good settlement, because I've gotten all my business from publicity about me and my cases. You don't get publicity from a settlement. Nobody even hears about it—nobody but me and my client. And I don't get a single bit of business from it."

"I don't want to settle cases," Carr said with the conviction and the stubbornness of a man who always meant what he said. "To me, the trial of lawsuits is the *summum bonum* of this business. This is an arena. It's combat. Me against the other lawyers. I want to win."

But his comments on that April day of 1984 would turn out to be more revealing than even Carr could have imagined, because Carr's innate antagonism toward the compromises and settlements that were an essential part of the legal process had plunged him into a trial that shouldn't have happened. It was a nightmarish legal war over the effects of a thimbleful—yes, a *thimbleful*—of a chemical compound called dioxin. And it was a war that Carr could not win.

By the time it ended three and a half years later, the case of *Kemner v. Monsanto* had done much more than set a record as the longest jury trial in history. It was bad news for the nation's legal system and for the trial lawyers who brought it. Carr's lawsuit over the traces of a potential poison had somehow become lodged in its own private Twilight Zone, a netherworld where those who entered became ugly and small: where a judge who lost control of his case was rewarded at the end by being put up for a big promotion, and where one lawyer's tenacity became his undoing.

Carr didn't know all that then, of course, when he made his prophetic observation about the merits of *not* settling cases. His trial against one of the world's industrial giants, the Monsanto Company, had only begun two months earlier, and, after all, there was nobody else in the courtroom with the cocksure swagger and the iron-pants endurance of the man whose name meant "king." What was there to worry about?

"If everything jells the way I think it will," Carr said then with his usual confidence, "it could be a super-duper verdict," surely the biggest verdict in Carr's three and a half decades as a lawyer.

The locus of Rex Carr's success wasn't some big-city legal barony, but, rather, the small, impoverished city of East St. Louis, Illinois, and the middle-class counties surrounding it. It seemed an improbable base of operations, and yet it was actually a place where juries were so obviously proplaintiff that lawyers like Carr enjoyed phenomenal success.

In 1983, the year before his trial against Monsanto began, Carr had earned $1 million, nearly five times the national average for partners in the nation's largest, most prestigious law firms. Now, at the peak of his legal career, Carr was litigating his most important case. He was seeking tens of millions of dollars from Monsanto for the damage he contended they had caused by spilling dioxin in a tiny Missouri town.

It was 11:10 P.M. on January 10, 1979, when the Norfolk & Western Railway freight train came rolling through the central Missouri farming community of Sturgeon. A bitter, cold night, five inches of snow on the ground, temperature five above.

Two railroad tracks ran parallel to each other, east to west, right through the center of town, past the white frame houses in the little town of 901 people. Norfolk & Western owned a right-of-way across the whole state, and its 88-car freight, pulled by three locomotives, was making the trip from St. Louis to Kansas City that night with a newly built tank car that was twenty-seventh from the front of the train.

That tank car and its brief, checkered history were at the epicenter of Carr's lawsuit. The car had been built by the GATX Corporation, a leading rail-car maker, and leased to Monsanto. At its plant in Sauget, Illinois, Monsanto had filled the tanker with 19,000 gallons of wood preservative for shipment to a chemical company in Tacoma, Washington. Norfolk & Western was hauling the car as far as Kansas City. There, it would be transferred to a Union Pacific freight for the rest of its journey.

But the Norfolk & Western freight train hadn't gone far when the new Monsanto tank car literally fell apart. It was a lemon, fresh from the factory with a defect that became apparent almost immediately.

A hundred miles out of St. Louis, right in the middle of Sturgeon, the tanker's front wheels fell off.

Since the wheels were attached to the car's coupler, their loss meant that the coupler instantly dropped down and gouged into the ties between the rails, derailing the train and upending the Monsanto tank car with such force that the tank ruptured.

Nineteen thousand gallons of smelly wood preservative spilled across a 2,400-foot stretch of the tracks.

At first, nobody in the hamlet knew what was in the car, and for safety's sake every one of Sturgeon's residents was evacuated for two days. To clean up the spill, men went in wearing gas masks and rubber suits, and they literally dug up and carted off the soil that had been contaminated by the preservative.

There was, of course, no doubting that *something* had befouled the tiny town. The snow turned yellow and orange, ponds turned black, fish died, and, worse, even after the soil had been bulldozed away and trucked off, a stench hung over the town. Residents of the hardscrabble town complained of watery eyes, difficulty in breathing, and nausea. People in the neighboring villages could actually smell when people from Sturgeon were nearby. They carried that foulness with them.

Then, in the month following the accident, Monsanto revealed that the tank car had contained traces of dioxin, an unwanted by-product created in the manufacture of some herbicides and wood preservatives.

There actually were a whole family of dioxins, each with its own peculiar chemical makeup and its own reputed dangers. But even though the particular form of dioxin, known by the scientific name 2,3,7,8-TCDD, that leaked out in Sturgeon was considered by some to be the most dangerous of all, there was then, as now, no conclusive evidence of its danger to humans. Dioxin could cause cancer in laboratory rats—what *couldn't?*—but there was no evidence that it caused cancer in humans.

That didn't prevent many of the town's residents from filing suit against the various big corporations—deep pockets, all of them—that had touched the tank car in one way or another on its maiden voyage. Sixty-four people joined with a retired teacher, Frances E. Kemner, in retaining a lawyer named Jerome W. Seigfried from neighboring

Mexico, Missouri. He was an affable, white-haired guy, the picture of a genial country lawyer and just the right speed for these working people and ordinary folk. Seigfried filed suit for them, for a one-third contingency, in the local Boone County court.

But forty-seven other people had a different idea about what would make for a good lawsuit. They joined together and hired another lawyer, Paul Pratt, whose East Alton, Illinois, office was right in Carr's backyard. At age forty-five, Pratt, along with Carr, was one of the wealthiest, most successful lawyers in the Illinois counties of Madison and St. Clair. Together, those two counties had come to be known as "Plaintiffs' Paradise," and, given the staggering verdicts that emanated from the two county courthouses, it was easy enough to see why.

Bottom-land flat, the Illinois counties of Madison and St. Clair were due east of St. Louis, directly across the Mississippi River. Belleville, Carr's home and a twenty-minute ride from his offices in East St. Louis, was a benignly middle-class city where the streets had names like Washington, High and Main, and where the county courthouse dominated the green-squared downtown. The tennis star Jimmy Connors was a hometown celebrity and Carr's client, at $250 an hour for contract and endorsement advice.

Carr kept his law firm in East St. Louis out of a sense of pride, loyalty and obstinacy. The city of 55,000 was 96 percent black, its median family income the lowest in the nation, its murder rate thirteen times greater than the national average for cities its size. But the real center for his firm was in the white enclaves of Madison and St. Clair counties. Fortuities of law, geography and commerce long ago made the area, in Carr's words, "just an ideal place to have lawsuits," and, in Corboy's, "a mecca for litigation in the Midwest."

Federal statutes enacted in 1910 and 1915 gave injured rail and barge workers the right to file suit anywhere the defendant railroad or barge company did business. Because both counties were major rail and barge centers—more than a dozen railroads had lines there, and the Illinois and Missouri rivers joined the Mississippi nearby—and because there was a high concentration of unionized blue-collar workers from whom to draw potentially proplaintiff jurors, the area's courts routinely produced huge verdicts for injured rail and barge workers.

"If you're hurt in California and that railroad passes through here, this is where you can file suit," Carr gleefully explained. "Railroading is hazardous work, so the types of injuries are always bad—legs off, arms off, deaths. A good lawyer, big defendants and sympathetic, working-man-type juries—all that laid the foundation for this area."

In 1982, the St. Louis *Post-Dispatch* reported that more than a thousand rail and barge lawsuits had been filed in the two counties during the prior two years alone and that, on the basis of a random sample of those cases, 80 percent involved accidents that had occurred elsewhere. Business was so good in the two counties that four hometown lawyers, including Carr and Pratt, were members of the trial lawyers' most elite million-dollar club, the Inner Circle of Advocates.

Carr's clients were from all over the Middle West. His partner, Sandor Korein, who represented the barge workers' National Maritime Union, got injury cases from up and down the Mississippi as well as from all the rivers flowing into it. By making his local courts the venue of choice for virtually all of their important cases, Carr and his fellow lawyers were "forum shopping," a perfectly legal practice as long as the court allowed it.

And so it was that after Seigfried commissioned a poll by a University of Missouri political science professor and found that a significant vein of sentiment among prospective Boone County jurors already was running against the Sturgeon townsfolk, Seigfried got his lawsuits dismissed in Boone County and went shopping for a more hospitable forum—in Plaintiffs' Paradise—with Rex Carr as his cocounsel.

But Paul Pratt had reached the courthouse first, and it was his case that came up for trial first, on March 15, 1982.

Even by the rough-and-tumble standards of justice in Plaintiffs' Paradise, Pratt's exploits in and out of the courtroom were the stuff of legend. As the officially approved regional counsel for the Brotherhood of Maintenance of Way Members and the Brotherhood of Car Men, two important railroad unions, Pratt had what lawyers called the union "ticket" to represent its members injured on the job, and he once had shown his gratitude for being given this exclusive franchise by entertaining some union officials, among others, in a Winnebago motor home rented by his firm. When a fight broke out between one of Pratt's associates and a prostitute, and the prostitute complained to the police, others around town took to calling the Winnebago the "brothelmobile." Almost a decade later people were still talking about it. There were also stories of a temperamental, hard-drinking Pratt routinely firing lawyers and office help, only to rehire them once he'd cooled off. And, it was also rumored in the small, close-knit Plaintiffs' Paradise fraternity, Pratt had persistent money problems despite the appearance, by his keeping not one but *two* private airplanes, that things were going every bit as well as they should have gone for a good lawyer who was eating off a union ticket.

Getting a ticket, as Carr's partner Korein had from the barge workers, was like being given a license to feast on manna from heaven, and what did it matter if, as some said, at least a few of the lawyers retained their union ticket by laying a little of the long green back into the hands of the union leadership? It was a rewarding symbiotic relationship. The lawyer got a lock on union personal-injury cases, and the union workers got excellent representation at a reduced contingency rate of 25 percent, instead of the standard one third.

That was exactly what had happened with Pratt's forty-seven dioxin cases. The lead plaintiff was a man named Richard Lowe, the local roadmaster for Norfolk & Western. He'd been sent over to Pratt by his union representative.

Pratt sued four well-heeled defendants. Conventional wisdom was that Monsanto was probably the most culpable. Then there were GATX, which built the tanker car, and Dresser Industries, which had furnished the cracked coupler. On the lowest rung of liability was Norfolk & Western, which had, after all, only been given a car to pull.

But on the night before jury selection was to begin, Pratt settled his case with every defendant except Norfolk & Western, the defendant whose legal team was probably *least* prepared for the trial to come. The three codefendants agreed to pay the plaintiffs $7 million in damages, more than half of which, $3.6 million altogether, went to Pratt for his 25 percent fee and expenses. Worse still for Norfolk & Western, the other defendants who had taken the lead in discovery and had promised to mount a spirited defense now started sitting on their hands, leaving Norfolk & Western to go it alone.

The result, after three and a half months of trial against an unprepared defendant, was a new record for Madison County: a $58 million verdict against Norfolk & Western, even though the railroad had neither made nor knowingly transported the dioxin.

Pratt stood to gain a $14.5 million contingent fee if his award were upheld on appeal—but the railroad had been so obviously hornswoggled in Plaintiffs' Paradise that even the Illinois Supreme Court felt compelled to step in. Instead of allowing the appeal to be heard, as it customarily would have been, by the Fifth Appellate District, in which Madison County was located, the justices transferred the appeal to the adjoining Fourth District, a rural area known for being much tougher on plaintiffs.

The justices had little choice but to do that. By taking advantage of laws that, in the past, had often allowed plaintiffs injured elsewhere to file suit in Plaintiffs' Paradise, Carr and a few other lawyers handling mainly out-of-town clients had capitalized on the generosity of local juries to such an extent that the embarrassing publicity was just too much for Illinois' elected judges to bear. Too much of a good thing was putting all the dioxin cases at risk.

When the appellate court ruling came down in Pratt's big dioxin case the following spring, it spelled trouble for the likes of Pratt and Carr. Pratt's entire $58 million verdict was thrown out under the legal doctrine known as *forum non conveniens,* a Latinism that meant "take your cases elsewhere." The justices told Pratt to send his claims back to Missouri, where the accident had happened in the first place. "Not even a gossamer thread binds this case to Illinois," they wrote.

But if that were bad news for Pratt, it also had ominous implications for Carr. He was finally getting his own case before a judge in adjoining St. Clair County after a five-year wait, but it was a case that involved the same dioxin spill and the same defendants as Pratt's. How could the appeals court rule any differently about his case than it had about Pratt's? Sure enough, the expected *forum non conveniens* argument was raised right away by the defendants in Carr's case, but the trial court judge wrote an opinion differentiating between the two cases and refused to dismiss. Carr had dodged a bullet, but even his fellow trial lawyers were worried that too much of a good thing in Plaintiffs' Paradise was sooner or later going to hurt everybody.

"I think guys like Rex are bad for the profession," grumbled Morris Chapman, another local trial lawyer who was also a member of the Inner Circle of Advocates. "How much money does he need, beyond a certain point? I've always taken the position that you have to live within the limits of the system. And if you go out and get these $20 million verdicts for a guy from Podunk, you're going to kill the golden goose! You may win that verdict, but you'll cost every other lawyer the system's viability because the system has only so much resilience. It's happening here because of the people who haul cases in here. The knee-jerk reaction of the courts has been to curtail that entirely. Now, it's unproductive for the rest of us."

Those were the first signs of the trouble in Paradise.

Having previously settled with Pratt in his Sturgeon case, Monsanto still found itself battling scores of other toxic-tort lawsuits over dioxin.

One such lawsuit was a class action brought in Brooklyn on behalf of 16,000 Vietnam War veterans and their families who'd been exposed to some of the 12.8 million gallons of the Agent Orange defoliant sprayed in Southeast Asia between 1965 and 1971 to clear jungles and destroy enemy crops. The lawsuit's main allegation was that dioxin had been formed as a contaminant in the manufacture of Agent Orange.

There was great disagreement over the long-term health effects of the veterans' possible exposure to the dioxin—cancer and nerve and liver diseases were alleged by the vets, while the chemical companies who made the stuff kept asserting that the maladies were what could generally be expected to be found in mostly middle-aged men.

But there was no disputing one fact: Win or lose, the seven corporate defendants, including Monsanto, were facing the spectre of perhaps $100 million in legal bills. Better to settle. With both sides playing their own game of chicken, jury selection was about to begin in the Brooklyn federal courthouse on a Monday morning early in May 1984 when the two sides finally compromised. They reached a $180 million settlement that, given the circumstances, was just about the best either side could hope for. Monsanto's share was $83 million, all of it covered by insurance.

That still left another series of cases pending against Monsanto that Pratt was also involved in. But, unlike in the earlier Agent Orange and Sturgeon cases, Monsanto wasn't talking settlement.

Led by a boyish-looking but tough-talking thirty-year-old in-house legal strategist named David Snively—quickly nicknamed "Snively Whiplash" by his foes—Monsanto had decided to *stop* settling. Although the giant chemical company didn't give any reasons for its change of heart, it was obvious enough. Potential plaintiffs were emboldened each time another settlement came down, and the way to end that was to stop settling. In a decision that would also have profound implications for Pratt and Carr, Snively started fortifying Monsanto's defenses, and the first place he went was the United States District Court in Charleston, West Virginia.

The West Virginia town of Nitro, nestled among the hills a little to the west of Charleston, was another of those burgs that the dioxin lawyers knew well by now. Nitro was a town of 9,000, and the Monsanto plant there that made chemicals for the rubber industry employed a good many of the ablebodied men and women in the valley.

Back in 1948, the plant had begun producing a herbicide called 2,4,5-T. Later, 2,4,5-T was used in Agent Orange, and, as Monsanto would come to learn, it would also be found to contain a small amount of dioxin.

The 172 separate lawsuits that were filed against Monsanto in the West Virginia federal court were related to what had happened at the Nitro plant in 1949, when some chemical-mixing equipment blew apart. The accident sprayed the inside of a building with a gooey coating of chemicals used to make 2,4,5-T. Within weeks, workers at the plant began developing chloracne, an erupting skin condition associated with dioxin exposure and the *only* human dioxin-exposure health hazard Monsanto had ever acknowledged.

But the workers claimed that, as the years went by, their health problems went far beyond minor skin eruptions. Aging workers blamed heart problems, lack of sex drive, blindness, general aches and pains, and a raft of other maladies on their long-term exposure to the dioxin and, beginning in 1981, they started filing lawsuits against their employer.

Ordinarily, workers who suffer on-the-job injuries aren't allowed to sue their employers. Such lawsuits were generally barred when the workers' compensation laws took effect. But the Nitro lawsuits were filed under a willful-misconduct exception to the law, which meant that those filing lawsuits had to prove not only that they'd been injured by Monsanto, but that the company had caused the injury *deliberately*.

Rather than trying all the dioxin lawsuits together, as had been done in Pratt's first case when it came up back in Plaintiffs' Paradise, the West Virginia federal judge selected seven representative plaintiffs from a list of fifteen that the plaintiffs' lawyers gave him. Even with such a small number of plaintiffs, it still took eleven months to present all seven cases to the jury. But when the evidence was in, the jury decided it wasn't much of a case.

Monsanto won on every dioxin count. Then, it played hardball against the plaintiffs and their lawyers by getting a court order making the plaintiffs pay $304,996 for what were known as "taxable costs" of the trial, sums Monsanto had to expend for witness fees, trial transcripts and the like. That would make future plaintiffs think twice before hauling Monsanto into court.

Such was Monsanto's "new look" in the courtroom. But Pratt wasn't around to see it. With his own shaky dioxin verdict to shore up back home, Pratt had left the Nitro case to his West Virginia cocounsel, who lost it on the last day of April 1985 every bit as proficiently as Pratt could have.

Now, Snively, who'd supervised the Charleston trial, was coming home.

Home to St. Louis, the headquarters of Monsanto.

Home to Plaintiffs' Paradise, where Rex Carr was trying to win his case against the only remaining defendant:

Monsanto.

Carr, fifty-seven years old when his lawsuit against Monsanto came to trial, was a bantam lawyer with a larger-than-life reputation and enough self-confidence to describe himself as "a knowledgeable lawyer, a forceful personality and a skillful talker." His voice had an imperious flatness to it, perfect for carefully parsed courtroom statements, but somehow unsuited to the coarse language he often used in private. Graying hair, combed back, framed an angular, softly lined face punctuated by a jutting, slightly cleft chin. In the courtroom, he favored dark suits and wore half-glasses.

Out of court, Carr relaxed in blue jeans, a turtleneck sweater, and a tattered, quilted navy-blue jacket. Who was there to impress in Belleville? But his choice of car betrayed an exceptional ego. His brand new BMW 733i—a $35,000 automobile, he proudly announced—sported a license plate that boldly proclaimed the name REX. With a radar detector on the dash, he dominated the interstate at speeds surpassing eighty miles an hour. Carr also kept a twenty-six-foot sailboat on nearby Lake Carlyle and sailed whenever he got the chance.

"He's a loner," said Korein, his partner of twelve years. "He says hello to who he has to talk to. At 10:30 he gets a cup of coffee. Gets a glass of juice for lunch. Urinates at 2:30. Stays until seven o'clock. Never shuts off the phone calls. A creature of very definite routine. Rex probably considers me one of his best friends, but we never see each other socially. And he really doesn't have any friends. He's just not gregarious in the slightest."

Korein remembered that Carr used to get his exercise by methodically running up and down the driveway in front of his house until he'd jogged a mile's worth. "He's obsessive," commented Jerry Schlichter, another of Carr's partners. "He even works at sailing, going out every weekend from April through November, which in this climate is stretching it. I went sailing with him once. I didn't like it. He was just too intense."

Carr sailed on a lake thirteen miles long and three miles wide, a solitary pilot resolutely setting his course for the same tiny island at the lake's far reaches. To circle the island and return was to reconfirm his dominion.

To look at Carr, whether in his sailboat or in the courtroom, was to see his steely will to win. But when people got close enough to the enigma, what they thought they sometimes saw were the stress cracks that weakened steel and eventually made it break. There was a hubris in Rex Carr that would be his eventual undoing in the Monsanto case. His bulldog tenacity, that all-consuming obsession with total victory, whatever the cost, could make him a caricature in his own battle plan.

Jack Carey, forty-two years old then, was in many ways the partner who knew Carr best, because Carey occasionally played crew member to Carr's skipper in weekend sailboat races on Lake Carlyle. Just as he had been doing during the week in the courtroom, Carr would try to win the race on sheer conviction. "If there were forty boats in the race and thirty-nine headed for the first mark, he'd start going in the opposite direction and expect them to follow *him,*" Carey recalled. "He just always expected that when the other thirty-nine saw him they'd assume that *they* were wrong, and it never seemed to bother him that we never finished anywhere close to first."

Inside the courtroom or out, that was the way it was with Carr. His karma was to succeed, and he had such an enormous ego that nobody could shake his resolve. "He's a brilliant lawyer," explained Bruce Cook, one of his former partners, "but like so many people who are that gifted, he thinks his opinions are the laws of nature."

"One day we were in this little mud puddle of a lake, ninety-eight degrees, and the wind just died," Carey remembered. "There were twenty boats but eighteen quit. We stayed out there, though, dead in the water behind another boat, and when the race was finally called he was *ecstatic!* He yelled out: 'This is the first time I've ever come in second!' And I said, 'Rex, you just came in last.'"

As it was for so many outstanding trial lawyers, Carr's will to prevail against his environment, be it physical, social or economic, was forged almost from birth. Carr grew up in East St. Louis, the fourth of five boys. His father, an Illinois Central Railroad fireman, deserted his family at the start of the Depression and later was jailed for nonsupport. Carr's mother provided for the family as best she could with a Works Progress Administration job as a mattress stuffer, while twelve-year-old Rex peddled newspapers. He later worked as an usher in a movie theater, and, at age seventeen, took a better-paying job chopping 300-pound blocks of ice for refrigerated railroad cars at the East St. Louis stockyards. To earn his way through the University of Illinois at Urbana, 163 miles away, he would hitchhike home each Friday afternoon to begin an enervating thirty-six-hour shift at the icing docks. Sunday evenings, he hitched a ride back. "I was sleepier than hell in my Monday classes," he recalled. "Didn't wake up until Wednesday."

Carr scornfully remembered that when an eighth-grade teacher asked him what he would be when he grew up, he cheerfully answered that he wanted to be a lawyer, "just like Daniel Webster and Abraham Lincoln."

"Oh," the teacher replied, "you want to be a liar!"

Carr attended the University of Illinois Law School on the G.I. Bill, graduating second in his class in 1949 only to discover that he could still make more money chopping ice than practicing law. He spent another year on the icing docks, leaving them for the more learned profession when he got married.

Carr's three children from his first marriage included a doctor in Chicago, a missionary in Colombia for a charismatic church (sarcastically described by Carr as a filial response to his atheism), and the owner of a limousine service in Malibu Beach, California.

Carr's second wife, Edna, was his former secretary, and at the time he began the Monsanto trial their sixteen-year-old son, Glenn, was a student at the local public high school. "Don't go out for football, son," Carr warned him with a grin. The school and its coaches were being sued by Carr for paralyzing injuries suffered by one of the school's football players during a game.

As the Monsanto trial approached in early 1984, business was booming at the firm of Carr, Korein, Kunin, Schlichter & Brennan. Gross income the prior year had been a record $10 million, and that was a lot to divide among five equity partners; four profit-sharing, or junior, partners; and nine associates.

Ninety percent of the firm's gross income was from contingent-fee cases. Most were settled, providing the cash flow to sustain the few big cases in hopes of a huge recovery years later at trial. The firm's associates made from $30,000 to $50,000 plus a share of the new business they brought in, and business was good enough that the firm's other thirty employees—including three investigators, a photography-lab technician and the pilot of the firm's $960,000 airplane —received bonuses of $2,000 plus one month's salary. Korein kept the books, paying the salaried help twice monthly, then drawing down the profits and distributing them to the nine partners "whenever I decide to. It's very much like keeping your household checking account."

Carr and his main partner, the fifty-two-year-old, Hungarian-born Korein, each earned a $1 million share of the profits.

But it was Schlichter, then thirty-five, who was on the fast track at the partnership. Having started out as a $9,000 a year associate thirteen years before, he had skyrocketed up to a $720,000 annual draw. The other six partners earned substantially less than the top three men, but "less" was a decidedly relative term, because even with a small share of the pie all of the partners were pulling down six-figure annual incomes.

Carr, Korein was the picture of a law firm feasting on the riches of its own success. But behind that facade was a law firm also beset by cliques, jealousies, power plays and infighting—a place where partners dreaded the annual setting of the shares for the forthcoming year because of the disputes that would invariably arise. If money was their way of keeping score, it was also the firm's most divisive influence. Even though the partners started meeting in November to vote on their respective shares for the coming year, it usually wasn't until the following spring that they finally hammered out a division of the profits that would be acceptable to everybody.

Carr and Korein were the odd couple of the firm, senior partners who had surprisingly little in common and who, in Korein's case, openly gossiped and kvetched about the other. Korein liked to play the stock market and talk about his big investments—"Return on investment," he'd chuckle, "an old Jewish custom"—whereas Carr had been forced to liquidate his entire million-dollar portfolio and sink every penny of it into a struggling tourist-barge business in France that he'd bought on a whim and that, he said, had made him "a victim of my own stupidity." Korein liked to tell people about that.

There was a rippling undertow of competition between the two. Korein had never had a million-dollar verdict and Carr had had a bunch, but Korein had the barge-worker's "ticket," generated thirty good cases a year with it and knew how to turn a respectable case into cash coming through the door. The two had a wary alliance: Every year, they each had to have exactly the same number of partnership points. The year the Monsanto trial began, each had 25 points, 25 percent of the firm's net profits, out of a total of 100.

But Schlichter was the real comer. "He knew how to spell greed in eight different languages," another partner said of him. Trim and muscular, with a neatly scissored moustache, an unlined face and a thick head of dark, gray-flecked hair, Schlichter was slick, all right, in the polished way that anybody who always seemed to get what he wanted and to do it without much apparent effort seemed slick. The other partners had stayed on the eastern side of the Mississippi, keeping their homes right where they made their wealth; Schlichter had moved with his pretty wife, Sue, and their two children to a three-story, elegantly furnished turn-of-the-century stone mansion with a limestone facade in downtown St. Louis, on the site of the old World's Fair grounds. Thirteen huge rooms, thirteen fireplaces, a dining room ceiling done in silver leaf on top of gold leaf: it cost him a thousand dollars a month just to heat the thing.

Schlichter was a local boy, the lower-middle-class son of a government worker. Working his way through UCLA Law School, he'd participated in antiwar protests and had even been arrested once, but when he joined Carr's firm in 1973, he brought in lots of cases and they moved him along fast, making him a partner in 1978.

When he read accounts in the legal newspapers about the partners' earnings at some of the eminent Wall Street firms, Schlichter would marvel that his was so much higher. "Think of those Wall Street lawyers," he'd say. "They're the ones getting all the publicity, and they're not making as much money as we're making." He knew that for a fact: Schlichter had a fat 18 partnership points—18 percent of the profits—at the law firm in 1984.

Even before *Kemner v. Monsanto* went to trial, Carr had secured a windfall settlement for his clients, who received a share in $5 million paid by the two companies, GATX and Dresser, who were responsible for making the defective tank car. After expenses were deducted, each plaintiff received an average of about $30,000, which wasn't bad at all considering that the Vietnam vets had gotten about $15,000 apiece in their Agent Orange settlement, and their exposure to dioxin had been much greater.

But the person who won the most money from the settlement was Carr himself. From that $5 million settlement, he took $1.7 million as his fee, turning half over to his firm and the remainder to the Missouri lawyer who referred the dioxin clients to him.

The settlements with GATX and Dresser provided a war chest for continuing the litigation. After advancing millions of dollars for expensive medical tests given to each of the sixty-five townspeople, the settlement was a restorative for the firm's cash flow. There were partners at the firm who believed that Carr's best strategy would be to encourage settlement by the remaining two defendants as well.

Norfolk & Western, in fact, was interested in a settlement. Even more important, Monsanto, was, too. Both had contacted Carr, telling him they wanted to talk. This was before the *forum non conveniens* chill moved in on the dioxin cases in Plaintiffs' Paradise, and before Snively entered the picture with his scorched-earth, take-no-prisoners policy. It seemed that a total settlement was possible.

If Carr could end the case without much more work, he would still garner one third of the settlement pot as his fee, and that would be an extraordinary windfall for him and his firm. So Carr replied to both Norfolk & Western and Monsanto that he wanted $12 million total from all defendants. Minus the $5 million that had already been paid, that left $7 million to be split by the last two defendants, and the expectation was that the bulk of it would be paid by Monsanto.

When Carr gave the Monsanto lawyers his settlement demand, he got another positive signal. They didn't blanch, indicating, instead, that it would be fruitful to talk. It would take some negotiating, no doubt about that, but Carr's partners thought he had a shot at inducing Monsanto to buy into the settlement.

But then Norfolk & Western presented its own settlement offer of nearly $4 million. The railroad, having been burned in the Pratt case, really wanted out and was willing to pay big money, given its relatively low culpability, to buy its way off the hook.

Now, Carr started backing away from his first settlement demand. If the railroad were willing to pay $4 million, that meant Monsanto would only have to pick up a paltry $3 million, far less even than the legal fees it was looking at! Carr acted like a man who had seriously miscalculated the value of his case. He wanted more money now, and he put pencil to paper and came up with a new settlement demand of at least *$9 million* for Monsanto. Korein was aghast and started telling the other partners that Carr was about to flush his best payday ever right down the drain. But nobody confronted Carr or told him to do otherwise, and the new, higher demand stuck.

Monsanto told him to shove it. "After that, they just said, 'Take your best shot,'" recalled Edward Brennan, then forty-three years old and another of Carr's partners.

"We don't settle dioxin cases. That's our posture," said Snively much later, giving a much too facile explanation to a matter that even in the early days was already tightly bound by ego as much as by principle. "We were litigating an important principle in *Kemner*. We don't settle meritless cases. In a case totally without validity, we're going to resist.

"Our company called it Orangemail. You have to draw the line at some point."

Monsanto *didn't* want to settle, and Norfolk & Western *couldn't* settle because Carr wouldn't accept the railroad's offer. The case of *Kemner v. Monsanto* was slated to go to trial with its two remaining defendants in February 1984.

And that was just what Carr wanted. Hell, no, he didn't want to settle, either. "I've *never* called up the other guy and said, 'I want to settle this case,'" he boasted, "probably because, basically, I don't want to settle the case."

Kemner v. Monsanto was his case of a lifetime, his one big chance to bring a $3.6 billion corporate monolith to the bar of justice in little Belleville, Illinois. And regardless of whether anybody else believed he could do that, Carr certainly did.

"I know that I am doing some good," Carr said as he sat one afternoon in his command post for the trial, an old medical building a few blocks from the Belleville courthouse.

Eight filing cabinets were crowded into what once was a nurse's cubicle, and a cast-off conference table and a gaudy striped sofa decorated a darkly varnished reception area along with a neon sign proclaiming PRESCRIPTIONS. Carr's office, a converted examination room, was impersonal except for a green-and-white plastic baseball cap emblazoned with I'M NOT PAID ENOUGH TO GET ULCERS that hung on the wall.

"It's conceivable that this might be the most important thing I ever do, if I really succeed in putting the onus on Monsanto, where it belongs," Carr said. "It's egotistical, maybe, to think that, but it's a possibility. And that's what I would be really proud of, if I could think that the insignificant role that I've played in life thus far could have some importance of that sort. I would like to think that that could occur. And it might occur; who knows?"

"This is Lenore Rush. She's George's mother. George is standing right behind Lenore. Barbara is his wife and then there is Glenn, Greg and Debbie. This is the Rush family. George is a farmer, lives near Sturgeon, Missouri. Thank you."

As Carr stood before the jury on a Wednesday, February 22, 1984, introducing each of his sixty-five clients, marching them in and out of the courtroom in shifts because there were so many of them, he sounded more like the glad-handing uncle at a family reunion than one of the finest trial lawyers in the world.

"Then the Bowne family, please. Now, Mildred Bowne, she's a widow, and John's mother. His wife is Carol—where is she? Oh, there you are, right in front of me!"

Carr had brought them all in to see his opening statement, putting them up the night before at the Town House Motel in Belleville, a place Korein grumbled "wasn't fit for a dog," but that was all right because dogs didn't have to stay there. Those who couldn't squeeze into the small courtroom sat in another room and watched the proceedings on a specially rigged closed-circuit television system.

Instead of being the high-ceilinged, darkly varnished place that people envisioned when they heard the word, Courtroom 14 in the new St. Clair County Courthouse was a much more modernistic affair, a small, windowless room with oak paneling and red wall-to-wall carpeting. But for the few symbols that marked it as a courtroom, the black-robed judge and the Illinois and American flags, it might have passed for a newly built classroom at the local junior college.

There were three closed-circuit cameras mounted to the walls of the courtroom, so as to pipe the proceedings down the hall for the rest of the *Kemner* plaintiffs. The lighting was recessed, and it wasn't so bright above the forty-five red-upholstered fold-down seats in the audience as it was above the judge, Richard Goldenhersh, whose bench was in the left-hand corner of the courtroom as you faced the front. To his immediate left, almost centered against the back wall, was the witness box. No more than a few feet farther left, all the way against the wall opposite Goldenhersh's bench, sat the jurors, twelve regulars and six alternates.

Privately, Carr said he had been thinking about his opening statement for weeks, but then he thought better of that declaration and revised it. No, it hadn't been weeks he'd been thinking about what he would say about Monsanto. It had been "months. Years."

He'd also used the past few weeks to get himself all worked up for the punitive-damage claim he would be mounting against Monsanto. It was an essential part of his strategy to prove that what had happened in Sturgeon wasn't an isolated incident. Looked at by itself, after all, the Sturgeon accident didn't seem so bad. Nobody had been killed, and, for that matter, Carr really didn't have much proof that the half-teaspoonful of dioxin spilled from that tank car five years earlier had done much of anything to his clients.

Carr contended that his clients suffered from liver damage, headaches, hearing loss, body aches and depression. "Crying episodes for no particular reason. . . . Nosebleeds. . . . A symptom or a complaint, if you will, of a large number of the men and the women alike —for want of a better word, quite frankly, it's dribbling of the urine. . . . They feel depressed. They don't feel as happy, if you will, as before the date of the spill. . . . Their systems are really fouled up inside." The list of relatively unremarkable maladies Carr attributed to the dioxin exposure was, itself, truly *remarkable*—so much so that, when Monsanto later alphabetically catalogued them all, it filled up all the space on an entire page, single-spaced, from "abnormal stool" to "wheezing."

"Half a teaspoon of dioxin," Carr told the jury in his opening statement. "Half a teaspoon. Perhaps even less. If you took a penny and lost it on the streets of downtown St. Louis, that is one part per billion in that entire area. And that's what we're talking about in this case—parts per billion of dioxin in this tank car."

So Carr would have to concentrate on building his case around what he saw as Monsanto's pattern of willful disregard for people's safety and health. He would put on trial the corporation's whole way of doing business. It would be a trial not just about the Sturgeon incident, but about Agent Orange, Nitro, even a dioxin spill in Seveso, Italy, that didn't involve Monsanto at all.

Carr believed in adding a half-dozen zeros to his potential damages by going after punitives, and he frequently sought, and won, large punitive damage awards. In that way, he differed from a lawyer like Corboy, who'd tried to get punitive damages just once—and then only on behalf of, and at the behest of, his good friend, a retired chief justice of the Illinois Supreme Court who'd been bumped from a flight to Florida!

The reason Corboy didn't seek punitive damage, was that the big judgments seldom stood up on appeal. Not only that, Corboy wanted juries to concentrate on the compensatory damages, because that money was *tax-free* to the client (unlike punitives, which were taxed just like one huge paycheck) and also easier to collect, since compensatory damages were covered by insurance but punitive damages weren't.

But in spite of all those infirmities and even though Carr's punitive damage awards were almost always diminished on appeal, they still gave him leverage in negotiating big settlements of his cases during the appeal process. Carr also genuinely believed that "a punitive verdict, even though you don't collect it, helps all of society, because the whole idea behind the punitive verdict is to punish for the past conduct and to deter similar conduct in the future." He definitely was going to go after punitives in the Monsanto case.

"Monsanto has consistently taken the position for its own economic reasons that dioxin's not really bad stuff; that the worst that can happen to you is chloracne, which is an outrageous lie, that's what it is!" he said out on his sailboat a few weekends after he'd finished his opening statement. Carr could really get himself wound up for a battle. He thought he had also discovered that Monsanto had tampered with the results of a scientific study on dioxin's toxicity. A potential smoking gun. "And that's just the tip of the iceberg! By the time we get through with Monsanto's case, we'll find them to be extremely culpable!" Culpable of what, he didn't say.

Carr was, indeed, the gifted orator that he saw himself to be, and as he stood squarely before the jury now, resting his notes on a lectern and occasionally glancing at them, he tried to move himself and his case a little closer to those average men and women in the box.

"This is not like a television program of Perry Mason or Judd for the Defense or a drama on TV," he told them. "There's not going to be a witness come in at the last minute that completely changes the whole complexion of the case and persuades you that what appeared to be a proper result is no longer a proper result. There are going to be little surprises—nobody can have a case as complicated as this is and not have some surprises—but there are not going to be any major surprises. I know what they know, they know what we know. And how it's presented is probably going to be the only surprise, and not going to be much of a surprise at that."

Carr also wanted to prime the jury for the cross-examination to come. He could be a relentless cross-examiner of an obstinate witness, the kind of questioner who, if he weren't stopped by the judge, could spend hours or even days asking the same question over and over until the witness finally gave him the answer he wanted.

Most trial lawyers would tell you that the best cross-examination was one that cut the witness like a stiletto, so pointed and razor-sharp that blood gushed even before the witness knew he'd been sliced. But Carr had a much different style. He would keep pounding away until the witness simply gave up. "Tenacity" was Carr's blunt description of his skill on cross. "I'll stick with the witness. I don't let him get away with an evasive answer."

"Now," said Rex, facing the jurors once more, "there's going to be something occur during the course of the plaintiffs' case which is important for you all to know that's going to occur, and to watch. There's going to be something called cross-examination. When the lawyer for the plaintiff asks questions of the witness, that's called direct examination. I'm supposed to know everything that witness is going to respond to a given question. I'd be a fool if I didn't know what he's going to say!

"It is the cross-examination, however, that is important in all of these cases, because the truth of what that witness is saying is tested on cross-examination. . . . If he said something differently on the earlier occasion than he is saying here now, that is called *impeachment*. It may not be important. It may be faulty memory. Maybe he was confused by the question. It may be he was just plain mistaken.

"But it may be that he's *lying*. All right?"

During his opening statement, Carr carefully walked the jurors through the process by which the most potent strain of dioxin—the

2,3,7,8-TCDD that was in that tank car—could be formed from other, more innocuous forms of the same basic substance. It was a tedious explanation of how chlorine molecules were rearranged, a presentation not easily grasped the first or even the second time around. But Carr also had a way to make the whole thing meaningful to his jurors: "It is two billion one hundred million times more toxic than the one that started out," he told them. "Now, that's the relative toxicity of it. It's been said that a couple of ounces of that in the New York water system would be enough to poison every inhabitant of New York City; that's how toxic this material is!"

That got everybody's attention. It made a half teaspoonful of dioxin seem a whole lot more dangerous than before, and it set the stage for Carr's finale, his demand the next day, during the last part of his argument, for punitive damages—"the way that ordinary citizens have of causing companies or defendants to do right, and that's what this case is about."

Right before he finished his opening statement, Carr had tried to take a little of the sting out of Monsanto's opening statement by starting to make it himself: "Monsanto will also take the position, I'm sure," he said derisively, "that our people are all liars and all not telling the truth and that Dr. Carnow"—the doctor who was being paid millions of dollars by Carr's firm to perform tests on the dioxin victims—"is a fraud. That's the position that they will take. They *have* to take that position! Otherwise, there wouldn't be a defense in this case!"

And Carr was pretty much right.

Monsanto's chief trial lawyer was Kenneth Heineman, a large, beefy, jowly man with slicked-down hair and heavy, dark-rimmed eyeglasses. He and three other lawyers in the courtroom for Monsanto practiced out of the Belleville offices of a big St. Louis defense firm, Coburn, Croft & Putzell. Carr was self-taught in the arcana of dioxin, but Heineman had earned his undergraduate degree in chemistry. Now, as Heineman walked up to the jury, he moved the lectern a little bit farther to his right, a little farther from the jury.

Heineman began straightaway with a direct attack on the plaintiffs and their only medical expert, Bertram Carnow, who, as Heineman put it, "charges two thousand dollars a day for every day of his deposition. For trial testimony he charges more. He publishes a sheet setting forth his charges. The sheet tells you that he must fly first-class wherever he goes. His fee per day of trial testimony is $3,000."

Carnow said all of the plaintiffs were brain-damaged and otherwise grievously ill. But Monsanto, Heineman said, had put them all through a battery of tests at the Northwestern University Hospital, and the doctors there couldn't find anything wrong with them. For hours on end, he talked about all the studies that proved how innocuous dioxin really was, and about how healthy everybody in Sturgeon really was. Why, said Heineman, in 1980, and again in 1982, the local high school baseball team had even won the Missouri state championship, and some of the plaintiffs in that courtroom were on the team! "One of the young men here, Tim Bowne, B-O-W-N-E, had the perfect athletic attitude. . . . He is a naturally very muscular boy, probably the strongest student in the high school. He can squat with barbells better than any other kid in the school," and he certainly hadn't shown any signs of illness. "One of the children, Laura Bolles, complains of having asthmalike symptoms, wheezing, and difficulty breathing. But she is a marvelous singer, and one of the elementary school teachers will tell you that she is very good in class, she has one of the stronger voices, she enjoys singing and never seems to be ill in class when she is singing." And so it went.

"I don't think [the plaintiffs] are lying," Heineman said with mock seriousness. "I think they've been scared to death by Dr. Carnow!"

"The evidence will further show," Heineman said when he was finished, "that there isn't enough dioxin out there at Sturgeon to hurt anybody, and the evidence will further show that these people, to the extent they have illnesses, those illnesses have not been caused by exposure to chemicals at Sturgeon, Missouri."

Only the opening statement of Norfolk & Western remained to be delivered. The railroad was represented by Albert Schoenbeck, a courtly, white-haired lawyer who was in partnership with his nephew. Schoenbeck had been trying to extricate his client from the case from the start, and he'd kept his $4 million offer on the table without so much as a yes or no from Carr. The shabby way Schoenbeck had been treated—first by Pratt and the other defense lawyers, including Heineman, who ducked out of Pratt's case, and now by Carr himself—amused Carr, even though in private he called Norfolk & Western, which had unknowingly hauled the dioxin, "a victim [of Monsanto], just like the people of Sturgeon are."

Still, Carr liked to repeat the story he'd heard about how an ill-prepared Schoenbeck had been the only lawyer in the courtroom the day the trial was to begin: "Monday morning, poor old Al Schoenbeck walks into the courtroom, says, Guess I'm early. No, you're on time. But where are the other lawyers? Well, they've settled!" Carr burst into a big guffaw. "I'd have given anything to have been there and seen Schoenbeck's eyes!"

There would be a time, soon enough after he saw how long the trial was really going to last, when Carr would finally accept Schoenbeck's $4 million offer. Having one less lawyer in the courtroom would speed things up and let Carr concentrate on his big tuna, Monsanto. For a while longer, though, Carr would let Schoenbeck dangle.

Schoenbeck put on his best country-lawyer act for the men and women of the jury, telling them he felt inadequate arguing against a guy like Carr who had "such a ready wit and a winsome manner that he could just charm the birds right out of the trees. And Mr. Heineman here took a very complicated chemical problem and complicated chemical processes and explained them so very well that even *I* was able to understand some of the things that he was saying!"

But Schoenbeck maybe wasn't quite so dumb as he or Carr would have people believe, because Schoenbeck did, in fact, use the "out" with the jury that Carr thought was the railroad's best defense.

"The defense of this railroad company," Schoenbeck said, "is that we cleaned up a spill which we did not cause and we cleaned it up as promptly and as thoroughly as was humanly possible and we spared no expense in doing it. . . . The defense of this railroad is that we did what we could."

The actual legal drama of the dioxin trial unfolded monotonously. One juror or another frequently nodded off. "Sleeping doesn't bother me," Carr confided. "The sleeping juror is not ordinarily a strong juror."

What did bother him was a young juror who appeared uninterested: "She's shaking her pencil; she's impatient. To me, that's the same as drumming your fingers. It's as if she's already made up her mind and thinks our testimony isn't important enough to listen to."

Carr stopped on one particular day to coach his expert witness from the Environmental Defense Fund, a group of lawyers, scientists, economists and computer programmers working to find solutions to environmental dilemmas: "Tomorrow, when you answer a question, I want you to look that juror in the eye. Speak directly to her. We need to bring her back to our side." Months or even years later, he would need that juror's vote.

In fact, Carr considered his symbiosis with the jury to be one of his greatest strengths.

Over the years, Carr's clients had included victims disfigured by burns, auto accidents and assorted other calamities, all allegedly caused by somebody else's negligence. "You really have to *sell* that injured person to the jury," he explained. "Once you get a jury's confidence in a trial, then in a closing argument you cash in on that confidence—you get things that you ask for. Who says that an amputated leg is worth $2 million? Where's the book that places a value on it? You can look up in the Blue Book and see the value of a used car, but you sure as hell can't look in a book and see the value of a cut-off leg! Who says the pain is worth a thousand dollars an hour? The *lawyer* says it."

And when juries gave him what he asked for, Carr benefited in lock-step with his client.

"The greatest thing about the trial business," Carr said, "is that I have the chance, if I get a million dollars for my client, of making $333,000 for myself—in one fee! Now, that's more money than many people will make in a lifetime. It simply is. And for me, a poor kid who was on relief, and who worked his way through law school, that's a lot of money. It gives me an incentive."

"It averages out," he said, referring to his standard one-third fee. "I've had some cases where I did so much work, I should have gotten 90 percent. Other cases, I got a third when I should have gotten 2 percent, because I did nothing."

But the greatest aspect of this system, as far as Carr was concerned, was that although he had no incentive whatsoever to drag out a case, he had *every* incentive to do his best so as to get a higher fee. His consideration was the bottom line. The efficient market was at work. "Suppose that fee was 10 percent instead of a third," Carr said. "There's a big difference in the incentive, and in what I will do for a third of a million dollars as opposed to 10 percent of a million dollars. A tremendous difference!" That higher percentage, he said, was what justified the risk of going for a big verdict at trial instead of settling a case.

But, just as with every other plaintiff's lawyer, even the strongest case couldn't get Carr's attention unless there were a deep pocket, that of an insurance company, private individual or corporation, from which the defendant's damages could be paid. As for anyone else, "The poor sucker goes without," said Carr matter-of-factly. "What good would it do for me to help him? I can't make money for him. He's S.O.L.," and Carr assumed everybody knew what that stood for.

Ultimately, a lawyer's won-lost record was determined by the finder of fact—occasionally a judge, usually a jury. "I never go into court with the belief that I'm going to lose a case. I settle the cases where I think there's a risk of losing. I can create my own won-lost record that way," Carr said. He favored a jury of poor people and black people: "Black people are the most compassionate people on earth.

"It's a myth among lawyers that poor people and black people won't give big money. Well, bullshit! Nobody's used to big money when you're talking about millions of dollars. And poor people would just as soon give away somebody else's money as anybody would."

Carr didn't want "the bank president, the insurance salesman, the small businessman or the doctor's wife, or any of those other people we consider to be big shots. You simply don't want those people. They don't have a heart. I try to get jurors that think as decent human beings ought to think—that is, like Democrats think: that humans ought to help humans."

Right before the Monsanto trial, though, Carr had used a body-language expert to guide his peremptory challenges in the jury selection for another trial, and the result was a verdict less favorable than the settlement he'd been offered.

"Really shook my confidence," he mused. So, in the dioxin case, he relied again on his own instincts. The result was a middle-aged and middle-class jury that included three black women and two black men, a racial proportion closely reflecting the county's 28 percent black population.

Carr won cases through what his former partner Bruce Cook called "intellectual clout. He presents a case very coldly, precisely and intellectually. If Rex says something is the law, even the judges will believe it's true. He dominates people through his intellect, his preparation and his aggression.

"One of the hardest things for a trial lawyer to do is to be an adversary—particularly in a small community like this one. To get the opposing lawyer down and kick him is difficult, but that's our obligation to our client. When most trial lawyers get the other guy down, they step back and give him some air. But Rex doesn't let 'em up. He'll slice 'em. He doesn't care what anybody thinks."

Carr certainly had more than his share of enemies, going all the way back to his days as the rabble-rousing negotiator for the local teachers' union (he led the teachers out on an acrimonious strike) and the head of the Human Rights Commission in East St. Louis during the racially tense late 1960s. "My reputation in the community was either as a nigger lover or as a teacher agitator. That was my reputation; not as a trial lawyer." Vacant buildings, boarded-up and crumbling, were eerie sentinels along lifeless streets in East St. Louis. The city's downtown resembled a combat zone, as, in fact, it had been: In 1967, Carr's brand-new office building was destroyed by a bomb, and the case was never solved.

Out of three hundred trials and thousands of cases Carr had handled since he began his practice, he could recall losing just ten—"never through my error, though. I don't know of any case that I've ever lost through my error." That, too, was typical of Carr, a man with such a towering ego that he couldn't admit to a mistake.

Instead, he insisted, any mistake that caused him to lose a case was always made by the judge, jury or client. Unlike many of his colleagues, he had never even watched another trial lawyer try a case.

Still, Carr wasn't above putting some space between himself and his reputation, and he could belittle his foes in the process by saying, as he often did, that the big, "super-duper" verdicts that he got weren't so much the result of good lawyering by him as of *bad* trial work by the other side.

That, he said, was what had happened in the trial he was proudest of, one that produced a $7 million verdict, the highest in the world at that time, against a Washington, D.C., hotel.

Carr's client was a Belleville-area Boy Scout who'd gone to the capital for a scouting jamboree and broken his neck on the hotel's high diving board. Carr did some investigating and found that the hotel had replaced the pool's original wooden board with a much more flexible Fiberglas board that propelled young Tommy Hooks head-first into the shallow water.

Carr was willing to settle with the hotel's insurance company for an even $1 million; that was the largest verdict in a swimming-pool case up to that point. But the primary insurance carrier, whose policy with the hotel also gave it the burden of defending any lawsuits, was liable for only the first $100,000 of any damages. A secondary carrier, though not required to participate in the lawsuit, had written a $10 million backup policy.

The first carrier immediately offered to settle with Carr for the full policy limit of $100,000. "Of course, we turned it down out of hand. But the insurance company's in it for the money! Why should they spend at least $50,000 defending the case when the most they're going to lose is $100,000, and they've already proposed to pay it!

"So the first company, Continental Casualty, asks the lawyer for the excess carrier if he wants to take over the defense. And he says No! To tell you how abysmal Continental's defense was, their lawyer liked my client, he was compassionate, he knew that my client was hurt because of the hotel's negligence, and he basically wanted my client to win! That doesn't mean that he lies down in court and gives up. But he wouldn't mind having his martinis at lunch.

"And I'm building me up a major case. I've got people coming in from all over the country to testify. All we had in this case to start with, mind you, was a kid who dived off a board into a pool that, from the licenses and everything else, met the requirements of the city ordinances. A board that was not defective. He just went down and hit the bottom of the pool and broke his neck.

"But this is the great thing about personal injury lawyers. When you have a major injury, you can afford to put a lot of time into thinking and analyzing whether there's a possibility of that kind of reward. So I had pictures taken of the diving board and I analyzed that case and made them produce the original plans and I found out that they had *replaced* the original board. The original board was wooden, and not near as flexible as this Fiberglas-and-aluminum board. The Fiberglas board did for AAU diving what the Fiberglas pole did for pole vaulting: sent people up higher, they got a lot more time to make their intricate dives. Much more flexible than the ordinary wooden board.

"The hotel let anybody who could swim dive off this high board. I also found out from diving coaches that it takes months of hard work for an Olympic diver to learn how to put his body down in one particular area in that water. So this diving board had the capacity to send divers not down into the deep part of the pool, but way out there! My kid ended up in water that was between six and eight feet deep! He knifed right down to the bottom and hit his head. I alleged that they simply overpowered this pool for ordinary, itinerant guests."

When the hotel's expert took the stand, even he didn't disagree that the diving board had been souped-up for an AAU competition, and that it had far too much spring for the average diver.

The excess-coverage insurer now was willing to settle, for $750,000. "I say: No! Things are going great! I want *$2* million."

Carr won the case after a three-week trial in Washington. Now, the insurer came back to Carr with still another offer: $1.75 million.

"But they didn't come up with the $2 million, so we didn't settle." The following week, a new hearing would be held to set the damages. Then, right before the damage hearing was to begin, the insurer finally *did* offer the full $2 million.

"Understand something," Carr commanded, his gaze narrowing. "Three million dollars, at that time, was the largest injury verdict on record. For *any* kind of injury. Here, they've offered $2 million. That's going to take care of him *great!*"

But Carr still turned it down. Never mind that it was what he'd demanded. If the other side was willing to pay it, he must not have asked for enough.

"So, what I tell the jury to do is, Look, these future medical payments will add up to $2 million. And his lost wages are going to add up to another $850,000. And that and everything else is going to add up to a little over $3 million. Now, that's what you're going to give him, basically, for *other* people. He's got to pay the medical payments out to doctors and hospitals; and he would have had the wages anyway. So, you're really not giving *him* anything. If you're going to give this much to other people, you've got to decide what you're going to give Tommy.

"And that's what they did. They *doubled* the $3 million. That much for the others, and that much for Tommy. And $1 million for his parents, which made for $7 million overall." The courts whittled the verdict down a little bit in post-trial proceedings, but Carr still collected $5 million for Tommy Hooks and took a $1.7 million fee for himself. Ten years later, he was still acting as Hooks' trustee, at no charge, helping him build a specially outfitted house and invest in some local pizza parlors.

Carr's career had produced a succession of such big wins and controversial cases: $3 million against a savings & loan that cut off a businessman's credit. Over $1 million on behalf of a woman whose foot was amputated after an improperly administered penicillin injection. And $5.75 million on behalf of a woman who entered a local hospital for a routine gynecological procedure and ended up having most of her small intestine removed instead when a surgeon made a mistake—a lawsuit Carr inelegantly referred to as "the guts-out case." There was also a $1.5 million verdict against the city of Alton, Illinois, a city that over the years had been slammed more than once by Carr.

Seventeen-year-old Hilton Perry had been out of reform school just one day when he walked into a Sears department store in downtown Alton in 1969 and tried to steal a five-dollar pair of cufflinks. When the black youth ran from the store, a policeman gave chase and shot him in the back, leaving him paralyzed from the waist down.

Perry's first lawsuit against the city of Alton had already ended in a mistrial. "He was represented by an incompetent lawyer," Carr said. "He tried the case as if it were a black versus white issue. In fact, it was cops against a human being."

A full seven years after the shooting, Carr took the case to trial once more, and again the all-white jury was deadlocked. "I made a mistake in that case. When I *voir dired* the jury, I asked each prospective juror whether he could set his prejudices aside. Each one said that he could. In my closing argument, though, I said, 'They would not have shot this young man if he were white. They shot him because he was black.' I said that. I made that mistake.

"After the jury was discharged, I asked them, 'Why didn't you convict?' The case, to me, was open and shut: The police claimed the officer shot him in self-defense, when, in fact, he was a couple of hundred feet away and had been shot in the back.

"They said, 'We told you we could try this case free of prejudice, and in your closing argument, you didn't believe us—you went on this racial business and we couldn't overcome that.' " The next year, Carr tried the case again, "but I stayed away from this racial business and I got a $1.5 million verdict." The city treasury didn't contain enough money to pay the verdict, and a $1.36 million bond issue had to be floated. Every taxpayer shared the burden of Carr's victory.

"I hope they're still paying it off," grumbled Carr, "because then they'll watch their goddamned cops and make sure they don't shoot people in the back when they have no right to."

Carr had always cast himself as the friend of the little guy, a lawyer battling hard against all the world's injustices. That made his libel lawsuit on behalf of one of his partners in a real estate investment all the more unlikely, because Carr's defendant was a struggling home-town newspaper that hadn't even published a story about Carr's client.

Sources had told two Alton *Telegraph* reporters in 1969 that an Alton savings & loan was laundering Mafia money from Chicago and then loaning it out to Carr's client, local building contractor James C. Green. As the two reporters started digging around for confirmation of the tip, they prepared a confidential memorandum containing what little information they knew and passed it on to Brian Conboy, a Justice Department lawyer in charge of an investigation of mob rackets in St. Louis. "We need to know where the big money is coming from," the reporters implored.

The reporters never got the information they were seeking, and they never wrote any stories about their own investigation. But the federal lawyer sent their memo up through channels to federal savings & loan regulators, who found other irregularities in the Alton S&L's dealings with Green and had his credit cut off. Several years later, when Green learned about the reporters' memo, he had Carr sue the 38,000-circulation newspaper.

It was hard to believe that a newspaper could be found guilty of libel for a story it never even published. But that's what happened to the Alton *Telegraph.* In 1980, eleven years after the *Telegraph*'s reporters wrote up their notes for the federal authorities, a Plaintiffs' Paradise jury slapped the small, family-owned newspaper with an astonishing $9.2 million libel verdict, nearly four times the paper's net worth and far more than what its $1 million libel insurance policy would cover. The family couldn't even appeal the judgment, because it couldn't find anybody willing to post the exhorbitant appeal bond—$9.2 million, plus interest—required by Illinois law. So the newspaper entered bankruptcy proceedings instead, resuming normal operations only when Carr and Green agreed to a $1.4 million settlement.

As usual, Carr made no apologies.

"The Alton *Telegraph* did a great job of brainwashing everybody," he said. "Just because it's a newspaper, it doesn't have a right to stay in business any more than anybody else."

Maybe there was something to Carr's theory that his best verdicts were, more than anything else, the result of bad lawyering on the other side. But if that was true, another pattern to Carr's courtroom record was also becoming evident: The word was out among the formidable defense lawyers in Plaintiffs' Paradise that the most effective way to neutralize Carr was to fight him with his own best weapon.

More than a decade before the *Kemner* trial began, Carr had tried what would be his first case against the family-owned U-Haul trailer-rental company. His client had been severely burned in a U-Haul trailer accident, and Carr's case centered on what he maintained was an unsafe trailer design. "He had a young kid that had been burned up like a cinder," recalled U-Haul's local attorney in that case, Morris Chapman. "Terribly burned. He wasn't dead, but he would have been better off dead from our standpoint." Damages for pain and suffering, after all, can be sought only for the living.

Carr wanted $150,000 to settle the case, but U-Haul refused. "Our main witness was a U-Haul vice president," Chapman explained. "I had schooled him because I knew Rex's proclivities. Most people are overawed by Rex. He just takes over. If he gets a witness on the stand, he may keep him there two weeks just to break him down. I told our witness, 'Don't even give him the time of day.'

"Rex kept him on the stand, hammering away, for weeks. The jury just got ticked. They gave him a couple of hundred thousand dollars, but the case was worth a lot more."

In other words, Carr had been beaten by his own tenacity.

"And after that, he set out to nail U-Haul," Chapman said, pursuing a vendetta that continued to the present day. "He had made his decision: I'm gonna get 'em."

Shortly afterward, a chance referral from another local lawyer gave Carr the chance to get even. A prospective client claimed she had suffered a muscle injury in another U-Haul trailer accident. "She didn't even have a broken bone; I told her to go down the street to see Rex," recalled the lawyer, W. Thomas Coghill, Jr.

"Rex caught the other side off guard," Coghill continued. "U-Haul had insurance, and the insurance company just treated it like some Mickey Mouse kind of case. But Rex's client in the *first* U-Haul case was permitted to testify. He was just so grotesquely burned that the jury brought in a punitive verdict."

Q. "Larry, what highway did you all—did you and Mr. Duvall start out on?"

A. "55."

Q. "And who was doing the driving?"

A. "Mr. Duvall."

Q. "And how old a man was Duvall?"

A. "Thirty-one."

Q. "Where was he going? New Mexico, was it? Or Texas?"

A. "New Mexico."

Q. "What was he going there for?"

A. "He was a minister and he had got this—the church, they had given to the—well, he was going to be a minister of this church. They had give [sic] him this church in New Mexico. . . .

Q. "Tell the Court how the accident happened, Larry."

A. "Well, we was going down a slight—down a slight hill, and the car started swaying right—back and forth and jumping up and down. It turned sideways and turned over."

Q. "How many swerves or sways did it take to your knowledge before it skidded around, turned sideways, Larry?"

A. "About, I think, two or three."

Q. "And did Mr. Duvall apply the brakes?"

A. "Yes, sir."

Q. "How do you know he applied the brakes?"

A. "Because it was swaying—well, I was looking over at him."

Q. "After it skidded sideways, was it struck by another vehicle?"

A. "Yes, sir."

Q. "And was the trailer attached to the car at the time it was struck?"

A. "Yes, sir."

Q. "And what was the other vehicle that hit it, Larry?"

A. "A semitrailer truck, a grain truck."

Q. "Was the hitch torn loose with the trailer when the truck hit the trailer?"

A. "Yes, sir."

Q. "And did the gasoline tank explode?"

A. "Yes, sir."

Q. "And you were—were you upside down in the Mustang, Larry, when this happened?"

A. "Yes, sir."

Q. "Seat belted in?"

A. "Yes, sir."

Q. "And were you able to get out?"

A. "Yes."

Q. "Before the seat belts burned loose?"

A. "I couldn't get it undone, and I just pulled on the window, and it seemed like it broke, and I crawled out the window."

Q. "And Mr. Duvall, he died subsequently, did he?"

A. "Yes, sir."

Larry Slightom was, by then, a man of twenty-nine who presented a shocking appearance. There was an abundance of scar tissue all over his face, neck, nose and even his lips, and he had lost part of his left arm. He was going to be Carr's living proof of the dangers of U-Haul trailers.

Schlichter was a young associate in Carr's firm then, and he assisted in what turned out to be his mentor's first million-dollar verdict. "I asked Rex during the trial, 'What do you think the jury's going to do?' And he said, 'I've got U-Haul's annual report. They've got retained earnings of $5 million—and that's what the jury's going to give me. I'm going to tell the jury to take the profit out of renting those trailers.' He was just unshaken in this conviction that there would be a $5 million verdict. And that's what the jury came back with: $5 million in punitive damages, plus another $225,000 in compensatory damages."

"It was an all-out, slashing attack," remembered Michael Shoen, one of the family owners of U-Haul who became its general counsel shortly afterward. The trial took place over three days in the meeting room of the local bank, and nobody but Carr took it very seriously until the verdict came in. "He blitzkrieged everybody."

U-Haul adamantly opposed the payment of anything to Carr, believing that to do so would just encourage him to file more lawsuits against the concern. To back up its resolve, the trailer-rental company even offered to pay any final judgment—taking the insurance company off the hook entirely—if its appeal failed. But by then the insurance company had already agreed to a $1.5 million compensatory-damages settlement with Carr, and that's what he took in order to forestall a U-Haul appeal.

Carr took the standard one-third cut of $500,000 for his firm. But what he did next strained credulity.

Carr asked his newly enriched client, Margaret Hayman, to give the horribly burned Larry Slightom a share of what she had won. It was only fair, he told her, because Slightom's mere appearance in the courtroom was what caused the jury to award such a huge punitive-damage verdict against U-Haul.

And her response to his request, for that matter, strained credulity a little bit, too: She gave Slightom $358,000, $108,000 in cold, hard cash, plus another $250,000 that was placed in a trust fund.

By then, Carr had already filed his next lawsuit in Plaintiffs' Paradise against U-Haul, seeking punitive damages of $10 million for an auto accident that had caused cuts and bruises to Sayers B. Johnson and his wife, Elsie, as they drove down a Missouri highway towing a U-Haul trailer.

The Johnsons' injuries hardly seemed serious. But when the case came up for trial in 1977 at the St. Clair County Courthouse, Carr tried to repeat his success in the previous U-Haul case. He wanted to put Larry Slightom on the stand again so that he could get another punitive verdict against U-Haul.

This time, though, U-Haul's lawyers fiercely resisted Slightom's testimony, and the judge, ruling that Carr's ploy "would produce passion and prejudice in the minds of the jury out of proportion to the probative value of his testimony," entered an order that not only kept Slightom out of the courtroom but prohibited Carr from even mentioning anything about the earlier case.

But Carr put on the best punitive-damage case he could, with the main allegation being that U-Haul knowingly rented dangerous trailers and installed unsafe hitches. As the desultory trial dragged on for month after month, it eventually set its own record that would stand until Carr broke it again: as the longest jury trial ever to be held in Belleville.

Shoen was just thirty years old then and working as both the chief in-house lawyer and the safety director of the Phoenix-based concern. As Carr's punitive-damage case against U-Haul stretched into a six-month war of attrition, Shoen took an apartment in Belleville and commuted weekends back to Arizona, setting a pace for himself that, Shoen said, drove him to exhaustion.

At one point, Carr accused Shoen of failing to give Carr some U-Haul records that had been subpoenaed, and, when Shoen denied he was holding out on the plaintiffs, Carr put Shoen himself on the stand and questioned him under oath about what had and hadn't been turned over, a tactic Carr would use again in the *Kemner* case. That was one of the most damaging things one lawyer could do to another, because a lawyer's credibility with the judge and jury was his main asset in a trial, and anytime a lawyer was forced into the witness box to answer charges of misconduct under oath it raised questions that wouldn't go away.

"Putting me on the stand was standard procedure," Shoen said later. "Get 'em on the run, and keep 'em on the run, that was Rex's strategy.

"Rex was powered by anger, because a punitive-damage case runs on hate," Shoen added. "You've got to get the jury to hate somebody, and he was trying to get them to hate us. I learned from Rex never to release the initiative. Seize it and ram it home!"

Shoen was so completely rattled by the whole experience of having to endure Carr's marathon cross-examinations of him and the other U-Haul witnesses that he started writing poetry about it. It was the only way he knew to articulate his own desperation. ("We fought through exhaustion . . ." one poem began. He has saved them, to someday give to his own young son.) And Shoen actually started saying prayers again, something he hadn't done since he was a teenager. He even tried to get himself some extra insurance from the Man Upstairs by shamelessly making a pact with God, telling the Lord that if He would give him a victory against Carr, "I'd promise to go back and work for safety at U-Haul like nobody'd ever seen!" That's what Shoen said.

And, as far as Shoen was concerned, that's what He did. The end result of Carr's $10 million punitive-damage case was a $100,000 settlement, a victory, in Shoen's mind, because that would hardly cover Carr's expenses in the case.

"There are no atheists in foxholes," Shoen said. "If I have to face Rex Carr again, I'm going to ask God for help. I used to wish the guy evil. Now, I wish him the best in life, but I don't want to be anywhere around him. I thank him that I started praying again.

"I always wanted to tell him that, to make him grind his teeth." Carr was an atheist.

After being so effectively shut down in his third U-Haul trial, Carr started suing the trailer-rental firm in any venue he could. He filed a lawsuit in Florida and another in Colorado, but between the two Carr only got another $250,000 in nuisance-value settlements from U-Haul.

Still another case involved what Carr alleged to be defectively designed lug nuts and bolts that caused wheels to fall off certain U-Haul trucks, a defect U-Haul acknowledged but blamed on the manufacturer, Ford.

Carr was rattling the saber all over again, boasting of his past victories over U-Haul and vowing once more to seek punitive damages.

"They knew about it for years! They got memos on it and said, 'No, it's going to cost too much.' Ford Motors was in on it, too. It is *criminal!* If they knew they had this defect in their trucks and let these trucks go out on the road. . . ." Carr's voice trailed off. "They have to learn. They have to learn not to do that."

"It's going to be Rex Carr's version of the Nuremberg trials," replied Shoen. "He'll go at it like an obsessed man."

The trial of *Carey E. Eyre, Jr., v. Mallinckrodt, Inc.,* in late 1983 was to be Carr's last tune-up bout before the main event against Monsanto the following year.

Carr's client was in the Air Force, stationed in San Antonio, when doctors at the military hospital there gave him a myelogram X-ray that required a dye called Dimeray to be injected into his back.

Mallinckrodt was the maker of Dimeray, a new, water-soluble dye that was considered far superior to the oil-based dyes that doctors had been using. Oil-based dyes had to be drawn back out of the spinal column once the myelogram was completed, but the new water-based Dimeray could be left in the patient.

But something went terribly wrong with Carey Eyre's myelogram at Lackland Air Force Base. Doctors there had typically injected much more than the recommended dosage of the old-style myelogram dye, because doing that helped them get sharper pictures of the patient, and they knew the dye was going to be drawn right back out anyway. What the doctors didn't realize was that overdoing it with Dimeray, which had never been tested by Mallinckrodt in dosages as high as the military doctors were using, would produce catastrophic results.

The overdose caused Eyre to develop such violent spasms in his lower back that both his hips were fractured. Even then, the Air Force doctors were so skeptical of his pain that they had orderlies come in and try to make him get back on his feet and walk around, so he could get well enough to be discharged. It was only when Eyre was wheeled down to the radiology department for an X-ray of his abdomen that the radiologist on duty exclaimed: He's got two broken hips!

There was no question that Eyre had a slam-dunk case against *somebody*, but Carr had a problem. The real malpractice was that of the Air Force doctors, but the military couldn't be sued by a soldier on active duty. So the only plausible defendant was Mallinckrodt. Carr also sued a small Illinois company that mixed and packaged the Dimeray for Mallinckrodt, though. By naming the smaller Illinois company, Carr could file his case in Plaintiffs' Paradise.

This was a case Mallinckrodt wanted to get rid of, just as it had with six similar cases. Before the trial, the drug-manufacturer's local lawyer, Carl Lee, made what he considered an excellent offer to Carr: $2 million, with an indication that his client might even be willing to offer more if settlement talks became serious.

"But Rex told people he was going to set a record and he didn't *want* to settle," Lee explained.

"They were really out for blood in that case, the plaintiff and Rex."

During jury selection, Judge Tom O'Donnell had asked each lawyer how much time he'd need to present his case. Rex Carr said a week; Carl Lee said two. So O'Donnell told all the jurors to plan on sitting for three weeks.

The trial lasted four months.

"Rex was *too* tenacious," Lee recalled. "The jury just got weary of it."

Even worse, Carr's disabled client, who was only able to get around by using a motorized three-wheeled cart, sat in the courtroom throughout the entire trial. Eyre's presence was a strategic blunder for a lawyer seeking, as Carr was, $30 million to $40 million in punitive damages. The best trial lawyers saved their horribly injured clients for one brief, heart-stopping appearance before the jury. But the jurors became so indifferent to Eyre's plight that some of them started calling him "Hot Wheels."

As Morris Chapman had earlier done in the first U-Haul case, Lee told his main witness, Mallinckrodt's medical director, a frail man with a heart pacemaker, to hold his ground against Carr. "What I really warned him about was the physical exhaustion that a witness feels around two or three o'clock in the afternoon. Rex uses cross-examination as a physical punishment. A witness wilts. I told him that Rex typically cross-examined witnesses for weeks at a time. 'Don't make mistakes because you're exhausted,' I said. 'Any time you can't take it, ask for a recess.'"

Carr kept the medical director on the stand for four full weeks of testimony, going over the same questions so many times that the jurors started mouthing the answers right along with him. "By the end of the third week, even the jury was rooting for my witness," Lee said. "Rex just overstayed his welcome."

The trial had its moments. As Carr was raking one Mallenckrodt expert witness over the coals, the expert kept acknowledging the patient's injury but said it wasn't Mallenckrodt's fault.

"If somebody puts arsenic on my cornflakes and the emergency room fails to save me," Carr shot back, "does that mean the person who used arsenic isn't guilty of murder?"

Lee broke in: "I object, your honor. That would *not* be murder. That would be justifiable homicide!"

Carr must have known what was coming, because during the trial he called the judge and berated him for evidentiary rulings that had gone against him. Talking to a presiding judge about the merits of your case anywhere but in the courtroom is an open-and-shut ethics-code violation, and yet none of the people involved seemed to think it was anything other than business as usual in this peculiar little pocket of the state where the litigation game was hardly played according to Hoyle.

"Tommy O'Donnell got me aside during the trial and said, 'Rex isn't going to set his record, but he's not going to take the blame and he's not going to give you the credit you deserve. I'm going to be the fall guy,'" Lee recalled. O'Donnell feared Carr was going to finance a reelection campaign against him the following year. Lee said he knew better than to report the matter to the Illinois attorney disciplinary board, which reported to the elected justices of the state Supreme Court. "I didn't think, no matter what happened, that anything would be done about it." Besides, his case was going better than expected. Why mess it up?

After three days of deliberations, the jury came back with a verdict of $1,850,000, *less* than Lee had offered Carr before the trial began. And it could have been worse: two jurors had been holding out for $25,000 to $50,000. (Mallinckrodt voluntarily paid the full $2 million anyway.)

"The whole four months of trial was for nothing," Carr grumbled, one of the rare times that he would feel compelled to don the hair shirt, even if he did still want to specify its size. "I let it go on too long. My fault. I cross-examined too long. But I found so much evidence against them that it took—I had their medical director on the stand for twenty-two days! The most recalcitrant witness I'd ever cross-examined! He wouldn't even admit that the word 'toxin' means 'poison'!"

Ed Brennan, Carr's partner, could only sigh in frustration. "That was the beginning of the 'Keep Him Before the Jury and You'll Beat Him' Syndrome."

When the trial of *Kemner v. Monsanto* began in 1984, the jurors were told it would probably last six months to a year. That was going to make it the longest jury trial in the country's history, longer, even, than Carr's earlier battle royal against U-Haul.

"Now, that boggles the mind, I know," Monsanto's lawyer, Heineman, had told the jurors when he first appeared before them on February 23, 1984, "but the plaintiff's case is very likely going to last that long, and it's going to be just a very long time before we get to put on our side of the case."

But even Heineman couldn't have possibly known how prophetic his admonition really was. It took Carr, working all alone in the courtroom save for the benign presence of his 50-percenter, Jerome Seigfried, a full eighteen months just to present the plaintiff's case. By the time Monsanto had proceeded just a quarter of the way through its defense case, *Kemner v. Monsanto* had already set a record as history's longest jury trial, not just in Belleville, but anywhere in America.

But even though pundits and scholars of the law cited it as the supposed manifestation of all that was wrong with a gridlocked legal system, the trial was really just an aberration that a place like Plaintiffs' Paradise was bound to produce sooner or later.

Kemner v. Monsanto was a trial out of control, a case that should never have made it to court, brought by an egotistical lawyer who couldn't be tamed and tried before a judge who lost control of his own courtroom.

To be a judge in St. Clair County was to be in the rough and tumble of an old-fashioned judicial system that forced every judge, from the Supreme Court elite to those on the lowest trial court, to run for office in partisan elections. To get the backing of the Democratic party organization, an action virtually tantamount to election in that working-class part of the state, the trial judges had to come up with a flat payment to the party that was usually at least $10,000, and they had to seek their campaign contributions from the same lawyers that practiced before them. More often than not, the major donors in Plaintiffs' Paradise were the plaintiffs' lawyers.

The system produced a log-rolling form of justice in which plaintiffs' lawyers helped the judges raise their money and judges, if nothing else, could return the favor by advancing some lawyers' cases for trial more quickly. Under the courthouse rules, lawsuits didn't have to be tried in a strict first-in-first-out order, because judges always had the leeway to take "hardship" cases out of turn. "That was the life blood of a firm, getting your cases tried," explained a local lawyer. It gave a plaintiff's lawyer leverage to get a bigger, quicker settlement. "Otherwise, you were at the whim of an insurance company."

When a respected former president of the St. Clair County Bar Association characterized the judicial system there as riddled with corruption, even one of the sitting judges came forward to affirm the allegation. And, whether it was apparent or real, the prospect of losing a lawyer's campaign support could make for a subtle kind of intimidation of any judge.

Local judges had to respect the clout of the plaintiffs' lawyers. In 1980, Morris Chapman, the renowned Plaintiffs' Paradise lawyer who had so effectively neutralized Carr in the first U-Haul case, got together with five other local lawyers and quietly formed the "Committee for an Improved Judiciary" which spent twenty-eight thousand dollars on a successful—to say nothing of false and misleading—advertising campaign to drive from the bench two judges they perceived as hostile to their interests and insufficiently proplaintiff in their rulings. When the attorney disciplinary board filed a misconduct charge against the six lawyers, as well as a second charge against Chapman and one colleague, Jon Carlson, for paying an investigator to "tail" one judge, who was hearing an appeal of one of Carlson's cases, the state Supreme Court simply affirmed dismissal of the charges on the ground that they weren't specific enough.

Even defense lawyers had to be wary, as Robert Owens, an out-of-town lawyer who defended International Harvester in a personal-injury case in which a St. Clair County jury awarded $15.1 million, found out after he angrily filed a confidential complaint about the presiding judge with the state Judicial Inquiry Board. The judge retaliated by hiring Carr to file a $17 million punitive-damages libel and slander suit against Owens, even though neither Carr nor the judge had seen Owens' complaint and neither knew what Owens had told the board. "Not having seen Owens' complaint, I [still] know exactly what's in it," Carr said with certitude, and he made no apologies if his lawsuit caused others to be wary of making what he deemed bad-faith complaints about local judges in the future. "I hope it does. That's the whole idea of it. It *should* have a chilling effect."

It was in this hothouse environment that Judge Richard Goldenhersh was going to try the most important case he'd had in his nine years on the Illinois circuit-court bench.

Goldenhersh, just forty years old in 1984, had the kind of booster's background that was to be expected from a lawyer who was the son of the most powerful jurist in the state, Illinois Supreme Court Chief Justice Joe Goldenhersh. He belonged to all the right judges' associations and committees, and he was definitely on the make for an appellate court judgeship.

Goldenhersh was a chipper guy, short and stocky, with curly black hair and a neat moustache. He wore half-glasses and when he peered through them at a lawyer or a witness from his elevated vantage point on the bench he could convey the impression of skepticism without really meaning to.

There were, in the words of one Belleville lawyer, "a whole ton of Goldenhershes" who'd become lawyers around the area, brothers and cousins and nephews and uncles who were known by the power of the family patriarch, Chief Justice Joe, but only son Richard had chosen to follow in his father's judicial footsteps. And if Goldenhersh had the reputation of being proplaintiff in his leanings, not exactly an uncommon rap in Plaintiffs' Paradise, he also was generally considered to be a competent, even-handed judge by those who appeared before him.

But that was before the *Kemner* trial.

Goldenhersh had, in a sense, doomed himself to a long trial from the very start, when he failed to do what the West Virginia federal judge did with the Nitro case and break it down to a manageable size. Even Carr wanted Goldenhersh to bring just a representative group of the sixty-five plaintiffs to trial first, a move that would probably have taken many months, or even years, off the trial time. (An uncooperative Monsanto refused to help Goldenhersh make his decision. The company opposed Carr's request, opposed the group trial that ultimately took place, and refused to specify an alternative it *did* favor.) But Goldenhersh ruled that the full case would go forward as one. That meant that Carr and the Monsanto lawyers had to litigate sixty-five separate lawsuits, putting on their proof for each individual claim and then, when that was over, arguing at great length the case for punitive damages.

But an even more fundamental flaw in the case didn't become apparent until months into the trial. Although it publicly refused to comment on its trial strategy, Monsanto had made its decision to stand and fight a war of attrition against the most tenacious attorney it could have possibly found. The deeper Monsanto dug in, the harder Carr scrapped and the longer the trial dragged on. Monsanto was going to make him spend it all.

"In these mass tort cases, the defendants have a very powerful weapon," Carr's partner Brennan said. "They can bleed a plaintiff to death, and Monsanto demonstrated it in *Kemner*.

"But Monsanto also met, in Rex, a force they hadn't reckoned with. A bulldog. Rex is as stubborn as they are, to the point of being self-destructive. They fought over whether the sun rose! But the other side loved it, because they were getting paid by the hour!" Brennan estimated Heineman's firm got as much as $6 million of the $10 million-plus that Monsanto admitted to spending on its defense.

"They were playing that delaying game intentionally, and he didn't even recognize it! His tenacity was his greatest asset, and it was his Achilles' heel in this case. They played him like a harp. He walked right into it! They said, 'Okay, Monster Man, come on!' They baited him. They caused controversy by refusing to agree on anything."

It turned into a case without boundaries. Goldenhersh didn't set limits on the amount of time the lawyers could spend presenting their cases or cross-examining witnesses, nor did he limit the number of expert witnesses that either side's medical team could produce. Monsanto presented *eight,* and when a reporter from the *American Lawyer* ambled into court one day to see what all the fuss was about, she encountered one of them, James Webster, Jr., the chief of medicine at Northwestern Memorial Hospital, whom Carr was grilling in Webster's fourth *month* on the stand.

That was several months *before* Webster was cited for contempt by Goldenhersh and ordered off to jail for failing to answer Carr's questions adequately.

Webster had been testifying since January. Now, on July 24, Carr was asking the Northwestern University physician whether anything besides dioxin could have caused the "hypoactive"—or slowed—reflexes found in his adult clients.

"The cause for these people's hypoactive reflexes that we've been assuming—" Webster began.

Carr cut in: "That's what I'm asking you, Doctor."

Webster: "—is a normal physiologic baseline state."

In other words, Webster was saying that the premise of Carr's question was all wrong; that there was nothing unusual about Carr's clients' reflexes at all in terms of earlier expert testimony and test results that Carr himself was using as a premise for his question. If the test results were normal, there obviously couldn't be a "cause" for an "abnormality."

Carr and the Monsanto lawyers huddled before the bench. "Whether it's normal or abnormal is not the question I'm asking," Carr told the judge, and he moved that Webster be jailed until he answered the question the way that Carr wanted.

Goldenhersh issued a contempt citation and ordered Monsanto's principal witness jailed until he answered Carr's question differently. Webster was taken to a holding cell in the courthouse, but after two hours Goldenhersh amended his order so that Webster could return to Chicago to see scheduled patients, and a little while later—before Webster could begin serving his indefinite jail term—an appellate court issued an order allowing him to remain free for the duration of the trial.

Word of Webster's jailing quickly spread through the courthouse, and the next day's newspapers were filled with stories about the trial's latest incredible turn. Goldenhersh accused *Monsanto* of creating all the hullaballoo in the press. One of the lawyers asked him why he thought Monsanto would do that.

"To get a mistrial," Goldenhersh angrily replied. "To get a mistrial. You asked a question and believe it or not I am going to answer you. You are not in the position to interrogate the judge who has ruled, but this one question I will answer: To get a mistrial that you tried dearly to get for three and a half years. We are done, gentlemen."

It wasn't the only time that Goldenhersh had accused Monsanto's attorneys and witnesses of trying to thwart Carr's case. He also threatened four other Monsanto witnesses with contempt and jail if they didn't conform their answers to Carr's wishes, and he levied a stiff fine on the company and its lawyers.

The fines against Monsanto and its lawyers came down in the serio-comic way that typified the style of the case. Carr had made an oral motion to Goldenhersh on May 8, 1985, asking the judge to fine Monsanto a million dollars for what Carr said was the contemptuous conduct of its witnesses. Carr was angry even then that the people testifying for Monsanto weren't "responsive" to the questions he was asking. That was an effective defense strategy, of course—a witness who stood his ground could provoke Carr into marathon questioning that delayed the trial and turned the jury against Carr.

Goldenhersh took Carr's contempt motion under advisement for *two years*. Then, on May 22, 1987, with Webster on the stand, the judge summoned Monsanto's lawyers to his chambers and told them he was fining Monsanto $100,000 and Heineman's law firm of Coburn, Croft & Putzell $50,000. The charge: not sufficiently instructing Monsanto's witnesses to be "responsive." When the lawyers requested a chance to respond to the judge's charges, he told them, "Those are not charges. They are findings. . . . No, sir. These proceedings are closed."

Another Monsanto witness, Raymond Suskind, didn't fare much better. He, too, was held in contempt, although Goldenhersh kindly spared the seventy-three-year-old physician, already suffering from stress and high blood pressure as a result, Monsanto claimed, of a tortuous cross-examination by Carr, from serving time in the lock-up.

Suskind testified for two and a half days as Monsanto's witness, whereupon Carr began a cross-examination that lasted an incredible twenty-one and a half days.

What provoked Goldenhersh was Suskind's slightly-less-than-gracious characterization of the credentials of Carr's most crucial witness, Bertram Carnow.

Carnow, who had an office in Chicago and described himself as an "industrial hygienist," had literally made a fortune from the dioxin cases brought by Carr and Pratt, and by now he had accumulated quite a record in their various trials. It was Carnow's testimony that was always used by the plaintiffs to establish that dioxin exposure had caused the alphabet soup of maladies the Sturgeonites allegedly suffered.

During Pratt's trial, Carnow also testified that one of the plaintiffs had become impotent as a result of the dioxin spill, whereupon, on cross-examination, it was brought out that the same man had fathered two children after the accident. When Carnow tried to stand by his original testimony, Pratt spotted one of the jurors' rolling her eyes in disbelief and asked the judge to dismiss her from the jury.

Carnow charged $3,000 a day for his trial testimony and billed upward of $1,500 (three to four times his actual cost) for each of the many dioxin-related tests that were regularly given to the plaintiffs. By Monsanto's reckoning, Carnow and his laboratory had received $4 million in fees for his testing and testimony on behalf of dioxin plaintiffs, and his "mind-boggling financial stake" in the cases made his efforts "inherently suspect."

Carnow, Monsanto also said, was a liar, a man who'd perjured himself on multiple occasions about the fact that he failed his internal medicine board exams five times. And Carnow's failure to publish any peer-reviewed articles on dioxin was "an act of pure cowardice."

On February 19, 1986, Carr introduced the terms *waxing* and *waning* to Suskind. Carnow had used the terms to explain why, when tests were performed on the Sturgeon plaintiffs, "dioxin symptoms" didn't always show up. According to Carnow's theory, if his tests didn't show an abnormality, the symptom was "waning" at that particular time.

Suskind, who wasn't in Carnow's monetary league but wasn't exactly a piker, either, when it came to witness fees—Monsanto paid him $2,000 a day—stood his ground against Carr: "I have never heard of the term 'waxing and waning' as far as TCDD is concerned."

Carr: "Well, Dr. Carnow has described dioxin as one in which the symptoms change, they wax and they wane from time to time. . . ."

Suskind: "Dr. Carnow is no expert on TCDD, sir."

Now the lawyers were huddled around Goldenhersh's bench again, out of earshot of the jury. Carr complained about Suskind's answer.

"It was not a response," Goldenhersh said. "It is the type of remark [on] which I should probably hold this witness in contempt and I may just do that unless you give me a damn good reason why I shouldn't. That remark was totally unresponsive and irresponsible."

Heineman took his best shot, but Goldenhersh was unpersuaded. He sent the lawyers back to their tables and then launched into a tirade at Suskind: "I am holding you in willful contempt of this court. I don't think—there is not a doubt in my mind that your action was deliberate, willful and contemptuous and no court in the state of Illinois can stand for that kind of behavior and that includes mine."

Suskind: "May I say something, sir?"

Goldenhersh: "Yes, you may."

Suskind: "I don't believe I was contemptuous. I really don't. I am a decent human being and I have been in the field of science for forty years and I know from where I speak and I know Dr. Carnow very well."

It was only after Carr told the judge that he didn't think Suskind was being contemptuous that Goldenhersh decided to reconsider his finding. The same thing had happened the previous year, when Goldenhersh had exploded in anger at a witness—"I've had it with this guy, and I'm going to hold him in contempt!"—only to have Carr ask him not to.

Goldenhersh: "Okay. At your request I'll hold it in abeyance."

When Monsanto filed a 20,000-page posttrial motion soon after the trial ended (only to have the judge throw it back, at Carr's behest, and order Monsanto to file a 200-page document), the document characterized Goldenhersh as guided "by what Mr. Carr believed was proper, and not by what was *legally* proper" in the dioxin case.

With Goldenhersh at the helm, the leaky vessel that carried Carr's case took some strange detours: The argument one morning over where each lawyer should stand when approaching the bench, the time court was suspended for a few days so Carr could fly to France to take care of a problem at his cruise-barge business, the "sick day" when court was recessed after a juror's horse dropped a foal—plus 184 other vacation and sick days, including the two weeks off that Goldenhersh gave everybody when one of the jurors was married.

There was also a year-long, tiring sojourn into the evidence about the Nitro blast and the Agent Orange case, because Carr's punitive-damage case rested on the theory that Monsanto had been misleading the world about the dangers of dioxin ever since the Nitro accident.

Carr didn't just ask questions when he had a witness on the stand. He frequently made speeches or cooked up bizarre analogies to which he demanded that Monsanto's witnesses respond. If the witness re-sisted answering one of Carr's far-fetched hypotheticals—and resis-tance was Monsanto's strategy, after all, so resistance was the norm—Goldenhersh usually told him or her to answer. That was what hap-pened when Carr launched into a polemical, rambling "question" of Suskind in 1985 that went like this:

"This study goes around and people, doctors go to court because this was published in an authoritative magazine. *The American Medi-cal Association Journal* published this table. And so it is accepted as evidence in every single court in this country, and I don't know where else around the world, but every single court where some person comes up and says 'I was exposed to dioxin and I got bladder cancer,' or 'I got skin cancer,' or 'I got bowel cancer.' This study can be used to show—well, here, look at it. Out of Monsanto, the people working there, only two people have bladder cancer, or eight people had skin cancer. It can be used to persuade juries that dioxin doesn't cause cancer. It can be used in every single—it can be used in the Vietnam cases to show that dioxin doesn't cause cancer.

"Doctor, it is a total fraud! Now, doctor, you know the extent that this can be used for, do you not, sir?"

Heineman broke in. "May I say my objection after you've given your jury argument . . . ? It is obviously a jury summation and I object to it. I ask that it be stricken, and I ask [that] the jury be instructed to disregard it, your Honor."

Goldenhersh: "The jury—the question was a proper question. Your objection is overruled. In the future, I would appreciate your objections to be made on the basis of the legal point that you are making. Mr. Carr, you may proceed."

Then there was the time in early 1985 that Carr was cross-examining another Monsanto witness by using the analogy that Monsanto's professed lack of knowledge about the dioxin hazard of its new tank car was like an ostrich's putting its head in the sand.

Carr: "Yes, and, doctor, the ostrich that puts its head in the sand and had no knowledge that the tiger is about to eat him, because he puts his head in the sand, he doesn't want to know, he thinks he's hiding. That's what Monsanto, I assume, thought it was hiding. The fact that you did not test guaranteed your continued ignorance of the facts, isn't that correct? . . . [A]ssume that the 2,3,7,8-TCDD [dioxin] is the tiger and Monsanto is the ostrich."

"I see no reason to make that connection," the witness replied, after the judge had overruled a Monsanto objection to the question. "Why is TCDD the tiger?"

Carr exploded: "Did Monsanto test for the tiger? Did they, Monsanto, take its head out of the sand and look around and have eyes to view and find out where the TCDDs were in its product? Did Monsanto do that before it inflicted this product on Sturgeon, Missouri?"

When the same witness was back on the stand two years later, Carr bolstered his case for punitive damages by telling the witness to assume a highly disputed fact that wasn't in evidence: that Monsanto was behaving "exactly the same as the cigarette companies" in denying that their products caused cancer.

Carr: "They both have a sizable stake in the outcome of this debate, whether or not cigarettes cause cancer and whether or not TCDD causes cancer, don't they, sir?"

"I suppose."

Carr also dusted off another ploy that he'd used before: Right at the beginning of the trial, he put the other side's lead attorney on the stand and interrogated him in front of the jury about the company's alleged failure to give Carr all the documents he wanted.

In an earlier trial, U-Haul lawyer Shoen had been Carr's goat.

Now, it was Heineman who was accused of deliberately withholding evidence, intentionally misrepresenting facts, tampering with evidence and lying under oath. The contretemps was supposedly over two missing documents. But, as Monsanto saw it, Carr was insinuating misconduct by Heineman "to abuse and belittle him in the eyes of the jury."

The evening after Heineman's last day on the stand, Carr "found" the "missing" documents, in his cocounsel Seigfried's briefcase. Heineman had been correct all along in his recollection that he'd given Carr everything he asked for. Carr never apologized.

Goldenhersh was clearly frustrated. But he acted as if the main culprit in the long trial were Monsanto, when, in fact, what had really caused the problem was the amazing synergy of Goldenhersh's own blunders, Monsanto's strategy of fighting the case by delay and Carr's incredible stubbornness. The judge even seemed to think the press was somehow to blame for his problems. After CBS tried to interview one of the jurors' employers, to show what a hardship the case was working on the companies that were still paying the salaries of their employees on the jury, Goldenhersh tried to ban reporters from interviewing employers. And he imposed a "gag order" on Monsanto, which the state Supreme Court later called unconstitutional, in an attempt to prevent anyone in the chemical company from talking to the press.

But, for all his frustration, Goldenhersh seemed to be the only one, other than Carr himself, who didn't see what Carr's shameless obstinacy in the courtroom was doing to the trial. From start to finish during the three and a half years of trial, Goldenhersh sided with Carr on 95 percent of the 8,878 evidentiary rulings the judge made.

Meanwhile, Carr's interminable jihad was having a devastating effect on his once-powerful East St. Louis law firm. Carr was so tied down by the case that he couldn't bring in new cases; referrals to Carr from other lawyers, once a major source of his business, all but dried up. And those cases that had been on Carr's desk when the *Monsanto* trial began had to be farmed out to other lawyers. Carr was taking big money out of the firm, but what was he bringing in?

Carr was also remote, working with Seigfried and another young lawyer and a secretary out of the Belleville cubbyhole while all of his partners and associates stayed in downtown East St. Louis. New associates who'd joined Carr's firm because of the allure of the master's reputation never saw him.

"The monster [trial] kept running," Brennan observed, "but there was no personal communication." When partners from the East St. Louis office did venture into the Belleville courtroom to watch the action, they were appalled by what they saw: Goldenhersh had become so enraged at the bickering between the two sets of lawyers that he had ordered them to make every objection, no matter how minor, in a sidebar conference at the bench. Since virtually every question engendered an objection—Question. Objection. Lawyers walk to bench. Mumbled sidebar conference. Lawyers walk back to their seats. Question is asked again—the lawyers were proceeding at the rate of about three questions an hour.

Back in East St. Louis, there was all manner of palace intrigue over what the partners could do about Carr's quixotic battle. "It was an ongoing bitch," one said. The partners already could see what Carr's towering ego prevented him from apprehending. "But nobody in the partnership ever tried to do damage control," said Brennan.

By 1986, gross revenues at the firm had dropped precipitously. From the $10 million, pre-*Kemner* peak of 1983, revenue had slipped below $7 million, and it was still sliding. Carr and Korein, still warily hewing to their unwritten agreement to keep their partnership shares equal, had agreed to take only 20 points apiece, instead of their former 25. Schlichter, meanwhile, was generating more business than ever and now, as the new power in the firm, *he* was getting 25 percentage points of the profit.

Excellent trial lawyer and business-getter though he was, Schlichter had even more leverage over the partnership because he was on the verge of a huge settlement in another dioxin case. While Carr battled away in the Belleville courthouse, Schlichter had been representing 110 plaintiffs who'd been exposed to dioxin in Times Beach, the Missouri town that became notorious when the Environmental Protection Agency ordered it abandoned because of dioxin contamination. (The two lawsuits, Carr's in the Illinois court and Schlichter's across the river in the circuit court of St. Louis, involved totally different spills. The only characteristic they had in common was their use of Carnow as an expert witness.)

Schlichter's fee agreements specified that he receive a whopping 40 percent of whatever he recovered—a percentage that Corboy considered "unconscionable," but also one that, for a long time, didn't appear likely to produce very much for Schlichter, because the main defendants were either out of business or in bankruptcy, and none of them was talking settlement. But that was before one of Schlichter's associates, Rob Bogard, learned while combing through hundreds of thousands of discovery documents that the tanks from which the dioxin had leaked at Times Beach had once been owned by Syntex U.S.A., a chemical concern that had stored Agent Orange in the tanks before they were used in Times Beach.

That was exactly the kind of evidence Schlichter needed to virtually guarantee a big win. The insurers representing the defendants knew that, too, and they also knew better than to get tangled up in what could have been an ongoing nightmare—the 110 plaintiffs were going to have their cases tried 6 at a time, and each trial was expected to last six months. So, on September 13, 1986, just three days before jury selection was to begin in the trial of the first 6 plaintiffs, the two sides began settlement discussions that ultimately produced, in early November of 1986, the law firm's biggest payday ever. The settlement was for $18 million, of which Schlichter's firm's share, after paying referral fees to a few other lawyers but *before* recovering the hundreds of thousands of dollars in expenses that his firm had advanced, was $6 million.

But any expectations that the salad days were returning to Carr, Korein, Kunin, Schlichter & Brennan were quickly dashed the following Tuesday, November 11, 1986. Korein had circulated a memorandum the previous day giving a day's notice of a special partnership meeting. Now, at 1 P.M. in the firm's small conference room, Korein began the acrimonious four-hour meeting with an exchange with Brennan over Brennan's decision to accept 1,000 new toxic-tort cases that had been referred to him by the tire-workers' union.

The lawsuits Brennan intended to file were going to allege that the workers had contracted a lung disease called asbestosis in their tire factories. Brennan would have to bring aboard three or more more lawyers immediately to work solely on those cases.

Korein said one quagmire at a time was all the firm could handle. "Send 'em back."

As the discussion continued, now Schlichter spoke up and said there were so many conflicts at the firm that he wanted to dissolve the whole partnership. Some of the partners thought that Schlichter's real motivation in breaking up the partnership was to keep as much of his newly-won $6 million Times Beach fee as he could for himself. Just how much of that money belonged to Schlichter was, in fact, the subject of acrimonious litigation, both between Schlichter's firm and his former partners and also between Schlichter and some of his clients who claimed they'd been coerced by Schlichter, after the settlement was virtually assured, into agreeing to pay him 40 percent instead of the previously-agreed-to 33 1/3 percent. A Missouri judge ruled against Schlichter's clients. One of the lawsuits between the firm and its former partner was settled in the partner's favor; another was still pending and proceeding to trial a year later.

"That's fine with me," Brennan had replied that day in November when Schlichter proposed breaking up the partnership. "It's going to happen anyway. That's what I was going to propose anyway, three weeks from now," when the firm was scheduled to have its first meeting to divide up the partnership points for the coming year. Brennan had been intending to quit then, anyway.

Most of the other partners just sat there dumbfounded. Another meeting, to fix year-end bonuses for the salaried workers and associates, was already scheduled for that coming Saturday, and the group decided to continue its discussion then. In the meantime, they all agreed to keep the firm's imminent breakup a secret at least until the end of the year, out of fear that a premature leak of the partnership's problems would hurt Carr's case.

Jack Carey hadn't been at the meeting. He was vacationing on Captiva Island, Florida. That afternoon, he received three separate calls from other partners, reporting what had happened and urging him to return. But Carey decided to stay put. He was already on the outs with Korein. Carey figured he was going to be thrown out of the partnership, too.

In all, three partners, including Brennan and Carey, left at the end of that year. But there was a new look to the firm now. Carr had always been the driving force behind keeping his firm in East St. Louis, an emblem, he said, of his commitment to the underdog. But Schlichter and Korein had always wanted to fly higher, and now they had enough clout to do that. For $24,000 a month, the two leased spacious new digs for themselves and a bunch of the firm's other lawyers on Olive St. in downtown St. Louis, a few miles from Schlichter's mansion. Carr stayed behind.

"Rex was always adamant about not leaving East St. Louis," Carey explained. "I've seen Rex swallow his principles for all the wrong reasons. Before *Kemner,* he would have said, 'You go to St. Louis but the firm stays here!' But he needs Korein and Schlichter now. He was too weak to say no. He had to let them go. So he's left with a skeleton office in East St. Louis and the city collapsing all around him."

Rex Carr moved the lectern right up in front of the jury so that he could eyeball each one of them as he began his closing argument on the morning of Tuesday, August 18, 1987. That was how Carr tried to take command of the courtroom. He liked to get up close.

Carr started out with a paean to the fourteen jurors, twelve regulars and two alternates, who'd managed to stick it out to the bitter end. Only four had dropped out along the way. "Maybe you don't realize it," he told them, "but once you sign your verdict in this case, this case will go down in the Guinness Book of World Records, and you will be the jury reaching a verdict, having served far longer, far longer than any other jury in the past—and probably, I would be willing to wager anything that I have on it, that there will never be another jury that will meet, or come close to equaling, what you have done here by your personal sacrifice and attention to this case."

Now that the case was over, even Carr acknowledged the worst of what the lawyers had inflicted on the jurors. "Mind-deadening repetition of the same thing and the same thing over and over again" was what Carr called it, not realizing that even now he was repeating himself. "I'm surprised that not all of our minds have turned to vegetables, to tell you the truth, because of some of the sameness of what you've heard."

Carr had asked the judge for twelve hours in which to make his closing argument. Monsanto's lawyers argued that there was no way they could cover three and a half years of evidence in a day and a half; they wanted forty-five hours instead and figured Carr had sought so much less time because covering all the evidence, or the lack of same, was the *last* thing he wanted Monsanto to do. Goldenhersh, as he almost invariably did, sided with Carr. Each side would be allotted twelve hours. Since the burden of proof was on Carr, he would lead off and also have the last word. Carr began with an eight-hour argument, saving his last four hours for the rebuttal.

Carr stuck to the strategy he'd adopted right at the start, putting Monsanto on trial not just for the Sturgeon spill but also for every other real or apparent hazard ever caused *anywhere* by dioxin. He was, after all, trying to get punitive damages, and that meant he needed to prove a pattern of misconduct on Monsanto's part. He tied Monsanto not just to the 1949 Nitro, West Virginia, accident, but also to later dioxin accidents in Germany in 1953, in Seveso, Italy, in 1977, and in Times Beach—accidents, except for Nitro, that Monsanto wasn't even involved in, but that, Carr claimed, should nonetheless have put Monsanto on notice as to the dangers of the dioxin byproducts that were being produced in its factories. Carr ascribed an array of Freudian maladies to those various dioxin incidents—"disturbances of vitality, disturbances of the basic psychic mood and affect, disturbances of drive, weakness of memory and concentration, a hyperesthetic tendency, vegetative hyperexcitability"—all of which Carr placed under the general banner of something he called "psychovegetative syndrome."

The Monsanto team had appointed as its "designated objector" Jack Musgrave, a forty-five-year-old partner in Heineman's firm who'd been sitting right alongside him at the counsel table the entire three and a half years. Every few minutes, each time Carr mentioned some other accident that Monsanto hadn't had any connection with, Musgrave would dutifully stand and object for the record. The judge always overruled him, of course, but Musgrave's objections had the effect, if nothing else, of keeping Carr off stride as the bantam lawyer marched through his final days before the jury.

Carr told the jury that "the bulk" of the dioxin-contaminated Agent Orange that was manufactured during the Vietnam War came from Monsanto (much of it did, in fact), and that even Lysol was contaminated with the nasty stuff.

"They had the ability, they had the knowledge, they had the know-how to stop," he said of Monsanto. "You would not have had any significant Vietnam problems. We would not have had Lysol contaminated with dioxin. . . . They knew. But, like the ostrich"—oh, God, here it came again!—"like the ostrich, they stuck their head in the sand so they would not be able to say that they in fact *specifically* knew it."

What the Sturgeon accident came down to, Carr was trying to say, was this: "Duplicity in Sturgeon was part of the pattern of conduct that they had with *everybody,* not just with the plaintiffs in this case." He contended that Monsanto's senior executives had made a decision to ignore dioxin's dangers so that they could maximize their own company's profits. "The big shots knew!" Carr insisted. That was the kind of populist rhetoric that usually went down well with the juries in Plaintiffs' Paradise. "They did it for no other reason than the big dollar!"

"I will tell you," Carr went on, "there are so many lies and so many deceits on the part of Monsanto in this case, to the workers, to OSHA, to the world at large! In an ordinary lawsuit, if you had just one of those, my biggest concern, my biggest fear about this case with you all is that you've seen so many lies and so many misrepresentations that you might come to believe it is the accepted way; it is the way things should be. That is my biggest concern. One of these lies in the ordinary lawsuit would be enough to condemn the defendant, to find the defendant guilty of the charges. My concern is, we have got so many overwhelming—it is like Doctor Goebbels! Nazi propaganda! If you tell the lie often enough, people will believe it to be true!"

Now, designated-objector Musgrave was on his feet again. "May we approach the bench?" Since Goldenhersh had insisted each objection be lodged in a sidebar, the trial had turned into a series of processions to and from the far side of the bench.

"I object to that inflammatory argument of trying to draw an analogy with the well-known Nazi criminal and the Monsanto witnesses. I request that the jury be instructed to disregard it and I move for a mistrial."

Goldenhersh looked at Carr. "I stand by what I say, your honor."

Goldenhersh: "Objection is overruled. And your motion is over-ruled. Let's proceed."

It wasn't until midafternoon of the next day that Carr finally got around to putting a price tag on his case for the jurors. When it came to compensatory damages, Carr was asking for $5,000 per year, per plaintiff, part of which was supposed to pay for annual medical check-ups by Carnow. Carr's formula meant everybody would get $40,000 for the time that had already elapsed between the 1979 spill and the present, and then a varying amount for the future, depending on his or her life expectancy. All in all, it added up to $35.4 million—"about a penny a minute is what it comes out to." Carr was rotating all his clients back through the courtroom again, so they could be present when the final pleas were made for them.

Carr wanted another $100 million in punitive damages. "Now, punitive damages, if it is, in fact, going to be punitive, has got to hurt them." Carr wanted the jury to send a message not just to Monsanto, but to all the chemical companies, drug companies and automobile makers who'd ever made a defective product. "We are under siege, if you will, from the ozone layer to the radiation problems to the defective automobiles!"

Monsanto's designated objector was all lathered up about Carr's ploy, but the judge overruled him, as usual. "It's proper punitive argument. Objection is overruled. I'll make it a continuing objection so you don't have to come up here."

Carr had given it his best shot with two days of florid speechmaking. But the problem with his closing argument was the same one with his whole case: it rambled all over the place, lacking any kind of cohesive theme to pull together in the juror's minds what he'd been trying to prove for three and a half years.

Carr's closing argument gave too little emphasis to Sturgeon and too much to all the other issues that even the jurors could see weren't relevant to the case they were deciding. Monsanto had had a connection with only one of the dioxin accidents that Carr kept harping on. The Nitro problem did belong to Monsanto, but a federal jury had already cleared the company of wrongdoing there. So, the jurors asked themselves, What the hell was Carr complaining about? Automobile pollution? Defective drugs? They knew that wasn't what the case was about.

To make matters worse for Carr, Monsanto's closing argument had a strong, clear theme that made the absence of one in Carr's even more obvious.

When his own turn came on Thursday morning, Heineman pulled an easel up close to the jury and put a big fiberboard chart on it that said:

THESE ARE THE REALITIES OF STURGEON

REALITY #1:   NOT ENOUGH DIOXIN TO HURT ANYONE.

REALITY #2:   MONSANTO DID NOT KNOW TCDD WAS IN THE TANKCAR.

REALITY #3:   THE E.P.A., THE CENTERS FOR DISEASE CONTROL & THE MISSOURI DIVISION OF HEALTH DISPROVE CARNOW'S CLAIMS.

REALITY #4:   PLAINTIFFS ARE NOT INJURED BY DIOXIN.

REALITY #5:   PLAINTIFFS DON'T TREAT STURGEON AS A HAZARD.

Heineman built his closing argument around those five "realities," all of which together boiled down to the assertion that nobody had been hurt in the Sturgeon accident and that Carnow, Carr's main medical expert witness, was a liar who stood to be greatly enriched by helping Carr to prove otherwise. Whenever Heineman or one of his partners made a statement during their three days before the jury—with breaks and delays, it took that long to finish twelve actual hours of closing argument—they tied it back to one of the five "realities."

To prove his first point that there wasn't enough dioxin to hurt anybody, for instance, Heineman used an illustration that he thought everybody could relate to. The small amount of dioxin that had spilled onto the track was found in a concentration of sixty parts per trillion. "Busch Stadium. Fifty thousand seats. Okay. What if there were 20 million Busch Stadiums? That would be 1 trillion seats in 20 million Busch Stadiums. One seat in 20 million Busch Stadiums is 1 part per trillion. One seat in 20 million stadiums! Sixty seats in 20 million Busch Stadiums is 60 parts per trillion! . . . Look how enormously, enormously small that amount is! . . . *One thousand* parts per trillion is the CDC's "no concern" level—that you can eat it every day in soil for the rest of your life! That's what they said!"

Heineman's closing argument was also effective because it put the plaintiffs and their chief medical expert on trial. Instead of just defending Monsanto, he went after the people who'd filed the lawsuit. He wasted no time in blasting Carnow for lying about flunking the internal medicine boards, and he brought it up again whenever he could, because once you've impeached a witness on even one question his credibility on everything else evaporates, too.

"Why would he lie about it? Because he knows it's important to his credibility. People will think he's not qualified. From these boards we learn he's not qualified and he's not believable.

"Let's test this. Do you remember when you were sixteen years old, you took your driver's test? I can still remember how nervous I was. You know, many people flunk it the first time and they never forget it. Never forget it! Oh, you're so excited. You go in and you can't wait to take that test because you're going to get to drive, and you flunk it and, oh, it's so embarrassing!

"What if you flunked your driver's test five times? Do you think you'd remember it? Now, think if it was a test that meant your livelihood, and you flunked it five times! Do you think you'd remember it? And when asked by me in court why he lied about it, he said he didn't lie; he just forgot! Do you believe that? Well, why is this important? Whom do you believe? Because in order to find for the plaintiffs in this case, you have to believe Bertram Carnow. You have to believe that they were injured, and the only person in this courtroom who has told you that the plaintiffs were injured by dioxin at Sturgeon is Bertram Carnow!"

Heineman ticked off a list of people he said the jury would be contradicting if it agreed with Carnow: the American Medical Association, the Centers for Disease Control, the Environmental Protection Agency, the Missouri Division of Health and all the family doctors who treated the Sturgeonites. "Everybody is wrong except Bertram Carnow—that's what you have to believe!"

Then, he burned the point home with a tabulation of what the "professional testifier" Carnow had made so far from the various dioxin trials: $875,000 for the Nitro trial, $974,250 for Pratt's trial, $580,000 for Times Beach, and at least $2.2 million so far for Carr's case. Plus, since Carr was asking the jury to pay for annual medical exams for all the plaintiffs for the rest of their lives, that was another $18 million or $19 million.

"That's a pretty good career he's had. About $21 million, the Bertram Carnow fund, and that's a nice reward for what? For telling you the truth? . . . Mr. Carr told you that he learned some things after this trial started that he didn't know at the beginning. One of the things he learned is that Bertram Carnow failed his boards five times and lied about it seven times. You think maybe that's why you didn't hear him hardly mention Dr. Carnow in his final argument? Barely mentioned the man's name!"

So much for the third "reality" of Sturgeon.

When it came to the plaintiffs, Heineman said they were just as healthy as anybody else, and he reminded the jurors about all the local witnesses that Carr hadn't called, but Monsanto had—neighbors, teachers, coaches, and family doctors who'd all testified that their friends and students and patients from Sturgeon were all just fine and healthy.

"Mr. Carr went first in this case. He had the burden of proof, and he could have brought these people before you, but he didn't."

That was the fourth "reality" of Sturgeon.

Heineman also had to deal with Carr's punitive damage claim, and he was ready with a clever way of dispatching it.

"You know, ladies and gentlemen, when I was a teenager in the 1950s, there was an expression that was used, and that expression was, 'If it won't run, chrome it.' And that referred to an automobile. A lot of us had crummy, old cars we fixed up that we could run, and some of them would really go, squeal away from a stoplight. And then some of them wouldn't. And, you know, you always could pick those out if the guys put, they put chrome parts under the hood.

"You remember those shiny chrome things? So, if it wouldn't run, chrome it! You make it look fancy. You overlook the shortcomings, divert attention from the shortcomings. Do you suppose that was some of what Mr. Carr did in this case? Why does he want you to retry the Nitro case? Is there something lacking in this case? Kind of makes you wonder, doesn't it. . . . We want to be tried on the Sturgeon case. That's why we're supposed to be here. Now, Mr. Carr wants to try a lot of other lawsuits. Why? Maybe it's because there's only half a teaspoon of dioxin in that tank car. You think so? You think the car wouldn't run, so he chromed it?

"Let's talk about what this case is and is not about. Okay. What is this case *not* about? This case is not about Nitro, it's not about Agent Orange, it's not about Weed-B-Gone, and it's not about Lysol. . . . It's about Sturgeon. None of those things were at Sturgeon. No Lysol there, no Weed-B-Gone, no Agent Orange, no Nitro."

When Carr finally rose to address the jury on the following Tuesday afternoon, he stuck to his formless strategy of attacking Monsanto's defense instead of arguing his own case. Monsanto, Carr said, was like a criminal lawyer defending a rapist: Instead of defending the criminal, they were going after the victim. He had his own chart, entitled the "Ten Realities of Monsanto," and what it said was that Monsanto had simply lied to *everybody* about the effects of dioxin.

Carr also had an explanation of why his clients weren't outwardly ill despite the dioxin exposure. He said they were like people who'd been bitten by a rabid bat: All their ill effects weren't going to show up until—poof!—one day, they just dropped dead.

That's what he said.

When both sides finally finished their closing arguments on Wednesday, August 26, after forty-four months of trial, it was eminently clear that Rex Carr had, indeed, had the poor trial that he always said he preferred when the choice was between that and a good settlement.

The jury had listened to 608 days of evidence; seen 2,232 plaintiffs' exhibits and 4,043 defense exhibits; and heard 91 witnesses presented by Carr as well as 86 by Monsanto. Right away, the jurors took a vote to see where everybody stood. There were eight votes for Monsanto. Three other jurors thought the plaintiffs had, indeed, been harmed, and one wasn't certain. But the important point was that a solid majority of the jurors had been sitting there in the courtroom already convinced that Carr had failed to make his case for compensatory damages. Some of them had long ago decided, as one put it, that Carr was "out to make a buck," and most of them didn't need any more persuading than they'd already had that the Sturgeon residents weren't injured.

There was, in addition, a surprising level of sophistication among the jurors about what had made the case drag on so long. They thought the big case should have been broken up and tried in small stages, and they blamed Goldenhersh for failing to exercise control over the lawyers. "Carr could say anything," one juror complained. "Carr ran that trial. If the judge had been fair, it would have been shorter."

And yet it was obvious that after three and a half years the jurors weren't in any better position to decide the case than they had been when the trial started. Nine jurors wanted to exonerate Monsanto on the punitive damage count, too, but the same three who had earlier voted for Carr on the compensatory damage count now started holding out for some kind of punitive damage verdict against Monsanto.

They took more than a hundred votes. Three times over eight weeks, the jurors reported themselves to be hopelessly deadlocked. The first two times, Monsanto asked for a mistrial. On the third, Carr, agreeing with Monsanto for the first time in anyone's memory, joined in and asked for one, too. Even he could smell what was coming. Goldenhersh could coerce a verdict—that was what he was doing each time he told the jurors to keep at it—but nobody really thought such an obviously coerced verdict would hold up on appeal.

There were those who thought Goldenhersh had his own good reasons for being so determined that the jurors reach a verdict. Goldenhersh, after all, was running for an appellate court judgeship, a promotion, and damned if he didn't hold the jurors until the county Democratic screening committee had approved his candidacy. At least there was no embarrassing mistrial or hung jury for the county Democrats to see.

Carr had asked for $35.4 million in compensatory damages in his closing argument. But the jurors, most of whom had discerned Goldenhersh's obvious tilt toward Carr throughout the trial and resented them both for it, ultimately decided that nobody but Bill Kemner and his mother, Frances, had been hurt by the dioxin spill. The Kemners received twenty-nine thousand dollars because their land was contaminated by the spill; all the other plaintiffs got one dollar.

That was part of the deal all the jurors agreed to in order to end the agony of their deliberations.

Carr had also asked the jury to award him $100 million in punitive damages, and the other part of the jurors' bargain was an agreement to award him $16.2 million in punitives. But it was anybody's guess how they'd arrived at that. Somebody'd taken a pencil and paper and calculated how much Monsanto ought to pay for each year it produced the Agent Orange and Lysol and Weed-B-Gone and all the other products that Carr had alluded to when he chromed up his case. Yes, yes, everybody had finally agreed. Do it. Get it over with.

The jurors said they felt pressured to do something to extricate themselves from the deliberations. It was a compromise.

A few reporters who didn't know any better called it a victory for the little people of Sturgeon. But punitive damages almost never held up on appeal, and this award—which wasn't even attached to any significant compensatory verdict—had even less of a chance than most of ever being paid.

Carr went back to the East St. Louis office. He gave a talk to the local bar association about his case. He had a trial date for his next case against U-Haul. God, people said with bewilderment, was Belleville ready for another one of *those?*

Mostly, Carr seemed his usual impassive self. If he had any regrets or self-doubts, he kept them all inside. He'd aged perceptibly during the trial, gotten old. Carr's own wife had become a recluse. "No friends," Brennan said of him. "No nothin'.

"Rex was the pure embodiment of the phrase 'The law is my mistress.' It gave him a tool to do what he does best: debate and argue. But they turned it on him. I don't know that Rex ever did recognize that."

Conclusion

To be a trial lawyer is to see the ignominy of slow justice in a system in which the *process* itself punishes all who come in contact with it: the winner as well as the loser.

In the case of *Wayne Newton v. NBC,* the singer's record-setting libel victory merely marked the start of an appeals process that will take years more to run its course. A month after the jury's $19.2 million award to Newton, another $3.5 million was awarded for lost income. That brought the total verdict to $22.7 million.

With NBC firmly dug in against paying the judgment or settling, Floyd Abrams made the lawyer's standard request for what is known as a judgment notwithstanding the verdict—essentially, a setting-aside of the jury's verdict as being wholly unreasonable. Failing that, Abrams sought a new trial.

Eleven months and hundreds of pages of briefs later, the trial judge rendered his decision: that Galane had, indeed, proved that Newton had been libeled by NBC, a real win for Galane, but that the jurors had gone way overboard in setting damages. He gave Newton an alternative: either accept a far more modest sum as damages or go through a whole new trial, this time in Los Angeles, on damages.

Galane and Newton faced a dilemma. Judge Myron Crocker was telling them that he would order a new trial in sixty days unless they filed a *remittitur,* or reduction, of the award down to $5 million for punitive damages, $225,000 for physical and mental injury as a result of the stomach ulcer Newton claimed NBC had given him, and

$50,000 for damage to his reputation. Newton's income had kept right on going up, not down, so Crocker said he was shocked that the Las Vegas jury believed the erroneous NBC stories had otherwise harmed Newton.

Galane went out to Newton's house the night before the singer was to leave for a USO-sponsored Christmas tour entertaining troops in the Middle East and explained what it all meant. NBC was going to keep appealing no matter what they did, so there was no real chance of collecting any time soon the $5,275,000 that Crocker was still allowing them. If they accepted the remittitur anyway, that would leave them with a big punitive damage award attached to two relatively small, and highly questionable, compensatory awards, and if some appeals court later struck them—as seemed likely—the punitive award would invariably have to be thrown out, too, on the ground that NBC shouldn't be punished if Newton hadn't been harmed.

"His chances of holding on to even the $5 million are slight," Abrams gloated as Galane and Newton pondered their next step. "Even if Newton wins on appeal, he'll have spent so much that he's unlikely now to even get his attorney's fees back."

Galane and Newton decided to do nothing. They simply let the deadline pass; that meant that there would be a new trial in Los Angeles on damages. Galane intended to build all over again his case for the harm to Newton's reputation, which the other jury said had been worth $5 million in damages but which the judge had cut to almost nothing. To support his case, Galane was going to take the deposition of James Watt, the hapless former Interior Secretary who'd invited Newton to replace the Beach Boys at a big July 4 bash on the Mall in Washington. The whole Beach Boys-for-Newton swap had been a joke, after all. Newton had never been invited back. That was harm enough to his reputation, wasn't it?

Abrams, who seldom attended depositions, definitely intended to be there for Watt's. It promised to be quite a show. "Can you believe it?" Galane cackled.

Likely to be excluded from the retrial was Newton's loss of past and future income, for which the Las Vegas jury had previously awarded $9,046,750 but which the judge had cut to zero. Galane also professed not to care that the trial was going to take place away from his home turf. "Don't forget," he said, "Los Angeles is where I won the *Maheu* case!"

Abrams wasn't forgetting that, but what was more important to him was the obvious implication of what Newton and Galane had just done. They had allowed the judge to take away all of their nearly $23 million in damages. The meter had been reset to zero. NBC now owed zilch to Newton, and in a new trial before a less sympathetic jury, Galane and Newton would have to take their shot all over again.

One more shot at scooping up all that scattered quicksilver and forging it into gold.

For John Coale, the Bhopal case was gone, but certainly not forgotten as it leapt on and off the front pages in synch with the vicissitudes of the Indian judicial system. The diary entry that he'd made in Bhopal on April 2, 1986, had turned out to have amazing prescience. "The actual victims, of course, as in most similar situations, are left out in the cold—as the real victims," he'd written then. Four years after the disaster, none of the Bhopal victims had collected a cent.

Coale said he had a plan to use political pressure to try to steal the case from the Indian courts and take it back to the United States, where he and his cohorts might be able to get their contingent-fee claws into it again. If he did that, though, he would be doing it without Lowy. The two had quarreled over Coale's refusal to give Lowy a share of the $375,000 fee that Coale had received for settling his lawsuits against Arrow Air, the military charter operator whose plane crashed in Gander, Newfoundland.

Mostly, Coale kept doing what he did best, drumming up publicity, getting cases and settling them. His biggest payday came when Conrail finally settled with the sixteen passengers who were killed in the 1987 train wreck. Coale's client received $3.7 million, and Coale a third of that—a cool $1,233,000, which he had already agreed to split fifty-fifty with Gauthier.

Coale's personal fortunes were rising, too. He'd traded up to a new Jaguar, "thanks to Conrail," and his draw at the law firm had been increased from $120,000 to $200,000. He'd also married his former legal assistant, Greta Van Susteren.

"I'm up to twelve cases in the Detroit air crash," Coale boasted, although he also lamented the demise of the one-third contingency in air-crash cases. There was so much competition that Coale had to cut his contingency to 15 percent in order to get the cases.

But an even bigger enterprise was in the making. Coale was going around the country, drumming up and filing class actions against the makers and prescribers of a drug called Ritalin, which is used to treat one million hyperactive children but which Coale claimed was causing side effects ranging from headaches to suicidal behavior. By the time he'd filed suits against the drug in Atlanta, Washington and Minneapolis, Coale and his lawsuits were prominent fixtures in the pages of *USA Today,* to say nothing of the local newspapers in the cities where he'd begun swooping in. "I'm trying to get this into a shark-feeding frenzy," Coale enthusiastically explained. He was being quoted in the papers as saying his Ritalin litigation would someday approach the dimensions of the Dalkon Shield case that brought about the bankruptcy of the A. H. Robins Company—a great boast to be making, regardless of whether it were true or not.

"Ritalin," Coale giggled confidentially, "has all the right ingredients for a real big case: children, drugs, and fraud."

When the general counsel of Lorillard appeared at a news conference the day after the *Cipollone* verdict, it was with the avowed intention of setting the record straight. The tobacco companies couldn't hold a news conference while the trial was in progress, he said. Now they could.

"We should all remember," Arthur Stevens told the reporters on that day, "that the real story of this litigation was not a woman from New Jersey who smoked, but about money. Money. And about three very big, very rich New Jersey law firms who decided to invest lots of their own time and their own money in the products-liability lottery. Sure, they posed as self-styled champions of Rose Cipollone, and, yes, they pandered to and were pandered by the whole crew of self-appointed antitobacco folks. But everyone knows what they were really pursuing. And it wasn't solely to benefit either Rose or Tony Cipollone."

But neither Stevens nor Murray Bring, the Philip Morris general counsel who accompanied him, would talk about the money spent by their side. Was it $50 million?, someone asked. Who knew. "Mr. Bleakley would be very embarrassed if I told how much he earned," Stevens dissembled. In the courtroom or out of it, the companies fell back on familiar tactics.

If the *Cipollone* case was about money, it was also about the scorched-earth defense policies of the tobacco companies, policies that only a lawyer similarly possessed of Edell's tenacity could overcome.

Stevens was a big, darkly handsome man whose features and flair for double-breasted pin stripes evoked the character actor Sheldon Leonard. "We have spent whatever was necessary to present our defense," he acknowledged solemnly.

The question was whether, knowing that, any other lawyers would rush in now that Edell had shown the way. Fighting the cigarette companies meant going up against a sophisticated litigation–public relations–lobbying machine that was capable of chewing up the opposition. The anti-*Cipollone* law that the companies sprang on Edell was proof of that. The cigarette makers had also lobbied successfully for the same kind of law in California after *Galbraith,* and there was great irony in the alliance that pushed through the law curbing antitobacco lawsuits there: The plaintiffs' trial lawyers themselves had supported the bill, in exchange for a new law increasing allowable contingent fees in malpractice cases.

The industry was, in short, still winning. In April, the Supreme Court had let stand a $3,050,000 libel award for Brown & Williamson against CBS and an anchorman at its Chicago station, the largest ever left intact against a news media defendant after appeal. The anchorman had delivered a commentary that said Brown & Williamson had a strategy of relating Viceroy cigarettes to "pot, wine, beer and sex."

And just one day after the *Cipollone* verdict, the federal appeals court in Cincinnati affirmed R. J. Reynolds' earlier victory in another cigarette liability case. That court, like all the other federal appellate courts that had considered the issue, said the 1966 federal labeling law insulated tobacco companies from any product-liability lawsuits from then on, "another indication of the strength of the position of this industry in this litigation," Bring boasted.

Edell had six more cases pending against the cigarette companies.

"Plaintiffs' lawyers will be able to successfully prosecute future cases without spending $2 million to obtain the evidence that we introduced," he said. But it would take many more years to translate Edell's breakthrough in *Cipollone* into the big money he envisioned.

"It's going to be a long time," defense lawyer Bleakley intoned even before the trial ended, "before there's any victory in this case." If nothing else, the truth of that statement had already been proved.

It had been an awful year for the Hunt brothers, but a great year for their guerrilla lawyer, Steve Susman.

Bunker, Herbert and Lamar were still trying to find a way to settle the myriad lawsuits emanating from their silver scam, but their options were limited because they were attempting to hang on to at least some of their assets and the plaintiffs seemed to want everything they had. Meanwhile, the Peruvian government's mineral-marketing company that had lost at least $63 million during the silver-price run-up sued the brothers under the antitrust and racketeering laws and, on August 20, 1988, won a $134 million judgment against them.

Bunker Hunt was also on trial in U.S. Tax Court. The Internal Revenue Service wanted more than $300 million in back taxes, interest and penalties for what the government claimed was another scam by Bunker: He had "loaned" his children $150 million to speculate in silver on their own, and when the market crashed he'd written off the debts. The IRS claimed his loans to the kids were really nondeductible gifts.

The Hunts' lender-fraud litigation against their banks was reaching an October 1988 showdown, too. That was when the federal court trial against the twenty-two banks was scheduled to begin.

The Hunt brothers' lawsuits against their banks had always been aimed at buying them more time, but with a trial looming and the banks not backing down on their repayment demand, even that precious commodity had finally played itself out.

The brothers must have realized that, too, because they were signing a settlement that would give the banks everything they were owed. The Hunts were going to raise the necessary cash by going even more deeply into hock, mortgaging or selling their Dutch North Sea operations, their daddy's huge Black Lake natural gas field in southcentral Louisiana, and their interest in Placid's Dallas head-quarters tower, and agreeing to turn over to the Penrod banks half their interest in Penrod Drilling if they failed to meet debt repayment deadlines. Herbert was being stripped of any operational role in Penrod. The IRS was going to get another $57.1 million from Placid (an amount separate from what the feds said Bunker owed), to be paid over seven years with interest.

It was time for the Hunts to finally limit their losses, to husband whatever assets the Hunts had left for one last run at the Green Canyon. The wildcatters were keeping the Green Canyon leases unencumbered, but that probably wasn't going to help them much because bad luck wasn't bankable. The Green Canyon project hadn't produced any oil yet. As one skeptical Susman, Godfrey lawyer put it, "the only thing in the Green Canyon is ten miles worth of pipe!" The huge piece of pipe the brothers had welded together, so crucial to their production plans, had come loose from its tow and fallen to the ocean floor in 1,500 feet of water.

Ask Susman what the Hunts gained in their litigation against the banks and he'd answer, time. But even their own lawyer couldn't say that the brothers were any better off now than they had been before the litigation started. As a delaying action, the lawsuits might have helped them if oil and gas prices had skyrocketed, or if they'd struck it rich in the Green Canyon play. Either outcome would have produced enough money to make everybody happy. But when neither happened, the only thing their lawsuits achieved was to bleed off more cash that the brothers couldn't afford to spend. The way out now wasn't through more litigation, but through settlement.

"When we were close to settling, and I asked the banks if we could stop discovery and save the money," Susman drawled. "But the bank lawyers won't do that. This was their good-bye kiss to their clients, running up the tab for the last two months on a case they knew would settle."

Which, of course, meant that Susman had made out quite nicely, too. He'd doubled his own annual income—it was now $2 million—in the one year he'd had the *Hunt* case. His firm, which was now up to thirty lawyers, was having its best year ever, and it was opening a permanent Dallas office. Gross revenue was a record $15 million a year, and the firm's profit was a cool $8.6 million.

More importantly, all the additional revenue wasn't coming just from the Hunts. He'd also had some spectacular victories—"it's been *all* victories, and I can't believe it!"—including a $536.2 million jury verdict in the TransAmerican take-or-pay natural gas case. It was, Susman boasted, "the first case in my life that the jury gave me, to the penny, what I asked for!" including $1.84 million in attorneys' fees. Best of all, Susman was being paid by the hour, so that he was getting his money up front, regardless of the outcome, and appeals be damned.

The Houston lawyer had also gone back to his roots, signing on as the lead trial lawyer in an antitrust lawsuit against a subsidiary of his old nemesis, the Mead Corporation. A Minnesota legal publisher, one of the original plaintiffs in the corrugated-box litigation, accused Mead's computerized legal research subsidiary of antitrust violations.

Mead, no stranger itself to guerrilla litigation, fought hard to keep Susman out of the new case, which was later settled. The paper company had paid him twelve thousand dollars in 1983 to lecture its executives on the evils of price fixing. "You know," Susman explained, "like the program 'Scared Straight': This is what I'm gonna do to you if you don't clean up your act." What Susman didn't realize was that the Mead officials would later try to claim, on the basis of that one-day seminar, that Susman was now *their* lawyer, and that he couldn't sue them again. Susman was trying to beat Mead's disqualification motion.

"Cute," he said of Mead's ploy. "Real cute. What goes around, comes around."

Philip Corboy was gloating after the Illinois appellate court reversed the medical-malpractice verdict in *Karsten v. McCray* and ordered a new trial, thereby not only reestablishing the Chicagoan's unbroken string of victories but also extending it to nineteen years.

In ordering the new trial, the Illinois appellate court vindicated Corboy's contention that the opposing lawyers had violated Joan Karsten's physician-patient privilege by speaking privately to two of her doctors, Menet and Dominguez, and then putting them on the stand to give damaging testimony against her. (Menet had said Karsten's sepsis had no connection to her brain damage; Dominguez had testified that Karsten "looked like" she had multiple sclerosis during a hospital stay years earlier.) Corboy had been saying all along, to anybody who'd listen, that the two doctors had given tainted testimony that helped a fellow doctor. He'd finally persuaded the only audience that counted.

To penalize the defense lawyers for what the appellate court called an impropriety, O'Reilly and Johnson would be precluded from using Menet's and Dominguez' testimony in the retrial.

Since there was no question that the two doctors' testimony had been pivotal in persuading the jury that Joan Karsten's problems had begun before McCray ever saw her or removed her appendix, Corboy was betting that a new trial, without them, would go much differently.

But it appeared that O'Reilly and Johnson were going to make him prove that. Although Corboy was once again trying to settle for the insurance limit of $3 million, their insurance company client had sliced the defense offer down to what, for this case, was a niggardly sum: $500,000. Corboy's investment in expenses alone now totaled $159,915.88.

A new trial date had been set.

Monsanto was definitely *not* interested in a settlement with Carr. Instead, it was asking Judge Goldenhersh to throw out the jury's verdict, and, in support of that request, the Monsanto lawyers filed what was probably the longest posttrial motion in history: 20,000 pages spread throughout 15 different volumes, plus appendices.

The Monsanto lawyers had obviously been writing their motion as the trial progressed, because the whole works was ready for submission to the judge almost as soon as the jury returned with its verdict.

Bad enough that Goldenhersh had to sit through the whole trial. Now, Monsanto was trying to make him read the judicial equivalent of *War and Peace.*

Nothing doing, Goldenhersh said. He granted a request by Carr that the chemical company be ordered to boil its motion down to 200 pages, a request Monsanto adamantly opposed on due-process grounds because, it maintained, all the errors of the trial couldn't possibly be covered in that allotted space, and appeal rights for any mistakes not specifically mentioned in the document would be forever waived.

Goldenhersh did temper his ruling, though, by allowing Monsanto to use its original 20,000-page motion as a supporting statement. Lawyers have a word to describe such statements in support of motions, but its oxymoronic use here by Goldenhersh showed just how far the absurdity extended in the case of *Kemner v. Monsanto.*

The 20,000-page statement, Goldenhersh ruled, would be considered a "brief" instead.

Notes on Sources

This book is based on official court documents and transcripts, and on my own interviews with the principal and supporting characters in each chapter.

The trials described here span many years. Many of the courtroom scenes in this book thus have been recreated, utilizing the precise language of the stenographic transcript; the recollections of lawyers, jurors, and others who were present; and contemporaneous newspaper accounts, where they were available. As to trials that I personally observed, *Kemner v. Monsanto* and *Cipollone v. Liggett,* the stenographic transcripts were used to authenticate my own notes.

Where someone is said to have "thought" or "believed" something, such an attribution is based on a comment by the person himself, either to me or to someone I subsequently interviewed.

A variety of sources was used in gathering financial information about each lawyer and his firm. Several lawyers discussed their finances openly, but most did not. More often, financial data came from legal newspapers and confidential law-firm sources.

This book benefited greatly from the excellent reporting of the *National Law Journal* and the *American Lawyer,* two newspapers whose reportage on the cases and lawyers described here added to the body of knowledge I was able to draw upon.

The notes that follow describe the significant material in each chapter derived from sources other than, or in addition to, trial records and personal interviews.

CHAPTER ONE

Newton v. NBC

Descriptions of money skimming at the Tropicana and the Stardust, and of how the mob operates in Las Vegas, are from "The 50 Biggest Mafia Bosses," *Fortune*, November 10, 1986, by Roy Rowan.

Meyer Blinder's brokerage business is described in "Blinder, Robinson —Blind 'Em and Rob 'Em," *Forbes*, April 20, 1987, by Matthew Schifrin.

The confrontation between Wayne Newton and Brian Ross is described in "Danke Schoen, Las Vegas," the *American Lawyer*, March 1987, by Diane Goldner. The article also explains how Ross and his producer, Ira Silverman, put together their broadcast on Newton, and it documents the key contention that Ross and Silverman knew before their broadcast that Newton's share of the Aladdin purchase price hadn't come from the mob, but, rather, from the Valley Bank of Nevada. See, also, "A Singer's Lament," the *National Law Journal*, December 15, 1986, by Penny Levin.

Morton Galane's two-hundred-dollar "gifts" to two newspaper reporters were first described in "Lawyer Reagan Wanted as Judge Is Said to Have Offered Reporters Gifts of Cash," *The Wall Street Journal*, October 18, 1983, by Edward T. Pound. An unbylined local follow-up the following day is entitled "LV Attorney Reportedly Offered Newsmen 'Goodwill' Money," the *Las Vegas Review-Journal*, October 19, 1983.

Floyd Abrams' trial and appellate record appears in an entry in the 1983–84 edition of *The American Lawyer Guide*.

The jury's reaction to Abrams and Galane is from the *American Lawyer* article by Diane Goldner.

Maheu v. Hughes

The decision of the U.S. Court of Appeals for the Ninth Circuit in *Maheu v. Hughes* is reported at 569 F.2d 459.

CHAPTER TWO

Bhopal

The opening quote from Ted Dickinson comes from "A Lawyer's Game of Chicken," *Newsweek*, December 24, 1984.

Disaster lawyer Stanley Chesley is profiled in "Master of Disaster," *Forbes*, February 22, 1988, by Deirdre Fanning.

Wendell Gauthier, another disaster lawyer and a friend of John Coale, is described in "One Year Limit Speeds Hotel Suits," the *National Law Journal*, April 27, 1987, by Marcia Coyle, and in "Anatomy of a Disaster," the *ABA Journal*, August 1, 1987, by Mark Diamond.

The hearing in Judge Keenan's courtroom during which Melvin Belli and Aaron Broder criticized each other is described in "Union Carbide Suits Put American Lawyers on Trial," the Washington *Post*, April 21, 1985, by Michael Isikoff.

The maneuvers of Michael V. Ciresi, who represented the Indian Government in the Bhopal litigation, against other plaintiffs' lawyers representing Bhopal victims were first described in "Bhopal Victims Lost in Morass of Legal Maneuvers," the Danbury (Connecticut) *News-Times*, April 30, 1986, by Bob Chuvala. *The Wall Street Journal* followed up with a story the next morning, "Lawyers for Victims of Bhopal Gas Leak Fight One Another," May 1, 1986, by Barry Meier. For additional reporting on this subject, see *A Killing Wind* by Dan Kurzman (McGraw-Hill, 1988). All three describe the jockeying among the various lawyers for a piece of the Bhopal litigation, and the unsuccessful attempts by Chesley and F. Lee Bailey to broker a Bhopal settlement with Ciresi.

For an overview of the Bhopal chase and its aftermath, see "Bhopal Journal: Only the Victims Lack a Strategy," the *American Lawyer*, April 1985, by Stephen J. Adler. Some background on the principals in this chapter, as well as information about the controversies among them, came from this article.

Amtrak Litigation

An article in the *Washingtonian*, "Life and Death on the Fast Track," November 1987, by Ramsey Flynn and Steven D. Kaye, contains the most thorough account of the Amtrak crash.

CHAPTER THREE

The opening quotes from Melvin Belli and Richard Daynard come from the May 1987 and December 1986 issues, respectively, of the newsletter *Tobacco on Trial*. The newsletter's editor, David Gidmark, provided valuable material for this chapter.

The estimate that tobacco companies spend $100 million a year defending cigarette liability cases comes from an interview with Richard Daynard in *Tobacco on Trial*, December 1986.

Tobacco industry defense tactics against Dollie Root are described in "Tobacco Firms Defend Smoker Liability Suits With Heavy Artillery," *The Wall Street Journal*, April 29, 1987, by Patricia Bellew Gray.

Tobacco industry advertising expenditures are from "Trying the Tobacco Case," *Trial Diplomacy Journal*, Summer 1987, p. 15.

Statistics on cigarette billboards and on cigarette excise taxes come from the PBS news show "Frontline."

Statistics on the number of American smokers are from "Smoking vs. Life Expectancy," the New York *Times*, November 1, 1987, by the Associated Press.

The comments of Richard Daynard concerning the defense tactics of the tobacco companies are from *Tobacco on Trial*, December 1986.

Tobacco on Trial, February 1987, quotes stock analyst Calvert Crary's speculation about the cigarette companies' ability to cover legal costs by raising prices a few pennies per pack.

Patricia Bellew Gray's April 29, 1987 article in *The Wall Street Journal*, cited earlier, quotes analyst Crary's theory that cigarettes are the most profitable product ever sold.

The forty-five thousand scientific studies documenting the link between smoking and cancer are characterized in "Antismoking Climate Inspires Suits by the Dying," the New York *Times*, March 15, 1985, by David Margolick.

Galbraith v. R. J. Reynolds

Melvin Belli's use of demonstrative evidence is described in "The 'Bigs' of Torts—Saints or Sinners," in the *New York Law Journal*, March 12, 1979, by Martin Fox.

Belli's admonition to "save your money and try your lawsuit" comes from *Tobacco on Trial*, April 1987.

Judge Bruce Dodds' comments about the Galbraith trial are contained in an interview with *Tobacco on Trial*, April 1987.

Comments of jury foreman Stacy Proft and other Galbraith jurors are from interviews published in *Tobacco on Trial*, April 1986. Belli assistant Paul Monzione's feelings about the jury deliberations are derived in part from comments he made to David Gidmark for interviews in *Tobacco on Trial*, April 1987, and "The Tobacco Juries—An In-Depth Study," *Trial Diplomacy Journal*, Summer 1987. Interviews of the jurors by an R. J. Reynolds consultant are described in *Tobacco on Trial*, May 1987.

Cipollone v. Liggett

Comparative-fault laws are detailed in "Where There's Smoke . . . ," *Forbes,* December 15, 1986, by Deirdre Fanning.

Characterizations of the liberal opinions of Judge H. Lee Sarokin appear in "The Hanging Judges of Business," *Forbes,* April 7, 1986, by Richard Greene, and in "I Am Flying: Hurricane Carter Rejoices in His Freedom," the New York *Times,* March 1, 1988, by Selwyn Raab.

A profile of Antonio Cipollone in the Washington *Post,* entitled "The War Over a Smoker's Death," May 27, 1988, by Paula Span, provides insight into his character and motivations in bringing the lawsuit.

The *Cipollone* jury's deliberations are described in detail in, "They Didn't *Really* Blame the Cigarette Makers," the *American Lawyer,* September 1988, by Amy Singer. An earlier article by the same author, "Cigarette Papers," the *American Lawyer,* May 1988, is also a useful reference on the *Cipollone* trial.

CHAPTER FOUR

Two books, *Beyond Greed* by Stephen Fay (Viking, 1982) and *Texas Rich* by Harry Hurt III (Norton, 1981), provided much of the background on the Hunt family history and on the origins of the Hunt brothers' financial downfall.

Descriptions of early skirmishes in the Hunt lender-liability litigation, including the departure of Weil, Gotshal & Manges from the account and the brothers' subsequent hiring of McCabe/Gordon and Philip Hirschkop, come from "The Hunt Suit: Noisy Nonsense," the *American Lawyer,* November 1986, by Ellen Joan Pollock.

The demise of McCabe/Gordon after it lost the Hunt account is chronicled in various articles published in the Boston *Globe,* including "Banned in Dallas," December 16, 1986, by Gregory A. Patterson and Todd Vogel, and "Boston's Fallen Legal Star," May 12, 1987, by Ethan Bronner.

Material about Stephen Susman's education, marriage and early legal career at Fulbright & Jaworski comes from a profile of Susman published in the *National Law Journal,* "Tackler of Texas Traditions," June 4, 1979, by David Margolick. The comments of Fulbright & Jaworski partners concerning Susman also are from this article. See, also, "Antitrust Lawyer Hopes Fee Will Confirm Vision," *Legal Times* (Washington), May 17, 1982, by

Larry Lempert, and "Fulbright Dropouts Build a Better Business," the *American Lawyer,* September 1986, by Claudia Weinstein.

Susman's first thoughts upon making partner at Fulbright & Jaworski are from "The $300-Million Paper Case," the *American Lawyer,* July 1979.

Jack Stanley, who first recommended Susman to the Hunt brothers, is profiled in "Endurance Test: Energy Firm Expands Even in Chapter 11, Wears Out Creditors," *The Wall Street Journal,* July 30, 1987, by Charles F. McCoy and Matt Moffett. The *American Lawyer* article "Noisy Nonsense," cited above, also describes McCabe/Gordon's earlier work for Stanley, and the subsequent findings of impropriety against Gordon by a federal district judge in Houston in connection with McCabe/Gordon's representation in bankruptcy of Stanley's GHR Energy Corporation.

Corrugated Carton Trial

The risk Mead faced by not settling the pending class action is described in "A Philadelphia Lawyer's Class Action Gold Mine," *Fortune,* September 7, 1981, by Irwin Ross, as well as in an affidavit of Susman's economist Richard Hoyt. The *Fortune* article also documents the lobbying campaign later waged by Mead in an effort to change the law relating to joint-and-several liability for price fixing.

CHAPTER FIVE

"Defending a Doctor Against All Odds," an article by defense lawyer Roger O'Reilly describing his strategy in the *Karsten* case, appears in the *ABA Journal,* May 1, 1986.

Material on the use of market research to evaluate potential jurors in the Randy Block case comes from "The Jury: Experts Set Sights on Finding Right 12," the Chicago *Tribune,* April 8, 1984, by Joseph R. Tybor.

Philip Corboy's use of market research to aid in jury selection in the *Marirose Johnson* case is described in both "Getting a Verdict on Jury Predictability," the *National Law Journal,* June 22, 1981, by Joseph R. Tybor, and "Mind Control in the Courtroom," the Chicago *Tribune,* March 28, 1982, by Lori B. Andrews.

Tom Demetrio's record-setting $12 million automobile-crash verdict is described in "Elements of a $12 Million Personal Injury Case," the *ABA Journal,* June 1, 1986, by Janine Warsaw.

Accounts of how Corboy twice turned apparent losses into victories appear in "Lawyers Specializing in Personal Injury Suits Find Business Is

Good," *The Wall Street Journal,* August 2, 1972, by Jonathan R. Laing, and "The Million-Dollar Attorney for the Maimed," the *Chicago Tribune Magazine,* April 3, 1977, by Jack Star.

Financial information on the firm of Corboy & Demetrio was first compiled by Francis Wilkinson of the *American Lawyer* for "Philip Corboy: Mastering the Science of P.I.," June 1987.

CHAPTER SIX

For a compelling account of what it's like to practice law in the environs of Madison and St. Clair counties, Illinois, see "Plaintiffs' Paradise," the *American Lawyer,* April 1983, by James B. Stewart, Jr. My account of lawyer Paul Pratt's earlier dioxin trial against the Norfolk & Western Railway draws heavily on that article. Stewart's article was preceded by a major investigative series entitled "The Hidden Industry" that ran in the St. Louis *Post-Dispatch* for five days beginning on February 7, 1982. That series by Bill Lambrecht also was essential to the research for this chapter.

Rex Carr's earlier cases are described in "Million-Dollar Master," a profile of Carr that appeared in the *National Law Journal,* September 20, 1982, by Greg Bailey.

Alleged corruption in the courts of Plaintiffs' Paradise has been well covered by the local Belleville *News-Democrat,* and the newspaper's stories concerning both the mishandling of cases in the local courts and alleged favoritism in judicial selection were used as source material for this chapter. Terry Hillig of the Alton *Telegraph* also provided research assistance.

The failure of Judge Richard Goldenhersh to control the *Kemner* case is documented in "A Judge's Default," the *American Lawyer,* July 1987, by Mary Billard.

Index

ABOUT THE AUTHOR

John A. Jenkins has been writing from Washington about the law and lawyers since 1971, when, shortly before his graduation from the University of Maryland College of Journalism, he went to work as a reporter covering the Justice Department for a prominent legal publisher. Four years later, his magazine writing career began with a series of investigative articles about the legal profession for the *Washington Monthly*. Since then, he has written widely about legal matters, becoming a regular contributor to the *New York Times Magazine*. His reporting has won six major journalism awards, including four Certificates of Merit from the American Bar Association Gavel Awards, one of the highest honors in legal journalism. He lives in Washington with his wife, Susan, and his daughters, Jennifer and Christina. *The Litigators* is his first book.